Counter-Thrust

**Great Campaigns of
the Civil War**

SERIES EDITORS

Anne J. Bailey
*Georgia College &
State University*

Brooks D. Simpson
Arizona State University

BENJAMIN FRANKLIN COOLING

COUNTER-
THRUST

From the
Peninsula
to the
Antietam

University of Nebraska Press
Lincoln & London

Library of Congress Cataloging-
in-Publication Data
Cooling, B. Franklin.
Counter-thrust: from the Peninsula to the Antietam /
Benjamin Franklin Cooling.
p. cm. — (Great campaigns of the Civil War)
Includes bibliographical references and index.
ISBN 978-0-8032-1515-3 (cloth: alk. paper)
1. Virginia—History—Civil War, 1861–1865—Campaigns.
2. Maryland— History—Civil War, 1861–1865—Campaigns.
3. Lee, Robert E. (Robert Edward), 1807–1870—Military leadership.
4. Confederate States of America. Army of Northern Virginia—History.
5. Offensive (Military science)—History—19th century.
6. McClellan, George Brinton, 1826–1885—Military leadership.
7. Pope, John, 1822–1892—Military leadership.
8. United States—History—Civil War, 1861–1865—Campaigns. I. Title.
E473.7.C66 2007
973.7'55—dc22
2007022761

Set in ITC New Baskerville.

To Nan and Ross Netherton
Northern Virginia historians
par excellence

Contents

Illustrations

Maps

Preface

Yankees called it Cedar Run; Rebels termed it Cedar Mountain. Confederates used the name Second Manassas; their opponents remembered it as Second Bull Run. Both sides spoke of Chantilly or Ox Hill, while Confederates preferred the name Boonsboro to denote what Federals referred to as South Mountain. Both combatants called the capture of Harpers Ferry a crucial event worthy of but one name, but Northerners memorialized the bloodiest single day in American history as Antietam while their southern foe stuck to the name Sharpsburg. However designated, these events come to us today as part of a critical Civil War epoch. It stretched from the Virginia Peninsula, through the piedmont, to the hills of western Maryland. The period covered July to November 1862. The story began quietly, the principal characters almost supine. It built slowly through battle—Cedar Mountain, Second Manassas, Chantilly, South Mountain, Harpers Ferry—reaching a crescendo at Antietam only to recede once more in the quiet of death and renewal. Yet throughout, it was a pivotal moment in time.

As part of the Great Campaigns of the Civil War series, this volume treats a period that Professor James A. Rawley once styled "perhaps the most acute crisis of the war." He suggested that the late summer and autumn of 1862 provided "a multiple crisis—military, diplomatic, and political." He cited (a) the triple military offensives of a resurgent Confederacy, (b) European overtures toward mediation and intervention on behalf of that emerging nation and the ramifications of border state allegiance, and (c) northern popular discontent with military failure, the high cost of waging war, and the abridgement of civil liberties on the eve of off-year elections. Although Rawley treated emancipation as a separate issue, that too was an integral part of the crisis.[1] He also might have included the changing nature of the conflict itself, passing as it did in this period from "soft" or conciliatory confrontation to "hard" or relentless subjugation. However defined, the period proved a decisive moment in the four-year struggle of national unification.

This book focuses on the major rollback of the Union offensives of Generals George B. McClellan and John Pope in Virginia and Confederate Gen. Robert E. Lee's subsequent counter-thrust that carried Confederate fortunes from the gates of Richmond to Union territory on the upper Potomac in Maryland. In short, it features the apex or high tide of Rebel fortunes at this stage of the war. Resurgent Union power parried the Confederate move, if not brilliantly at least sufficiently so that Abraham Lincoln might issue a presidential directive that forever changed both the course of the Civil War and eventually the future direction of human rights in a reunified country. The Confederate counteroffensive failed to deliver the resounding proof of sovereignty necessary to gain European intervention in an increasingly bloody struggle. Accelerating mobilization of northern will and power did convince British and French leaders not to join in overt intervention. Even then, it was a remarkably close-run thing.

The story has essentially four parts. In the first part, Lee determined to drive an invader from his native Virginia and redeem the northern part of the Old Dominion. The people and events speak to this theme, associated with the dramatic engagements at Cedar Mountain, Second Manassas, and Chantilly. They underscore Lee's vow to punish Gen. John Pope and his perpetrators of a harsh war on innocent civilians. From the Tidewater to the Potomac, battles and maneuvers reflected new leadership at work on both sides. Buffeted by the coalescing field generalship of Lee and his chief lieutenants, James Longstreet and Thomas "Stonewall" Jackson, Pope's headlong rush into central Virginia (only tepidly supported by his uncooperative partner, McClellan) represented disparate personalities and leadership styles. Moreover, a new general in chief in Washington, Henry W. Halleck, plus mounting pressure from abolitionist politicians for stronger suppression of the rebellion caused problems for President Lincoln and his administration. Lee's classic triumph at Second Manassas—perhaps his greatest battle—capped a two-month operation whereby he and his army relieved pressure on Richmond and chased their opponents back to the suburbs of Washington.

Still, Lee and his Confederates could not annihilate the Federal armies or attack the enemy capital. An unheralded but key setback at Chantilly reflected that salient fact. So a second part of the story encompasses Lee's first ill-fated attempt to carry the war across the Potomac. The invasion of loyal border slave-states like Maryland in the east and Kentucky in the west formed part of a grand Confederate strategy. High stakes attended Lee's offensive into Maryland (as well as those of Braxton Bragg and other Confederate generals in northern Mississippi aimed at west Tennessee and southwestern Kentucky). In each case, southern success hinged partially on the speed of Confederate moves but also on the recovery of their antagonists. Lee failed to anticipate how rapidly McClellan, reappointed to unified field command, could rejuvenate defeated Federal forces around Washington and begin the pursuit that would end on the banks of the Antietam. Discovery of the famous "Lost Order" produced a foot-race to save Harpers Ferry, sharp fighting on South Mountain, and, finally, the seminal day of carnage at Antietam. McClellan's subsequent failure of nerve to destroy his opponent provided a strangely pyrrhic victory in turn. Underpinning the actions of an overstretched Lee and the ever-hesitant (yet confident) McClellan lay political and logistical issues and the omnipresent question of defending Washington, not to mention the anxious waiting by Americans and the issue of European intervention. Above all, the deceptive "Lorelei" of Maryland secession (together with acute resource issues) diverted Lee's celerity of movement and singularity of purpose on enemy soil. Controversial decisions on both sides became hidden in the fervor of the Confederate invasion.

The third part of the saga features measurement of performance and results. From whatever combat success he obtained in Maryland—and McClellan remained convinced that he had saved the Union by his bloody victory at Antietam—the primary result was Lincoln's issuance of a preliminary Emancipation Proclamation. This singular event aimed at destroying the economic fiber of the Confederacy's war-making apparatus and the southern way of life. However, other actions by the president at this time held equal portent. His willingness to suspend the writ of habeas corpus throughout the Union in order to stifle opposition to the war and to prosecute conscription evasion in the loyal states produced equal controversy. Moreover, the impact of the Proclamation, the continuing sanguinary character of the war, and the inability of either side to consummate annihilative battles kept both North and South off balance. The refusal of Confederate leaders, soldiery, and populace to regard Lee's abortive expedition (as well as those in Kentucky and elsewhere) as defeats renders questionable modern assertions that Antietam in particular was the pivotal turning point of the war. The *New York Times* might well suggest on September 21, 1862, that the effects of Antietam "will be seen and felt in the destinies of the Nation for centuries to come." Approximately a hundred thousand casualties incurred by both sides in the eastern theater alone from July to November underscored that point. The conflict remained unresolved as McClellan and Lee resumed maneuvers back in Virginia by fall. McClellan's lackluster performance after Antietam led to his replacement—a move that meant other campaigns would continue the story of the war. Hence this series of books.

There is a fourth part to the story, however muted by the predominantly operational flavor of the series. It remains critical to broadening our understanding of the period. This dimension involves civil-military relations. On one end it surfaced at the local level whenever the populace rubbed against military authority. At the national level, on the other end, the issues reflected larger questions of war and politics, the interplay of elective officials with professional soldiers and with one another. Cut a different way, as National War College professor Charles Stevenson suggests, such relations involved a "reluctant dictator" (in this case, Lincoln), "a coalition of rivals" (at both ends of Pennsylvania Avenue), an evolving national institutional and organizational team for victory (management and administration in both mufti and uniform), and even an emergent new strategy for that victory (a fateful shift from conciliatory to relentless conflict).[2] Behind the operations, then, lay wartime considerations of civil-military tension absent the modern structure, policy, and strategic synthesis more familiar to us today. Transformational techniques from militia mobilization to conscription, confiscation to emancipation of property, and states' rights localism to national centralism emerged against traditional democratic checks and balances in American governance.

Conduct of the war and politics necessarily spotlighted Lincoln and the Radicals, the president and his search for a winning general, as well as Lincoln's personal role in preparing both domestic national will and the international environment for his shift from constitutional reconciliation to expansion of the Rights of Man in the conduct of the war. The Confederate experience pales in comparison, although Confederate President Jefferson Davis shared similar travails of a chief executive plagued by balky military and political teams, citizen concerns about government intrusion via conscription, confiscation, and a discernable inability to defend hearth and home of the realm. Davis's principal military and civilian difficulties lay distant from Richmond and the Virginia theater of war in this period, just the reverse of Lincoln and the Union. Yet almost perversely, the actions and issues of Lincoln and the Union as seen through the prism of the eastern campaigns of 1862 would ultimately contribute to the Confederacy's demise, notwithstanding the South's apparent success at the time.[3]

Most certainly the period from the Virginia Peninsula to Antietam Creek underscored Professor James McPherson's contention that "the American Civil War could not end with a negotiated peace because the issues over which it was fought—Union versus Disunion, Freedom versus Slavery—proved to be non-negotiable."[4] Perhaps only Lincoln and Davis saw this hardening of the conflict's direction at the time; certainly many of their contemporaries in uniform and sack coats did not. Indeed, the Civil War continued for another two and a half years following the events covered here. A revolution in firepower on the battlefield stalemated the quest for a single military stroke to end the carnage. Neither side was ready for peace following the Seven Days, after Second Manassas, or at the end of the Maryland campaign (with or without outside mediation, a mediation that evaporated suddenly as Europeans became concerned with their own strategic needs and fear of becoming mired to little purpose in America's conflict). Victory thus remained elusive, and the months between June and November reflected that fact in the changed nature of the war itself.

Conciliation and moderation were swept aside by a new sternness, even harshness, of a people's war, fought not merely for restoration of the Old Union but for creation of something new, governed by new people with new purpose under redefinition of the sacred Compact and God's beneficence. From it all shone forth the singularity of purpose and strength of conviction driving Abraham Lincoln in particular past the bitter defeats of summer and indecisive victories of autumn toward his elusive goal of national unity and freedom for man. Was this the ultimate meaning behind Professor

McPherson's contention that Antietam provided the battle that changed the course of the Civil War? Or, as one reviewer queried, should we term Antietam's legacy "the event of the war," with a question mark? Hopefully, *Counter-Thrust* and the study of the period from the Peninsula to the Antietam will suggest answers. As such it builds upon such pioneering efforts as the original Scribner's *Campaigns of the Civil War* volumes *The Army under Pope* by John Codman Ropes and Francis Winthrop Palfrey's *The Antietam and Fredericksburg*, published in 1881 and 1882, respectively.[5]

Acknowledgments

Special thanks go to Marilyn and Ron Snyder of Annapolis, Maryland, for making available the soldier letter that begins the book. Joseph Rubenfine of West Palm Beach, Florida, similarly provided a copy of the John Wotring diary. National Park Service staff members Jim Burgess of Manassas National Battlefield and Ted Alexander of Antietam National Battlefield were helpful in guiding me through material from their park libraries and discussing aspects of those battles with me. The editors and anonymous readers of the University of Nebraska Press provided welcome direction and guidance; Judith Hoover's copyediting of the manuscript was invaluable. Responsibility for errors and varying interpretations remains mine alone.

Series Editors' Introduction

Americans remain fascinated by the Civil War. Movies, television, and video—even computer software—have augmented the ever-expanding list of books on the war. Although it stands to reason that a large portion of recent work concentrates on military aspects of the conflict, historians have expanded our scope of inquiry to include civilians, especially women; the destruction of slavery and the evolving understanding of what freedom meant to millions of former slaves; and an even greater emphasis on the experiences of the common soldier on both sides. Other studies have demonstrated the interrelationships of war, politics, and policy and how civilians' concerns back home influenced both soldiers and politicians. Although one cannot fully comprehend this central event in American history without understanding that military operations were fundamental in determining the course and outcome of the war, it is time for students of battles and campaigns to incorporate nonmilitary themes into their accounts. The most pressing challenge facing Civil War scholarship today is the integration of various perspectives and emphases into a new narrative that explains not only what happened, why, and how, but also why it mattered.

The series Great Campaigns of the Civil War offers readers concise syntheses of the major campaigns of the war, reflecting the findings of recent scholarship. The series points to new ways of viewing military campaigns by looking beyond the battlefield and the headquarters tent to the wider political and social context within which these campaigns unfolded; it also shows how campaigns and battles left their imprint on many Americans, from presidents and generals down to privates and civilians. The ends and means of waging war reflect larger political objectives and priorities as well as social values.

Historians may continue to debate among themselves as to which of these campaigns constituted true turning points, but each of the campaigns treated in this series contributed to shaping the course of the conflict, opening opportunities, and eliminating alternatives.

By July 1862 George McClellan's thrust toward the Confederate capital at Richmond had been turned back in a week's worth of battles orchestrated by Robert E. Lee and the Army of Northern Virginia. Still, McClellan's Army of the Potomac remained close enough to Richmond to pose a real threat, and John Pope's Army of Virginia was approaching from the north. Once more Lee exploited divisions in the Union high command. Learning that the new Union general in chief, Henry W. Halleck, had decided to withdraw McClellan's command from the James River, Lee rushed north to strike at Pope, perhaps the only Union general he truly detested. At Second Manassas the Confederates smashed into the nearly unguarded Union left, sending Pope reeling back toward Washington. Lee decided to take the war north of the Potomac, as images of foreign intervention, northern war-weariness, and Marylander support for the Confederacy tempted him. It was a critical moment for the Lincoln administration: the president had been debating all summer whether to strike at slavery. All depended on whether McClellan could rally a defeated and disheartened force, forge a new army from Union forces around Washington, and defeat Lee in battle. Aided by a little luck, McClellan forced several passes at South Mountain, gathered his forces east of Antietam Creek, and attacked Lee's lines east and north of Sharpsburg, Maryland, on September 17, 1862. The result was the bloodiest single day of combat during the war. Lee barely hung on: after remaining in place a day, he withdrew southward over the Potomac. Lincoln seized the moment to issue the preliminary Emancipation Proclamation; eight weeks later he fired McClellan when that general did not move quickly enough to bring Lee to battle.

In the East the summer of 1862 proved a critical moment in the war, between Lee's effort to turn the tide of the conflict and Lincoln's decision to embrace waging hard war against the Confederacy and striking a blow at slavery. Benjamin Franklin Cooling recounts these events, yet questions to what extent one can call Antietam a turning point, given the persistence of the conflict. That escalation and emancipation changed the nature of the conflict is clear, Cooling argues, and yet that simply set the stage for what would come next.

Counter-Thrust

→ 1 ←

Summer Impasse

A UNION SOLDIER known only as John wrote to his father on July 13, 1862, from a "Camp near Harrisons Landing" on the Virginia Peninsula. He was well, he said, and hoped the home folks were also. "Everything is quiet here now," with "no firing of cannon and musketry" as "there was this day three weeks ago." President Abraham Lincoln "was here last week, taking a view of his Boys," accompanied by army commander Maj. Gen. George B. McClellan and his bodyguard, who all looked splendid. Today they had undergone a brigade inspection, with troops receiving four months' back pay that he hoped to send home "by Adam's Express" Company as it "is not safe to send by mail." He understood that his parents "were getting quite a nice little home on the hill," and he hoped to see it before many months. He was content, he wrote, "as long as I keep my health." The sun was hot, "and on a march, there is a good many gets sun-struck."[1]

John then enumerated his comrades' condition and how their captain had returned from his wounding at the battle of Fair Oaks earlier that summer. He told his father, "I expect you are harvesting by this time and perhaps you are done." He then recounted seeing oats fit to cut, but what harvesting was done was "done very quick by the Army of the Potomac." There were wheat fields "as high as 40 and 50 acres" with first-rate wheat, "all destroyed," including one in which his unit had camped and another where a thousand head of cattle, as well as six horse teams and the cavalry's horses, "all turned in to take a good feed." In a half-hour's time "a whole 40 acre field would be tramped to the ground." "It looks hard," he concluded, "but it can't be helped." Already, war and the armies had turned from merely fighting and killing one another to de facto destruction of civilian property under the guise of "military necessity." John's letter captured well the changing tone of the second summer of America's Civil War.[2]

For the past year, operations had shifted from the banks of the Potomac to the shores of Chesapeake Bay and from Washington's suburbs to those of Richmond. Soldiers in blue and gray had developed what was called "the eastern theater" of the conflict. The battle at Bull Run (Manassas) had produced a resounding Rebel victory during the first summer of the war. Then McClellan (dubbed "the Young Napoleon" both for his perceived affectations of the Great Captain and his initial achievements in mountainous western Virginia) went to Washington to build a formidable fighting machine. That machine became the Union Army of the Potomac. A superb organizer and charismatic leader, "Little Mac," as he was also called by his supporters, conveyed his Grand Armée by water to the Virginia tidewater in March 1862. This joint army-navy endeavor forced his opponent at the time, Gen. Joseph E. Johnston, to hastily retire from northern Virginia to protect the Confederate capital. That retreat had been costly. Self-inflicted destruction of supplies and railroads weakened southern morale already stunned by defeats at Roanoke Island in coastal North Carolina, Forts Henry and Donelson, and then Shiloh and New Orleans and the loss of the strategic rail junction at Corinth, Mississippi, in the West.

By June, however, the Union juggernaut slowed, plagued by long distances and Confederate raiders' interdiction of supply lines as well as lack of unity of command. McClellan's five-week slog up the Virginia Peninsula ended with unanticipated defeat during the Seven Days' battles outside Richmond. Suddenly, by midsummer, affairs from the Mississippi River to the shores of the Atlantic suggested an impasse. Anxious Northerners complained about their government's inability to finish the task of suppressing the rebellion. Southerners now spoke confidently of shifting the war back northward, even beyond the Potomac frontier perhaps.

In some ways, the pivotal event occurred on the final day in May at Seven Pines (Fair Oaks) near Richmond. There Johnston stopped McClellan and his legions within sight and sound of the city's church spires. But the southern general was severely wounded in the fight and forced to relinquish army command, opening the way for a new leader. That leader, Robert Edward Lee, was also a native Virginian, scion of one of the Old Dominion's best families, older than Johnston and calmly serene yet inwardly aggressive. As presidential adviser on a daily basis, he developed "a rapport, even a trust" with President Jefferson Davis. "Genl Lee acts in accord with [me]," the chief executive told an aide. Castigated for failure in western Virginia the year before against McClellan and subsequently able to produce only meager results on the South Carolina–Georgia coast, Lee in the battles of Seven Days reversed his fortunes—fortunes that would grow as the summer progressed. He inherited what, under his tutelage, would become the premier fighting force of the youthful Confederacy, known ultimately as the Army of Northern Virginia. True, the high-water mark for both general and army might lie a year away at Gettysburg. By then, McClellan would be a memory and Lee a wiser field commander. Meanwhile, from June until November 1862, the fate of these two warriors and their armies, the two presidents and their nations' fortunes as well were inextricably linked. The story of the war in the East from the Peninsula to the Antietam became largely their story. And it shaped one of the crucial periods of the conflict.[3]

Militarily, McClellan and Lee needed to recuperate after the costly Seven Days' battles. Meanwhile, Richmonders rejoiced at their deliverance. True, they could never forget that excessively hot month of July, wrote thirty-four-year-old Sallie Brock Putnam, "for they lived in one immense hospital" and "breathed the vapors of the charnel house." Political prospects had brightened, she noted, "but death held a carnival in our city." Alexandrian Judith W. McGuire, seeking haven in the capital, recorded, "Our people are suffering too much; they cannot stand it." Saloonkeeper Gottfried Lange added that his pen was too weak to describe "the great lamentation" that had befallen the city. Refugees had swarmed into town before the invader's arrival, and McGuire noted that "a number of servants" from several properties, "indeed from the whole Pamunky River, went off with their Northern friends," including her driver and hostler, whom she had helped raise from childhood.[4]

Mournful strains of the "dead March and muffled drums" played incessantly for military funerals taking place everywhere. The Chimborazo hospital complex at the eastern end of Broad Street and its counterpart, Winder hospital on the city's western fringe, as well as beautiful Hollywood cemetery overlooking the James River received the battlefield's largesse. Both sides had lost nine thousand men in actions even before the Seven Days' combat. More than twenty thousand men in gray and perhaps an equal number of Federals fell during that bloody week: fifty-three hundred Rebels and half that number of Yankees at Malvern Hill alone. Lee's aggressiveness had saved the city, but at a heavy cost. At least the forty-six hundred new Union prisoners at Belle Isle in the James River enjoyed better accommodations than internees from actions the previous year, who endured stuffy warehouses like Libby prison. They might even have been better off than McClellan's throng huddled on swampland around Harrison's Landing.[5]

Just as after Manassas, "fervent cheerleaders" in Richmond managed to inflate the meaning of the Seven Days' victories. The *Richmond Enquirer*, for one, beamed that Lee's success had opened the path to ending the war. Southern independence seemed assured, announced its editor, even permanent, as negotiations with Washington would open ways to acquire Maryland, Kentucky, and Missouri. From the field, Maj. Gen. Daniel Harvey Hill's division headquarters praised those high and heroic qualities for "which the Southern soldier is so remarkable." President Davis proclaimed in a victory dispatch "to the Army of Eastern Virginia" on July 5 that within the previous ten days it had marched to attack the enemy in his entrenchments "with well-directed movements and death-defying valor." That enemy had been driven back thirty-five miles and despite reinforcement had been compelled to seek safety under cover of gunboats, "where he now lies cowering before the army so lately derided and threatened with entire subjugation." Confederate fortitude and gallantry would be held in "loved remembrance" by a grateful people, promised their leader. Lt. William Nathaniel Wood of Virginia echoed the president: "We had an army of *soldiers* and a general worthy of the men he commanded." Louisianan R. A. Pierson wrote his father, "The Federals are meeting some reverses that will check their onward march in the South for at least this year," and Samuel A. Burney of Cobb's Georgia Legion wrote, "The help of God has been vouchsafed to the arms of the Confederacy."[6]

Some critics nonetheless claimed that Lee "does not follow up his blows on the whipped enemy," commented War Department clerk John B. Jones. Personally, he disagreed, for "this 'grand army' of the North" would soon die on the Peninsula, "after sunset, or when it thunders," the victim of heat, malaria, and mosquitoes. The commanding general "neither sleeps nor slumbers," in Jones's view, but had begun reorganizing Maj. Gen. Thomas Jonathan "Stonewall" Jackson's command "for a blow at or near the enemy's capital." Let Lincoln "beware the hour of retribution," trumpeted the government civilian. But hopelessly muddy roads, the powerful Union defensive position at Harrison's Landing on the James covered by Federal naval guns, and Confederate arms too "battle thinned" themselves deferred completion of victory. Lee sent able cavalryman Maj. Gen. James Ewell Brown Stuart and a battery of horse artillery, along with an observation balloon, to scout McClellan's positions. Little came of it except destruction of a fledgling Confederate aeronautics corps. Episcopal clergyman-turned-artillerist Col. William Pendleton's mid-July impromptu shelling of the Federal encampments proved more promising. They stirred up a fine "rumpus," according to Jones, as "Lee has turned the tide" with the promise of "a long career of successes." Elsewhere, Generals Braxton Bragg and Edmund Kirby Smith as well as William W. Loring were "in motion at last" to redeem Tennessee and Kentucky and Appalachian Virginia. Missouri seemed to be rising again in "rebellion." Still, Jones croaked about a Richmond citizenry "too jubilant over recent success," with too many "skulkers" and draft dodgers and strangers from Maryland in the city.[7]

Disturbing reports from lower down on the Peninsula told of how fleeing slaves now baffled their white masters. Arrival of the Yankees had stoked such unrest, and an alarming incidence of latent Union loyalism had even surfaced in the cradle of tidewater correctness. The war's destructive path suddenly suggested something besides glamour and glory. One soldier, William Nathaniel Wood, saw in a body of old field pines that "every tree seemed to have been struck by many bullets or shells," and South Carolina surgeon Spencer Welch complained to his wife, "There are no crops or fences anywhere, and I saw nothing which had escaped the Yankees except one little Guinea fowl." Welch thought the Confederates were bad at this game, "but the country over which the Yankees have been looks like some barren waste." Still, everyone rejoiced that Lee had made Richmond temporarily safe. If not tactically brilliant, he had displayed a talent for raising hope for miracles despite staggering losses. His attacks against McClellan had cut down the flower of his fighting men, thus abrogating any opportunity to annihilate the foe. His subsequent entrenching of Richmond City led a peevish public to derisively label him "king of spades." Yet if nothing more, the Seven Days "cemented Lee's reputation as an aggressive and stubborn fighter." Though he was not as yet of Napoleonic stature, many people sensed his destiny. The *Richmond Dispatch* told its readers, "The rise which this officer has suddenly taken in the public confidence is without precedent." Gone were the days of Joe Johnston's retreating before the foe.[8]

Just how Lee and his victorious army as well as the government and people of the Confederacy would respond to future challenges remained to be seen. The lengthening casualty lists and continued presence of McClellan's leviathan on the banks of the James occasioned "restless anxiety." For his part, Lee (with presidential dispensation) utilized the post–Seven Days' period to withdraw the army to the defense line around Richmond. He reconstituted the fighting ranks with returning stragglers and reinforcements from other theaters. He realigned the army's divisional organization and placed new generals in positions of authority. Stonewall Jackson and James Longstreet advanced in stature as his principal lieutenants, along with Stuart as chief of cavalry. McClellan's passivity after Malvern Hill gave the Confederate government an opportunity to take stock of the situation, even revisit the idea of undertaking a strategic offensive. Perforce, to some it was not just a question of recapturing northern Virginia. The idea of going on into Maryland and even Pennsylvania had floated through high government circles and the army for over a year. Jackson in particular had argued for that course as a means for ending the war and achieving independence. He had importuned Johnston and utilized Virginia congressman Andrew Boteler to press the scheme in Richmond. Davis and Lee appreciated bold thinking, notwithstanding McClellan's continued presence. Lee especially saw merit in moving away from the capital and grain-rich central Virginia.[9]

The shift could be seen on July 5 when Davis enjoined Lee's men not only to drive the enemy from the sacred soil of Virginia but to "carry your standards beyond the outer boundaries of the Confederacy, to wring from an unscrupulous foe the recognition of your birthright, community independence." On the eve of the anniversary of the Manassas battle Davis wrote to critic John Forsyth that he deplored public doubt of the advantage of "invading over being invaded" and repeated an earlier "declared purpose and continued hope" that Confederate forces might "feed upon the enemy and teach them the blessings of peace by making them feel in its most tangible form the evils of war." "The time and place of invasion has been a question not of will but of power," the president intoned. Later that month officials from Secretary of State Judah P. Benjamin to army Adj. Gen. Samuel Cooper spoke of reinforcement for an offensive "beyond the Potomac in a very short time." By this point, Lee and his lieutenants were ready to set the offensive in motion. Frankly, Lee had advised the president as early as June 5, "it would change the character of the war." Nonetheless, Lee could not leave Richmond exposed—nor would Davis allow it with a Yankee army nearby.[10]

Following an inauspicious night retreat in pelting rain and darkness after Malvern Hill, the Army of the Potomac recovered sufficiently to reoccupy Evelington Heights. This prominent ridge commanded what became the vast Federal encampment around the Berkeley plantation at Harrison's Landing on the James River below Richmond. By Independence Day, Lee determined that further attack on the enemy would be suicidal. McClellan's own exhortation to his troops sounded much like the victory pronouncements of Davis and Lee. He too spoke of glory, not defeat: "Attacked by vastly superior forces, and without hope of reinforcements, you have succeeded in changing your base of operations by a flank movement, always regarded as the most hazardous of military expedients." Your conduct "ranks you among the celebrated armies of history," he told them. "On this our Nation's Birthday we declare to our foes, who are rebels against the best interests of mankind, that this Army shall enter the Capital of their so-called Confederacy, that our National Constitution shall prevail; and that the Union which can alone insure internal peace and external security to each State must and shall be preserved, cost what it may in time, treasure and blood." Granted, the cost—human carnage and the loss of forty artillery pieces, thirty-one thousand small arms, hundreds of wagons and ambulances, and quantities of supplies and equipment of the campaign—hardly suggested success. Barely a fortnight before, the men in blue had heard the Richmond clocks chime out the hours. Now they were thirty-five miles away and chastened about the lost opportunity. Well might some wonder "whether this is strategy or defeat" or why their general seemed deified by "a *masterly* retreat."[11]

Lt. Oliver Wendell Holmes Jr. of the Twentieth Massachusetts wrote his parents, "The anxiety has been more terrible than almost any past experience." Many in the ranks blamed the War Department, even the president, for insufficient support. Others, like Col. Francis C. Barlow of the Sixty-first New York, thought McClellan and other senior army leaders derelict. He told his mother that McClellan had been completely outwitted and the army's survival attributable more to "the severe fighting of some of the Divisions than to any skill of our Generals." Yet there was little time to belabor these issues. Earthworks needed digging, fresh uniforms and equipment required issue, and reorganization had to be effected. Debilitating heat, swarms of flies, overcrowded living conditions, and bad water soon produced nearly forty-three thousand names on the army's sick list, leading Medical Director Jonathan Letterman to issue instructions to improve sanitary and cooking conditions. Yet the Yankee army seemed to weaken by the day, just as Rebel war clerk Jones had predicted. Only the navy's gunboats dashed about, flushing shorelines with desultory fire to keep the Confederates at bay. One positive note came when Brig. Gen. Daniel Butterfield and his brigade bugler, Oliver Norton, teamed to produce the quieting melody that would officially close out the army's day, "Taps." Meanwhile, a "worn out and war worn" McClellan seemed incapable of reasonable decisions. His anxiety was obvious. True, he had saved his army and never tired of informing Washington to that effect. Lincoln thanked him for "the heroism and skill of yourself, officers and men," yet McClellan could not admit that Lee had out-generaled him. "We have failed to win only because overpowered by superior numbers," he rationalized in an annoyingly predictable way.[12]

McClellan's relations with Washington spiraled downward after Malvern Hill. Now situated in a virtually unassailable position at Harrison's Landing (supported by naval gunfire and with logistical support from the river), his continuing presence near Richmond completely neutralized any Confederate move toward Washington. To resume the offensive, Little Mac repeated his customary requests for massive reinforcement. Lincoln wired him on July 2, hinting at how absurd were such requests when only sixty thousand troops might be found elsewhere in theater and these hardly discretionary in mission. The president might have added that the government's closing of northern recruiting stations in April due to McClellan's promising advance on Richmond had caused such shortages. But he did not. The president merely suggested that he was not asking that Richmond be taken just now. "I am satisfied that yourself, officers and men have done the best you could," he wrote the general, adding that by all accounts "better fighting was never done," so "ten thousand thanks for it." Merely save the army, its material and personnel, Lincoln insisted, "and I will strengthen it for the offensive, as fast as I can." Just don't expect reinforcement within a month or even six weeks. McClellan persisted, however, raising the fifty thousand figure for reinforcements and informing Secretary of War Edwin M. Stanton on July 3, "Reinforcements should be sent to me rather much over than much less than 100,000 men." Strength figures for the army on July 10 showed 98,631 officers and men "present for duty, equipped" with 335 artillery pieces; days later the figures stood at some 101,692 "aggregate present for duty" from a total present-and-absent statistic of 158,314. McClellan and Washington debated all month as to the meaning of those numbers and how to succor the army.[13]

Despite the impressions of Colonel Barlow and some senior officers, the army itself had not lost confidence in its leader. McClellan was nothing short of inspirational in the eyes of his men. He instituted inspections to restore élan and ordered regimental band concerts once more. "We see General McClellan nearly every day," recorded Sgt. Maj. Elisha Hunt Rhodes of Rhode Island, "and he often speaks to the men." Not only had the general graced the Independence Day national salute with fanciful proclamation, but he trooped the line as the soldiery "cheered and put their caps on the bayonet points," suggesting that the army's morale "was ascertained to be much better than supposed." Three hundred naval guns roared, making the earth tremble and echoing up and down the James. Whiskey rations were issued and music played until midnight, remembered Pvt. Robert Knox Sneden of the Fortieth New York, the "Mozart Regiment." McClellan addressed the men and spoke of victory—not over Lee and the Rebels, but over adversity. Such adversity was not of his doing, McClellan claimed. Few observers might deny that McClellan expressed great concern for his army. Few could agree, however, as he claimed to wife, Mary Ellen, on July 7, "We have accomplished one of the grandest operations in Military History."[14]

McClellan seemed to drift off in his own personal war. He imagined numerically superior enemies. He battled with himself (physically and psychologically) and especially with the administration in Washington. He found his true enemy, "heartless villains" in the capital, who "have done their best to sacrifice as noble an Army as ever marched to battle." In McClellan's mind, it was he, not the Confederacy, whom Secretary Stanton and his Radical clique wanted defeated. "If I had succeeded in taking Richmond now the fanatics of the North might have been too powerful and reunion impossible," he observed, mixing political result with military affairs—always dangerous for a general in a democracy. He considered himself indispensable, the savior of the government and the nation. Emitting a West Pointer's disdain for politicians as amateurs dabbling in a world better left to professionals and discounting Lincoln's and Stanton's abilities and strategic acumen, McClellan courted favor with administration opponents while at the same time seeking validation from his commander in chief. For those civilian leaders he was now something of an embarrassment. He had been their supreme commander, their general in chief overseeing the whole military element of Union grand strategy, until reduced to mere field commander in March. If, as historian Gary Gallagher contends, "despite Lee's important role, George B. McClellan indisputably stood as the central figure of the Richmond campaign," then for that reason alone his post–Malvern Hill barrage of excuses, subterfuges, and continuous requests for reinforcement merited attention.[15]

Thus Lincoln would personally visit Harrison's Landing in early July, seeking to brace his principal field commander for returning to his main task. Indeed, the president and his advisers may well have wanted to sack McClellan by this point. The general was schooled in the art of preparation, often confusing that necessary ingredient of victory with execution. True, as the general informed Washington, the Army of the Potomac may not have been ready yet to renew the offense. Lincoln understood this when he telegraphed McClellan immediately after Malvern Hill to save the army first where he was, or by removal if necessary. "If, at any time, you feel able to take the offensive, you are not restrained from doing so," however, quipped the president. But McClellan's overcautiousness ("the slows," in Lincoln's words) became aggravating. Perhaps Maj. Gen. Ambrose Burnside might be persuaded to return from coastal Carolina operations to take over the beleaguered army on the Peninsula. Burnside declined on grounds of inadequacy, deferring to his friend Little Mac. Moreover, McClellan's earlier job commanding the whole U.S. Army (which in his mind he had never relinquished) had accustomed him to offer policy advice when the government simply sought a more operational focus. McClellan wrote the president on June 20 hinting that he wanted "to lay before your Excellency by letter or telegram my views as to the present state of military affairs throughout the whole country." That wasn't on Lincoln's agenda as he sailed down the Potomac aboard the vessel *Ariel.* Rather, he wanted a new general in chief and a coordinated two-pronged offensive in Virginia that involved McClellan. The president arrived at Harrison's Landing on July 8 seeking solutions. McClellan met him with an unsolicited position paper on "the existing state of the Rebellion." The paper said nothing directly about the Army of the Potomac or its particular mission.[16]

That army rather poorly greeted its commander in chief, said soldier Robert Sneden. McClellan agreed, writing his wife a fortnight later, "I *had to order* the men to cheer & they did it very feebly," although in that interval the general's feelings toward his commander in chief and those around him had soured further. Other commentators claimed to have cheered the "Grand Old Man," as one New Yorker called Lincoln. Looking ungainly in his high silk hat and dust-covered black suit, the president paraded the line on horseback. He gave no hint of his intentions for their beloved commanding general. McClellan wrote his wife after Lincoln left that he did not know how much the president had really profited by his visit, "for he really seems quite incapable of rising to the height of the merits of the question and the magnitude of the crisis." In fact, his manner "seemed that of a man about to do something of which he was much ashamed." Thus McClellan skirted asking Lincoln for reappointment to his old position as general in chief and hinted that he would serve where needed. The two men talked about the state of the army and (much to McClellan's chagrin) how it might be removed from the Peninsula. The chief executive then left, having also chatted with key corps commanders. Just two of those commanders, Erasmus Keyes and William B. Franklin, favored evacuation; Edwin Sumner, Samuel Heintzelman, and Fitz John Porter, like McClellan, felt removal of the army would prove disastrous to the Union cause.[17]

Three days later, on July 11, unbeknown to McClellan, the administration resolved the unity of command problem by ordering Maj. Gen. Henry Wager Halleck, the successful western theater commander, to Washington as the new supreme commander. The newcomer would learn more about McClellan's thorny relations with Washington when he too visited Harrison's Landing later in the month. By that time, other issues crowded the agenda, further screening the contents of McClellan's position paper. Not that Halleck was much concerned with that document. Others were, however, as they saw the purpose of the war shifting from its constitutional base. On July 1, Lincoln had asked northern governors for a new 300,000-man levy "to bring this unnecessary and injurious civil war to a speedy and satisfactory conclusion." That same day he signed two significant acts revising income tax rates to help defray the costs of the war and initiating a transcontinental railroad to open the West. The next day, Lincoln signed two more laws. The Morrill Act provided states with twenty thousand acres of land for each senator and representative as an endowment for proposed agricultural and mechanical schools that would become a land grant college system for a reunited nation. The second law demanded a loyalty oath from every elected or appointed government official. Later in July, Lincoln would sign legislation dealing with confiscation of Rebel property. He was employing the war powers of his office to promote activist government for modernizing and improving the nation even while that nation struggled to survive on the battlefield. Here then was a new political economy of war that discomfited many people.[18]

Other transformational forces were at work that hot summer. Before Malvern Hill, the conflict had been controlled or limited. Thereafter, it began to evolve inexorably toward unrestrained warfare. The change was slow and evolutionary and actually began that spring in the western theater. For both sides, it extended past voluntary manpower mobilization to conscription, substitution, or recruitment of local defense battalions called "partisan rangers" that meshed fighting and home front in yet uncharted waters. Change went even beyond the economic warfare of the Union's naval blockade and embargoes and Confederate decrees about burning cotton and denying such commodities to the enemy—affecting both the hinterland and coastal regions. It could be seen in reaction to the previous year's Union military disasters at Bull Run and Ball's Bluff that had spawned a congressional star chamber called the Committee on the Conduct of the War. Political dimensions of the struggle for both sides increasingly involved expanding presidential war powers, diminishing civil liberties, and more sophisticated political economies of war. Beyond Washington and Richmond, civilians felt smothered by an all-engulfing immersion in the unending conflict. War had coalesced military, political, and socioeconomic dimensions as never before by the summer of 1862. Perhaps it had been moving in that direction ever since John Brown stormed the Harpers Ferry armory in 1859 to incite the slaves to revolt.[19]

Definitions of the nature of war, the status of combatants, and what a particular war is all about always translate into change in laws, statutes, and process to contain the carnage. It made sense in 1861 and 1862, for instance, to question why, if an early end to the bloodshed without conciliation could be found, the Union should risk alienating the southern citizenry. We have taken New Orleans "and are fast getting every important place," Federal Capt. Hans C. Heg wrote his wife from Tennessee in late spring. The war would soon be over, for "when Richmond falls, the Confederacy is played out." Accommodation would make reconstruction so much easier. Then something went terribly wrong. Richmond did not fall, nor did strategic strong points like Chattanooga, Tennessee, and Vicksburg on the Mississippi. Southern resistance stiffened. Northern politicians and some in uniform questioned McClellan's generalship as well as government policies and the performance of the Lincoln administration. The Seven Days' defeat provided a watershed for accommodation with the South. Failure on the Virginia Peninsula persuaded many people that little hope existed for reconciliation. A firmer and even harsher war was needed against a determined enemy. Property confiscation, enforced loyalty oaths, arrests, and banishment from occupied territory, even allowing the army to subsist on the southern economy might break the backbone of rebellion.[20]

Moreover, the issue of slave property had surfaced. Southern black labor undergird the Confederate war effort, as many Federal officers and men soon discovered. The term "contraband of war," or just "contraband," became the sobriquet for refugee blacks (however indefinite their legal status) when every patrol reappeared in camp with those victims ostensibly seeking asylum. Return or protection of such private property became less likely as the First Confiscation

Act (signed the previous August) authorized the president to seize any property used in support of insurrection and a second such measure (adopted on July 17, 1862) specifically spoke to confiscation of human property—slaves—of Rebels. A militia bill also adopted by Congress that day enabled Federal utilization of blacks for any military duties within their capabilities. Together with congressional passage of an Article of War on March 10, 1862, forbidding military officers to return runaway slaves to their owners, followed by emancipation of slaves in the District of Columbia in April, the floodgates of abolition and emancipation had begun to squeak open, essentially legitimizing the liberation practices of northern soldiery. Still, Lincoln and others shrank from taking the nation too far toward total emancipation at this time.

Ersatz emancipation (as liberation), like confiscation (or pilfering) of other Rebel property, marched into Dixie with the first blue-clad soldiers. Contraband blacks quickly saw men in blue as their ticket to escaping slavery and attached themselves in defiance of laws, the Constitution, and general white prejudice against blacks. The urge for harsher treatment of rebellious Southerners, including freeing slaves as a war-ending device, confronted conciliation when politicians and generals squared off on such issues that second summer of the war. Professor William Freehling claims that the confiscation acts gave the U.S. government "a law-enforcing bureaucracy and loyal slaveholders a federal police" via the army for separating Unionists from Rebels and either rewarding or punishing them via protection or legal taking of their property. Other historians claim that the weaknesses of the confiscation acts rendered them useless. Professed southern loyalty as well as tepid enforcement by Lincoln and his military officials screened the effort. The soldiery saw it more simply, however: Southerners were rebels; their property could be liberated and used to Union benefit. Civilians resisted accordingly and bloodshed occurred. Thus conciliation and restoration of the Union under the Constitution fused with punishment and retribution via confiscation that summer. Emancipation lurked in the shadows.[21]

This hardening direction of the war could be found on the Virginia Peninsula. One northern humanitarian working among black refugees at "Tyler House, Camp Hamilton" would write a friend at home later in September, "We have been in such a turmoil ever since McClellan came down here with his hordes of plunderers and commenced rolling [*sic*] the people." New York soldier Robert Knox Sneden noted earlier that the nearby Westover house and grounds at Harrison's Landing had been wantonly vandalized by his comrades-in-arms. He claimed that this would never have occurred had the overseer's family remained instead of fleeing the invaders, "as guards are always placed on occupied houses to prevent this very thing." Individual acts of theft and destruction in barnyards, icehouses, fields, and water mills were one thing. But such hooliganism bred citizen resistance (leading even to partisan or guerrilla warfare in portions of the South mostly beyond Virginia). A revolving door of episode, blame, and counteraction engulfed civilian and soldier alike, distinct from set-piece battles between recognized combatants. The situation caught the Davis government's attention after Seven Days.[22]

Responding to a Gloucester County citizens' petition in early August for protection from "the ravages of the enemy," Lee explained that reaction by the main army would only result in attracting a larger force of the enemy, "and their ravages would be more extensive and ruinous." He recommended a "corps of rangers," that quasi-regular organization, along with conscription, authorized as a sort of local defense force by the Confederate Congress back in the spring. He also suggested removal of property such as slaves, cattle, horses, and foodstuffs beyond the Federals' reach. That aside, Lee could envision no relief from an enemy "who are now under orders from the President of the Washington Government to subsist their army upon the country" (alluding to hardening Yankee dictats that had been put in place just since the conclusion of the Peninsula campaign). In fact, official Union policy still hung in the balance, as some generals like McClellan and Don Carlos Buell in Tennessee, while accepting the "contraband of war concept," remained convinced of the rightness of accommodation. McClellan advocated taking Richmond, thereby destroying the Confederate army and government, and then negotiating reconciliation with a southern people overwhelmed by irresistible Federal power. He deplored making war on those people. Truth was that for the Lincoln government, war policy had begun moving in opposite directions. McClellan's famous "Harrison's Landing letter to the president" surfaced this fact.[23]

Therein McClellan pointed out that the cause of free institutions and self-government should never be abandoned and that preservation of the Constitution and the Union stood paramount. He lectured

Lincoln that the president had to assume and exercise "the responsibility of determining, declaring and supporting such civil and military policy and of directing the whole course of national affairs in regard to the rebellion." The Constitution "gives you power sufficient even for the present terrible exigency," he advised. McClellan's words placed limits on the exercise of such executive power, however. For one thing, the general called for continued restraint in conduct of what he now saw as not merely rebellion but war. This should not become a war of subjugation or a war on the populace, but one conducted by "the highest principles known to Christian civilization." Military and political organizations should remain the target, with private property and the unarmed populace protected regardless of political or ideological considerations. Military appropriation of goods should be paid for, and there should be no military arrests or loyalty oaths. McClellan believed in protection of constitutional freedoms as a prerequisite for winning back support of the white masses and, incidentally, approval of foreign nations. Neither property confiscation, political executions of persons, territorial organization of states, nor forcible abolition of slavery "should be contemplated for a moment." The slogan "For the Union as it was and the Constitution as it is" acquired almost gospel meaning for believers like Little Mac. Such a policy should be clearly announced and followed, he urged.[24]

Historian Ethan S. Rafuse attributes McClellan's attitude to familial Whiggish political preference for order and stability, his Philadelphia upper-class snobbery, and West Point elitism. "Any declaration of radical views," especially on slavery," will rapidly disintegrate our present Armies," warned the general. Focusing on what he styled "concentrations of military power," McClellan offered a plausible view that "national forces should not be dispersed in expeditions, posts of occupation and numerous Armies; but should be massed and brought to bear upon the Armies of the Confederate States; those Armies thoroughly defeated, the political structure which they support would soon cease to exist." Washington might agree with the principle of concentration against enemy forces, realizing McClellan needed resources for his Army of the Potomac above all else. More disturbing to the Lincoln administration, of course, was the general's blatantly crossing the thin line of civil-military separation. If the general was trying to parry what he perceived to be a threatening riptide of political radicalism sweeping the halls of government, his opponents—hard-war emancipationists among the Republicans—sought McClellan's removal from command for ineptitude, if not outright treason. To them, he represented soft-war appeasement. The general should confine his attention to winning military victory, they advanced, a viewpoint shared by Lincoln. In any event, the president thanked McClellan for his frank observations, pocketed the Harrison's Landing paper, and said nothing.[25]

Back in Washington, the president declared, "McClellan would not fight." The city's rumor mills immediately touted government uncertainty about army affairs and how slavery was the "chief component of the difficulties." In fact, Lincoln could not fire McClellan directly for fear of inciting the army to attempt a coup against the government. On the other hand, if the slave issue underscored the civil-military quandary contained in McClellan's missive, it was Lincoln's job, not McClellan's, to worry about larger war policy. The general's letter no doubt had its value. It reflected a distinctly polarized populace. It clearly defined what might be called the political moderate or conservative position. It underscored powerful border state legislators' sentiments—those of Kentucky senator John J. Crittenden, for instance—as well as those from Democratic sections of the Midwest and northeastern business interests. The conservatives feared social revolution and afforded a moderating influence to more fanatical radical hard-war subjugationists and emancipationists. Officers in McClellan's army like Col. Gouverneur K. Warren of the Fifth New York wrote his brother on July 20 that Lincoln should "discard" New England and Horace Greeley abolitionists; doing so "would remove the cause for resistance from the minds of the masses South, and we could crush out the Secession Leaders." Warren thought the soldiers were "fighting for the Union which was unattainable without permitting southerners their constitutional rights." Such views reflected growing enlisted-rank disillusionment with disease, battles, and no end to the war in sight, he claimed.[26]

On the hand, the very vocal Radical camp included reformist zealots like Greeley, William Lloyd Garrison, Wendell Phillips, and African American spokesman Frederick Douglass, hard-line politicians Thaddeus Stevens, Charles Sumner, Benjamin Wade, and Zachariah Chandler, and Generals John C. Frémont, Benjamin Butler, and Ormsby MacKnight Mitchel. They saw slavery as the

Confederacy's backbone, morally and economically as well as politically. These advocates of emancipation saw property confiscation as a method and loyalty oaths and arrests as intimidating tools for separating Unionists and secessionists. It made perfect sense to direct the Union military to subsist off southern resources and even enlist liberated slaves as combatants. Lincoln's task included controlling the Radicals' influence.[27]

Caught in the middle were so-called moderates of the War Democrat stripe and newspapers like the *New York Times*. Accommodation to the constitutional rights for Rebels struck many in this camp as traitorous and incompatible with the sacrifices of northern soldiers on the battlefield. They felt less concern with southern sensibilities while urging a more resolute pursuit of military victory. As IV Corps division commander Erasmus Keyes wrote Union Quartermaster Gen. Montgomery Meigs in late July, "The South has been made a unit by the mere continuance of the war," and "to think of starving them out is simply absurd unless we can destroy their rail and water lines of communication," whereby their armies would starve on account of bad roads in wet weather. Nobody said anything about changing southern institutions and culture, however. Emancipation hardly entered this group's lexicon. Moderates, particularly in Congress, held up debate on refining confiscation legislation while McClellan struggled before Richmond. Such divided counsels (as Keyes termed it) and the Seven Days' defeat simply increased southern antipathies to ending the conflict.[28]

Lincoln personally continued to skirt the emancipation issue when signing the Second Confiscation Act (but sent a draft veto message to Capitol Hill signaling his lingering doubts). Confiscation continued to trouble him because it failed to address a slave's freedom past the death of the erstwhile owner. Moreover, confiscation reflected the developing contest as to whether the legislative or executive branch of government would handle slavery and reconstruction of the nation. As did most others, Lincoln viewed the legislation as a war-fighting measure, aimed at a rebellious, slaveholding, southern white oligarchy who had caused and now abetted the war. He envisioned confiscation for military purposes only during the war and solutions in the courts after the war. Emancipation would belong to executive branch action when the time was right. Thus Second Confiscation gave the chief executive power to employ all forms of rebel property, including slaves, for suppression of the rebellion. True, the act also provided for freedmen colonization "in some tropical country beyond the limits of the United States." Yet overall, the Second Confiscation Act seemed a "repudiation of the conciliatory policy." To soldiers like John Beatty in one of the western armies, it would "enable us to weaken the enemy and strengthen ourselves, as we have hitherto not been able to do." Slavery was the enemy's weakest point and key to his position; once that institution was torn down, Rebels would lose all interest in the Confederacy and "be too glad to escape with their lives." Confiscation appeared to be a step in an evolutionary process toward victory, not toward emancipation.[29]

The president signed yet another significant piece of legislation that same day. A militia bill amending the Force Bill of 1795 further suggested that both unsatisfactory combat results and growing radical fervor had found their mark in Congress and at the White House. This new move empowered the commander in chief to call militia into service for up to nine months, to set manpower quotas on the states, and, where a state failed to fulfill its quota, to issue "all necessary rules and regulations" "to provide for enrollment" for "otherwise putting this act into execution." The new law never mentioned Federal manpower drafts or conscription per se. The details of mobilizing manpower remained with the governors. Yet the vague wording "all necessary rules and regulations" allowed an activist administration to move the Union closer to national conscription (already embarked on by the Confederacy). Moreover, the president could now enlist African Americans, assuredly moving freedmen's opportunities from labor to combat employment, although nobody really talked much about that for the moment. Jurist Frank Williams cites an obscure Lincoln memorandum of the time wherein the president professed no objection to recruiting free Negroes, slaves of disloyal owners, or slaves of loyal owners (with the owners' consent) but objected to recruiting slaves of loyal owners without consent unless necessary. He most strenuously objected "to conducting offensively, while recruiting, and to carrying away slaves not suitable for recruits." Lincoln continued to walk a tightrope.[30]

The Confiscation and Militia Acts expanded Lincoln's tool kit. Even the aged yet respected former General in Chief Winfield Scott (himself a Virginian) weighed in by telling people in New York that it was now a war of conquest. To historian William Blair, the Union had accomplished more in the Seven Days' period "by losing than it might have through winning." Perhaps a turning point, the period certainly brought slow rationalization of a new war policy—an anathema to McClellan and his kind. Still, Lincoln moved circumspectly on the issue of outright emancipation. Four days after receiving McClellan's Harrison's Landing letter and returning to Washington, the president again introduced the idea of compensated emancipation to border state senators and congressmen. Otherwise, "the institution in your states will be extinguished by mere friction and abrasion," he told them. Colonization and recompense for slave owners remained possible. When again rebuffed by those legislators, Lincoln retreated, fearful that any form of emancipation would fan the spirit of resistance and even secession in loyal slave states. Furthermore, emancipation under Lincoln's scheme would hardly lessen Radical pressure for "unconstitutional" emancipation by presidential decree for the remaining three million slaves in the seceded states—a move totally unacceptable to a majority of Southerners. A frustrated president turned to yet another approach.[31]

Within a fortnight, Lincoln decided that he would issue an emancipation proclamation using his war powers. Short of constitutional amendment, he had no other device at hand beyond property confiscation. Presidential secretary John Hay recorded on July 20, "The President himself has been . . . the bulwark of the institution he abhors, for a year," but he would not preserve slavery much longer. So, after hinting at some action during a carriage ride with Secretary of State William Seward and Secretary of the Navy Gideon Welles on July 13 (the day after his final plea to the border state politicians), he aired the first draft of an executive decree ending slavery before the full cabinet on July 22. It included warnings of the consequences of confiscation. It renewed the compensation idea for loyal states undertaking gradual emancipation and proposed that as of January 1, 1863, slaves should be free in all the rebellious states. Only Postmaster General Montgomery Blair, a product of border state politics, objected, predicting political fallout in the autumn elections. Secretary Seward wisely advised postponing the proclamation "until you can give it to the country supported by military success," lest it be viewed "as the last measure of an exhausted government, a cry for help . . . our last *shriek*, on the retreat."[32]

Seward was correct. He recognized not only domestic danger,

but shifting international sentiment. European newspapers trumpeted emancipation as a Radical Republican ploy to spawn a bloody servile uprising in the South. European governments, concerned about repercussions of possible racial strife within their colonies, felt extreme pressure to intervene in or mediate the American struggle. Declining cotton supplies threatened economic distress for influential mercantile interests, especially in Great Britain. Napoleon III of France had met with Confederate commissioner John Slidell on July 16, and the commissioner requested recognition of the Confederacy and military aid in the form of warships to break the Yankee blockade. As the Confederacy hovered on the verge of attaining its independence via the battlefield, British and French intervention seemed likely. Lincoln later recounted that the wisdom of Seward's counsel to postpone "struck me with very great force." He admitted, "In all my thought upon the subject, I had entirely overlooked" the international factor. Keeping his counsel, however, even the new general in chief, Henry Halleck, knew nothing of Lincoln's plan. Writing to McClellan on August 7, Halleck fully agreed with him "in regard to the manner in which the war should be conducted," adding, "I believe the present policy of the President to be conservative."[33]

Professor Freehling may be correct in suggesting that although Lincoln signed the two July bills from Congress, political and military survival required a presidential stall to "allow time for a final and definitive test" on conciliatory policy that could induce the "rebels' voluntary return to a Union that protected slavery." Ultimately, that test had to be some singular military victory. Just where and when and which general and his army could effectively deliver that victory remained unclear. Was Lincoln even interested in amicable settlement with the South by this point? On July 25, while promulgating the Second Confiscation Act, he called for suppression of the insurrection, urging persons in rebellion to cease "on pain of forfeitures and seizures"—hardly conciliatory words or tone. By this time too a new combat team had been installed to pursue the war more vigorously in Virginia. In addition to McClellan, Major Generals Henry Wager Halleck and John Pope were brought in from the West to sort out eastern affairs. Lincoln's focus never shifted very far from the operational demands of winning the war and suppressing rebellion, especially when such demands stood out so close to Washington.[34]

Heading the new military team would be Halleck, former departmental and theater commander, reputedly the smartest officer in the Old Army and previously McClellan's subordinate. Now their roles would be reversed, with "Old Brains" (as Halleck was styled) commanding Little Mac. This promised some difficulty for both men. Actually, Lincoln had first introduced Pope, another veteran of the war in the greater Mississippi Valley, before Halleck's arrival. Pope's role was to organize the new army in Virginia; both he and Halleck reflected pragmatic experience dealing with recalcitrant southern slave owners. Pope and McClellan promised fealty and cooperation in a new drive on Richmond. Yet probably neither believed the words of the other. Pope's telling phrases should have alerted McClellan to the Westerner's role as new mouthpiece for the administration. "Your position on James River places the whole of the enemy's force around Richmond between yourself and Washington," Pope wrote his new comrade-in-arms on Independence Day. Were McClellan to move with his whole command directly on Richmond, "I must fight the whole force of the enemy before I could join you, and at so great a distance from you as to be beyond any assistance from your army," Pope noted. "If my command be embarked and sent to you by James River," he stated, "the enemy would be in Washington before it had half accomplished the journey." He concluded that under such circumstances of "insuring the safety of the capital," "my position here is difficult and embarrassing." McClellan answered patronizingly that Pope was doing the right thing by concentrating his dispersed commands, as "departure from this wise principle has been the cause of all our trouble in front of Washington." He underscored his own plan to preserve the morale of his men by maintaining his present position as long as possible and vowed that he would "not fall back unless absolutely forced to do so."[35]

Meanwhile, the Army of the Potomac passed the days and nights in debilitating heat and sickness, monotony and watchful waiting, as patrols and a cordon of outposts and earthworks screened Harrison's Landing and vicinity. The summer heat also affected southern troops. North Carolinian W. C. Henslee recalled that "sickness of epidemic proportions and nature" in his regiment struck down "81 lives from our ranks" while encamped at Drewry's Bluff below Richmond. Lee rebuilt his army, stretching it defensively from Louisiana camps on the railroad north of Richmond eastward around the city to places like the Washington Artillery of New Orleans's Camp Longstreet,

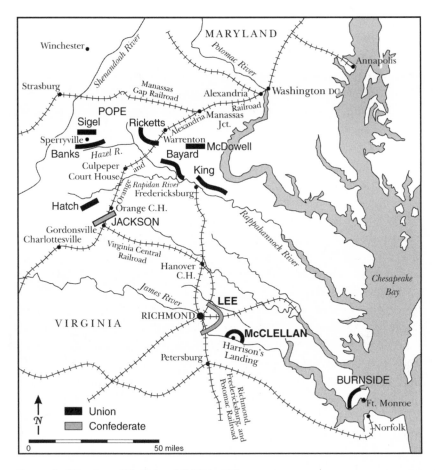

Strategic Situation—Virginia—Mid-July 1862

and then southward thirty miles to Petersburg, covering his logistical line to the Carolinas. He wanted to prevent Federal advance on
either side of the James (precisely what McClellan had in mind, if yet
imprecisely). Reinforcements bolstered Lee's numbers. Lt. William
H. S. Burgwyn, one of those arrivals, filled letters home about dusty
marches and countermarches to deter the enemy from filtering across
the James or assaulting river defenses like Drewry's Bluff. Staff officers
like Capt. Charles Minor Blackford had it easier, taking advantage of
free time to visit Richmond City. He caught glimpses of Confederate
deities from President Davis (who "looks like a statesman") to Lee
("the highest type of Cavalier class to which by blood and rearing he
belongs"). His direct superior, Stonewall Jackson, "on the other hand

was a typical roundhead," alluding to a Cromwellian pose of a different age. Transferring in from coastal Carolina, Brig. Gen. Nathan G. "Shanks" Evans wrote his wife at the end of July about the army's "fine spirits" and suggested that if God would grant another victory, "I think the war in Virginia will stop for awhile."[36]

According to Vermonter Marshall Harvey Twitchell, "Rest, reinforcements, and discipline soon brought us again into fighting trim." Despite Confederate officer Edward Porter Alexander's postwar contention that he could not recall a single incident of interest as occurring during that month, fighting resumed at the end of July when Lee sent a combined arms expedition under Daniel Harvey Hill to Coggins Point across the James from which to bombard McClellan's camps at Harrison's Landing and cut off river communications. The thirty-minute barrage by Hill's forty-three guns unnerved the Yankees and ripped up camps and supply boats but hardly caused McClellan to shift base. In fact, three days later, he sent an expeditionary force of his own to seize Cole's plantation on the point to prevent any further disruptions as a naval flotilla steamed upriver and anchored threateningly off Malvern Hill. Such moves bothered Lee, who dispatched Hill back to divisional field command and withheld reinforcement of Jackson, now parrying Pope's concentration in the Warrenton area as well as a Federal buildup at Fredericksburg on the Rappahannock River. Unpredictably, McClellan suddenly became even more menacing when he ordered "Fighting Joe" Hooker with seventeen thousand infantry and cavalry on a reconnaissance to Malvern Hill. The Army of the Potomac no doubt felt the pressure from Washington to do something.[37]

Early August appeared to witness resumption of a Federal offensive against Richmond. Cavalryman Stuart reported an ominous column moving out of Fredericksburg on the telegraph road, threatening the vital Virginia Central Railroad and the lower end of the Richmond and Fredericksburg Railroad. Hooker's reoccupation of Malvern Hill by August 5 was uncomfortably close to the capital, and Lee positioned nearly half his army against Hooker while at the same time continuing to watch his southside communications with Petersburg. Both army commanders personally discovered one another to be full of fight and prepared to give battle in much the same manner as a month earlier. But the day was late at Malvern Hill, the weather hot, and the Confederates could do little to maneuver Hooker out of position or threaten his communications with Harrison's Landing. Still, Lee's prompt reaction spooked McClellan, as usual. Claiming he could not get his whole army to Hooker's support before Lee attacked and suggesting a major battle would only uncover the fortified camps at Harrison's Landing anyway, McClellan glossed over the real reason for not better supporting his subordinate. Withdrawal orders had arrived from Washington. "Under advice I have received from Washington I think it necessary for you to abandon the position tonight, getting everything away before day light," he told Hooker at 10:00 p.m. on August 6. By the next morning, the Federals had pulled out, and Lee was baffled as to McClellan's real intent. Aggressive Federal brigadier Philip Kearny still urged immediate movement on Richmond, while Capt. Theodore Dodge of the Tenth New York jotted in his diary, "We are ready to march at a minute's notice, with wagons packed and 8 days rations on hand." The march would occur, but not as Kearny or Dodge wanted.[38]

McClellan had overreached himself scheming and fretting in the July heat. Instead of developing and then acting promptly on a new offensive plan, he had passed too much time penning "soft" policy advisories to superiors and letters of apology to staunch local secessionists like Hill Carter of Shirley plantation for his soldiers' property transgressions. He additionally wrote politically inflammatory missives to influential friends and revealing private letters to his wife. While toying with Washington over statistical counts, in the end McClellan had moved too late. The withdrawal telegram from Washington on August 3 reflected corps commanders' opinions of army morale and the dreadful health in the James River camps as well as Lincoln's displeasure with the entire situation. Halleck's assumption of his duties on July 23 had been followed quickly by conferences with the president, Stanton, Pope, and Burnside and then departure for Harrison's Landing the next afternoon. Burnside and Quartermaster General Meigs went along. Long-distance telegraphic and letter communications had not moved the army nor resolved strategic and operational differences. Halleck carried with him Stanton's instructions that he could keep or fire McClellan at his discretion.[39]

Halleck's team visit found the Army of the Potomac safe, still believing in itself and its commander, and prepared to do battle. At first, Halleck gave McClellan the benefit of the doubt, leaving it to Burnside and Meigs to query staff and subordinates. In awe of his former superior, Halleck admitted that the meeting was awkward as he listened patiently to McClellan's latest scheme for an advance south of the James. That would not do, said Halleck, for it was necessary that McClellan and Pope unite forces and attack Richmond while shielding Washington. Little Mac wanted thirty thousand reinforcements; Halleck said that was impossible. Attack or withdraw from the Peninsula were the options, and McClellan had until the next morning to decide. McClellan reluctantly agreed to attack north of the James (thus leading to Hooker's movement), and Halleck's party then returned to Washington. No sooner was Halleck back in the city than he received new aid requests from McClellan. Lincoln may have been more perturbed at Burnside's intelligence of Army of the Potomac officers threatening to march on Washington and clean out the politicians.[40]

Halleck hardly wanted field command himself, and Burnside continued to brush aside such an opportunity. Yet something had to be done. The situation was in violation of the precepts of Halleck's own tract, *Elements of Military Art and Science.* He concluded that Union forces in Virginia were dangerously dispersed and that distinct danger might lie behind comments like those of Sgt. Thomas W. Smith of the Sixth Pennsylvania Cavalry that "the men fairly idolize [McClellan] and are more eager to be led into battle by him than ever." Whether that fealty also meant supporting some sort of military coup was never clear. More than one senior officer shared the view of Brigadier General Keyes, who told Meigs on July 21, "The newspapers will tell you that the health of this army is improving," but "it is only apparently improving." Officers and men were beginning to droop: "To pen up more than 100,000 men and animals in a space so small that you can find no point of that space which is a mile distant from its outside boundary on the James River in the months of July, August, and September is to secure disease, weakness, and nostalgia as a certain crop." Unless massively reinforced, "they will succeed in ruining this whole army, and this army lost, the North is necessarily from that moment at the mercy of the South." Better to carry the army away "to a healthy distance and build it up to return the whole to the James River next October," was Keyes's view. If the army could take a position between the enemy and "our own possessions, we might allege health as a motive for the movement, bid defiance to the South, and by and by to England and France also, but by remaining here in our present condition we submit to chance the ark of our safety." The "sickliness of this country in August and September being one of the strongest reasons for withdrawing" found a receptive audience in Washington.[41]

Halleck and McClellan remained cordial, although neither trusted the other. To his wife Halleck wrote, "[McClellan] received me kindly" at their meeting at Harrison's Landing, but "our interview was from its nature necessarily somewhat embarrassing," particularly because "I was obliged to disagree with him as to the feasibility of his plans." Halleck found it "unpleasant to tell one who had been my superior in rank that his plans were wrong, but my duty to myself and country compelled me to do so." Though the army commander was "in many respects a most excellent and valuable man," he did not understand strategy and "should never plan a campaign." Halleck believed that he and McClellan "can get along well together, if he is so disposed," though Halleck feared "that his friends have excited his jealousy and that he will be disposed to pitch into me." So be it, he wrote his wife. Just as he had sustained McClellan from the west, McClellan "ought now to sustain me." "I hope he will," Halleck concluded, "but I doubt it." This was a far cry from sentiments Halleck had expressed to a traveling companion while coming east on July 21. "McClellan was the ablest military man in the world," he said at that time. Perhaps trading western simplicity for the mare's nest of eastern politics, duplicity, and mistrust had not been such a good idea after all. Arrival in Washington confirmed such misgivings, further exacerbated by McClellan's obsession that the true defense of Washington lay "in a rapid and heavy blow given by this Army upon Richmond."[42]

An exasperated Halleck finally directed Burnside to move his IX Corps from the base of the Peninsula to reinforce Pope. Then he ordered McClellan on the last day of July to immediately begin transferring his sick northward and two days later to abandon Harrison's Landing—not for a march on Richmond, but for transfer to the line of the Rappahannock River. McClellan and Burnside would cooperate with Pope's army, and Halleck gave McClellan reason to believe that he would eventually command the whole force. McClellan reacted predictably that Halleck's dispatch had caused him "the greatest pain I ever experienced." He pleaded for continuation of his present position, a scant twenty-five miles from the city. Any transfer would demoralize his army, deprive it of naval support, signal northern weakness, and trigger European recognition of the Confederacy, advanced McClellan. Assume the defensive everywhere else but in tidewater Virginia, he advised, for "here, directly in front of this Army, is the heart of the rebellion," and "it is here on the banks of the James that the fate of the Union should be decided." The order would stand, Halleck shot back. Using McClellan's own overestimation of the enemy, Halleck told him, "You are 30 miles from Richmond and General Pope 80 or 90, with his superior numbers upon one or the other, as he may elect." Neither army could reinforce the other in case of attack. "If you or anyone else had presented a better [plan] I certainly should have adopted it, but all of your plans require re-enforcements, which it is impossible to give you." Halleck advanced, "I find the forces divided and I wish to unite them." Later he told his chastened field commander, "I deeply regret that you cannot agree with me as to the necessity of reuniting the old Army of the Potomac." Lee, made aware of the appearance of Burnside's men at Aquia Creek landing east of Fredericksburg, wrote Jackson at Gordonsville on August 7, "I have no idea that [McClellan] will advance on Richmond now." The Peninsula campaign was over. The campaign for northern Virginia was about to begin.[43]

The question may be fairly posed whether Washington should have ended McClellan's Richmond campaign at this point. McClellan had offered an eleventh-hour plan at the time of the Harrison's Landing meeting with Halleck that, ironically, was the device that Ulysses S. Grant used to circumvent Lee's stubborn defense of central Virginia two years later. Perhaps enhanced by such intervening events, McClellan's death-bed reflection in the mid-1880s was this: "Had the Army of the Potomac been permitted to remain on the line of the James I would have crossed to the south bank of that river, and, while engaging Lee's attention in front of Malvern, have made a rapid movement in force on Petersburg, having gained which I would have operated against Richmond and its communications from the west, having already gained those from the south." Moreover, as early as July 10, the Union army commander had requested from Brigadier General Meigs, the quartermaster general in Washington, "as many large ferry-boats as possible to be sent to him at once." However audacious and unlike McClellan, the scheme had merit. It would prove the very operation that eventually led to Union victory three years later. The elements of success seemed present even in 1862. But of course, McClellan was no Grant, and it still took some nine months of bitter fighting in 1864–65 to capture Richmond and destroy Lee's army.[44]

Certainly Little Mac could produce brilliant plans. As general in chief he had envisioned how a capture of Richmond would collapse southern military resistance and permit a grand sweep down the eastern seaboard of the Confederacy, securely anchored by Union sea power and Union coastal operations on his Atlantic flank, with linkages to the western forces of Don Carlos Buell and Henry Halleck beyond the Appalachian mountains, eventually reestablishing Federal institutions in the Deep South. Now, in July 1862, Union naval power controlled the tidewater and squadron commander Commodore Charles Wilkes expressed confidence that it could support any offensive movement undertaken by the army. If the army had sufficient transports—estimated to be thirty steamships and over one hundred sailing vessels—to carry both invalid and able-bodied troops away from the Peninsula, then it had the means to either project a river crossing of the James or convoy sufficient force by boat to the Appomattox River for expelling any Confederates defending Petersburg. Meigs told McClellan two weeks after the army commander's initial request that though ample craft might move up to twenty-four thousand men at the time, these were not ferryboats. Quartermaster agents went to Philadelphia and New York seeking to procure more shipping. Meigs meanwhile thought the steamers and half-dozen available ferries plus several tugboats were sufficient to tow the sailing vessels and barges anywhere desired by the army commander. Nonetheless, the question arises: At this stage of the war, were such an operation and its sophisticated logistics even possible for getting a jump on Lee, who enjoyed the interior lines of more rapid rail movement to counter such a thrust?[45]

The Army of the Potomac's trimonthly strength returns on August 10 showed more than ninety thousand men with thirty-seven heavy and 343 field guns available for such an operation. This posed a formidable task for logisticians. Within the week, the impending army withdrawal itself produced panic that the quartermasters would not find sufficient steamships necessary for accelerated debarkation. In principle, a revived army should have been able to move quickly overland once it got across the river barrier. That barrier would be breached in 1864 via pontoon bridges secured by naval presence. Just how quickly that might have been done two years earlier is conjecture. Lacking details of McClellan's scheme, it cannot be determined if railroad interdiction between the two cities might also have been contemplated. Uncertainty existed about several rumored Rebel ironclads abuilding at Richmond that could range downriver to disrupt Union control of the waterways. Federal intelligence was unsure of the flow of reinforcements coming from the south to enhance Lee's strength and placement of such units to counter any Federal advance using the James as a direct avenue to Richmond. McClellan seemed to imply a divergent strike: southward across the James to Petersburg and north of that river to Richmond from Malvern Hill. One thing seems sure: Brig. Gen. Alfred Pleasonton alerted McClellan's chief of staff (and father-in-law) Rudolph B. Marcy on August 13, "The enemy have, no doubt, the idea we are about to advance on Richmond."[46]

The central question was one of speed. Could McClellan and his subordinates even manage a difficult river crossing and change of base after the unsatisfactory results achieved on the Peninsula? Could the quartermasters develop a new base from which the army might operate, especially when Meigs dismissed McClellan's call for more logistical support and the construction of additional wharves? In retrospect, that same army two years later under a far more aggressive Ulysses S. Grant, while heavily battered by prolonged and bloody combat since the Wilderness, yet still capable of stealing a march on Lee across the James, proved incapable of quickly accomplishing what in essence was McClellan's 1862 plan. No indicators in mid-1862 suggested that McClellan would have been any more successful in securing quick and conclusive victory over Lee, capture of Richmond, and the end of the war in Virginia. The fact was, of course, thanks to Halleck, Stanton, and Lincoln, McClellan would never be given the chance to even try.

McClellan had a point in tirelessly contending, "A decided victory here [before Richmond], and the rebellion is crushed." "Here is the true defense of Washington," he preached. "It is here on the banks of the James that the fate of the Union should be decided." The fact was, by midsummer the Lincoln administration had tired of McClellan's opinions, promises, and complaints. Lee had beaten back Little Mac's juggernaut within sight of Richmond. A lull settled over the fighting. Sickness swept through both camps in the heat of a tidewater summer. At the same time, a different heat hung over Washington.

Badgered by changing political winds as northern Radicals sought a stronger prosecution of the war, Lincoln prodded the Army of the Potomac commander to renew operations. The president and secretary of war brought in new generals from the Mississippi Valley. Henry Halleck would take charge of Union armies everywhere while John Pope organized a consolidated field force both to shield Washington and to open a second line of advance on Richmond. Halleck's managerial task was to bridle two balky horses, McClellan and Pope, for a single concerted drive on the enemy capital. New faces did not necessarily mean new results.

The Union high command all but handed the initiative to the Confederates. Lee, working with President Jefferson Davis, stood on the cusp of forging a well-oiled Confederate fighting team: the future Army of Northern Virginia. Lee not only turned the tide against McClellan, but earned recognition as a victorious leader in a season that elsewhere had witnessed only retreat and defeat. He chose two superb wing commanders in Jackson and Longstreet for his rejuvenated strike force. Still, a measured actor, Lee could not act beyond Richmond's protection as long as McClellan's army remained on the city's doorstep. Offensives to redeem lost Virginia territory must wait, notwithstanding President Davis's fiery words that there could be "no difference of opinion" as to the "advantage of invading over being invaded"—except, perhaps, to a delusional group of politicians "who feared to excite the hate of our enemies."[47]

By July the changing nature of the war began to impact the grand strategy of both sides. The Lincoln administration introduced the first stirrings of official emancipation and the policy of hard-line subjugation of the South. Confiscation, draft statements on compensated manumission as well as colonization of freed people, and gradual tightening of guidance on manpower procurement all pointed to new roles for the government and the people. Such a shift held great portent for field commanders, bound technically by separation of civil-military relations and fighting front from home front. Personalities and policies, plans, actions, and words had increased importance in the hot summer of 1862. And the McClellan–Lee standoff before Richmond permitted Pope to replace McClellan at the forefront of the war in Virginia.

→ 2 ←

From Tidewater to Cedar Mountain

GEORGE MCCLELLAN spent the two weeks following receipt of Halleck's order trying desperately to avoid evacuating the Peninsula. Privately, he wrote letters excoriating Lincoln and other superiors for stupidity, duplicity, and culpability for what he took to be impending disaster. He dramatically reduced his estimation of enemy strength (perhaps reflecting the fact that Lee had already begun shifting forces to counter Pope to the north). Halleck meanwhile expected prompt compliance with his directive. The Army of the Potomac finally decamped on August 14. Rhode Islander Edward W. Stone noted. "The shadow of coming events at Harrison's Landing was resolved . . . into tangible substance." Preparations had been made with baggage and upwards of eleven thousand convalescing sick and wounded placed aboard river transports and sent downriver. Fate had intervened to assuage the ghosts of the Byrd and Harrison families, declared one Confederate, "that their *ancestral* marshes are yielding their malaria and mosquitoes with an unstinting hand, and aiding unsparingly the sword of the South in relieving it of invaders." No tents were to be carried but only five days' cooked rations and movement to be in light marching order. The general impression, said Union III Corps topographer Robert Sneden, was that "we will move on Richmond by way of Petersburg." Turning their backs on the Rebels beaten at Malvern Hill "and the entomological tribes that shared our tents and disturbed our repose," Sneden and his comrades took up the march. The route lay away from rather than toward Richmond.[1]

The officers in particular, Sneden observed further, anticipated that they would move on "Malvern Hill and Richmond, or cross the James above Petersburg, and move on Manchester," where lack of protective defenses gave access to the enemy capital. All this caused consternation, for, as another Rhode Islander, Elisha Hunt Rhodes, observed, "[We are no] nearer the end of the war than we were when we first landed at fortress Monroe five months ago." Capt. Theodore Dodge of New York remembered that in June, "if anyone had told me we were not going to Richmond, I should have laughed in his face." But now, "'tis best no doubt," for the "little mounds behind each regiment" attested to the fact that "this place is by no means healthy, and the worst months are to come." Sneden agreed: "All were glad to know that the army would move out of these burning acrid plains and go *somewhere* no matter where!" They were retiring before "overwhelming forces and fearful disease," Dodge concluded. At least some of Samuel Heintzelman's corps sported new uniforms and canvas leggings, their kepis adorned with snappy red diamond corps identification badges—the first such in the army. Still, many questioned whether a renewed offensive against Lee and Richmond rather than another "change of base" might have had a more salutary effect.[2]

No matter, the movement would be made, and it was a hot one. The temperature stood at ninety-two degrees on August 15, and four degrees higher three days later. "Our greatest enemy was dust," recounted Edward Walker of the First Minnesota, as the march back down the Peninsula met with "sullen and defiant remarks" from local women on all sides. The women were irate about the loss of slaves and servants, which now forced them to do their own tasks, noted Sneden. Why didn't the Yankees leave us alone, the women asked plaintively. "You will never subjugate us," they told their perceived oppressors, all the while asking for coffee and sugar and the ever-present snuff tobacco. Sneden deplored this peculiarly southern habit, for it "serves to excite them in the same way that strong tea does old women." Turning away empty-handed, the females would sneer, "Curse this war, but you 'uns will never conquer us." Devastation was everywhere. Williamsburg, the colonial Virginia capital, stood closed up, with stores sacked and no business being conducted. Only safe-guard sentinels ensured that the residents remained unharmed. Sneden commented that the column mustered barely six miles a day on average, ten at most, as McClellan "is taking things easy," although "Pope is badly in want of reinforcements."[3]

Sneden's observation indicated that his comrades knew another Federal force now operated elsewhere in Virginia. For the moment, though, he and the marchers concentrated on the immediate trek to embarkation points where river transports like "the little Schuykill steamer *Reindeer*" could convey them northward to a rendezvous with Pope. Precision and order attended the embarkation at Yorktown, Fortress Monroe, and Newport News. The army had retired through Charles City Court House and over the Chickahominy River at its mouth. There Federal technical proficiency and the Fiftieth New York Engineers had constructed a fourteen-hundred-foot crossing, "One of the best pontoon bridges we ever saw," pronounced William Westervelt of the Twenty-seventh New York. The structure conveyed a train of artillery or wagons in the center with two ranks of infantry on each side. Overall the ninety-mile march had not seemed "an agree-able prospect" to men like Theodore Dodge. Yet they had made it with more time lost to liberating surviving cornfields, springhouses, and chicken coops than in enemy action. Rhodes concluded that the populace "are very poor indeed," but that "they are reaping their reward." A last-minute bath and fishing restored everyone's spirits, with whole regiments of soldiers as well as horses and mules in the water together. Then they went aboard troop ships like the Hudson River steamer *Coatzacoalcos*.[4]

Shipboard quarters offered succor despite crowded conditions. "Bands were playing and men cheering, flags flying and the show grand," said Sneden, as they steamed down the York River and into Chesapeake Bay. Still, "our spirits were not so buoyant as when another much larger fleet, filled with expectant troops [had] left Alexandria in March last," with "On to Richmond" on their lips, he observed wistfully. Heavy swells in the bay caused resort to demijohns of whis-key. Some units, like the Second Pennsylvania, slept well on the over-night run to Aquia Creek, well fortified before departure with bread, cakes, watermelons, oranges, and even coconuts. The Federal army always ate better than their Confederate opponents, even in retreat. Probably more than a few of the departing Yankees wondered why

Lee and his generals had allowed them to escape unscathed. But Capt. Charles Wilkes of the navy concluded, "The facility and energy with which McClellan executed this retreat was in truth one of the most remarkable events of the war, and it [subsequently] served to save the country." By this time, Robert E. Lee and President Jefferson Davis viewed McClellan's departure with relief. Pope's army near Culpeper now demanded attention.[5]

Watching McClellan depart, Lee began to shift his own army toward the new threats on the Rapidan and Rappahannock rivers. He had been constrained from doing so as long as McClellan and a sizable body of Federals loomed so close to Richmond. Stonewall Jackson had gone ahead with two or three divisions, but that was not enough to ensure Richmond's safety from the new threat. Timing was crucial, and the new opponent promised possible interdiction of communications with the rest of the Confederacy through Gordonsville and Charlottesville as well as the crucial Shenandoah Valley granary. The rail junction at Gordonsville became the critical point. Lee could not abandon the Confederate capital completely. He would gamble that a residue of Federals left in the Hampton Roads area might be bluffed by two divisions and a cavalry brigade that would remain behind for protection for the Richmond–Petersburg area. By midmonth, Lee moved his headquarters to Gordonsville, then to Orange. He left behind a capital struggling to return to normal, terrorized as much by Brig. Gen. John H. Winder's eagle-eyed detectives harassing vagrants, rooting out illicit liquor trade, and fretting Maryland refugees as possible traitors as by fears about the Yankees. Like its counterpart, Washington, one hundred miles to the north, Richmond had become a fortified logistical and manufacturing as well as political center. Its residents watched apprehensively as Lee's army marched away to open a new front.[6]

On June 26, the very day that Lee had launched his Seven Days' offensive against McClellan at Beaver Dam Creek, Lincoln and Secretary of War Edwin Stanton established a new eastern army. Merging units of the old Mountain Department and departments of the Rappahannock and the Shenandoah, they styled it the Army of Virginia. The president prescribed its mission: the force would "operate in such manner as, while protecting Western Virginia and the national capital from danger or insult," it would also "in the speediest manner attack and overcome the rebel forces under Jackson and

Ewell, threaten the enemy in the direction of Charlottesville, and render the most effective aid to relieve General McClellan and capture Richmond." Here was an offensive–defensive mission that required delicate coordination and impeccable timing. Absent the guiding professional hand of a general in chief, however, an abiding question persisted: How to achieve success? The track record of civilian amateurs Lincoln and Stanton had left something to be desired, even if advised by an aged and eccentric Maj. Gen. Ethan Allen Hitchcock as head of an Army Board comprising the heads of War Department bureaus. In fact, tired of Lincoln and Stanton's meddling, Hitchcock finally departed his assignment. The need for professional soldiers directing the military effort eventually resulted in the arrival of the two Westerners, Henry Halleck and John Pope.[7]

Pope actually preceded Halleck east and received a warm welcome in Washington on June 24. A veteran of Missouri and Mississippi Valley service and Union success in capturing Island Number 10 and Corinth, Pope had political connections and a changing manner of warfare that had much to do with his selection. Like Lincoln, he was a product of the Midwest. He and Mary Todd Lincoln were distant cousins, and Pope had accompanied Old Abe on part of his trip east to the inauguration. As a West Pointer with topographical engineering and Mexican War experience, he exuded soldierly manner and confidence, even bombast, in the eyes of many. His wife, Clara Horton, was the daughter of an important Ohio congressman. Best of all, in the eyes of Republican activists, Pope had proven an outspoken critic of the lame-duck Buchanan administration's soft handling of the secession crisis and openly advocated abolition of slavery. To historian T. Harry Williams, Pope was "pugnacious and confident and conceited." Certainly Lincoln wanted a fighting general at this point, one who could introduce some backbone and cohesion to the invertebrate effort in Virginia. Stanton, Secretary of the Treasury Salmon P. Chase, and congressional Radicals viewed Pope as the kind of "general who would fight their war—a hard, relentless contest, unsparing of the Southern populace, especially in Virginia," to quote Pope's biographer Peter Cozzens. Willing to come east to advise the administration, Pope wasn't sure he wanted the task of command. Leaving a grievously ill infant daughter and her mother back in St. Louis, the Westerner sensed that an outsider might have great difficulty bridling other generals seething from lack of success at catching Jackson in the valley. He told Stanton it was command "of a forlorn hope under the most unfavorable conditions for success."[8]

Stanton took Pope's case to Lincoln. The president decided the general should stay in the east. Still, everyone recognized that the basic problem was lack of command unity. Winfield Scott and Pope advised the president to call on yet another western figure for a new general in chief: Henry Wager Halleck. As author of treatises on the conduct of war and international law and more recently the Union's most successful department and theater commander, Halleck, like Pope, may have been the best the Union had to offer for top command at this stage of the conflict. He too balked at moving from western success to a highly questionable situation in Virginia. Both Halleck and Pope wished to avoid what one would come to call the "political-hell" of Washington and the other would style "a sort of moral odor of sewer gas in the air" of the capital. When contacted by Lincoln's special envoy, Governor William Sprague of Rhode Island, Halleck wired the president that if he were to go to Washington to assist the administration, he "could advise but one thing: to place all the forces in North Carolina, Virginia, and Washington under one head and hold that head responsible." This was the kind of common sense Lincoln wanted, so the president directed him to report for duty in Washington. "I am very anxious—almost impatient—to have you here," Lincoln wrote Halleck. So it was little wonder that the latest arrival demanded and received full power and responsibility to plan and direct operations and was told first to supervise the raising of new troops under Lincoln's order for a draft of state militia. Before long, however, Halleck became ensnared not only in McClellan's touchy situation on the Peninsula but in Pope's unfolding saga in central Virginia.[9]

In a sense, Pope confronted the same difficulty as McClellan: advancing south while adequately protecting Washington. McClellan had been quite cavalier about that responsibility. To him—and with a certain degree of truth—the city's safety rested chiefly with the field army's offensive against the enemy's capital, although he was willing to assign to that mission what he considered an ample protective force together with a growing and sophisticated fortification system. The administration differed in interpretation of just how much of a garrison would adequately constitute the formal "defenses of Washington." The forts themselves, begun early in the war and perfected by McClellan's chief engineer, Brig. Gen. John G. Barnard, still lacked connectivity. Hundreds of cannon, miles of earthworks, and large numbers of expert heavy artillerists and their support troops were simply part of a statistical game anyway, manipulated by either the administration or the field commander to support a particular stance on the issue. When Jackson's diminutive Army of the Valley had so unhinged the efforts of three separate Union armies sent against him in May and June, the moment seemed propitious to consolidate them to shield Washington while McClellan and the Army of the Potomac labored so intensively before Richmond. Once Jackson left the valley to join Lee before Seven Days, Lincoln and his advisers moved decisively to do so and subsequently to open a second approach to Richmond. The two purposes were complementary in their view.[10]

Three separate contingents—those of Franz Sigel, Nathaniel Banks, and Irvin McDowell, perhaps fifty-seven thousand effective troops (Civil War statistics are suspect and variable)—came together as *corps d'armée* under Pope's command. In truth, the first casualty of Pope's appointment had been a third Westerner, John C. Frémont, previously commanding one of the three separate operating forces against Jackson. This general had fallen out of favor with the administration over his premature emancipation attempts, his incompetence and corruption in Missouri, and his abject failure to defeat Jackson. When Frémont refused to serve under Pope, his former junior in the West, Halleck rebuked him, saying, "The obligation of duty is the same upon all officers in the service, whatever the rank." The good of the country came first. But Frémont departed, and the administration was happy to be rid of him and his intrusive, ambitious wife, Jesse. Brig. Gen. Rufus King temporarily succeeded him. Two days later, Stanton (not Pope) named Sigel as Frémont's replacement. It was all quite political: Sigel carried weight with German American voters in the North and had achieved some battlefield success at Pea Ridge, Arkansas, in the spring. Unfortunately, Pope remembered Sigel from the West and doubted his abilities. As Michael C. C. Adams has noted, this period of the war witnessed as much concern among West Point professionals about amateur volunteer generals as about the enemy. Sigel and Banks were amateurs and a political anathema to conservative soldiers in the Union army.[11]

Seeds of difficulty, if not outright disaster, germinated with the establishment of the Army of Virginia. McDowell, however competent, was hardly a pillar of success because of the previous year's rout at First Bull Run. Banks, like McDowell, was loyal, serious, and well intentioned but also tarred by defeat at Jackson's hands. Furthermore, he was a "bobbin-boy" who had risen from the factory floor through Massachusetts's political office to military rank. Sigel spoke with a pronounced accent; when Pope took to hectoring the Baden native, Sigel determined that his commander was not only offensive, pompous, and even arrogant, but afflicted "with looseness of the brains as others with the bowels." Over the course of the coming campaign, Sigel claimed later, the new army commander would manage by "mere fancy and desperation," not sound judgment. He would prove ignorant of distance and topography while playing favorites with subordinates and talking behind people's backs. Pope would reciprocate by declaring Sigel "the God damnedest coward he ever knew" and vowed to arrest the German "the moment he showed any signs of cowardice." Pope embraced McDowell as his principal adviser. Such disparate individuals scarcely promised success.[12]

Here then were four potentially dysfunctional personalities about to launch a major new field force. Like Lee as a result of Seven Days, Pope faced organizational problems. He took over a widely dispersed, segmented group of independent commands with a legacy of failure. Cobbled together, the force needed time to build cohesion, confidence, and élan. In short, the Army of Virginia was unproven, portions of it habituated to defeat as well as neglect at the hands of the War Department. All of this became apparent during the first month of its existence. The separate commands moved sluggishly to coalesce and coordinate their efforts. It helped little that Pope remained in Washington for several weeks advising the administration. Direction by telegraph and dispatch proved unavailing, and his underlings proved unresponsive to distant command. In Pope's mind, they were too sensitive to shadows and rumors of Jackson and other Confederates once again traversing the valley to descend upon them. Put your cavalry out on reconnaissance, Pope ordered Sigel at Sperryville on July 18, and spare no cost in securing information about every movement of the enemy. Seize all horses and mules not absolutely indispensable to inhabitants of Culpeper County, he told Banks and Sigel four days later. Don't protect houses or property and arrest disloyal males. Brusque and blustery, Pope wanted to establish control and energize a fighting machine worthy of meeting old and new adversaries. At least some of his soldiers called Pope "a man we all like, and have great confidence in." One, named "Plump," wrote the *New York Sunday Mercury* from Warrenton that Pope had issued an order that "gives us assurance that he will prosecute the war in earnest, that no (rebel traitor) will receive protection from him." The soldiers appreciated that. Like the administration, they anticipated that Pope would bring rigorous war to the Old Dominion.[13]

Pope misread his soldiers, however. Soon after assuming command, he courted controversy with his legendary proclamation about coming from the West, "where we have always seen the backs of our enemies," and having his "headquarters in the saddle." In some ways, that sounded innocent enough, for he also proclaimed concern for the soldier's well-being and preparation for offensive, not defensive, operations. He even sent barbs in McClellan's direction by suggesting that there would be no more "phrases . . . in vogue amongst you" like "'taking strong positions and holding them,' of 'lines of retreat,' and of 'bases of supplies.'" "The strongest position a soldier should desire," he preached, "is one from which he can most easily advance against the enemy." Let the enemy worry about retreat: "Success and glory are the advance, disaster and shame lurk in the rear." Unfortunately, Pope's words produced derision and animosity in the ranks on both Union and Confederate sides. As citizen-soldiers, they looked to actions, not words. What everyone got with John Pope was a new general, according to an English publication, who was "vain, imprudent, and not proverbially truthful; but shrewd, active, and skilled in the rules of warfare." Pope tightened discipline by reducing baggage trains, increasing punishment for straggling, and threatening courts-martial for any commander who failed to ensure that one hundred rounds of ammunition per infantryman and two hundred rounds of ammunition per artillery piece were maintained at all times, thus incurring the soldiers' displeasure. On the other hand, his men particularly applauded new rules for collaring Virginia's civilians.[14]

What quickly became the vortex of a nasty controversy across the lines were Pope's General Orders 5, 7, 11, and 13, all signed (with the administration's tacit blessing) between July 10 and 25, 1862. They reflected a new direction to the war, reorienting Federal arms toward the Confederacy's resource base, its people and property, signifying militarily and politically that the conflict was turning "harsh" in its blurring of combatants and noncombatants. These directives profoundly disturbed Davis and Lee, eventually leading the Confederate president to claim, "The military authorities of the United States [had] commenced a practice changing the character of the war from such as becomes civilized nations into a campaign of indiscriminate robbery and murder." Pope undoubtedly told his army "to subsist upon the country in which their operations are carried on." But actually they were to reimburse via vouchers, redeemable at the conclusion of the war "upon sufficient testimony being furnished that such owners have been loyal citizens of the United States since the date of the vouchers." None of this was new; requisitioning with cash or vouchers or outright stealing had already attended operations elsewhere. Yet eastern soldiers previously had shied away from pillage. Lt. John Meade Gould of the Tenth Maine, for example, recorded how liberation of livestock and produce as well as searches for firearms and other weapons had trampled citizens' rights without governmental authority. Want of firewood had led to vandalism when his unit barracked at Harpers Ferry in late March, and Gould considered, "Such a shameful destruction of everything makes a man wish himself a Confederate." The idea of calling Federals "protectors" seemed a farce, he said, for they had done three times the mischief as the Confederates. His tone had changed by July.[15]

Gould now suggested that the Union should give up the "senseless, intensely foolish, idea that this is a war of 'restoration.'" Punish the rascally spies, farmers, women, and children who constantly pass through the lines informing the enemy of every movement of the Federals, he suggested. The army was losing men every day to guerrillas. For the sake of showing the people of the Shenandoah that this was a war of restoration, the government troops had been soft—and what was the result? "It is positively proven that an easy policy is a poor one, the natives laugh at us, jibe us, and when we are gone, pick up our stragglers and sick," said Gould. War "is a great and terrible game," so let the terror be with our enemies and not among ourselves. "[I] thought exactly opposite on all these points before I came in contact with the rebels, natives and soldiers." Pvt. James T. Miller of the 111th Pennsylvania wrote his brother on July 26, "The soldiers begin to think that we are going to have war in earnest and that we are to be supported by the Government and that no false notions of mercy are to save the scoundrels that have caused this war." If the "powers at Washington" would only continue such good work, "I shall think that the lesson though a severe and bloody one was the best thing that could have happened to the Country." Raise another five hundred thousand men and "teach the rebels that we have the power and disposition to crush this rebellion," he mused, and "make France and England know and respect us." Pope's orders merely codified what many soldiers had come to regard as necessary: firm suppression of the Rebel populace.[16]

The war truly had entered a new phase by summer. Back in April, along with conscription, the Confederate Congress had passed a partisan ranger law that blurred the distinction between civilian and enrolled soldier. Consequently, "on the pretext of being peaceful citizens," irregulars of partisan or guerrilla stripe began attacking the rear of Union armies, killing straggling soldiers, molesting supply trains, destroying railroads, telegraph lines, and bridges, and committing "outrages disgraceful to civilized people and revolting to humanity," as Pope announced in General Order 7, dated July 10. Lawless, evil-disposed persons and "lack of maintenance of peace and quiet among themselves" introduced Pope's blunt policy that Virginians living within a five-mile radius from such depredations would be held responsible and assessed for damages or be impressed to repair physical destruction. Anyone caught in the act of depredation would be "shot, without awaiting civil process." Any avowedly disloyal individual would have to take an oath of allegiance to the United States or be extradited south, with oath violations punishable by execution and the violators' property seized.[17]

Two weeks later, Pope expanded the guidelines, stating that subordinate commanders "will proceed immediately to arrest all disloyal male citizens within their lines or in the rear of their respective stations" and require an oath of allegiance and security for obedience so as to permit their remaining at home, pursuing their "accustomed avocations" without harassment. Those refusing would be expelled beyond Union lines; violators would be shot, their property confiscated. Communication with anyone "living within the lines of the enemy" was prohibited except as specified by military law, and persons writing or carrying letters or messages other than according to such law would be considered spies. Two days later, Pope ended the practice of guarding private houses and property because "soldiers were called into the field to do battle against the enemy and it is not expected that their force and energy shall be wasted in protecting private property of those most hostile to the Government." Still, commanding officers would be responsible for the conduct of their troops in order to preserve discipline and efficiency. There was nothing really new here, as army practice, sanctioned by the Lincoln government, actively pursued such an approach in other areas of the occupied South. The president himself issued an executive order on July 22 reflecting the new confiscation acts. He sent a stern public warning on July 25 that anyone guilty of aiding, countenancing, or abetting the Rebel cause would immediately cease or suffer forfeitures and seizures of property. Treasury Secretary Chase noted after dining with Pope on July 21, "Genl. Pope expressed himself freely and decidedly in favor of the most vigorous measures in the prosecution of the war," employing every instrument "which could be brought to bear against the enemy."[18]

Such a statement stood in sharp contrast to McClellan's conciliatory position. Indeed, McClellan issued a wordy lecture to his own army on August 9, railing as much against Lincoln's executive order and the confiscation legislation as Pope's implementing orders. Of course, those directives had no effect at all outside the Army of Virginia's operating precincts. "We are continually in camp," wrote Vermonter Edwin R. Reid from Camp Ferrero near Fredericksburg on August 7, living under "the most stringent orders that we ever were." Besides, it was simply too hot to forage and intimidate the local populace. Nonetheless, McClellan complained to Halleck about the hardening war policy passed by Congress "and practically enunciated by General Pope." As he had done with Lincoln, Little Mac advised Halleck, "This contest should be conducted by us as a War and a War between civilized nations," with combat "directed towards crushing the armed masses of the rebels," not against the people, who (as far as military necessities permitted) should "be protected in their constitutional, civil, and personal rights." Halleck agreed that some of Pope's utterances seemed "very injudicious." They had been shown to the president before issue: "I felt unwilling to ask him to countermand them."[19]

Davis and Lee too thought Pope's manifestos were most sinister. Confederate artilleryman Edward Porter Alexander called Pope "a blatherskite," but division commander Richard Ewell fretted that the Yankees were "bent on starving out the women and children left by the war." Murmurs of reprisal began to rumble ominously. Davis wrote Lee on the last day of July, "[Pope] directs the murder of our peaceful inhabitants as spies if found quietly tilling their farms in his rear *even outside of his lines.*" In Luray, Virginia, one of Pope's brigadiers, Adolph von Steinwehr, had seized "innocent and peaceful inhabitants to be held as hostages to the end that they may be murdered in cold blood if any of his soldiers are killed by some unknown persons whom he designates as 'bushwhackers.'" Adj. Gen. Samuel Cooper immediately clarified that the term applied to "the citizens of this Confederacy who have taken up arms to defend their homes and families." Rumors mounted that for every citizen murdered as a result of Federal orders, a captured Union officer would be hanged. Lee spoke menacingly of wanting that "miscreant Pope" suppressed. Pope's orders, if reported correctly in the newspapers, he told Jackson on July 27, "cannot be permitted and will lead to retaliation on our part."[20]

Indeed, the Confederate president was apoplectic about Pope's uncivilized methods. Praised by the former U.S. vice president and now serving Confederate officer John C. Breckinridge for his "patriotism, courage and dignity," Davis also had "the highest and the hardest task of any living public man," in the Kentuckian's view. Davis told Cooper to issue general orders declaring Pope and his commissioned officers "to be in the position which they have chosen for themselves—that of robbers and murderers and not that of public enemies entitled if captured to be considered as prisoners of war." Enlisted men in Pope's army remained exempt as yet, said Davis. Should the U.S. government persist in its steady progress toward "a savage war in which no quarter is to be given and no [age] or sex to be spared," then the Confederacy "shall reluctantly be forced to the last resort of accepting the war on the terms chosen by our foes until the outraged voice of a common humanity forces a respect for the recognized rules of war." Confederate General Order 54 of August 1, 1862, signaled this stringent reaction, although it was applicable only in Virginia, not other theaters of war. When Lee forwarded the official Confederate government position through the lines on August 2, Halleck rejected the missive, claiming a week later, "These papers are couched in language exceedingly insulting to the Government of the United States." Still, Halleck softened Pope's blunt orders by mid-

August and engaged a Columbia College legal scholar, Francis W. Lieber, to codify guidelines for waging partisan warfare; the resulting "Lieber Code" (promulgated as General Order 100) would emerge the next year. Pope claimed on August 14 that his orders had been "entirely misinterpreted" and "grossly abused," but he tempered their implementation.[21]

In truth, Halleck reflected the U.S. government's position. The general in chief condoned Ulysses S. Grant's policy of confiscation in western Tennessee. On the very day of Lee's letter, he directed Grant not only to detain all active Confederate sympathizers and seize their property for public use, but to get all the supplies he could from Rebels in Mississippi: "It is time that they should begin to feel the presence of war on our side." Halleck suggested not merely cleaning out western Tennessee and northern Mississippi of all organized enemies, but, "if necessary, take up all active sympathizers, and either hold them as prisoners or put them beyond our lines. Handle that class without gloves, and take their property for public use"; get "all the supplies you can from the rebels" in Mississippi, he ordered, and "see that all possible facilities are afforded for getting out cotton," as it was thought important "to get as much as we can into market." Yet he ostensibly felt that Pope's policies were injudicious. Was this a double standard in Union policy: hurt them intensely in the West; go softer in Virginia? Richmond made no effort to curb partisans or guerrillas operating behind Union lines, thus making hypocritical any southern protests about "rules of civilized war." Pope, in fact, proposed nothing contrary to traditional laws governing combatants and noncombatants on face value except in comparison to conciliation.[22]

Still, Union soldiers apparently used Pope's orders to cut a swath of confiscation, property destruction, and intimidation through central Virginia. Homes, businesses, even churches were pillaged, families deprived of even the coarsest food and shelter. "Our men know every house in the whole country," said one officer in Stafford County. "They now believe they have a perfect right to rob, tyrannize, threaten & maltreat any one they please, under the Orders of Gen. Pope." No one seemed immune from Pope's concept of the new warfare, concludes Daniel Sutherland, chronicler of the struggle in Culpeper County. Naturally the populace was aghast; Myrta Lockett Avary observed, "Civilians, women, children and slaves feared Pope." Some citizens moved quickly to take the hated Yankee oath of allegiance. Others turned to "bushwhacking" lone Union sentinels or soldiers bathing in streams. Many Virginians merely adopted passive or sullen resistance, and a smattering of latent Unionism surfaced in central Virginia as it had in the tidewater. Confederate soldiers soon spread the word that the Federals were "systematically destroying all the growing crops and everything the people have to live on," Capt. Ujanirtus Allen wrote his wife. The devastating marks of the enemy were visible along their march route, said Louisiana Catholic chaplain James Sheeran: "The fences are torn down, corn trampled under foot and houses gutted of their furniture." A few Union officers like McDowell and the military commander at Fredericksburg worked to stop "indiscriminate marauding," while Pope feigned surprise that his orders had given license for "acts of pillage and outrage."[23]

The spirit of the First and Second Confiscation Acts had begun to be practiced in earnest. Lincoln still shied from offers of privately raised African American units and even bluntly told one group of free blacks that there would be no war "but for your race among us." Nonetheless, an optimistic Brig. Gen. John P. Hatch wrote his father from central Virginia in mid-August, "I believe the resources of the south are about played out." But McClellan's conciliatory position, the defeats before Richmond, and concern that hard war might have a negative effect on wooing the hearts and minds of Southerners back to the Union tempered confiscation. Unrestricted warfare could backfire in diplomatic efforts abroad as well as with the swing-vote moderates and neutrals in the North or southern Unionists whom Lincoln still felt existed in pivotal numbers. In fact, the *Memphis Appeal* (exiled to Grenada, Mississippi, at the time) declared that Davis's threats of retaliation had "inspired confidence throughout the Confederacy." Heavy-handed Union invasion forces had the effect of hardening, not relaxing, civilian resistance in some places. Conversely, the Rebel president's threats apparently steeled some Union hearts; the *New York Herald* proclaimed that the very consideration of retaliatory measures seemed "an open confession of the weakness of the rebel cause." If Davis and his colleagues "were not mad they would be down on their knees begging for mercy instead of defiantly threatening retaliation."[24]

Lee now intended Pope's utter destruction. "I would rather you should have easy fighting and heavy victories," he told Jackson, who was at Gordonsville observing the Union advance on August 7.

Nevertheless, Lee left "the matter to [Jackson's] reflection and good judgment." Much of the uproar about Pope's demeanor, verbiage, and relationship to others would derive from his subsequent failure and defeat. At the start, these were merely omens, leading one of the early deans of Civil War historians, Kenneth P. Williams, to observe simply, "The operation that lay ahead was both delicate and difficult, and it was to put a heavy test on Halleck, Pope, and McClellan." Clear thinking, quick reaction, and professionalism were the key because "the generals were to be given full rein." Events on the Peninsula had already destroyed Little Mac's reputation; events to come would eclipse Pope's renown. As for Halleck, the gargantuan task of coordinating east, west, and everywhere else in the war seemed "a three-dimensional chessboard." So a wily opponent moved to parry the latest Federal moves in central Virginia, while the hornet's nest stirred by Pope's obnoxious dicta coupled with McClellan's petulant, even intransigent behavior. No one knew if Halleck could coordinate two eastern armies any better than Lincoln and Stanton had done previously with five.[25]

Lee chose to contain Pope's drive south on the axis of the Orange and Alexandria Railroad while blunting other Union forces gathering under Ambrose Burnside in the Fredericksburg area. In addition to Jackson, who had been serving as advance guard since July 13, he ordered cavalry commander Stuart both to encourage "our people to bring up from the Rappahannock Valley corn and grain of all kinds" and to "give what protection you can to the families of our citizens and every facility in your power to get within our lines." The Federals seemed to be arresting all citizens in the Fredericksburg area, "thereby causing great distress and alarm." The weight of responsibility for stopping McClellan lifted from his shoulders, Lee could gradually transfer Longstreet and the rest of his army northward on the line of the Virginia Central Railroad. He could cover the direct rail and highway route from Fredericksburg to Richmond while at the same time reinforcing Jackson and pressing him to be more forceful. Move northward from Orange through Culpeper and into Fauquier County to blunt Pope while drawing the enemy from Fredericksburg, he instructed Jackson. By this time, "Old Jack," as his men now called Jackson, had already seized the initiative. With determination and a sense of the enemy's center of gravity, Jackson moved forward to smash the lead element of Pope's marauding Yankees: Banks's command.[26]

Logistics became critical for both armies. The rail line of the Orange and Alexandria and nearby turnpike became Pope's axis of advance when he finally took the field personally at the end of July. He planned to concentrate his forces at the critical county seat of Culpeper on the railroad. Mindful of Washington's desire that he await McClellan's linkup, Pope wanted his army to engage and beat Jackson before Lee could reinforce him. Meanwhile, opportunities to seriously damage the Virginia Central farther south at Gordonsville and Charlottesville had evaporated in a bungled cavalry raid by John Hatch. Another group of raiders under Col. H. Judson Kilpatrick destroyed a supply dump at Beaver Dam Station to the east of Gordonsville on the Virginia Central Railroad on July 19 and 20. Such success proved fleeting, as the energetic Rebels quickly rebuilt the mutilated line of track and Lee reported that the incursion "did no serious damage." Pope soon replaced Hatch with a promising newcomer, Kentucky-bred John Buford, who would work well with McDowell's cavalry brigade chief, George Bayard. Hatch went off to the infantry while this younger duo assumed a screening mission for Pope's army strung out on an east–west line between Sperryville and Warrenton.[27]

Many of Pope's subordinates chafed at the delay in advancing to meet the enemy. They poorly understood Washington's instructions to concentrate Union power. One restless brigade commander, Robert Milroy, wrote home from Woodville in Rappahannock County on August 2 that over twenty days had elapsed since crossing out of the Shenandoah Valley. "Lying idle in camp" seemed criminal: "How horrible it is, that our generals will thus recklessly waste the resources and energies of our country" by miserable delays. They dangerously hazarded "the very existence of our Glorious Government by holding back and not trying to crush out the wicked rebellion, or only trifling with it." European nations seemingly clamored to recognize the Confederacy and destroy the Union. This citizen-soldier blamed a few "scientific" West Pointers whose war management proved as "detrimental to the Nation as Treason." Down easter John Gould worried that the vast amount of Shenandoah grain "will find too good a market" in Richmond, "to be kept back [merely] by broken down railroads." He and others looked for Jackson to dispatch "5 or 10 thousand laborers and afterward secure the grain by holding the valley." Meanwhile, Pope finally got moving. By August 8, with the exception of King's division of McDowell's corps still at Fredericksburg, his forces advanced toward Jackson at Gordonsville.[28]

Bayard and Buford now covered a front from Madison Court House to Rapidan Station (with pickets stretching from the Blue Ridge on the west to the juncture of the Rappahannock and Rapidan rivers closer to Fredericksburg, termed "the forks" in dispatches. "Our Northern cavalry has a fine set of men as a general rule," Gould commented, but "are terribly deficient in discipline and their officers want the dash and imprudence so requisite for this branch of the service." Nevertheless, the mounted force plus lookouts in a signal station atop Thoroughfare Mountain that commanded a view of the entire countryside from Culpeper southward to Orange Court House soon spotted Confederate columns crossing the Rapidan at several points between the railroad and Liberty Mills. They were moving northward at measured pace. Local citizens remembered that the widely dispersed Yankees in the neighborhood seemed more bent on foraging than on noticing the oncoming enemy. The Confederates hanged some of the perpetrators when they found them. Pope personally worried most about the direction of Jackson's advance, whether through Madison Court House or more directly toward Culpeper. The Federal commander finally determined on the latter and concentrated his full strength to protect communications with Fredericksburg and the lower Rappahannock, whence Burnside and McClellan would come from Aquia Landing.[29]

Pope directed Banks to push forward Brig. Gen. Samuel Crawford's four-regiment brigade accompanied by two artillery batteries to Cedar (Slaughter) Mountain, south of Culpeper and between the main road to Orange and the railroad. Bayard's cavalry would support Crawford while Buford's horsemen would continue to screen the Madison approach. Pope also ordered the rest of Banks's and Sigel's men to march immediately to Culpeper from Hazel River and Sperryville, with James B. Ricketts's division of McDowell's corps closing on Warrenton from Fredericksburg. Banks's foot soldiers lost no time completing the march by August 8, but Sigel's command was another matter. Notwithstanding brutal summer heat and dust, the German American gained no points at headquarters by asking which route he should take. There *was* only one; the maps showed that fact. So the ever-maligned Sigel would reach Culpeper a day behind Pope's schedule. Pope was furious, for only Banks would be fully available to combat the advancing Rebels. Even then, Pope thought Banks had fifteen thousand men in his corps when little more than half that amount, or about eighty-eight hundred, were actually available. Furthermore, King could rejoin McDowell from Fredericksburg only by forced marches overland or via the circuitous river-rail route via Washington. Pope finally ordered him forward and wired the War Department of his dispositions while asking for more cavalry. Paper returns at the end of July show a force of 77,779 available for the Army of Virginia, but Pope's actual strength in the field numbered fewer than forty-four thousand.[30]

This was more than enough to cope with Jackson, but Pope would be seriously handicapped should Lee's whole army come at him. Intelligence reports from a former employee at the Tredegar Iron Works in Richmond alerted Pope to sizable troop transfers from Lee's army and the fact "that public attention in Richmond is now mostly turned upon Jackson and Pope." This information suggested that some quick reversal of McClellan's movement from the Peninsula might capture the Confederate capital. In fact, McClellan would continue to hammer that very point during the first half of August. But the die was cast, rapid reversal of movement was not possible, and so the opening stages of the new campaign went on. Pope characteristically boasted to Washington of King's rapid raid on Frederick's Hall on the Virginia Central, where his men ostensibly ripped up two or three miles of track, blew up several culverts, and destroyed water tanks, thus making "the road impassable for a number of days." A similar foray from Fredericksburg down the telegraph road toward Hanover Court House on the direct route to Richmond had been less successful, however. Brig. Gen. John Gibbon's march in grueling heat yielded only hordes of stragglers, who were quickly gobbled up by Stuart's hovering horsemen. None of this seriously interfered with Lee's movements, as he quickly informed his superiors. The actions did prompt concern on both sides for overextension of their forces in the face of the enemy.[31]

Halleck telegraphed Pope worriedly on August 8, "Do not advance, so as to expose yourself to any disaster, unless you can better your line of defense, until we can get more troops up on the Rappahannock." He hoped to do so quickly, but "be very cautious." In the meantime, Pope should keep up connections with Burnside, now closing on Aquia Landing, and "do not let the enemy get between you." In similar fashion, Lee cautioned Jackson on August 7 and 8 to avoid prematurely attacking Pope in his strong and chosen positions, "but to turn his position at Warrenton, &c. so as to draw him out of them." Lee believed greatly in maneuver, and he hoped that Jackson would "be able to strike him moving." Relying on "your judgment, courage, and discretion and trusting to the continued blessing of an ever-kind Providence, I hope for victory," he counseled. "I must now leave the matter to your reflection and good judgment," or make up "your mind what is best to be done under all the circumstances which surround us," Lee concluded. "Let me hear the result at which you arrive."[32]

At this moment, Lee, like Halleck, continued to advise his chief executive on affairs beyond the Virginia theater. Confederate Secretary of War George W. Randolph plied Lee with numerous communiqués concerning coordinated movements in southwest Virginia and Kentucky by Generals Humphrey Marshall and Edmund Kirby Smith, as well as those of William H. Loring in the Kanawha River region of western Virginia. Lee worried that diverting manpower reserves to such operations might affect his own ability to stop the major Union invasion forces in his most immediate front. Halleck too fretted about other Confederate activities in Tennessee and Kentucky, although the shifting fortunes in Virginia remained his uppermost concern. Both sides could only let affairs involving Jackson and Pope play out on their own for the moment. Yet these two pawns could affect the larger game. And problems soon developed for both these field commanders, largely of their own making. Jackson, for one, ran afoul of his personality—that legendary Calvinist, taciturn, lemon-sucking iconoclast, the "Cromwell of the Confederacy," grimly determined to strike the enemy with a vengeance.[33]

Jackson had been at Gordonsville since July 19 with essentially two divisions, those of Ewell and Charles Winder. Lee sent A. P. Hill's so-called Light Division as reinforcement, with the enjoinder to Jackson on July 27 that he should utilize the strengths of these subalterns and share knowledge of his plans with them. Old Jack did nothing of the kind. That was not his style. He always treated his lieutenants more as "children unable to think for themselves," observed military analyst Edward Stackpole many years later. By this point, Jackson commanded fully half of Lee's force with Hill (twelve thousand, which Lee thought what he had sent augmented to eighteen thousand),

Ewell (seven thousand), and Winder (four thousand), plus Brig. Gen. Beverly H. Robertson's twelve-hundred-strong "Laurel Brigade" cavalry. Jackson never could abide the hesitant Robertson after losing a more intrepid Turner Ashby as his cavalry leader earlier in the valley. Moreover, the fiery battle chieftain Powell Hill came with baggage of his own: pending resolution of disputes with James Longstreet and his staff over conduct in the Seven Days' battles. Seemingly only "Old Baldy" Ewell was not rankled by the domineering Jackson. He may well have originally considered his commander as "crazy as a March hare," but Ewell came to venerate the man and almost blindly follow his instructions. On the whole, however, Jackson's unwillingness to delegate and allow discretion among his subordinates, much less tutor them, would plague his performance until his death the following spring at Chancellorsville.[34]

For the moment, there seemed to be almost as much dysfunctionality south of as north of the Rapidan. Jackson's force took to the road early in August, a move that may have been occasioned at least partially by its commander's need to attend courts-martial at Liberty Mills, west of Orange. Jackson had pressed charges against one of his best brigade commanders, Richard B. Garnett, for misbehavior at the March defeat at Kernstown in the valley. Amid the stormy courts-martial affair on August 7, scouting and spy reports of Pope's activity caused Jackson (apparently losing his case against Garnett anyway) to break up the proceeding and begin his offensive. As he reported later, "Having received information that only part of General Pope's army was at Culpeper Court-House, and hoping, through the blessing of Providence, to be able to defeat it before re-enforcements should arrive there, Ewell's, Hill's and [Winder's] divisions moved in the direction of the enemy from their respective encampments near Gordonsville." Then Jackson's shortcomings, plus frustration at the Garnett business, almost undid his initial work against Pope.[35]

Jackson had drawn up sketchy marching orders on the evening of August 7. Perhaps absent-mindedly, he neglected routine logistical considerations such as relative strength and road distance required for his three divisions. He also overlooked the positioning of divisional wagon trains. The next morning, as Ewell led off with Hill and Winder following in order, Jackson then changed the route of Ewell's lead division. Worse, he failed to inform the other division commanders. So Hill's people became stuck at Orange awaiting passage of what purportedly was Ewell's column but in fact was that of Winder instead. An irate Jackson and a fuming Hill both failed to even ask whose men blocked passage. The result put Ewell well in advance up the Culpeper road while Hill's men simply retired to biv- ouac at the end of the day (having accomplished scarcely two miles of marching for their effort). The whole army completed only about eight of the required twenty miles to Culpeper. Jackson's timetable stood in disarray, mostly by his own doing. Born from this episode was "a spark of mutual mistrust" between A. P. Hill and his superior officer, which would lead to the former's arrest and increasingly sour relations between two of Lee's best combat commanders.[36]

It was not an auspicious beginning for Jackson's vaunted foot cavalry. Their optimistic commander thought the odds still favored the enterprise, although he admitted to Lee the next day, "I am not making much progress." Jackson said nothing about fouled orders, the heat, sunstroke, and concern for enemy cavalry to his west and rear that caused him to "fear that the expedition will, in consequence of my tardy movements, be productive of but little good." Yet he wanted to be in Culpeper "this forenoon." A chagrined Hill accord- ingly force-marched his men to catch up with Ewell and Winder at the Crooked Run Church crossing of the Rapidan. Then they finally began a slow march northward together, steadily pushing Bayard's cavalry vedettes, and by early afternoon arrived at a critical junc- tion of the Orange and Madison highways into Culpeper. Off to the Confederate right loomed Cedar Mountain. Straddled by school- house and farm gate bearing the name of nearby thirty-nine-year-old farmer William Major, the intersection lay in the crook of the head- waters of Cedar Run that flowed together just north of the mountain. Nearby stood the prosperous farm of Catherine Crittenden, "a high- blooded dame of the Virginia pattern," according to Rhode Island chaplain Frederick Denison. The farm gate to her property gained so much attention in the subsequent clash of arms as "to be a battlefield landmark deserving of capitalization," in historian Robert Krick's colorful phrase. Other residents in the area included the Reverend Philip Slaughter on the eastern slope of the mountain, from whom the promontory acquired an alternative name. Local people wel- comed the reappearance of protective Confederates in their area.[37]

Sugarloaf-shaped Cedar (Slaughter) Mountain captured the visual appeal of Virginia's piedmont. Private Gould thought, "Altogether

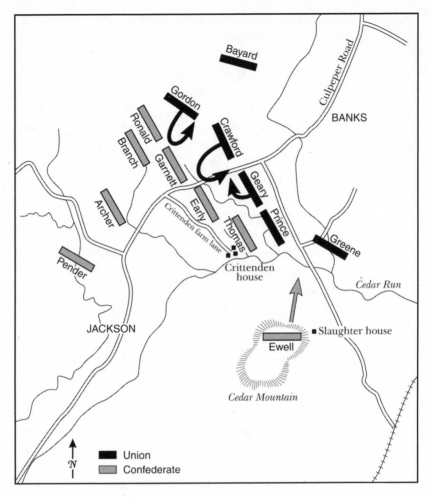

Battle of Cedar Mountain—August 9, 1862

the scenery is rather tame and depends upon the foliage alone for beauty." Van Rensselaer Willard of the Third Wisconsin declared that the country around Culpeper "resembles a large plain over grown with a stunted growth of oak and pine," with very sandy and dry soil, yet somewhat broken by small hills and ridges toward Cedar Mountain. Even today the gently rolling ground appears ideal for troop maneuvers, broken up only randomly by groves of trees, a few ridgelines, and ample defilade space. Chaplain Denison observed that the battle space "was an open valley" encompassing three large farms, perhaps two miles in length and one and a half miles in width, stretching north and northwest of the mountain. The southern branches of Cedar Run, yet a third name applied to the contest in some contemporary accounts, bisected the site, as did a side road to Mitchell's Station on the Orange and Alexandria to the east. A few dense woods farther up the mountain and just northwest of the Culpeper road slightly obstructed fields of fire. Otherwise, the area was mostly cropland—corn and wheat awaiting harvest—an ideal spot for Napoleonic-style combat.[38]

Robertson's horsemen and Brig. Gen. Jubal Early's brigade of Virginians moved forward first, as a broiling sun and humidity steamed the central Virginia countryside. Thermometers in the region recorded temperatures in the nineties at battle time. It was, to use Krick's quaint expression, "the sort of heat that feeds on itself day in and day out in the Virginia summer." Delays quickly developed at the Crooked Run crossing, where mud snared men, beasts, wagons, and artillery pieces. Jackson's appearance and the hard swearing of his chief commissariat, Maj. William Harmon, had only marginal effect on the roadblock. The devout Jackson cautioned his cantankerous quartermaster about his language but soon deferred management of the balky mule teams to Harmon's "fluent damnation." The traffic jam abated eventually, but none too soon for Jackson's taste, as Union resistance appeared to stiffen by 1:00 p.m. Then Jackson's aide, Sandy Pendleton, informed Early that he should advance immediately on the enemy. Winder would provide support. "Old Jube," as his men called their gruff, hard-swearing bachelor commander, soon set about dispersing what appeared to be more Yankee cavalry. Deploying over the sloping Major farm up to the mountain, Early opened the battle of Cedar Mountain as directed. Within an hour, bloodless skirmishing gave way to the heavier throbbing of a nascent artillery duel. The widow Crittenden implored Chaplain Denison to let her escape the fusillade of shells to Culpeper, but to no avail. He informed her that she had to "fare as well as we did," in fact silently rejoicing when the battle actually caused her house to shake. Such cacophony apparently was "not as pleasing to her as the theory of secession," Denison caustically observed later.[39]

Banks arrived in person on the field in due order with Christopher C. Augur's thirty-two-hundred-man division, which took position under cover of cornfields with his cannon banging away at the Confederates. Jackson personally would spend the later part of his afternoon on the battle line. Initially he had established a command post at thirty-four-year-old Cornelia Petty's house on the road up from the Crooked Run crossing. Ewell was already on her porch playing with the Petty children when Jackson and his staff rode up. Soon the generals crouched over maps spread out on the porch floor, agreed on options, and then stretched out for a quick nap in the seductive heat. Knowing that time would elapse before Winder and Hill arrived, a confident Jackson permitted Early to develop the situation. He could depend on having about fifteen thousand troops to deploy against what he thought might be the enemy's nine thousand. Moreover, as he had told his trusted physician and staff-mate, Hunter McGuire, the day before, if they faced Banks, that general was willing to fight, and "he generally gets whipped." To Jackson's men, this brought back warm memories of "Commissary" Banks in the spring, whose rout had always provided good spoils of war. They joked about getting requisitions ready, as "Old Stonewall's Quartermaster has come with a full supply for issue." Some of that overconfidence would manifest itself when the battle matured.[40]

Jackson's full-blown advance confirmed Pope's worst fears. His intent had been for Crawford and Bayard to simply delay the advancing Confederates until the entire Army of Virginia was concentrated at Culpeper. He could then move confidently to defeat Jackson before Lee's arrival. Pope later suggested that lacking numbers to confront both Lee and Jackson, he intended to draw back against the Blue Ridge. This would force the enemy to either attack him in a strong position or permit withdrawal back toward Washington, although Pope was unclear whether he meant the capital or tiny Washington, Virginia, "to have me on his flank and rear." To do any of this required the presence of Banks, Sigel, and all of McDowell's corps. Sigel disrupted the intent not only by arriving late at Culpeper but by bringing unfed and weary troops, contrary to Pope's orders that the men had to be well-victualed and ready for action beforehand. Still, early on the morning of August 9, Pope ordered Banks to take his corps forward to reinforce Crawford, push skirmishers to feel out enemy positions, and (in one of the more confusing and controversial instructions of the whole war) attack with them and notify the army commander immediately of what transpired. Anxious to make clear his intent, Pope sent several aides to ensure Banks's compliance while he personally continued to marshal the rest of his forces at Culpeper. Those aides included Louis H. Marshall, an old friend from prewar campaigning on the western plains and, ironically, Robert E. Lee's nephew, whom, his uncle decided, "I could forgive fighting against us if he had not joined such a miscreant as Pope." In addition to Marshall, the starchy army regular of questionable abilities and scruples acting as Pope's inspector-general, Benjamin S. Roberts, may have also muddled Pope's orders in discussion with Banks. Nonetheless, Banks's arrival in the early afternoon blocked Jackson's advance.[41]

Banks's fighting spirit was up that day. He was determined to avenge Jackson's earlier indignities. It did not help that Roberts goaded Banks with the barbed statement, "There must be no backing out this day." Banks remained silent at the time, although he later recalled, "I heard the sound of his voice" and its referral to the retreat from Strasburg in the valley "before the same Stonewall Jackson." In any event, the politician-general did not shirk his duties and displayed admirable personal courage setting up his command post just north of Cedar Run and riding conspicuously along the battle line to show his presence as well as ensure proper troop placement. Banks would escalate a mere encounter to general engagement status within minutes, thereby compelling Pope and McDowell to interrupt their own afternoon repose in Culpeper. Sounds of Banks's heavy gunfire in the distance caused the two Union generals to exchange cigars and conversation for their horses and hasten toward the front. Even out on the edge of the developing battle, brigade commander Alpheus Williams had found matters so quiet before the battle started that he and old officer friends partook of a leisurely lunch prepared by their cook, and then "all lay down under a shade [tree] and talked over the events of the ten months we had been together." Everyone seemed as unconcerned and carefree "as if he was on the lawn of a watering place instead of the front of a vastly superior enemy." To Williams and compatriots, sorrow and misfortune seemed far distant, yet, he told his daughter later, of all present that warm afternoon, "not one, five hours afterwards, was unhurt."[42]

Jackson planned to envelop both Federal flanks, using Early to fix the enemy on the Culpeper road while Ewell took two brigades to the right and passed over the base of Cedar Mountain to strike the enemy left. Winder meanwhile executed a similar maneuver west of the road to strike Banks's right flank. Hill would act as army reserve. Winder, a well-respected thirty-three-year-old West Pointer out of Maryland's Eastern Shore (who happened to command Jackson's old division that day), and Ewell held the keys to success, although Jackson, as an old artillerist, determined that his batteries would apply flanking enfilade fire on both ends of the Union line. These maneuvers would take time, and Winder's appearance touched off the lively two-hour cannon exchange, almost unhinging Jackson's whole battle plan. Just as the fierce cannonade got the worst of the Federal batteries, Winder went down with a gory wound. Both he and Jackson liked to dabble in tactical direction of the Confederate guns, and the Marylander paid the price. Carried to the rear, where surgeons pronounced his wound mortal, a chaplain told him, "General, lift up your heart to God." Winder replied that he did so and expired. His Stonewall Brigade then moved to attack with the battle cry "Remember General Winder," according to aide McHenry Howard. Jackson would subsequently grieve at the loss of a man who "seemed to many observers to be among the brightest prospects in Jackson's army and perhaps the most distinguished Marylander in Confederate service," added Howard. Apparently not many of Winder's men shared such lamentations, however, for the strict professional had been promised fratricide by less adoring volunteers in the ranks. Yankee guns had now relieved them of that opportunity.[43]

Winder's loss temporarily disrupted Confederate fortunes. His successor, William B. Taliaferro, inspired little confidence among senior commanders and had no sense of Jackson's battle plan or Winder's role in it. Confusing and uncoordinated, even disjointed tactical maneuvers consumed the afternoon until about 5:00 p.m. Then, unaware that he was outnumbered more than three to one, Banks seized the initiative. He had seen nothing from the Confederates except skirmishing and jockeying for position, he later told Pope. Perhaps the enemy was weaker than supposed. So he directed both of his divisions forward without reserves, expecting Pope to fulfill his promise of reinforcements. Banks's movement became a general advance in full array with infantry, screened by regular army battalions as skirmishers, supported by artillery. The Federals marched straight into the cornfield jaws of death at the hands of Rebel batteries and infantry. Then Hill's Confederates arrived inconveniently to turn the tide of battle.[44]

Banks sensed victory, at first. The temperature stood near one hundred degrees; the corn was dense, uncut, and so high that the troops could not see where they were going. Augur and Pennsylvania brigade commander John Geary both went down early with critical wounds, and the action south of the Culpeper–Orange road disintegrated into a free-for-all. North of that road, Crawford's brigade slashed across a wheat field and into the Confederate brigades of Thomas J. Garnett and Charles A. Ronald, crumpling them in disorder. Gathering momentum, Crawford's attack wheeled south, knocking Taliaferro off guard as well as collapsing Early's brigade, which melted in precipitous rout. By 6:00 p.m., Banks's earlier assessment seemed proven. The Rebels were weak; rolling up their whole battle line appeared quite possible. Reversal of Old Jack's vaunted reputation lay within reach. Then, suddenly, the tide of battle shifted.[45]

With his line collapsing, Stonewall Jackson's "combat intelligence and inherent battle sense" alerted him to potential disaster, according to military analyst W. J. Wood. Riding quickly to the Crittenden farm gate intersection with the Culpeper road, he surged among the routed elements of his command. Brandishing his unsheathed sword above his head (supposedly for the only time in the war) and grasping a battle flag in the other hand, "Old Blue Light" (another of his sobriquets) shouted, "Rally brave men, and press forward! Your general will lead you. Jackson will lead you. Follow me!" Friend and foe stood fascinated by what they saw. One newly captured Yankee, hatless and with broken sword in hand, asked Capt. Charles Minor Blackford, "What officer is that?" When told, and "fully appreciating the magnetism of the occasion, he seemed carried away with admiration," noted Blackford. Waving his own broken blade around his own head, the bluecoat reputedly shouted, inexplicably, "Hurrah for General Jackson! Follow your General, Boys!" Blackford could only graciously reward him: "You are too good a fellow for me to make prisoner." His captive "disappeared in an instant."[46]

In a scene reminiscent of First Manassas, where he had earned his immortal sobriquet "Stonewall" the year before, Jackson now stemmed the rout at about the same time Crawford and Augur ran out of steam. Berating Hill for his tardy arrival, Jackson expertly directed the latecomer to attack the Federal right flank as it wheeled southward across the highway, thus exposing itself to counteraction. Hill's Light Division accounted for fully half of Jackson's strength, making it, in one historian's view, "the ideal weapon to turn the battle around, perhaps even turning defeat into victory." Moreover, Union casualties were high, ranging from 30 percent of Col. Henry Prince's brigade to over 50 percent of Crawford's command. By 6:30 to 7:00 p.m., with Jackson brandishing his sword and banner, Hill stripped to his bright red battle shirt. With the tired but reinspired Confederate infantry rallying to the fray, the scene was exhilarating. For Capt. Hugh Lawton of the Liberty Hall Volunteers going into battle seemed panorama-like, as "the fire from both sides flashed fiercely at one another." Pvt. John Wotring of the Thirty-third Virginia in the Stonewall Brigade noted, "The enemy are driven back with great slaughter." Neither Gordon's late-arriving brigade nor Ricketts's division could stanch Banks's collapsing line. Banks's attack, which had netted such stunning and unexpected success two hours before, evaporated. Jackson (thanks mainly to Hill's arrival) had snatched victory from defeat.[47]

Could Jackson complete destruction of his foe? After reversing the situation on his left, he turned to Ewell to complete the anticipated double envelopment. But the Confederates lacked a large, organized cavalry force to exploit success, despite the arrival of several mounted units after the main action ended and dusk closed over the battlefield. The retiring bluecoats might well have wondered what had happened to Pope's reinforcements, twelve thousand to fifteen thousand men of McDowell's and Sigel's corps. Some, like Brigadier General Williams, believed that if they had arrived "an hour before sundown, we should have thrashed Jackson badly and taken a host of his artillery." Instead, a fighting retreat by stalwart units like the Tenth Maine and a suicidal mounted attack by part of the First Pennsylvania cavalry simply caused more casualties (the Keystoners losing 50 percent of their number for the trouble). Both sides were exhausted by twilight, and Jackson seemed satisfied to merely hasten Banks's departure, even though "victory perched on our banners," in the words of Mississippian James Hardeman Stuart, a signalman on J. E. B. Stuart's staff. Thermometers still recorded eighty-six degrees an hour after sunset, so that such details as John Wotring's avowed fifteen-mile march to battle, plus the hard fighting, negated Jackson's personal leadership in trying for a final annihilative blow. The army commander pushed two unengaged brigades from Hill's division, supported by young Willie Pegram's guns, across Cedar Run. They ran into stiff resistance from Ricketts's infantry and fire from three Union batteries. The final sparring contest in the darkness underscored the fact that nothing more could be accomplished by either side at this point.[48]

Ironically, it may have been a case of mistaken identity that finally shut down the fighting around midnight. Pope, now on the scene, assumed Pegram's offending guns were really Federal pieces and sent a staff officer to stop the racket. Pegram, not realizing who was delivering the demand, did so and limbered up to leave the field. This same darkness cloaked the arrival of William E. "Grumble" Jones's cavalry, which nearly captured Pope, Banks, and their staffs as well as division and brigade leaders Williams and George S. Greene. The Union brass stampeded, with Pope and Banks both missing for a time. Eventually they reappeared to discuss the day's events with McDowell and Sigel atop a pile of fence rails. Across the lines, Jackson was so worn out by the day's events that he slumped by the roadside to catch some sleep. He could barely mumble to his staff, "I want rest, nothing but rest." His men echoed that thought, aide Charles Minor Blackford commented: "They were so tired that the men were lying about in line of battle and asleep." Not waiting even for food, "I do not believe anything short of the enemy could have revived them to action," he observed.[49]

Both sides claimed victory. Each had stopped the other's advance. Jackson, however, retained possession of the battlefield. Stuart's arrival enabled the army commander to ascertain the next morning that Pope had now consolidated on Ricketts's position just north of Cedar Run. The two armies faced each other passively for the next two days, too fatigued to resume fighting and content to merely police the battlefield for reusable weapons and equipment, bury the dead, and tend the wounded. Stray soldiers from both sides scavenged bodies for clothing, food, and trinkets. Father Sheeran of the Fourteenth Louisiana found great delight in debating the issues of the war, particularly Lincoln's violation of the Constitution, with a captured Yankee captain during this interlude. In general, though, the terrible heat, the stench of rotting bodies, and the postbattle shock prevented many pleasantries passing among contending veterans from Cedar Mountain. Armies and generals knew how to fight; they were remarkably unsure about how to follow up success or failure and what to do with the debris of the battle afterward. The generals reflected; the privates dug burial pits. All awaited the next move.[50]

Jackson realized how close his army had come to defeat. He had not conducted the battle especially well, nor had he assessed the initial stages of the action properly. His neglect of his flanks and underutilization of Ewell's command both in combat and during the pursuit stood in sharp contrast to his valiant effort to rally a disintegrating battle line at the moment of greatest danger. Hill's biographer James I. "Bud" Robertson condemned Jackson's orders that day as "so garbled and incomplete" that disposition of the army's reserve devolved upon that subordinate. Yet Banks's conduct, though "marked by great coolness, intrepidity and zeal" (in Pope's view), also proved weak in reconnaissance and impetuous in attacking without reserves, though negating Roberts's cutting admonition about running away. Mainly the heat and the men in the ranks determined Cedar Mountain. Perhaps analyst Wood said it best by declaring that the battle showed that "a skilled professional [Jackson] had met a courageous amateur [Banks]." The professional came "within a razor's edge of disaster, saved by strong reserves and the rashness of his opponent, who had attacked without them."[51]

Pope declined to renew the battle until Sigel arrived. Finally, on August 11, the Federal commander asked for a truce to bury 450 dead and retrieve the remaining wounded of some twenty-four hundred casualties he had sustained. Such numbers amounted to about 28 percent of his strength at Cedar Mountain. Jackson counted fourteen hundred casualties, and both armies had lost key unit commanders through death, wounding, or capture. Alpheus Williams told his daughter a week later that all brigades' field officers had been cut down; the Tenth Maine was badly chewed up, and among the Second Massachusetts, "whose officers are of the Boston elite, four captains were killed outright, all of them young men of great fortunes and of the highest standing." Nonetheless, the human toll dimmed before the laurels of victory bestowed upon the near-legendary Jackson. He sent Lee a dispatch proclaiming, "God blessed our arms with another victory," a refrain repeated by war correspondent Peter Wellington Alexander when writing home about Cedar Mountain. Lee answered Jackson, "The country owes you and your brave officers and soldiers a deep debt of gratitude." Mourning the loss of gallant officers and men, said Lee, "I hope your victory is but the precursor of others over our foe in that quarter which will entirely break up and scatter his army."[52]

Jackson's aide, Charles Blackford, showed more prescience when he remarked, "The victory was decided but the results, beyond the moral effect on the men of both sides will not be much." Pope's congratulatory communiqué to his army a week later gave no hint of any setback. He was delighted and astonished at the gallant and intrepid conduct of his command, especially Banks's corps: "Success and glory are sure to accompany such conduct, and it is safe to predict that Cedar Mountain is only the first of a series of victories which shall make the Army of Virginia famous in the land, and draw very close [to] the hearts of their country every officer and soldier who belongs to it." Pope's words rang false with many of his men. One of Banks's lieutenants thought that if Cedar Mountain could not constitute a glorious victory, "it was a glorious defeat provided such an adjective could be used with that noun."[53]

Capt. Ujanirtus Allen from Georgia assured his wife soon after the battle that combat would be renewed quickly. "The enemy I think will make a desperate stand," inasmuch as they had an overwhelming force, though "crushed in spirit." While acknowledging themselves whipped, observed C. Dabney of Stuart's staff, his commander could not get a captured surgeon to take a bet that the next issue of the *New York Herald* would not claim it a Yankee victory! In the end, however, under the deceptive cover of blazing campfires on the night of August 11, Jackson retired back to Gordonsville to await the arrival of Lee and the rest of the army. Both Jackson and Banks had badly bloodied their forces. Yet the campaign for central Virginia had barely begun, suggested General Williams. The Rebels could bring more reinforcements from Richmond than Pope could counter. "I hope to see the day we shall meet them with at least equal numbers and on fair grounds," he said. "Our generals seem more ambitious of personal glory [than] of their country's gain, at least some of them." Many Federals would have agreed.[54]

So the hot dry days of midsummer witnessed two armies pulling out of their lines before Richmond and moving to reinforce gathering hosts on the Rapidan. The Confederate capital was no longer directly threatened. Instead, a new Union force advanced overland from Washington. Seeking to punish the man he despised as a "miscreant," Lee personally delighted that Jackson had bested Pope's advance guard at Cedar Mountain, not knowing that victory had been achieved only by his subordinate's personal courage and A. P. Hill's arrival to rally the Confederates. Nearly four thousand Federals and

Confederates fell in a brutal, stand-up fight in the blistering heat of corn and wheat fields astride the Culpeper–Orange highway. Banks retired, Pope reinforced him the next day, and Jackson awaited the arrival of the rest of Lee's army.[55]

On the war's larger stage, Lincoln countered abolitionist heckler Horace Greeley that if he could save the Union with slavery intact he would do so; conversely, if it took freeing some or all slaves to preserve the Union, he would do that likewise. But he made no move beyond Second Confiscation and, more concerned about available manpower for the fighting, implemented his war powers on August 4 by announcing an additional quota for three hundred thousand new nine-month volunteers to augment three hundred thousand three-year volunteers already called for on July 2, 1862. Across the Atlantic, the British prime minister, Lord Palmerston, solemnly intoned to a banquet audience that his government would continue with "a strict and rigid neutrality." McClellan tried one final time, wiring Halleck three days after Cedar Mountain that he could "in forty eight hours advance on [Lee] and either drive him into the works around Richmond or defeat and capture his forces." This effort, said McClellan, would seem to "have the effect to draw back the forces now before Genl. Pope and thus relieve Washington from all danger." He may have been right. But Cedar Mountain closed McClellan's options. By August 18, the Army of the Potomac had left Harrison's Landing, heading off down the Peninsula.[56]

⇢ 3 ⇠

Stonewall and a Virginia Reel

CLARISSA HARLOWE BARTON had not intended going into nursing. The daughter of an old New England Indian War veteran, Clara taught school and remained single. She eventually found a niche as a copyist at the Patent Office in Washington. When the war came, she became obsessed with voluntarily carrying supplies to the troops in the field—nourishing food, but more especially hospital items like bandages, salves, sheets, bed shirts, and stimulants. She cut through army and Sanitary Commission bureaucracies that claimed war and battlefront were not places for women. She conveyed her supplies to Ambrose Burnside's debarking troops at Fredericksburg in early August. Then, on August 9, she learned of Cedar Mountain. By August 13, she had reached the gore and suffering of Dr. James L. Dunn's blood-splattered hospital in Culpeper. For two days, without sleep, she scrubbed floors and passed out supplies. Dunn wrote his wife, "If heaven ever sent out a homely angel, she must be one, her assistance was so timely."[1]

One captain at a neighboring hospital told her, "Miss Barton, this is a rough and unseemly position for you, a woman, to occupy." She shot back, "Is it not as rough and unseemly for these pain-racked men?" Returning to Washington, she penned an impassioned public letter, dated "Culpeper Court House, August 14, 1862," portraying the pathos of the post–Cedar Mountain scene. She also spoke of "the nobility of soul, the resignation, and bravery of our gallant troops" that she found in the impoverished field hospitals. She needed new sources of supplies for her crusade. Newspaper publication of her letter would inspire the home front. "It is well to be a soldier," she pronounced, but later admitted that a "sense of propriety" had kept her from the actual battlefield.[2]

Cedar Mountain left a distinct impression on participants. For many it was their first battle; for others it was their second or third experience. Pvt. James Miller of the 111th Pennsylvania claimed that it had captured the "enthusiastic dream of my boyhood," a battle filled with "glorious pomp and stern reality." But the carnage also translated into lost friends and colleagues. As John Mead Gould, newly promoted to first lieutenant in the Tenth Maine, recorded bluntly, it took "thirty minutes to drop 170 out of 460" combatants in his unit. One officer had been shot before even entering the fight, a victim of his high-crowned black regulation Hardee hat with ostrich plume and brass emblems. Gould described robbing the dead of boots, clothing, and valuables and the fact that almost every survivor had some scratch on him. His regiment's noble performance had been to little purpose, as the enemy "had us completely at their mercy." By regulation he should have been mounted, but an accident kept him on foot. "I would as soon have blown my brains out as to have gone into that musketry fire mounted."[3]

The last trainload of wounded arrived in Alexandria from Culpeper on August 18. Rumors had John Pope abandoning the town and environs and pulling back behind the Rappahannock River. Both sides spent time the fortnight following Cedar Mountain planning and jockeying for position. The stakes were high, as Louisianan Reuben Allen Pierson indicated to his brother in Mississippi, four days before Cedar Mountain. Everyone looked to England and France "for mediation or at least recognition," he wrote. Pierson personally had little faith in mediation but thought that public clamor would demand recognition and separation "from the vile Fanatics of the North." Pennsylvanian James Miller, by contrast, felt that if any of the folks at home thought they were experiencing hard times due to the conflict, they should come to Virginia and see the desolation, with thousand-acre farms stripped of all fencing, crops, and livestock in a single day. The only way that the owners could get payment, he thought, was "to prove that they are union men and this is going on in thirty places at once." Since leaving Harpers Ferry to reinforce Pope, Miller had not seen twenty able-bodied young men because the Rebels had conscripted them all.[4]

Miller thought it a pity if loyal Northerners could not make as large sacrifices to support the Constitution and the laws as the Confederates could to destroy them. He preferred to draft every able man from fifteen to sixty and put them in the field. Virginia would not recover from the effects of the war for a century, he predicted, and if combat continued another six months, two-thirds of the inhabitants would be starving. Still, they had only themselves to blame for the war and its consequences. Moreover, in Miller's view, "Secesh as most of them are[,] they say that our soldiers are gentlemen when compared with soldiers of Jackson." His own comrades had "unbounded confidence" in Pope, but not Irvin McDowell, whom, together with Secretary of War Edwin Stanton, Miller blamed for McClellan's not taking Richmond. He hoped General in Chief Henry Halleck would give McClellan half a chance, for he was not only a good general, "but one of the best that the world ever saw." He was, in fact, a "prince of Generals," who "will yet vindicate his claim to be considered the greatest General of modern times." This army, contended Miller, "feel[s] perfectly able and willing to flog an equal number of the rebles [sic]," for they had held their own at Cedar Mountain while outnumbered two to one, "and they had the choice of position and the fight that we have had only makes us anxious to have another turn with them."[5]

Pope gathered his forces until he clearly outnumbered Jackson. Yet, surprised by the enemy's audacity, he was torn between continuing his offensive as he promised to his political patrons and securing his position. Mentally he passed from offense to defense. His concentration around Culpeper temporarily made sense. Jackson withdrew to Gordonsville on the night of August 11, relinquishing his gains but with his mystique undiminished. Neither Jackson nor Pope intended retreat; operational plans called for the opposite. But only senior leadership could decide whether the time was propitious for further advance. Pope had informed Halleck of the situation that morning, stating, "One-third of the enemy's whole force is here, and more will be arriving unless McClellan will at least keep them busy and uneasy at Richmond." Able to get by with numbers on hand, he nevertheless asked revealingly, "Please make McClellan do something to prevent [Confederate] re-enforcements being sent here." Halleck merely

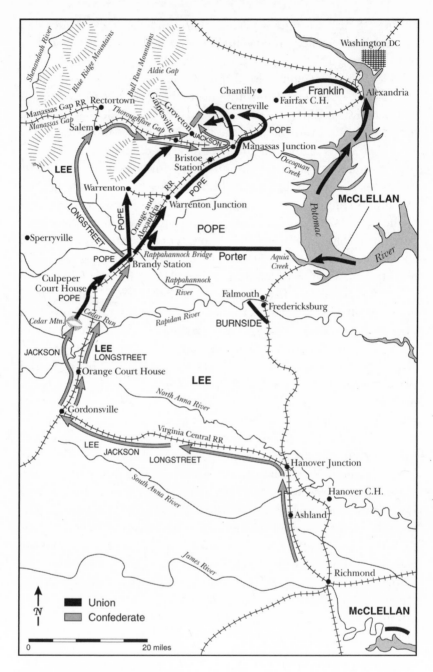

Movements—August 9–28, 1862

replied that Pope should "keep the enemy in check till we can get re-enforcements to your army" and authorized withdrawal behind the Rappahannock.[6]

Enter Robert E. Lee, again wearing his strategic cap. Like Halleck, Lee sought alternatives and reinforcements to cope with the unfolding situation in central Virginia. As long as he stayed in Richmond, he could advise on Confederate grand strategy and comment on operations in other theaters. Moving to Gordonsville, however, he necessarily refocused on Pope and to some extent lost touch with the details of operations in other theaters. He seconded Department of Southwest Virginia commander William W. Loring's scheme to advance into the Kanawha Valley to draw attention away from tidewater and piedmont predicaments. Conversely, Pope at this same moment wanted Brig. Gen. Jacob Cox, the Federal leader in the Kanawha, to reinforce his Army of Virginia at Culpeper. But above all, Lee sought to destroy Pope and then redeem northern Virginia.[7]

In reality, grand strategy and matters beyond the Appalachians belonged to Richmond authorities anyway, although they implicitly affected Lee's operations. The Davis administration had not developed good strategic control of its far-flung military operations, although, as in Washington, the technology was at hand for doing so. Field armies could be managed by the telegraph, although that device had its limitations in precisely where it went and who controlled it. Perhaps Lincoln, Stanton, and Halleck were better attuned to the utility of such technology. Possibly Davis and his secretary of war, George W. Randolph, were less inclined to interfere with their independent commanders. In any case, when Lee left Richmond (hardly having time to say goodbye to his wife and family) he concentrated his attention on Virginia. The capital's protection from lingering Federal forces on the Peninsula and the need to drive back or annihilate the miscreant Pope took precedence.[8]

Before departing town, Lee shifted another ten brigades under James Longstreet to support Jackson. Here was a calculated risk, given the Federals' lingering presence in the lower tidewater. Lee also moved two additional Confederate brigades to Hanover Junction to watch Burnside when he eventually appeared at Fredericksburg. Gustavus W. Smith took charge of Richmond's close-in defense with seven thousand men (many green troops shifted from North Carolina). Lee saw the chance to defeat the Federals in detail. Although Longstreet

ranked Jackson, Lee's presence rationalized command and organizational arrangements for his two wing commanders and established the coordination mechanism for proper planning and implementation. Jackson's independence might now be reined in. When
the three discussed the situation, Lee, like Old Jack, looked to an
immediate move northward against Pope's seemingly vulnerable
left flank. Nicely boxed between the Rapidan and Rappahannock
rivers, the Federal army invited destruction. If properly executed, a
Confederate maneuver could sever Pope's umbilical via the railroad
to Alexandria and Washington as well as the lateral line of reinforcement from Burnside and McClellan. Longstreet demurred, urging
that the army sideslip along the Blue Ridge foothills to the west, thus
gaining Pope's rear. Lee won out, only to discover that his army and
its generals were unready for bold execution.[9]

Logistics became a major problem at this point. Stretched far out
on lines of communication, neither army received adequate supplies via traffic-clogged railroads to their rear. Pope's supply route
proved particularly inadequate to his needs, despite earlier managerial success under a civilian railroader in uniform, Col. Henry
Haupt. The enigmatic Pope declared him superfluous (Haupt *was*
difficult to deal with), sending him home only to discover quickly
that Haupt's successor, the "too old and easy" Col. Robert E. Clary,
as well as freewheeling interference by his own military subordinates,
botched things to a fare-thee-well along the sixty-mile single track
back to base. Complaining as usual to Washington, Pope swallowed
hard and wired Haupt, "Come back immediately cannot get along
without you; not a wheel moving on any of the roads." Meanwhile,
Orange and Culpeper civilians felt the impact of voracious soldiers
raiding their livestock pens and granaries. Father James Sheeran of
the Fourteenth Louisiana commented at the time, "Whenever we
stop for twenty-four hours every corn field and orchard within two or
three miles is completely stripped." How feeding two armies might
affect their celerity of operations remained anyone's guess.[10]

One thing was sure: Lee's men did not respond readily when
ordered to advance at daybreak on August 16. Sudden concern
about rations and straggling arose as the Confederate columns filed
northward toward Somerville and Raccoon fords on the Rapidan.
Longstreet complained loudly about feeding an army moving
covertly behind sheltering Clark's Mountain (a key piece of terrain

for the Confederate high command north of Orange Court House). Everything depended on rendezvous and timing. Arrival of Fitzhugh Lee's cavalry and R. H. Anderson's infantry from Beaver Dam Station on the Virginia Central became crucial to consolidating Lee's strike force. Yet both parties diverted through Louisa Court House looking for resupply. Such a detour, though necessary, proved poorly coordinated and poorly timed with higher headquarters. Several days' delay resulted while Jackson's disgust with Longstreet's apparent sluggishness frayed tempers and Lee reluctantly deferred the advance across the Rapidan until late on August 18. Jackson made his displeasure well known while offering to share rations with other commands until the planned advance could tap Union supply dumps at Brandy Station to the north. He even suggested that the ground beyond the Rapidan would be "rich with apples and corn," as if the enemy had not already harvested those delicacies.[11]

Then, suddenly, Pope learned of Lee's plans. An amply financed spy network, alert cavalry scouting, and stray prisoners of war gave the Union commander notice of Confederate intentions. These factors became even clearer when Thomas O. Harter of the First Indiana Cavalry (part of Sigel's escort troop) penetrated the Confederate inner circle, learned of Lee's intention to attack Pope before he could retire behind the Rappahannock, and so informed the Federal commander on August 18. Pope told Harter after the war that he was "the first person" to provide such information, and McDowell substantiated Harter's help in enabling the army to escape Lee's trap. A combination of miscues (blamed on Georgia politico Gen. Robert Toombs, who left unguarded the critical Raccoon ford) furthered opportunity for Union reconnaissance when so ordered by Pope. The fact was, Pope was alerted to Lee's intentions.[12]

Pope responded not only to his own intelligence but to Halleck's August 16 suggestion that it would be better if the Army of Virginia retired behind the Rappahannock: "We must not run risks just now, but must concentrate." Pope replied that the line of the Rappahannock as far up as the forks with the Rapidan was safe. He ordered Brig. Gen. Jesse Reno, commanding the IX Corps coming with Burnside from Fortress Monroe and holding the sector in the path of Lee's planned advance, to send part of his attached cavalry across the Rapidan to watch all approaches from Louisa Court House and Hanover Junction and to employ spies and scouts "without regard to expense." Entrusted with one such overnight mission, Col. Thornton F. Brodhead led the First Michigan and Fifth New York cavalry splashing across Raccoon ford early in the morning of August 18 and surprised a sleepy Stuart and his staff awaiting arrival of Fitzhugh Lee near Verdiersville on the Orange plank road east of Orange Court House. Brodhead nearly captured the *beau sabreur* himself and did snare Stuart's newly acquired red-lined cape and feather-adorned hat (taken from old West Point classmate and later Union brigadier Samuel Crawford during the Cedar Mountain truce on a bet that the *New York Herald* would report that battle as a glorious Yankee victory). More to the point, however, Brodhead brought back a satchel containing, among other papers, Lee's blueprint for the operation.[13]

Stuart would avenge this affront to his honor within a fortnight by making a similar raid on a Yankee supply trove at Catlett's Station. For the moment, though, the damage to Lee's plans seemed incalculable. The captured papers confirmed Pope's worst fears: that the Rebels intended turning his left flank. Hesitant about being cut off from his supply base at Manassas and reinforcement from Fredericksburg, the Army of Virginia leader told Washington on the afternoon of August 18 that he would withdraw behind the line of the Rappahannock. Brodhead's caper provided suitable cover for Pope's clandestine spy operation and a belated corroboration of Harter's report. At least Pope did not duplicate McClellan's tendency to inflate enemy numbers. Halleck wired back that he fully approved Pope's actions. "Stand firm on that line until I can help you," enjoined Old Brains. "Fight hard and aid will soon come."[14]

The elongated ridge called Clark's Mountain hid Lee's concentration from a prying Union signal station atop Thoroughfare Mountain, where it could observe the country for miles in the direction of Gordonsville and Orange Court House. "No indications of the enemy in force in that direction," was the word sent back to Pope. But Brodhead and an ample purse for dissident Virginians willing to spy for the Union saved Pope's army with their early warning via the captured plans. When Lee and his staff ascended Clark's Mountain about noon on August 18, they found Pope's army in plain view before them, stretching in "fancied security," and to all appearance "in utter ignorance of the vicinity of a powerful foe," according to Confederate staffer Armistead Long. The opportunity slipped from Lee's grasp. He could not know of Pope's impending retreat. What he did know was that his nephew's cavalry was not up, and further delay resulted. Both sides beat tattoo that evening and bedded down as usual. At about 11:00 p.m. the entire Federal army stole quietly out of camp along assigned routes, headed for the Rappahannock.[15]

Reno made straight for Kelly's ford on the Rappahannock via Stevensburg. Pope's other contingents became helplessly snarled in traffic jams trying to neck through Culpeper. Matters got ugly, thought staff officer David Strother, with "one heterogeneous mass of vehicles" clogging the road and broken down vehicles pushed to the side and set afire so as to be seen for miles by their light. Still, the sleeping Rebels apparently failed to catch on, and hard-working leaders like Pope and McDowell had unsnarled the mess by midmorning on August 19. Some twelve hours were lost in the process. Citizen-soldier Robert Milroy might grumble to his wife about "our miserable humbug-bag of gas" Pope now showing "our backs to the rebels" while his tired and hungry soldiers marched dejectedly. Yet the Army of Virginia saved itself. Van R. Willard of the Third Wisconsin declared later that whatever Pope's subsequent misfortunes and "whatever may be his other faults," one could not but admire the skill and the promptness "which he manifested in conducting this retreat." Early on August 20, the Army of Virginia stood securely on the north bank of the Rappahannock, ready to take on its pursuers. Those pursuers were a day behind schedule. Lee's indulgence for subordinates' tardy arrival cost him the chance to destroy his opponent.[16]

Word reached Lee about the Federal retreat only at noon on August 19. He and Longstreet rode again to the summit of Clark's Mountain. They watched silently as the Union dust clouds faded into the distance. Sadly, Lee put down his field glasses and turned to his lieutenant: "General we little thought that the enemy would turn his back upon us this early in the campaign." It was a bittersweet comment and reflected Lee's frustration. The hour was too late to start now; better to march "at the rising of the moon." Jackson at least wreaked vengeance, executing three deserters by firing squad before his paraded corps to set an example of much-needed discipline and determination. A citation in John Wotring's diary said it simply: "18th cook four days rations remain till morning of 20th at 10 o'clock am, we move toward Culpeper C.H." Even then, Powell Hill's command became a scapegoat, caught oversleeping and in the middle of breakfast when Stonewall appeared and ordered everyone onto the march.

Only sharp skirmishing at Kelly's ford and Rappahannock Station on the turnpike and rail line marked the extent of action that day.[17]

Culpeper residents, for the most part, rejoiced at the Yankees' departure. They plied the enemy with thinly veiled taunts about hurriedly "returning from Richmond" while greeting arriving Confederates with cheers and singing as well as flowers and baskets of produce and sweets. Such pleasures proved fleeting as Lee pushed pursuit of Pope. Passage of the Rapidan cooled marching feet and restored spirits, but there would be no repeat at the Rappahannock. Pope's forces (arrayed from Kelly's ford past Rappahannock Station to Freeman's ford and bridges at Warrenton Sulphur Springs and Warterloo to the northwest) occupied generally favorable high ground and contested passage. Moreover, Pope's awareness of enemy movements allowed him to dispute all crossings. Lee could not find alternative ways across the river. Historians have cited the ensuing maneuvers as "waltzing" along the river. Allusion to a boxer's jabbing better reflects the two armies' actions.[18]

Pope claimed that the Rappahannock line was very weak, fordable almost everywhere, and "runs through a flat country." An engagement with the enemy here, he wrote Halleck on August 19, "will be simply a pitched battle in the open field, the river presenting scarcely any impediment, while the country is very open." Noting that his army was much fatigued "but in good spirits," Pope positioned his forty-five thousand men well: from Reno's Second Division, IX Corps (eight thousand) at Kelly's ford ("one of the best on the river"), to McDowell's eighteen thousand defending the railroad and turnpike at Rappahannock Station and Sigel's twelve thousand further upstream and ready to sideslip as events required. He held Banks's battle-worn seven thousand men in reserve. Actually chafing to advance back across the river and assault the enemy, Pope accepted Halleck's continuing enjoinders to hold until reinforced. Of course, Pope might be outflanked by a maneuver-oriented Lee. The character of the country became more rolling upstream from Rappahannock Station and Beverly ford (the next available crossing). It would be there, on Pope's right, where Longstreet had originally urged action, that Lee now slid his legions. Seeing that he could no longer separate the Union left flank from reinforcement via Fredericksburg, Lee decided to crab to his left, poking, probing, and attempting to get across the river without major engagement. In the process, Lee would draw his own army farther away from covering Richmond. He would also pull Pope away from Burnside at Fredericksburg.[19]

Lee ordered Jackson and Stuart to attempt crossings at Beverly's and Freeman's fords while steadily intensifying artillery exchanges up and down the river line. Col. Thomas L. Rosser, a promising twenty-six-year-old West Pointer with his Fifth Virginia Cavalry and two cannon from Jackson's lead division under William B. Taliaferro, drove across at Beverly's only to provoke a heated counterstroke by McDowell, who sent a brigade with artillery support under Marsena Patrick, a hard-bitten old army regular, even if characterized by one observer as "the finest existing fossil of the cenozoic age." A brisk fight filled the air with Minié balls and artillery projectiles. At the other end of the line that day, a similar "handsome skirmish" took place in reverse when cavalryman John Buford tested Longstreet's and Hill's resolve on their side at Kelly's ford. As one Confederate surgeon put it simply, "Each army is trying to get the advantage of the other, and it is difficult for either to cross the river while the other opposes it." Everything tended to confirm Halleck's earlier admonition to Pope to "keep scouts well out on your right." That night Pope learned that at least some of McClellan's veteran troops, namely, John Reynolds's Pennsylvania Reserve division, would join him the next day, August 22. Further confirmation of Lee's shift upstream came that day at Freeman's ford, when possibly the heaviest fighting thus far involved Robert Milroy's division of Sigel's corps. Stuart tested the Ohio politician's pluck, but additional artillery exchanges convinced Lee that Freeman's ford offered no opening. Besides, the army commander had something else in mind for his cavalry.[20]

At this point, the Confederate leader suddenly agreed with Stuart's suggestion that he take his fifteen hundred troopers off against the enemy's line of communications as he had done on the Peninsula. The goal would be to interdict the railroad behind Pope, thus causing him to retire from the Rappahannock line and into the open field, where Lee could defeat him in pitched battle. Jackson would continue slipping upstream on what one participant called a "hot fatiguing march" in heavy gear along sultry river bottoms. By afternoon, Jackson's wagon train stretched from Beverly's ford past Freeman's and Fox's crossings to the one at Warrenton Sulphur Springs. It was an inviting target, and the Federals at Freeman's suddenly decided to interrupt the march. With a lull in the artillery duel about 3:00 p.m.,

Sigel pushed infantry and cavalry across the river to fret the Rebel movement. Col. Alexander Schimmelfenning and the Seventy-fourth Pennsylvania in particular took the high ground beyond the ford and disrupted passage of Jackson's wagon train, cutting out eleven pack mules and a handful of dusty soldiers as trophies. Schimmelfenning sent back for reinforcements, and two additional regiments from Henry Bohlen's brigade splashed across the shallow ford, led by yet another of those German American politicians in uniform, Carl Schurz.

Schurz, like Sigel, Julius Stahel, and other émigrés in Union blue, had fled the 1848 revolutions in the fatherland, arriving in America with strong patriotic and antislavery sentiments as well as pronounced accents. Schurz's soldierly qualities received immediate testing this day south of Freeman's ford, when his advance ran into Isaac Trimble's brigade of Ewell's division, positioned by Jackson to protect against any enemy sortie on the supply train. The battle at Freeman's ford became more memorable among the participants than in the history books. Bohlen and his command were quickly overrun, the general killed right on the firing line and the men in blue sent scampering back across the river. It was a scene reminiscent of the Ball's Bluff rout of November 1861 that had led to the establishment of Congress's infamous Committee on the Conduct of the War. No such result came from Freeman's ford. However, "pouring a dreadful fire into their crowds of confused and broken lines, as they were huddling together to cross," noted the Reverend Nicholas A. Davis of the Fourth Texas, "many were shot in the back, and others drowned by the crushing crowd which pressed for the other shore." The work took only a few minutes, leaving hundreds of Schurz's dead and wounded on the ground and in the river. Only timely employment of Capt. Hubert Dilger's artillery battery staved off a Confederate breakthrough.[21]

By this time, Jackson had gone further upriver to supervise a crossing near the prewar Warrenton Sulphur Springs spa. These richly furnished white buildings, enclosed by expensive carved marble fencing, had been a prewar vacation spot for Virginia gentry. Guests had long since given way to Union wounded on the 188-foot-long three-story promenade portico of the main hotel building, and the grounds of the place showed the effects of wartime neglect. The buildings now fell prey to salvoes of artillery fire designed to dislodge snipers. Sigel's people had already burned the bridge at the crossing, but Jackson told Ewell to get Alexander Lawton's and Jubal Early's brigades with two batteries across the river during a momentary break in a passing thunderstorm. Old Jack wanted to quickly establish a bridgehead that could be widened further for passage by the rest of the army the following day, but he miscalculated on a flooding river. In the words of John Wotring of the Thirty-third Virginia, "It is said to be a race between Gen Jackson and Gen. Pope which shall get to the head of the River first." The Rappahannock's rising waters isolated the vanguard on the north side. Early took position on high ground fronting Great Run (equally swollen by the rain) covering the road to Rappahannock Station while Lawton commanded the road to Warrenton. Jackson could only hope that Sigel's Federals would react slowly to this situation. And so they did, much to Pope's disdain.[22]

Sigel, whose colorful pronunciation of English often mixed with the elixir of battle to dramatic effect, was said to be everywhere, "with more fidelity and sleepless activity." But how was it possible to decide where the enemy would strike and thus meet him with adequate force in every instance, wondered one of Sigel's staff, James Lyons. Prejudiced nativist sycophants close to Pope, including McDowell and Col. David Strother, determined their scapegoat: "the nervous little German" whose "timid soul" and lack of "dash of the offensive spirit" typed him as "excitable, helter-skelter and unreliable as a military leader." Strother especially decided that Sigel had been "pounding away continuously with artillery to little or no purpose" and that "only some hardheaded common sense men with him would save him from disaster." Sigel remained preoccupied at Freeman's ford that stormy night of August 22. The rain poured down and cut off Early and Lawton on the north bank at Warrenton Sulphur Springs, but the feisty little German could not travel the inundated roads to do anything about it. By 9:00 p.m., cavalryman George Bayard's scouts carried word of the Rebel intrusion at the springs to Pope's headquarters.[23]

Pope pondered what to do now. His flank and rear threatened by Jackson, the blustery general wired Washington suggesting options and asking for instructions. He could retire behind Cedar Run, fifteen miles north on the railroad, and link up with elements of McClellan's army transiting by boat to Washington and thence down the Orange and Alexandria to meet him. Samuel Heintzelman's III

Corps of the Army of the Potomac had disembarked at Alexandria on August 22 and was moving south by train. William Franklin's VI Corps remained on transports in the Potomac (as did William Sumner's II Corps further downriver). Fitz John Porter's V Corps was also ashore and marching overland from Aquia Landing. Pope learned from the War Department that Jacob Cox's Kanawha division had entrained at Parkersburg in western Virginia en route to helping him. Or the Union commander could take his opponent's lead and knife across the Rappahannock at Kelly's ford to cut Lee's right rear. Such a move would leave the Army of Virginia with a river at its back and separated from reinforcement, however, while Jackson stood poised for some wide-swinging move on Pope's supply route. Another, less risky option would be to destroy that part of Jackson's force that was apparently isolated from its parent command by six-foot floodwaters. Indeed, an expectant Pope directed Sigel to spare no time in doing so. Halleck, usually noted for avoiding just such a decision as Pope sought and who had twice counseled earlier that day to ensure the safety of the railroad at all costs, suddenly wired that he approved Pope's option of striking at Lee across Kelly's ford.[24]

At that moment, events stymied the Federal counterploy. About mide-vening Pope's telegraph line went dead at both ends. Stuart's horsemen had descended on Catlett's Station. Railroader Henry Haupt thought rumored gunfire meant nothing more than teamster panic spread-ing to the small cavalry guard at the place. He could not have been more wrong. This was a major raid that changed the character of the campaign. Indeed, Stuart had reached Catlett's through helpful intercession of liberated Warrenton citizens and a Federal officer's captured black servant. He arrived in the same thunderstorm that isolated Early and stymied Sigel. His troopers routed civilian workers and a small military guard just sitting down to supper at the station. Redeeming himself for the Verdiersville surprise, Stuart's Catlett's Station haul included supply wagons, horses and mules, prisoners, thousands of dollars in Federal payroll for Pope's army, and the con-tents of the army commander's headquarters wagons. In addition to Pope's dress uniform coat, Stuart also found a fistful of orders and telegrams that gave Lee a clear sense of the timetable for the concen-tration of Pope, Burnside, and McClellan. The rain prevented Stuart from destroying the nearby railroad bridge over Cedar Run, and so he drew off by 3:00 a.m. Lee and Pope both dismissed the affair as marginal, but Union morale sagged again. Pope realized how vulnerable was his line of communications.[25]

Pope had worried all day about the railroad. Just about the time that Stuart wrecked Catlett's, Pope wired Halleck to quickly forward a brigade for bridge protection duty as well as Heintzelman's corps. He also directed McDowell to send back two cavalry regiments to protect the baggage train. Obviously, Pope was too late, and so he played down Stuart's impact by wiring Halleck over a restored telegraph link that damage at Catlett's was "trifling; nothing but some officers baggage destroyed," while the railroad, "as far as I know," was in perfect condition. Such news, if true, was vital. Pope and Halleck as well as numerous intermediaries had so plagued railroad operatives over the past few days as to cause Assistant Secretary of War P. H. Watson to wire Pope testily the previous morning, "You can use the cars for either warehouses or for transportation, but not for both." If everyone wanted McClellan's army brought forward through Alexandria, they would have to pay more attention to the care and condition of the line. Stuart had not closed it down with the Catlett's raid. Yet communications had become snarled between headquarters and the field. Nobody, neither Halleck nor McClellan nor even Burnside, seemed to know exactly where and what Pope was doing in the wake of the Catlett's mess. Perhaps historian Kenneth P. Williams was correct: just as the armies of Virginia and the Potomac composed what later would be an "army group" during World War II, a single commander would have been in order. Eventually, Pope sent Washington a specific disposition of his troops indicating a concentration closer to Warrenton so as to counter Jackson.[26]

Pope was correctly more concerned about Jackson's whereabouts than Stuart's raid. He received word from Sigel the next morning that the army's right flank had been turned at Sulphur Springs. Pope now abandoned the notion of attacking Longstreet. Seeing the floodwaters as heaven sent, he prepared his army to move quickly upstream to dispatch Jackson's bridgehead. He told Sigel to "stand firm, and let the enemy develop toward Warrenton." Reinforcements would be constantly arriving in the rear, and he did not "wish any further extension of our lines to the right" but desired "the enemy to cross as large a force as he pleases in the direction of Warrenton." Then, by 7:15 a.m., Pope changed course, ordering Sigel, together with Banks and Reno, to march at once upon Sulphur Springs and thence toward Waterloo Bridge, "attacking and beating the enemy wherever you find him." McDowell would go to Warrenton and, together with Sigel, crush whoever had crossed the Rappahannock. Pope's game plan for the rest of the campaign aimed at independently crushing Jackson. This was what Lee most feared.[27]

The weather continued to plague both armies, however. Sigel and the others struggled through rain and mud. Jackson sent engineers to rebuild the Sulphur Springs bridge and found himself supervising the actual work as floodwaters swirled around his mount in midstream. He said little to anyone and nothing by way of small talk, observed his loyal aide, Capt. Charles Blackford, but apparently suffered acute anxiety about Early's and Lawton's safety north of the river. Downstream, Longstreet and McDowell dueled with their artillery as the Confederates again tried to force passage at Rappahannock Station and Beverly's ford. Milroy, leading Sigel's corps, confronted Early late in the day but could not push the issue. Old Jube worried that Jackson might not recall him in time to escape disaster. He need not have been concerned, as Sigel's main force took so much time moving into position that by 3:00 a.m. the next morning Early's wet and bedraggled men managed to escape back across an ersatz bridge to rejoin Jackson. Still, the close brush with disaster in this sector spurred Lee's further sideslipping to the Warrenton Sulphur Springs and Waterloo Bridge. The Army of Northern Virginia now seemed to shift away from rather than directly toward Pope's railroad lifeline. Pope, despite Stuart's embarrassment and assisted by twenty-four hours of rising waters, once more seemed poised to elude Lee's grasp.[28]

Pope relinquished the Rappahannock Station position as he shifted northward. Lead elements of Fitz John Porter's V Corps of the Army of the Potomac closed on Kelly's ford from Aquia Landing near Fredericksburg. They then languished in splendid isolation for several days, a fact their disgruntled commander communicated forcefully to Washington and which further heightened McClellan's disgust with Pope and Halleck. Sigel finally crossed Great Run to find Early and Lawton gone, so Pope ordered the German American to continue upstream to cover Waterloo Bridge. The river valley echoed to the crescendo of increased artillery exchanges. Smoke filled the hollows between contending forces in what another of Jackson's aides, Maryland staff officer Henry Kyd Douglas, styled "the noisiest artillery duel I ever witnessed" that "accomplished little and was not expected to accomplish much." Virginia artillerist Greenlee Davidson, however, marveled at the Federal guns' "remarkable precision." Their shot would just graze the top of a promontory and come whizzing down the rear face to endanger the Confederate gunners. He wondered if they had a gun like Davy Crockett's fabled rifle, "which would shoot around a hill." It took two days to "exhaust this artillery fusillade," but Pope could afford to wait. The standoff permitted the Army of the Potomac's lead elements to arrive by foot or rail. Affecting a swagger when they did arrive, Col. Orlando Poe, one of Maj. Gen. Joseph Hooker's brigade commanders, wrote his wife on August 23 that his men felt good and "are chock full of fight." That same day, in the afternoon, McClellan wrote his wife from the steamer *City of Hudson,* "I take for granted that my orders will be as disagreeable as it is possible to make them—unless Pope is beaten, in which case they may want me to save Washington again." A tone of noncooperation attended those words.[29]

Official Washington remained unaware of this friction for the most part. President Lincoln personally seemed bothered more by *New York Herald* editor Horace Greeley's column "The Prayer of Twenty Millions," which had expressed disappointment with administration policy with regard to the "slaves of the Rebels." Greeley had proclaimed that the administration should execute the laws, particularly the "emancipating provisions of the new Confiscation Act." Lincoln should stop catering to the wishes of border slave-state politicians and make the army fight rather than arresting fugitive slaves. Lincoln answered with a public letter of his own on August 23 in Washington's *Daily National Intelligencer.* The chief executive projected the rather conservative stance that he would save the Union, "save it the shortest way under the Constitution," and the sooner the national authority could be restored, the nearer "the Union as it was." His paramount object in the struggle "*is* to save the Union, and is *not* to save or to destroy slavery." He reiterated that he intended "no modification of my oft-expressed *personal* wish that all men every where could be free." He might have resolved the slave issue in his own mind but gave no hint publicly on such a move. Lincoln scholars ever since have scratched their heads as to Lincoln's purpose and meaning at this point. Perhaps battlefield victory might point the way. Yet two generals brought east to secure victory were no closer to that goal than before. Lincoln too was increasingly perplexed by the singular lack of military success in central Virginia and its meaning for the larger scope and issues of the conflict.[30]

On Saturday, August 23, Lincoln, McClellan, Pope—even Lee—all seemed frustrated by stalemate. Forced to relinquish the offensive and withdraw from central Virginia, much in the manner that McClellan had been ousted from the Peninsula, Pope had thwarted Confederate attempts to trap him but seemed unable to regain the initiative. In parrying Lee's upriver maneuvering by concentration back toward Warrenton in Fauquier County, Pope had exposed his own line of communications to the type of cavalry raiding that benefited Confederate fortunes elsewhere in the war at this time. Stuart merely replicated in the East what the exploits of John Hunt Morgan, Nathan Bedford Forrest, Joseph Wheeler, and others accomplished in the West. Western theater Federal generals, like Pope, customarily dismissed threats to their supply lines and relegated defense of those lines to uninspired, poorly disciplined, and static rail and depot guard units. At some point, they all paid the same price as Pope had paid at Catlett's Station. Moreover, Lee, frustrated by Pope's dogged rebuffs and the weather, wrote President Davis that maneuver room east of the mountains was shrinking and his own communication line back to Gordonsville more exposed with every flank move westward. "If we are able to change the theater of the war from the James River to the north of the Rappahannock," Lee mused, it would be possible "to consume provisions and forage now being used in supporting the enemy." Within twenty-four hours Lee discovered a bold if dangerous plan to dislodge Pope from the Rappahannock.[31]

On Sunday, Lee studied the Yankee dispatches Stuart had garnered at Catlett's. Such luck rivaled the famous Lost Order of the Maryland campaign a month later, as Lee recognized that Pope's August 20 report to Halleck afforded both dangers and brilliant opportunity. On the one hand, those dispatches suggested that Lee would face upwards of two hundred thousand Federals within the week. Yet that week afforded Lee a window to destroy his nemesis. From headquarters at Jeffersonton near Warrenton Sulphur Springs, Lee at once wrote Davis outlining a plan to concentrate all available manpower for some as yet unannounced stroke. Richmond would be stripped of troops and Loring's command in western Virginia would transfer from the Kanawha to "descend the Valley of Shenandoah, so as to threaten

[Federal] possession of the Valley." The Confederate capital's safety had been ensured by the spadework of hard-working hired slaves who built forts garrisoned for field batteries, Lee observed. He confidently wrote wife Mary Custis, "I think we shall at least change the theater of war from [the] James River to north of the Rappahannock." Still, he said nothing in either letter about the venue or the manner in which he might destroy Pope.[32]

Sometime on Sunday afternoon, Lee, Longstreet, and Jackson pored over maps atop a flat field desk set up on the Jeffersonton village common. Their resulting plan would cut loose Jackson from the main army with twenty-seven thousand infantry, artillery, and cavalry. With space shut down east of the Bull Run mountains, Old Jack would move rapidly northward via Amissville and Orleans to Salem on the Manassas Gap Railroad. There he would turn east, and moving down that rail line through Thoroughfare Gap in the mountains descend upon Pope's vital, but exposed, supply base at Manassas Junction. That event would surely cause Pope to pull back from the Rappahannock. Lee with Longstreet and the Richmond reinforcements would follow Jackson's trail and regain the direct route to destroy Pope and threaten the northern capital. There might be risks. Pope might undertake a counterstroke across the Rappahannock and overwhelm Longstreet in Jackson's absence. He might even sideslip and return to Culpeper. Or he could rapidly retire north of Bull Run, beyond Manassas, and escape entrapment. But Lee's reading of the captured dispatches suggested that Pope simply awaited McClellan and Burnside. Jackson and Longstreet agreed. The plan went forward. Longstreet moved to relieve Hill's lines at Waterloo Bridge. Twenty-five select couriers would ensure that the army's two wings remained in constant touch during Jackson's march.[33]

Jackson's famous "foot cavalry" struck out promptly in the predawn darkness the next morning. Their march was to be rapid, secretive, and logistically unencumbered. Only ambulances and ordnance wagons for sixty cannon accompanied the flying column. Each man carried sixty rounds of ammunition and three days of cooked rations. John Wotring had complained for two or three days previously that both armies had been short of rations, especially flour, and were eating saltless meat. Now Confederate quartermasters provided amply for Jackson's march. The hot sun soon turned the operation unpleasant, but Jackson had decreed no straggling (as had plagued his force before Cedar Mountain) and no removal of clothes or shoes when crossing streams. Not that the trek proved entirely onerous; local citizenry saw to that. Pleased with deliverance from enemy presence, they showered the marchers with cheers for the soul as well as food and drink for weary bodies. Capt. French Harding of the Thirty-first Virginia recounted, "On the day we started we breakfasted on abbreviated rations, dined on half rations of unripe corn and fried green apples, and supped about midnight on half rations of fried green apples and unripe corn." Until reaching Salem, Jackson's foot soldiers thought they were headed for the Shenandoah Valley.[34]

So too did Pope, apparently. On August 25 and 26 he essentially lost control of the campaign that would drag on for another week and end, in the words of Pvt. Luther E. Alden of Massachusetts, with the "disaster and shame" of Second Manassas. Naturally, nobody knew this at the time. Rather, each day began with customary artillery fire at Waterloo Bridge. Then Union signalers from a nearby hill confirmed that a large enemy column, stretching an estimated fifteen miles into the distance, could be seen marching northwest toward Amissville. Suddenly the fog of war dropped upon Union intelligence gathering. Pope lost sight of Jackson's movement for fully twenty-four hours. His spy network faded, and Union cavalry, penny-parceled out to the corps commands, came up lame—overworked and with horses taxed to the end of their endurance. Infantry reconnaissance proved a poor substitute. Aided only by reports from the Shenandoah, Pope concluded that Jackson was headed for the valley. He also decided that Lee's whole army was moving that way and shuttled units accordingly.[35]

At first, McDowell was to chase Jackson. Then Pope decided that he should stay at Warrenton while Sigel marched away from the river to Fayetteville, six miles south of Warrenton. Banks would go over the railroad at Bealeton and double back to Kelly's ford. Lee's worst fears about Pope either striking Longstreet or returning to Culpeper seemed in the offing. Luther Alden's caustic perception that "we were moving hither and thither" in circles was true. By nightfall, additional reports trickled in to headquarters that Jackson had made Salem on the Manassas Gap Railroad, and the Union commander decided instead that McDowell should cross the Rappahannock at first light the next day and discover just who was left at Jeffersonton. The flooded river again precluded much action, but Pope wired

Halleck confidently that Jackson was headed to Front Royal and the troops at Salem posed merely a flank guard. To Pope and his subordinates and Brig. Gen. Julius White commanding at Winchester in the Shenandoah, it appeared that Lee and his army might be headed in that direction.[36]

Federal lookouts clearly could see Jackson's column disappearing in the distance, the composition of that column, and what Confederate forces had been left behind. Still, Pope's army had been driven to distraction by the constant and arduous movement over the previous several weeks. Fatigue showed on both the general and his soldiers. Pope complained to Halleck that only McDowell's corps provided a reliable maneuver element. Cedar Mountain had weakened Banks, while Sigel, as Halleck knew, was "perfectly unreliable, and I suggest that some officer of superior rank be sent to command his army corps." Sigel's conduct "has occasioned me great dissatisfaction," undoubtedly because of his sluggish response to Early's bridgehead at the Sulphur Springs. Pope concluded, "Sigel's corps although composed of some of the best fighting material we have, will never do much service under that officer." Such negativity suggested an inability to undertake any action pending relief by the Army of the Potomac. Yet Pope was not completely surprised when reports from Sigel's scouts, Buford's vedettes, and escaping slaves confirmed Jackson's breakthrough at Thoroughfare Gap the next day.[37]

Lee and Jackson had worried that the Federals might have defenders in the notch itself. Not so, and by 2:00 p.m. on August 26 the Confederates had reached Gainesville, although, said Henry Kyd Douglas, "the march had been a rapid one and the soldiers were weary, faint, and footsore." Pope meanwhile did little but shift from one foot to the other on the Rappahannock to the south. By now Lee had set Longstreet in motion toward Salem. Only R. H. Anderson's division and Stephen D. Lee's artillery would deceptively hold the line against Pope until D. H. Hill and Lafayette McLaws could arrive from Richmond. By this time, Jackson had moved to cut the Orange and Alexandria first at Bristoe Station, four miles below Manassas, and then at Manassas itself. Having covered fifty-four miles in less than two days, he was in position to seriously damage the enemy. According to Douglas, "Never in the history of warfare has an army shown more devotion to duty and the wishes of one man, than the followers of Jackson exhibited during these days."[38]

Always ready to fight, Pope nevertheless delayed on August 26, writing dispatches to subordinates and Halleck while awaiting developments along the river line. Waterloo Bridge and the Sulphur Springs crossing fixed his gaze as McDowell's artillery continued to pound Longstreet's positions on the opposite bank. Reynolds and Reno moved into supporting positions for the Union assault on Longstreet as Banks remained off to the southeast, recuperating near Fayetteville and ostensibly protecting the railroad. Poor Sigel could do little to regain favor at army headquarters except stay out of the way. On the previous day Pope had penned a lengthy missive to Halleck in which he iterated three times his understanding of his mission: undertake no independent action pending consolidation of the Army of the Potomac with his own (presumably under Halleck's general command, although Pope feared it might be under McClellan). He had complained about not being kept informed of McClellan's departure from the Peninsula as that affected his own timetable. He judged Halleck displeased, although the general in chief replied on the morning of August 26 that he was not. "Just think of the immense amount of telegraphing I have to do," Old Brains told his subordinate (and repeated the thought separately to McClellan). "Then weigh whether I can be expected to give you any details as to movements of others, even when I know them." Federal unity of command was fast breaking apart.[39]

Pope's biographer uncharitably accuses Halleck of moral cowardice "at a time when strength of will was imperative." More accurately, the general in chief complained of being "broken down every night with the heat, labor, and responsibility." He no doubt lagged in communicating fully with and managing skillfully McClellan's fast-closing elements and their commander. Little matter, at this point, for Pope's flat-footed inattention to his line of communications now rose to change the picture dramatically. True, Pope had taken desultory measures since Cedar Mountain to post guards for his supply depots, as was military custom. He had anticipated arriving reinforcements as adequate to stop merely cavalry raiders. He had allocated three infantry companies to Bristoe Station and another three plus an artillery battery and an untested cavalry regiment to Manassas. They proved too little too late. Not only had Stuart smashed such forces at Catlett's Station, but Jackson now descended with half Lee's army on two hapless new targets. Jackson's brilliant audacity coupled with Pope's miscalculations determined the course of events.[40]

Jackson's legions traversed Thoroughfare Gap and linked up with Stuart at Gainesville just to the east on the morning of August 26. Longstreet poised to follow upon Lee's order as soon as Pope's men reacted to the new development. Still, the Federals remained stolidly in place. Meanwhile, Jackson sent Col. Thomas T. Munford's Second Virginia cavalry with the lead brigade of Louisianans under Henry Forno from Ewell's division to capture Bristoe. Newly arrived horsemen under Fitzhugh Lee and Beverly Robertson would screen the country toward Pope. Munford and Forno quickly overcame the detachments at the station and immediately began to disrupt the main track toward Warrenton Junction. Inasmuch as Haupt was quickly transferring locomotives and rolling stock back to Alexandria to forward McClellan's arriving troops to Pope, the Rebels had a field day with train bashing. Successive wrecks of equipment rendered the Orange and Alexandria impassable, but not before one alert train crew rammed through their particular train behind the locomotive *Secretary*. They spread the alarm about this latest raid. Ironically, the same badly shaken civilian engineer poured on too much steam and plowed into the rear of another train about two miles east of Bull Run bridge north of Manassas. In one historian's words, "From that moment until the end of the campaign the railroad was of no further use to the General who believed in letting his own lines of retreat and of communication take care of themselves."[41]

By evening that day, both Pope and Washington realized that something was amiss. The Bristoe prisoners underscored the rich prize and inadequate force protection that greeted Jackson's men along the railroad. No matter how tired from the fabled march, Rebels like Captain Harding (mostly living off green corn and apples and dining "on a tightened cartridge box belt") relished "a reasonably good supper, furnished by the Yankees, that evening" at Bristoe. Brig. Gen. Isaac Trimble now offered to take Manassas Junction with his "twin Twenty-ones" (Twenty-first Georgia and Twenty-first North Carolina, perhaps five hundred men total). Jackson readily assented, assigning some of Stuart's men to help just in case. The Federal commander at the junction, Capt. Samuel Craig of the 105th Pennsylvania, counted only 115 men of his regiment plus eight guns of the Eleventh New York battery and the untried Twelfth Pennsylvania cavalry for defense. As at Bristoe, this force, which had just bedded down for the night, folded quickly before the Rebel onslaught. Manassas yielded a treasure trove beyond the Confederates' wildest dreams. A mile of railroad sidings counting over a hundred brand-new boxcars plus numerous warehouses promised a cornucopia of delicacies like oysters, pies, and liquor and staples such as flour, coffee, and tobacco. Stuart's boys quickly fell to plundering while Trimble's infantry held back, pending Jackson's instructions. When Jackson arrived, he clamped a lid on dispersal of spirits and set about guarding against any Federal countermoves. Hill and Taliaferro arrived at dawn to support Trimble while Ewell's three remaining brigades and most of the cavalry stayed at Bristoe, subsequently providing a rear guard at Kettle Run.[42]

Jackson netted a rich haul at Pope's expense. Eight pieces of light artillery, caissons, and ammunition plus seventy-two artillery horses and harnesses and 175 draught horses were only the spear tip. Forty-two wagons and ambulances, two hundred new tents, at least four sutlers' stores and contents, large stores of oats and corn and whiskey, two trainloads of what Trimble called "promiscuous stores, clothing &c," two thousand barrels of flour, a similar number of barrels of salt pork, one thousand more barrels filled with corned beef, and fifty thousand pounds of bacon added to the inventory. Jackson also noted recovery "of over 200 negroes," obviously runaway slaves in the employ of Union quartermasters. Still, he worried about other Federal units that would begin probing back toward Manassas to see what the cannonading and break in telegraph traffic was all about. As Jackson's men enjoyed the bacchanalia, news of this latest raid prompted action from Washington.[43]

Alarmed Union authorities, particularly railroader Haupt, moved immediately to protect what remained of the railroad between Manassas and Alexandria. Scattered blue-clad columns began converging on the junction. Jackson had not marched completely unopposed into the area, and escapees from the garrison (cannoneers and two guns from the New York battery) had fled up the Centreville road, encountering Col. Gustav Waagner's Second New York Heavy Artillery at the Blackburn's ford pontoon bridge on Bull Run. This oversized unit, originally recruited for duty in Washington's fortifications, had just detached men to guard Banks's baggage and supply train parked at the stream. The "Heavies," now acting as infantry in the field, crossed the creek and proceeded cautiously toward the junction under the impression that only "a party of guerrillas were committing depredations at Manassas." Although Waagner dispersed a party of Fitz Lee's cavalry in the yard at Liberia plantation, around daybreak on August 27 he soon encountered Hill's entire division of nine thousand men and twenty-eight cannon. Waagner retired in good order north of Blackburn's ford sometime after 10:00 a.m. "Having had nothing to eat, no sleep, and having been constantly on their feet for over 24 hours," the New Yorkers began to flag a little, according to their regimental adjutant. They struggled on to Centreville and then to Fairfax Court House, harassed by mounted Confederates (many of them Fairfax and Prince William County youth who knew the countryside).[44]

Meanwhile, back at Liberia, an even larger Federal force stumbled piecemeal into similar disaster. Haupt had prevailed upon Halleck and McClellan (now aboard his headquarters boat off Alexandria) to do something. An order went to one of VI Corps commander William B. Franklin's brigades to move by rail to secure the Bull Run crossing and protect a construction train that would go forward to repair track damage on the line. Again, nobody was thinking about Jackson, merely that guerrillas or cavalry had descended on the line. So Brig. Gen. George W. Taylor's New Jersey brigade steamed out of Alexandria at dawn and moved slowly west toward Manassas. The *Secretary* train wreck forced Taylor to detrain a mile east of the Bull Run bridge. By this time he had learned of the Rebel occupation of the junction. Leaving the Fourth New Jersey, Taylor and his other three regiments (plus two of Col. E. Parker Scammon's regiments, recently arrived with Jacob Cox's Kanawha division from western Virginia) pushed across Bull Run, deployed into battle lines, and advanced toward the distant noise of Waagner's battle. Taylor's men were veterans and naturally disdainful of Pope's rear echelon units, but they lacked cavalry and artillery support and, like Waagner, received a thorough drubbing from Hill.[45]

Taylor desperately ordered a charge. It caught a withering blast of musketry and cannon fire, after which Jackson boldly rode out with a white flag to demand Taylor's surrender. The Federals were uninterested and whipped a volley past Jackson's head, continuing the uneven fight for a bit longer. Soon they too were badly used up, and Taylor ordered a withdrawal that remained orderly until reaching the Bull Run railroad bridge bottleneck. Pressed hard by Confederate infantry and artillery, the retreat disintegrated into rout. Taylor fell mortally wounded along with at least 150 of his men; two hundred more became captives. Only Scammon's Buckeyes saved the survivors as the Confederates filed into old rifle pits on their side of the stream and the Federals scrambled to high ground between Union Mills and Johnny Moore creek. Scammon escaped along the railroad, and Hill's men burned the bridge and returned to the junction. In all, Jackson's command had mauled three separate Federal commands, inflicted more than five hundred casualties, and incurred but twenty of their own. Scant solace came later from Jackson's comment that Taylor's "advance was made with great spirit and determination and under a leader worthy of a better cause." In truth, Taylor had failed miserably.[46]

Fitzhugh Lee's cavalry continued to range behind Federal lines after destroying Waagner's command. They cut the railroad link to Alexandria between Fairfax and Burke's stations at about 6:30 p.m. and intercepted another of Haupt's construction trains sent forward to pick up wounded at Bull Run bridge. They also destroyed a small span over Pohick Creek before melting into the woods and returning to Manassas Junction. There they found Jackson's army plundering everything in sight. Jackson had supervised the transfer of property from Federal to Confederate hands and continued his vendetta against liquor. "I fear that liquor more than General Pope's army," he told one captain. But he also realized that his time at the junction was limited. Pope as well as Washington authorities would surely dispatch heavier forces to intercept Jackson's raiders. A third, larger Federal column did threaten to disrupt Confederate activities as August 26 became "the watershed of the short life of the Army of Virginia."[47]

Pope had handled his army well enough up to a point when faced with Lee's relentless pressure. Reinforcements from the Army of the Potomac seemed to be on their way. When reports of Jackson's raid came in, the brash Midwesterner moved quickly to counteract the damage. Alerted to the danger afforded by the Thoroughfare Gap corridor to his rear and when telegraphic traffic with Washington ceased, Pope had to make choices. Slipping eastward to link up with the Fredericksburg reinforcements or rushing across the Rappahannock and attacking whatever Confederates remained there no longer seemed feasible. Both options left Washington uncovered, and Pope remained unwilling to take that gamble. Of course, he could simply retreat back northward on the railroad. More appealing to this fighting general, he might "crush any force of the enemy that had passed through Thoroughfare Gap." He could still cover Washington, as McClellan's forces were ostensibly in place to help in that regard. Trapping Jackson at Manassas *was* tantalizing! Moreover, it made sense. There remained the matter of trying to determine precisely the Confederates' location and then implementing action against them.[48]

Pope issued orders early on August 27 for Sigel, McDowell, and Reynolds to march northeastward from Warrenton to Gainesville (thus cutting the Confederate line of communication through Thoroughfare) and block the retreat route of the Manassas raiders. He envisioned these commands as providing an anvil on which his other units would hammer Jackson. Heintzelman and Reno, followed by Porter and the still-recovering Banks, would proceed along the railroad from Warrenton Junction to Catlett's Station and then strike northwestward for Greenwich, about four miles away. The full sixty-five-thousand-man Army of Virginia would concentrate at Gainesville, where Pope hoped to soundly defeat all Confederate units east of the Bull Run Mountains. Frankly, Lee feared just such an eventuality. Yet he could do little more than urge Longstreet forward quickly and watch closely the course of events during August 27. By evening McDowell stood squarely between the two wings of Lee's army, although he did not know it. Longstreet, accompanied by Lee, lay about ten miles to the northwest, just beyond Thoroughfare Gap, while Jackson stood eight miles to the southeast at Manassas Junction. Heintzelman meanwhile had reached Greenwich, but a sluggish and still-peeved Porter had hardly moved from Warrenton Junction, thus upsetting Pope's timetable. It was Hooker's division from Heintzelman's corps that most immediately threatened Jackson's activities at the Junction. Hooker's advance party from the Seventy-second New York discovered that the enemy lay in heavy force at Bristoe. It would be imprudent to continue on. This report led Heintzelman and Hooker to anticipate heavy fighting.[49]

The ever-combative "Fighting Joe" Hooker pushed his whole division to help the New Yorkers and immediately confronted Early's brigade of Ewell's division positioned behind Kettle Run, two miles out of Bristoe toward Warrenton. He was there in the first place because Jackson feared just such a move as Hooker's advance. Ewell deployed most of his force at the station proper, facing west with outposts on the road to Greenwich. But Early and Forno's Louisianans, enjoying superior supporting artillery, picked a fight with Hooker. Eventually Ewell feared being cut off from Jackson's main force and retired, firing the railroad bridges over Kettle and Broad runs and causing three hundred enemy casualties to about 250 of his own. The summer heat sapped the strength of Hooker's men; they did little about the Confederate sappers destroying the bridges except to snipe at Ewell's departing men. If the Kettle Run affair accomplished nothing more, it bloodied Hooker's nose and further confused the Union command. It most certainly bought Jackson more time. Dick Ewell had conducted a very skillful rear-guard action on behalf of his chief.[50]

By 7:00 p.m. that muggy August evening Jackson wearied of preventing drunkenness, worrying about Yankee interception, and dividing up goods and equipment taken at Manassas Junction. He had planned to hold back on the food distribution until Lee and Longstreet joined him. His soldiers set the pace, however, as everything but hard spirits had gone into a barter trade among participants at the feast. Hardtack, bacon, coffee, sugar, soap, even elegant linens and clothing went into haversacks or were freely divided. No Confederates anywhere else for the next three years would have it so good, not even in the fall in Maryland or on the Pennsylvania campaign the next year. In a feast of eating and frolic, the legend of Manassas Junction was born. As one bedraggled soldier put it, "To see a starving man eating lobster salad and drinking rhine wine, barefoot and in tatters, was curious; the whole thing was indescribable." Eventually it had to end as Jackson, perhaps belatedly, gave orders at sunset to break away and escape northwestward to the environs of the previous summer's battleground. Everyone was to bivouac in the vicinity of Sudley Mill and nearby Groveton on the Warrenton turnpike. Typical of Jackson's poorly communicated desires as well as the difficulty of night marches, Hill and Ewell took the road to Centreville, eventually spending the night between Blackburn's ford and that crossroads, much to Jackson's dismay. Back at Manassas, everything left went up in flames: ammunition, warehouses, and railroad cars. The first phase of Jackson's mission was complete.[51]

Rapid movement, a decisive strike at the Union supply line, and capture of the enemy's principal base—even stopping Union countermoves—all had been achieved. True, if Kyd Douglas was to be believed the overnight getaway was "a martial masquerade by night."

He recounted commissary, quartermaster, and sutler stores carried along on the soldiers' backs. One fellow bent double beneath numerous boxes of cigars, "smoking and joking as he went"; another similarly labored with boxes of canned fruits, still others with coffee sufficient for a winter's encampment or strings of shoes hung like beads around their necks. At this point, the second part of Jackson's mission—reunion with Lee and Longstreet, leading to Pope's destruction before unification with McClellan—now moved to the top of the agenda. An increasingly irritated Pope could see the flames of Old Jack's handiwork from his Bristoe command post barely five miles away, and prisoners taken at Kettle Run told him that the Confederate chieftain and twenty-five thousand men had done the deed. What now was to be done about Jackson, however? Hooker might be too played out and low on ammunition for further action, but Pope knew the rest of his army could respond. At 8:00 a.m. on August 27 he wrote Porter that the enemy seemed to be advancing along the line of the Manassas Gap Railroad: "We will probably move to attack him tomorrow in the neighborhood of Gainesville." An hour later Pope issued what one writer has termed the decisive orders of the campaign: to converge on Manassas "at the very earliest blush of dawn."[52]

Prodded by McDowell (who also sensed a golden opportunity to defeat the Rebels in detail), Pope told Heintzelman's first division commander, Philip Kearny, to be prompt and expeditious and forget wagon trains or road march until the matter was resolved. Porter would support, with Reno moving in from Greenwich. McDowell and Sigel would go through Gainesville toward the north before cutting toward Manassas. If he marched promptly and rapidly, Pope told McDowell, "we shall bag the whole crowd." Here then was Pope's plan, and a good one at that. Thinking Jackson's raiders would still be at the junction, he wanted to concentrate most of his army there before moving en masse to destroy him. Disregarding the problems of night movement and the distinct possibility that the enemy might have left the locale, Pope moved ahead without benefit of sufficient reconnaissance. Indeed, except for Bayard's cavalrymen with McDowell on the Warrenton turnpike, Pope's cavalrymen provided little help. Screened off by Stuart's horsemen, they failed to provide intelligence to Pope in his hour of greatest need.[53]

Pope and his Army of Virginia remained in good shape. They still might unite with McClellan's Army of the Potomac before Lee could strike a decisive blow. Both sides sought to defeat a portion of the other before reinforcements could lengthen the odds. But where were Longstreet and McClellan in the equation? While Jackson knew precisely what he intended doing—taking a strong position near the Groveton crossroads on the Warrenton turnpike to await Longstreet—Pope appeared less sure at this point. He could do nothing now about the wreckage that lay from Kettle Run to Bull Run on the Orange and Alexandria or the smoking ruins at Catlett's and Bristoe stations and Manassas Junction. Clearly intending revenge as he encamped that night at Bristoe, Pope had an operational plan in his own mind. Yet he delayed until morning in order to have Porter and Kearny on hand to pitch into Jackson at Manassas Junction. "I reached Manassas Junction with Kearny's division and Reno's corps about 12 o'clock in the day of the 28th," he later recorded, "less than an hour after Jackson in person had retired." Incorrect in his time, Pope now became unsure just where Jackson had gone. Ironically, the Confederate leader was equally unaware of how narrowly he had escaped Pope's snare when he drew up north of Groveton.[54]

Lee's post–Cedar Mountain strategy had been to overwhelm Pope at Culpeper before the "miscreant" could be reinforced by McClellan and Burnside. But Pope eluded the trap, pulling back behind the steep banks of the Rappahannock and parrying Lee's search in vain for a way across that river. Both sides lost possibly three hundred men testing each other for weaknesses. Meanwhile, McClellan and Burnside transferred their forces up the Potomac with all due speed given the availability of shipping and the fog of war, which hid the serious nature of events confronting Pope's Army of Virginia. New bases of operation were prepared for the arrivals at Aquia Creek Landing and Alexandria, while McClellan fumed at having to retire from the Peninsula to support Pope and lack of clear guidance from the new general in chief Halleck. Unbeknown to his generals, and to few political colleagues, President Lincoln engaged in his own moral and political battle—over slavery. His decision awaited a military victory.[55]

Pope then misread a key move by Lee. Stuart's descent upon Pope's supply line at Catlett's Station not only interrupted rail traffic but also enabled Lee to read Pope's mail. Those dispatches foretold Union movements, thus causing Lee to take bold action. Determined to root the Federals out of their Rappahannock position, he divided his forces, keeping Longstreet to fix Pope in place while Jackson stole a rapid flank march behind the Bull Run Mountains before slashing through Thoroughfare Gap to fall upon Pope's principal supply depot at Manassas Junction on August 26. Rail and telegraphic contact with Washington disrupted, both the Union high command and McClellan unclear as to condition and whereabouts of Pope and his army, the campaign disintegrated. Jackson seemed to hold the key, but where was he?

Southern war correspondent Peter Wellington Alexander wrote his Savannah editor from Richmond on August 18, "I feel authorized to assure you and your readers that our prospects [in central Virginia] under Divine Providence, are all that can be desired." In the end, though, it may have been George W. Taylor's New Jersey brigade tragedy at Bull Run bridge that determined future events. To historian Ethan Rafuse, this event "was a major turning point in the campaign." It provided McClellan the excuse not to rush remaining unallocated troops from his own army to aid a colleague whose politics and way of war Little Mac despised. Another historian, John Hennessey, merely saw McClellan "emboldened to immobility" by Taylor's disaster, which "hardened McClellan's dilatory tendencies." Either way, Little Mac soon gratuitously advised the president, "Concentrate all our available forces to open communication with Pope" or "leave Pope to get out of his scrape and at once use all our means to make the Capital perfectly safe." In his mind, there could be no middle course.[56]

⇒ 4 ⇐

Lee and Pope at Second Manassas

STONEWALL JACKSON'S RAIDERS left Manassas Junction a smoldering pyre by midnight on August 27–28. John Pope now tried to counter the disaster. His previous orders to subordinates to either reinforce the junction or scout toward Thoroughfare Gap had come to naught for reasons beyond his control. Believing that he could catch the intruders, Pope now directed Major Generals Philip Kearny and Joseph Hooker of Samuel Heintzelman's III Corps, Army of the Potomac, to reopen the rail line from Bristoe Station to Manassas and destroy Jackson's raiders. He especially wanted Fitz John Porter, "with your whole corps, or such part of it as is with you," to close up from Warrenton Junction as quickly as possible. He could then bolster Hooker, who "has had a very severe action with the enemy, with a loss of about 300 killed and wounded" at Kettle Run. Pope told Porter to march at 1:00 a.m. so as to reach Bristoe Station for a dawn offensive. Surely only the enemy's advance guard had rummaged the supply dump, thought Pope. He wanted to block the rest of Lee's army from reinforcing Jackson, defeat the isolated Stonewall, and then retire north of Bull Run. To subordinates like Porter, however, Pope appeared lacking in "confidence in the plan and management of the campaign," even taken aback by the "late serious disasters."[1]

A crisis of confidence overtook the whole Federal command structure. Merging two armies shaped by different personalities, styles of command, and philosophies of war proved challenging enough; Bristoe and Manassas only aggravated the situation. Pope's Army of Virginia had yet to congeal as a unified fighting force. Amalgamation with units from George B. McClellan's Army of the Potomac bred mistrust and dissent as well as personal animosities and varying allegiances among the general officers. Senior division commanders Kearny, Hooker, and especially Porter worked at cross-purposes with Pope as they moved under his operational command and control. McClellan's clique wanted little success to accrue to the midwestern braggart who competed for Washington's favor. They further stoked Pope's already high-strung nervousness about his situation and displeasure with his own subordinates Sigel and Banks. General in Chief Henry Halleck might have better clarified the status between the two armies. He had all but promised McClellan ultimate command of the unified force but made no move to confirm that impression. Halleck also failed to ensure that McClellan's subordinates' understood their role to be "co-operating with and supporting General Pope against the enemy."[2]

And what of McClellan himself? Events very much hinged on the game the general seemed to be playing with Washington. His procrastination after Seven Days had not set well. His own view was that this was the old conspiracy waged by politicians against him. When Halleck ordered that he move his army back to where "it could unite with that of General Pope, and cover Washington at the same time that it operated against the enemy," Little Mac shifted his venom to his new boss. McClellan's dispatches and delay aroused suspicion. Eventually he begrudgingly complied with all due speed. Some things lay beyond his control: trying to rapidly transfer sixteen thousand sick as well as perhaps one hundred thousand fit soldiers with their baggage and equipment, artillery, horses, and wagons proved very difficult. McClellan tried to tell Washington officials, but they never appreciated logistical problems attending that effort.[3]

Halleck authorized McClellan "to assume control of all vessels in the James River and Chesapeake Bay, of which there was then a vast fleet." Indeed, approximately five hundred vessels of various sizes and types substantiated Quartermaster Gen. Montgomery C. Meigs's claim to McClellan that "nearly every available steam vessel in the country is now under your control." Many of the craft were too large to ascend the James River to Harrison's Landing, where the army lay bivouacked. Smooth embarkation would not be possible, as McClellan's chief quartermaster in charge of ship movements informed his superiors. Yet Washington badgered the army commander with dispatches urging speed, since Pope's situation seemed to be disintegrating quickly. When McClellan marched overland to embark at Yorktown and Fortress Monroe, he also complained to his wife that corps commanders William B. Franklin and William B. Smith were slow, inefficient, and disappointing. Delay could not be entirely attributed to McClellan's obstructionism, yet it certainly affected the course of events as Lee and Jackson descended upon Pope.[4]

McClellan genuinely believed that only he could save the Union. He confided privately to his wife on August 21 that with Pope and Burnside hard-pressed in central Virginia, the administration "seem to want the 'Quaker,' the 'procrastinator,' the 'coward' & the 'traitor'" (epithets thrown at him by radicals, opposition press, and other ill-wishers) to save the situation. Ever convinced that "the herd" in the capital was out to do him in, McClellan's private thoughts and words began to exude impertinence bordering on insubordination, although not so his official correspondence. Still, Little Mac liked to think that he remained the War Department's senior general, whose advice was not merely requested but actually needed by a disorganized administration. Halleck tended to encourage such expectations. For his part, McClellan was as blunt as Robert E. Lee in wanting Pope's demise, since "such a villain as he ought to bring defeat upon any cause that employs him." Very soon Lincoln, Stanton, and Halleck began to seriously question McClellan's teamwork in meeting and defeating their mutual enemy. Devotion to *his* Army of the Potomac as well as implicitly promoting Pope's failure intermixed in disastrous fashion.[5]

Arriving off Alexandria on August 27, McClellan was as perplexed as Halleck about Pope's actual situation. He tended to embrace rumors and hearsay from stragglers encountered during the erratic transfer of his troops and passed them on in dispatches to Washington. Hardly averse to casting aspersions on Pope's predicament, Little Mac shamelessly promoted the defense of Washington. His advice to Halleck was sound enough: don't parcel out reinforcements to Pope without accompanying artillery and cavalry, especially considering the fate of Waagner and Taylor. Like Pope, McClellan sought constant guidance from higher authority. An overworked Halleck provided few specifics. By August 28, except for Sumner's and Franklin's corps plus artillery, most of the Army of the Potomac had been sent piecemeal to help Pope while McClellan's generals helped undermine cooperation. A fiery if often inebriated Phil Kearny duplicitously warned Pope not to anticipate help from Porter and the McClellan clique. Porter and Burnside fed anti-Pope rhetoric to the War Department and Congress, complaining bitterly that Pope "ran away from the Rappahannock, shamefully abandoning" them without a word of warning that the Army of Virginia was shifting upstream with the Confederates. McClellan refused responsibility for events "unless," he said, "I receive authority to dispose of the available troops according to my judgment."[6]

The disasters along the Orange and Alexandria led McClellan to tell superiors that above all else, "we should first provide for the immediate defense of Washington on both sides of the Potomac." He implied that Pope's field operations were already a dismal failure. Halleck stood at the center of this swirl of events, the man who wanted to avoid, but was now party to, Secretary of War Edwin M. Stanton's vendetta against McClellan. Unclear about Pope and McClellan, worn down by Washington's August heat, in delicate health, and beset by a deteriorating military situation in Kentucky as well as the perfidious nature of capital city politics, Halleck swung back and forth between being assertive and equivocal. Tempers were on edge when Halleck finally acknowledged that McClellan's overall knowledge of the country around Washington best qualified him to defend the capital while helping save Pope's army and defeat Lee. Most tellingly, the general in chief admitted to McClellan that he could provide no details on Pope's location or the state of Washington's defense, as more than three-quarters of his time was devoted to raising new troops and dealing with matters in the West. As ranking general in the field, Halleck told him, "direct as you deem best; but at present orders for Pope's army should go through me." Meeting some of Halleck's overworked staff in a Washington hotel bar, Capt. Charles Francis Adams Jr. wrote his father, the U.S. minister to England, that he was discouraged and terrified: "Small men with selfish motives control the war without any central power to keep them inbounds."[7]

In truth, Halleck was caught in the unenviable position of having to be concerned with disintegrating situations in two major theaters of operations at this time. Confederate fortunes *had* begun to rebound beyond the mountains as well as in Virginia. Successful maneuvers by Braxton Bragg, Edward Kirby Smith, and others threatened Union gains in Tennessee and Kentucky. As Halleck accordingly had so little time for details, he essentially gave license for the Army of the Potomac commander to regain control over the whole eastern theater. A precocious McClellan (sounding now much like his own former incarnation as general in chief) ultimately would advise President Lincoln directly at 2:45 p.m. on August 29 that there seemed to be two courses of action. His own preference was to let Pope get out of his scrape and at once use all means to make Washington "perfectly safe." But Lincoln was no fool, and he whipped back a wire at 4:10 that same afternoon: "I think your first alternative to wit 'To concentrate all our available forces to open communication with Pope' is the right one." He did not "want to control," he continued; "that I leave to Genl Halleck aided by your counsels." Yet McClellan's offhand comment about Pope's plight incensed the commander in chief. Presidential secretary John Hay jotted in his diary that Lincoln bluntly felt that "McC. wanted Pope defeated." At this point, McClellan was building a case for his own dismissal. Lincoln and Stanton wanted him kept on a tight leash.[8]

A galvanized Halleck suddenly sent what McClellan took as accusations of disregarding orders. McClellan quickly fired back that he had only been exercising "discretion you committed to me" and irritably told his superior to give distinct and definite instructions. The butt of this controversy lay with the dispatch of railroad repair crews to Manassas and the remaining two corps of Franklin and Sumner to reinforce Pope. McClellan had responded prudently, although whether he did so willingly was another matter. Somehow Franklin halted midway at Annandale; Halleck raged at the interruption while McClellan again counseled that lack of proper reconnaissance of the countryside dictated caution given reports of Confederates ranging about freely north and east of Manassas and Centreville. Both generals remained ignorant of the real-time situation as Union and Confederate armies now locked in major conflict. Clearly McClellan could not abide the role of mere movement coordinator. He had expected to assume supervisory command of both armies; Halleck had intimated as much. McClellan was unhappy at relinquishing his precious army piecemeal to an upstart. Notwithstanding Lincoln's direction, McClellan would ensure that John Pope would have to get out of his own fix.[9]

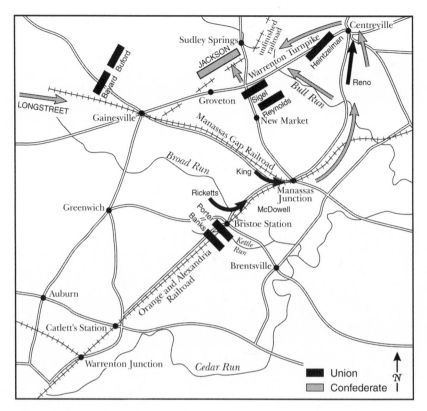

Situation—August 28, 1862

Pope, for his part, experienced difficulty getting organized to do so. His plan for concentrating the widely dispersed army and bagging Jackson at Manassas had flaws. For one thing, it depended on speed; for another, it hinged on up-to-date intelligence about his opponent. Both proved difficult to achieve with worn-down, ineffective cavalry. Besides, Jackson's men had vanished from the junction (something apparently never contemplated by the bull-headed Federal commander). Moreover, just as Pope had not anticipated Jackson's flank march in the first place, he now repeated the fatal error of not sealing Thoroughfare Gap against passage by the rest of Lee's army. A lone brigade remained at Warrenton to watch for telltale signs of a moving enemy as Banks trailed Porter coming north on the railroad. Similarly, McDowell followed Sigel several miles to the west on the Warrenton turnpike, bent on concentrating at Gainesville, where the road from Thoroughfare Gap joined the turnpike. Pope remained convinced that he could crush Jackson before Lee appeared with Longstreet's wing. Only the much-maligned Sigel and equally pilloried McDowell really worried about Longstreet, it seemed. McDowell shifted toward Thoroughfare Gap at 11:30 p.m. on August 27 only to receive Pope's instructions, written two hours earlier, telling him to hasten the army's concentration at Manassas Junction. McDowell left James B. Ricketts's division at Gainesville as support for Col. Percy Wyndham's First New Jersey Cavalry, actually screening the gap. Neither force would be sufficient to prevent Longstreet's pushing through to help Jackson, however.[10]

The wording of dispatches, the widely dispersed units, and the fact that both the Warrenton turnpike and a wagon road adjacent to the Orange and Alexandria Railroad were clogged with Federal baggage trains all loomed ominously. Pope's evening guidance on August 27 to both McDowell and Porter—"Jackson, Ewell and A. P. Hill are between Gainesville and Manassas Junction," and "if you will march promptly and rapidly at the earliest dawn of day upon Manassas Junction we shall bag the whole crowd"—could not be effected. Unfamiliarity with the countryside plagued Union movements. One of Sigel's reconnaissance teams stumbled into the Confederates and was captured, thus uncovering Pope's maneuvers to Jackson. Then Sigel mistook orders to put his right flank "on the Manassas railroad" to mean the Orange and Alexandria, not the Manassas Gap spur line, where he permitted his men a leisurely breakfast at Gainesville while blocking the march route for everybody behind him. Porter apparently showed no desire for pushing a rapid night march. Even when everyone eventually found his proper place and movements began around 10:00 a.m. on the hot morning of August 28, Pope's timetable stood in complete disarray. Sigel finally headed off in the direction of Bristoe, while McDowell moved north on the Warrenton turnpike so as to turn right onto Pageland lane, the main Gainesville–Manassas road, paralleling but north of the Manassas Gap track and out of supporting distance with Sigel. Porter arrived at Bristoe six hours behind schedule. Railroad resupply remained badly jammed back in Alexandria and Washington as Fitzhugh Lee's demonstrations on the Little River turnpike northwest of Fairfax Court House not only convinced the government that the capital was threatened but "helped fix Pope in his idea that Jackson was still headed northeast."[11]

Meanwhile, Old Jack clearly kept to his role in preventing Pope from retiring safely north of Bull Run. Leading elements of Brig. Gen. John Reynolds's Pennsylvania Reserves division stumbled onto Confederates in force about a mile east of Gainesville on the turnpike to Centreville at a place called the Brawner farm. This 319.5-acre spread, owned by Mrs. Augusta Douglass, included a four-chimney house known as Bachelor's Hall, some outbuildings, and an orchard. John Brawner, a sixty-four-year-old crippled farmer, rented the place for his wife and three daughters. Because the house sat atop a low ridge overlooking the turnpike, it immediately caught Jackson's attention as he aligned his troops against an unfinished railroad grade and hill known locally as Sudley Mountain. Brawner and his family fled when the Maryland cavalry brigade of Col. Bradley Johnson opened suddenly on the marching Federals at 10:00 a.m. The subsequent firefight riddled the Brawner buildings but also perplexed McDowell, who did not realize that he had found Jackson. Ignorant of the countryside and uncertain about both the location of the enemy and Pope's ever-changing instructions, all the corps commander knew for sure was that a body of Rebels had delayed his movement. He ordered nearby artillery to suppress Confederate fire. Nobody realized that these were the opening shots of the Second Battle of Manassas.[12]

Had Jackson unnecessarily brought on a fight? His withdrawal from the junction had been anything but masterly. For one thing, Hill's march to Centreville initially drew Pope in that direction. Eventually Jackson's own widely separated divisions had collected between Sudley and Groveton hamlets. The morning of August 28 found him trying to determine Pope's intentions. The wily Confederate might have used the sylvan landscape of farm and woodland to simply await the arrival of Longstreet and Lee. At some point, Jackson and Lee had probably determined that a decisive battle would be inevitable. To bring it on prematurely appeared foolhardy while the two army wings were separated. Yet Jackson realized some action was necessary to fix Pope's attention and leave open the way through Thoroughfare Gap. The Confederate wing commander could not allow Pope's escape to high ground at Centreville or merger with the Army of the Potomac. At about noon Jackson reinforced the firing line engaged with McDowell at Brawner's place.[13]

McDowell almost upset Jackson's scheme. Thinking the enemy might only be "some rear guard or cavalry party, with artillery," he studied area maps for about an hour and then directed Reynolds to break off the action and strike for Manassas Junction via nearby Pageland lane. Jackson's fresh troops arrived to find the Federals gone. The tired newcomers, bolstered by Ewell's men, then filed behind the railroad embankment west of Groveton to await developments. In the meantime activity in the early afternoon shifted back to Pope's field headquarters. Having passed the night at Bristoe, the Union commander was up at dawn, pacing restlessly while smoking cigars incessantly and pressing subordinates as to why no sound of gunfire indicated the "bagging" of Jackson at Manassas Junction. An annoyed Pope studied reports that had Jackson at Centreville and Longstreet closing rapidly through Thoroughfare. By late afternoon Pope suddenly changed his mind, perhaps due to Fitzhugh Lee's activities around Fairfax. The army would now concentrate at Centreville, not Manassas, to catch Jackson. Even the ever-trusting McDowell began to have misgivings about Pope's focus. Nevertheless he complied with the army commander's directive. Nothing could compel a "befuddled" Pope to "take stock, and evaluate matters dispassionately."[14]

Pope, in fact, became dimly aware of heavy fighting off to the west by late afternoon, when he and his staff rode up the Manassas–Centreville road and set up a new command post near Blackburn's ford. The firing came from Thoroughfare Gap, where Longstreet's advance guard had reached the key passage at 9:30 a.m. For two days they had been following Jackson's end-around move through Salem, where, commented Rebel John Dooley, ladies waved their kerchiefs from the lighted windows, and "more than one voice is heard at the piano singing fortissimo 'Dixie,' 'Bonnie Blue flags,' etc." They had not paused to savor "the cheering and brilliantly lighted parlours" but were driven on by their officers, sleeping in an open field one night where a stampede of headquarters staff horses left many of them stunned and bruised. Indeed, Longstreet's forced march may have been more arduous than that of Jackson's foot cavalry. Robert Campbell of the Fifth Texas in John B. Hood's brigade recalled tramping well into the night while the highway "for miles back" was lined with sleeping Confederates, "who unable to move farther had fallen by the road side." In this march, the eighteen-year-old soldier remembered later, "3 out of every 5 had fallen off—from pure exhaustion—and unable to march farther." Lee and Longstreet kept in touch with Jackson by courier and remained confident about the separated portions of the army. Still, most of Longstreet's men would not approach the gap before midafternoon.[15]

Confederate scouts initially reported the passageway undefended, but that situation had changed by late afternoon. Union scouts from British mercenary Sir Percy Wyndham's cavalry noted Longstreet's approach, then spent the morning felling trees to block the passage while awaiting the arrival of Ricketts's five thousand infantrymen from Gainesville. The sweating foot soldiers made Haymarket, three miles east of the gap, by 2:00 p.m. They found that Wyndham's men had withdrawn from the gap itself. Undaunted, Ricketts drove his men as well as Longstreet's advance back toward the defile, deploying his command with artillery support on Quarry Ridge, about a half mile from the eastern end. They effectively disputed Confederate occupancy of the gap. Sharp fighting then broke out at Chapman's Mill, adjacent to the railroad track and road near the eastern end of the gap and key to Ricketts's position, soon spreading up the slopes as both contenders scrambled to gain advantage on Pond Mountain to the south and Mother Leathercoat Mountain to the north. Longstreet also sent Wilcox's division to Hopewell Gap, the next pass to the north, for he could ill afford lengthy delay in reaching Jackson. John Buford's and George Bayard's cavalry disputed various smaller gaps along Bull Run Mountain, but all of this effort came to naught when the Rebels, enjoying superior numbers, not only gained the high ground ahead of Ricketts's people but quickly outflanked the main Federal position east of the pass.[16]

By midafternoon the heavily outnumbered Federals simply lost any chance to confine Longstreet. With orders from Pope to pull out and make for Centreville, Ricketts's artillery continued to blast away at the gap until after dark, when everyone retired to Gainesville and eventually to Bristoe Station. Casualties numbered scarcely over a hundred on either side. Longstreet's weary men, now in complete control of Thoroughfare, bedded down for the night just east of the mountain. Longstreet and his staff took lodging at a mountaintop cottage, and Lee, having supped at one local landowner's house, spent the night at William Beverly's nearby Avenel estate. With hundreds of stragglers seeking to rejoin the ranks, there would be time enough to reach Jackson the next day, they surmised. Ricketts might well have arrived too late to do anything about stopping Longstreet's twenty thousand Rebels, but worse, Pope had forfeited his best chance at beating Lee in detail. McDowell had the right idea: Pope failed to see the need and, lacking detailed reports on the precise situation at the Gap, chose to "pursue" a presumably trapped Jackson. McDowell's whole corps possibly could have held Longstreet at bay long enough for Pope to complete the task of inflicting irreparable damage on Jackson. Nothing like that took place, so the major confrontation would occur near the old battleground of First Manassas.[17]

Frankly, it may have been a second fight at the Brawner farm in the late afternoon that preoccupied Pope with Jackson to the neglect of Longstreet. McDowell's strung-out corps further reaped the whirl-wind of Pope's blizzard of confusing orders. Rufus King's division (its commander unfortunately plagued with epileptic seizures yet not relieved of field command) proved a case in point. Delayed by Sigel's morning traffic jam, King's men lay about in temporary bivouac on Pageland lane about a mile south of the turnpike cooking dinner and resting at midafternoon. They had covered scarcely seven miles in the day's search for Jackson. Then, at 5:00 p.m., came orders to return to the main road and march to Centreville. King's four bri-gades proceeded, stretching for about a mile of road space, with McDowell and his staff in the van. Zouaves in red trousers acted as flankers on the column's left, largely due to the morning encoun-ter at the Brawner place. Finding no lurking enemy, the marchers relaxed. McDowell even rode off to find Pope and got lost, claim-ing later, "The country between the Warrenton Turnpike and the Manassas railroad, on which we were now marching, was unknown to us." Suddenly a lone rider appeared in the distant fields. Brigade commander Abner Doubleday wanted him taken under fire, but to no avail. It was Jackson, about to spring a trap.[18]

Old Jack had been napping in a fence corner when a courier brought word that a large body of Federals could be seen marching along the turnpike only a few hundred yards away. Earlier, "toward evening," Jackson had learned that Lee and Longstreet would pass through Thoroughfare Gap in the morning. Delighted, his fight-ing spirit rose once again. Springing to his horse, the general rode audaciously out across broomsedge fields to within musket range of McDowell's column. He cantered back and forth, surveying the foe. "We could almost tell his thoughts by his movements," observed Rebel surgeon Dr. Hunter McGuire as he watched the general from afar. Finally, satisfied that the opportunity was too good to be missed,

Jackson wheeled and galloped back to his own lines. He touched his hat in salute to subordinates and said simply, "Bring out your men, gentlemen!" It was about 6:00 p.m. on a warm summer evening.[19]

Jackson had watched King's strung-out column unsuspectingly crossing his front. His own men lay poised less than a half-mile away. So, with banners unfurled and drums beating, Jackson and his men stepped forward from the wooded shelter of ridge and railroad embankment. William B. Taliaferro's four brigades promptly advanced to the northern edge of the Brawner farm, skirmishers in advance, three artillery batteries in support on the lower slope of Stony Ridge to their rear. By the third shot, the gunners had bracketed the dusty Federals, sending them scurrying for cover in the ditches beside the turnpike. A New York battery quickly deployed with counterbattery fire from a position just to the northwest of the six-house Groveton settlement. Before long the rattle of musketry and black powder smoke joined the din. A second preliminary aspect of renewed combat at Manassas had been joined. A Federal brigade of Midwesterners would be featured—the only such contingent in the eastern army at the time—opposing Jackson's old "Stonewall Brigade."[20]

The weather and the ground were right for battle that evening. Thermometers at Georgetown in DC recorded temperatures in the high seventies, and both armies spoiled for a fight after weeks of toilsome marching and maneuvers. The smell of heat and dryness in soft farm country found King's men leaderless, their division commander prostrated by yet another seizure. McDowell had left the vicinity to search for Pope. Hatch's own brigade in front of the column unknowingly slipped past Jackson's ambush. But John Gibbon's brigade, next in column when caught suddenly by fire from Jackson's artillery and infantry, deployed out of the roadside ditches and Brawner's woods on the south side of the highway. Aided by two regiments from Abner Doubleday's following brigade, the Federals formed into battle line, guiding on the Brawner farm structures. Taliaferro's five thousand men, their red battle flags flapping over a dirty tan-and-gray battle line, stood nearly tooth by jowl with the two Yankee brigades. Securely anchored by Gibbon's iron men (clad in regulation army uniform, with feathered high-crown black hats, one side pinned up by a brass eagle), the battle was a classic linear contest. Standing, firing, and dying all took place in two lines scarcely 70 to 150 yards apart. By 7:15 p.m. Jackson had secured Maj. Gen. Richard Ewell's division and fifteen minutes later directed a frontal assault by those troops already on the field. The Federals calmly blew away what enemy sprang forward and continued to hold the line. Superior firepower, grit, and determination gained the day. The fighting further damaged Brawner's farm buildings, killed livestock, and mauled orchards. Just before dark Jackson attempted to hook around Gibbon's left flank, using intrepid southern artillerist John Pelham's horse artillery to support Taliaferro's final attempt to wrest victory from the impasse. Gibbon held, however, and both sides called it a day in the gathering dusk.[21]

There was "no maneuvering and very little tactics" in the ninety-minute fight, merely "a question of endurance, and both endured," said Taliaferro. Some 1,250 Confederates fell, as did more than a thousand Federals, with loss percentages ranging from 33 to 70 in stalwart units like Gibbon's black hats and Isaac Trimble's vaunted "Twin Twenty-ones" (Twenty-first Georgia, Twenty-first North Carolina). Both Confederate division commanders, Taliaferro and Ewell, were wounded, the latter losing a leg but securing an eight-month recuperation period away from the army. In fact, Ewell never would fully regain his reputation for ability and combativeness. The action at Groveton (Brawner farm) trailed off into the summer night with desultory musket fire mixing with the cries of the wounded. King, recovering from his seizure, queried his brigade commanders and, bolstered by the arrival of Reynolds's Pennsylvania Reserves, considered standing firm overnight. Prisoner reports of overwhelming Confederate strength, however, narrowed his options. Nobody quite knew where the rest of Pope's army lay, as some commands occupied the old 1861 battlefield on the Henry and Robinson farms closer to Bull Run and others were further away at Centreville and presumably at Manassas Junction. A battered Gibbon counseled withdrawal, although he later recanted the notion. Despite Pope's interim order to hold fast, King decided to withdraw toward Manassas rather than continue marching across the enemy's front or even await developments in the morning. So Jackson missed a splendid opportunity to obliterate one of Pope's divisions. "Our Brigade is cut up badly," noted Stonewall Brigade member John Wotring, "nearly half its number killed and wounded." Maj. Rufus Dawes of the Sixth Wisconsin thought the fighting had "eradicated our yearning for a fight."[22]

Night descended over the smoky landscape of the Brawner and Dogan properties, cloaking the dead and wounded. Brawner would seek recompense for damages from the Federal government after the war. But for the moment, he and his family were absent from their war-torn property. Those in uniform also departed, the Confederates back to the sheltering defense line along the railroad grade, their opponents searching for the main army. Sometime after the battle, at about 8:00 p.m., King sent a courier to find Pope, who, along with his staff, had watched the Groveton fight in the distance from their vantage point at Blackburn's ford. Pope actually continued with plans to concentrate at Centreville, until the appearance of King's courier. The army commander understood the man to say that "King's division of McDowell's corps had met the enemy retreating from Centreville, and after a severe fight had remained masters of the field, still interposing between Jackson's forces and the main body of the enemy." Here was something quite promising, thought Pope. He had his quarry trapped. Porter and McDowell might regain the Gainesville area and blunt the rest of Lee's army coming through Thoroughfare, while Sigel and others could destroy Jackson in the morning. The fluidity of the situation had obviously eluded Pope. From King's dispatch unfolded the next wave of baffling orders, piques at mistaken movements, attendant delays by subordinates, and the whole jumble of actions that would undermine Pope's renewed efforts to destroy the enemy. Pope confidently told Washington, "The game [is] in our hands." Jackson could not "escape without very heavy loss, if at all."[23]

Pope's immediate response to King, "to hold his ground at all hazards and to prevent the retreat of the enemy," never reached its intended recipient. Hence King left Jackson unattended. The whole army "would fall upon the enemy at daylight" from the direction of Centreville and Manassas, Pope ordered in separate dispatches to Kearny, Hooker, Reno, and Sigel. Speed, night marches, and coordination were critical (and improbable) in this gigantic convergence of force. Compliance with orders in principle could not translate to compliance in practice. Subordinate commanders had wearied of Pope's preemptory shifting about the countryside. Uncertainty about their commander's true intent translated into a constant sense of urgency and barometric fits of temper on everyone's part. At one point the ever-colorful Kearny exploded upon receiving a Pope order, "Tell General Pope to go to Hell. We won't march before morning." Kearny meant what he said. Even the enlisted ranks projected an image of "shuffling, half-starved somnambulists" after days of heavy marching with meager rations in the August heat. Perhaps only Sigel spent the predawn hours preparing to carry out Pope's orders.[24]

Pope termed King's withdrawal "a most serious and unlooked-for mistake" when informed about it by Gibbon at daybreak on August 29. "Where is McDowell?" he asked Gibbon, flailing wildly. "Goddamn McDowell, he is never where he ought to be!" Gibbon feigned shock at the remark as everyone in the army supposed that Pope "liked, trusted and leaned upon McDowell very much." All of this reflected still another fundamental problem: Pope's shifting command center was poorly positioned for facilitating the kind of coordination envisioned for trapping Jackson. An eight-mile arc of operations proved too great for properly managing an army with a balky command team in unfamiliar country at night. Aware that McDowell no longer fixed the enemy at Groveton and thinking Jackson was trying to flee, Pope sent a dispatch to Porter, still at Bristoe Station: "Push forward with your corps and King's division, which you will take with you, upon Gainesville." "I am following the enemy down the Warrenton turnpike," he added typically. "Be expeditious or we will lose much." Earlier Porter had been told to march at once to the perceived danger point at Centreville. Taking pen in hand upon receipt of the new order at 5:20 a.m., he began to write what the courier Col. David Strother thought were marching orders. But as Strother quickly discovered when asked by Porter how to spell the word "chaos," the V Corps commander was really writing his friend Ambrose Burnside at Aquia Landing, who would shuttle-pass information along to Washington and provide the only data of Pope's actual operations consistently received in the city at this point. Porter observed that the Rebels were apparently wandering around loose, although "I expect they know what they are doing, which is more than any one here or anywhere knows." He had already told Burnside, "All that talk of bagging Jackson, &c., was bosh." He now added, "I hope Mac is at work, and we will soon get ordered out of this."[25]

By the time Porter's men reached Manassas Junction from Bristoe at 8:30 a.m., McDowell had resurfaced, having spent the night trying to find headquarters. He was as poorly informed as Pope about the Groveton fight but finally located both Porter and Gibbon at Liberia plantation, just north of the still smoldering supply dump. Together they studied Pope's latest directive. Realizing that the order effectively dispatched most of his own corps off under different leaders,

McDowell sent Pope a note protesting what he hoped were merely temporary arrangements. He stalled Porter, but when no reply came from the army commander, the pair eventually got moving by 10:00 a.m., with V Corps and one of McDowell's brigades under Brig. Gen. A. Sanders Piatt. After about an hour's march toward Gainesville they ran into Confederate resistance crossing Dawkin's Branch. Another courier arrived with a new dispatch from Pope. This proved to be the famous "Joint Order" that would prompt controversy for decades into the future.

Intended by its author to clarify the command situation, the order displayed a new tack that had not appeared before in the army commander's thinking. Pope now wanted Porter and McDowell to "establish communication" with Heintzelman, Sigel, and Reno, then moving westward on the Warrenton pike, and "the whole command shall halt." "It may be necessary to fall back behind Bull Run at Centreville to-night," Pope added incongruously, as "I presume it will be so, on account of our supplies." Still believing Jackson to be retiring toward Gainesville to rejoin Longstreet, Pope had been brought up short by his logistical deficiencies. "One thing must be kept in mind," said Pope, "the troops must occupy a position from which they can reach Bull Run to-night or by morning," since "indications are that the whole force of the enemy [Lee and Longstreet] is moving in this direction at a pace that will bring them here by to-morrow night or the next day." The brash Pope left a loophole that would subsequently haunt both him and Porter: "If any considerable advantages are to be gained by departing from this order it will not be strictly carried out."[26]

Pope's testimony at Porter's subsequent court-martial for disobedience of orders in December 1862 better explained his thinking on that August morning. It also clarified the immense difficulty of timely communication in response to changing conditions on the ground. As Pope stated at the trial, the situation all afternoon and overnight on August 28 and 29, which had determined troop dispositions, fluctuated so widely that "it was not until toward daylight in the morning of the 29th that I became thoroughly satisfied of the position of the enemy, and of the necessary movements of troops to be made in consequence." Had the Manassas Junction debacle awakened Pope to his army's inability to effectively carry out "bagging the whole crowd"? Was the Union pursuit bogging down principally because the Army of Virginia was hungry and lacked a means of resupply? In Pope's mind, there still might be time to annihilate Jackson, although cavalryman John Buford had sent word through Ricketts that very morning that Longstreet's "seventeen regiments, one battery, and 500 cavalry passed through Gainesville" at 8:15 a.m. Pope knew nothing about this news, as Ricketts relayed the intelligence to McDowell only to have the corps commander pocket the document and forget about it until evening. Both McDowell and Porter clearly saw the clouds of dust in the direction of Thoroughfare Gap—stirred up by enterprising Confederate cavalry farther out the Manassas–Gainesville road in front of the pair—viewed by even some of Pope's staff from a vantage point near Centreville. Everyone apparently discounted its importance, even the army commander when he eventually learned of the news, so confident was he that he could annihilate Jackson alone.[27]

Wishful thinking pervaded Union headquarters all day on August 29. Preoccupation with more immediate problems plagued subordinates on the ground. Once again dispersal and distance haunted the Federals. Headquarters would be "with Heintzelman's corps" or at Centreville, a difference of several miles in those locations, as it turned out. Pope claimed later that he wanted Porter and McDowell to quickly hit Jackson's right flank, pinned in position by Heintzelman and Sigel on the turnpike to the east. This was clearly hindsight, for the Joint Order contained no words to that effect. Moreover, by the time McDowell and Porter had received the order, Stuart had already dipped into his bag of tricks to stymie their large column on the Manassas–Gainesville road. Directing Fifth Virginia troopers to cut all the brush they could find and drag it along the road in the rear to simulate dust rising off a marching column, Stuart's ruse worked superbly. Porter and McDowell hesitated to press on and stopped to await developments. Any chance to strike Jackson evaporated. Of the lot, only Sigel moved according to Pope's orders to "attack the enemy vigorously at daylight and bring him to a stand if possible." Heintzelman and Reno, taking a circuitous route via Centreville, were two or three hours behind schedule. Carl Schurz's division from Sigel's corps had already initiated the main battle against Jackson.[28]

Sigel knew nothing about King's engagement at Groveton and consequently had spent an unsettling night isolated on Henry House hill facing Jackson alone. He sent skirmishers and scouts to discover the Rebels "in considerable force" on the wooded ridge north of the turnpike. The reports lacked detail as to the precise location, length, or depth of the Confederate position. So the next morning, August 29, Sigel launched probing attacks all along Jackson's two-mile front with the divisions of Schenck, Schurz, Steinwehr, and Milroy. The open, gently undulating farmland provided good maneuver room for infantry, although intermittent breakthroughs, repulses, and counterattacks all underscored the futility of the task. Robert H. Milroy bore in on "the dump," a gap in the Confederate line filled with stone and rock debris from the aborted prewar railroad construction, at the seam between the divisions of William E. Starke (Taliaferro) and Alexander R. Lawton (Ewell). Schurz attacked farther up the line toward Sudley Church, where A. P. Hill's division anchored Jackson's left flank abutting Bull Run. Kearny responded to Sigel's plaintive requests for help by even sending a brigade north of Bull Run to outflank the Confederate position, a weak move badly reflecting on the one-armed general who harbored a personal grudge against Sigel, rooted in native American bias against foreigners. A single brigade could accomplish almost nothing in that sector anyway. Eventually the noise of fighting on the Union right caused McDowell to leave Porter by early afternoon and move circuitously with Ricketts's and King's divisions (now commanded by Hatch) to reinforce Sigel.[29]

Escalating combat thus marked the morning's passage, with Kearny's and Hooker's divisions of Heintzelman's corps and even Reno's command slowly entering piecemeal into the fray. The bloody Union attacks continued as Sigel desperately tried to keep his own corps under control. Jackson's young staff officer, Henry Kyd Douglas, later wrote, "Unless [one] has been under the fire of a desperate battle, holding on, as it were by his teeth, hour after hour, minute after minute, waiting for a turning or praying that the great red sun, blazing and motionless over head, would go down," nobody quite understood how slowly timed passed. The temperature was not nearly as hot as at Cedar Mountain. Recordings taken in Georgetown DC, some thirty-five miles away, were in the low eighties the first morning at Second Manassas. By noon, however, the sunny and sultry August day typically began taking its toll of men and beasts as much as the cannon fire and musketry. Jackson's well-fed, rested Confederates offered dogged resistance as both Lee and Pope soon arrived in person on the unfolding battlefield. The stage was set for a grand contest between them.[30]

Pope found "the two armies confronting each other, both considerably cut up by the sharp action in which they had been engaged since daylight." Up to this point, leadership on both sides had left the fighting to subordinates. Pope set up headquarters on Buck Hill, "the hill immediately in rear of the center of our line, immediately east of the Sudley Spring road, and north of the Warrenton turnpike," near a local landmark stone house of ruddy color. Sigel reported in, asking that his badly spent command be withdrawn from combat. Pope demurred, as there were no replacements and he assumed that Porter and McDowell were about to attack the enemy's right flank and rear. He then rode out to inspect the firing line, informing Heintzelman and Reno that they must hold Jackson in place to assure the others' success. Eventually returning to his command post, Pope remained confident that Jackson had been "brought to stand" and the enemy position developed. He waited impatiently for sounds from the west on the turnpike, where he assumed Porter and McDowell were carrying out his earlier orders.[31]

Jackson received word shortly after 8:00 a.m. that Longstreet's column had passed through Thoroughfare Gap, having departed at an early hour. Breakfast on "mutton corn" and nearby ripening fruit left many loose bowels among Longstreet's marching ranks that morning, although Robert Campbell of the Fifth Texas reported a sumptuous "two crackers and a slice of bacon" as his fare. Lee and Longstreet conferred with Stuart near Gainesville, agreeing that they must press ahead to aid Jackson as the sounds of battle echoed to their front. The cavalryman passed off on his mission against Porter and McDowell, while the gray-haired patriarch of the Confederacy's premier army personally moved ahead with Longstreet's marchers. Troops to their front were supposed to be Confederates, but at least one account claimed that Lee rode unescorted, suffering a grazed cheek from an enemy sharpshooter's bullet for his trouble. He established his command post atop Stuart's Hill, where Pageland lane bisected the Warrenton turnpike. Longstreet soon fused his men "at a wide obtuse angle" to Jackson's right flank, while Lee and Jackson consulted. The five-day movement had ended, thus marking the culmination "of one of the most daring undertakings of the war," in historian John Hennessy's words. The Army of Northern Virginia had reunited for the testing battle.[32]

Jackson and Longstreet joined ranks at the Brawner property overlooking ground still littered with Gibbon's untended wounded and unburied dead. Longstreet further overlapped the turnpike facing east. As more reports arrived from Stuart, detailing Porter's and McDowell's actions, Longstreet shifted other arriving units farther to the right and established a reserve on Pageland lane. Most of his artillery wheeled into position on the lower slope of Stony Ridge, about two hundred yards northeast of the Brawner house, where they could enfilade Pope's developing battle line. The Federals' inability to make progress in this area should have alerted Pope's headquarters to the presence of new Confederate units. Similarly, the onset of a crisp artillery duel between Longstreet's batteries and nearby Federal guns at Groveton could have warned Reynolds and others nearby to the new presence. All this was apparently lost in the fast-igniting firefight, where dry grasses set aflame by exploding shells consumed the Federal fallen from the Brawner farm fight the night before.[33]

When John Bell Hood's Texans moved into line, Robert Campbell, on picket duty, selected a good tree for protection from Union sharpshooters about eight hundred yards away from his own company. "Pope had halted and on the bloody ground of '61—intended to make a repetition of crushing the 'Rebellion,'" Campbell caustically remembered. The Confederate battle line now stretched southeastward for nearly three miles from Sudley Church ford on Bull Run in the north to the Pageland crossing of Warrenton turnpike before dropping gently beyond the Warrenton–Alexandria–Washington road, crossing the Manassas Gap rail line, and ending just beyond the Manassas–Gainesville road. Stronger on its left flank because of higher ground and the unfinished rail bed defended stoutly by Jackson's men, the open fields toward the lower end of the line proved perfect for Lee's preferred delivery of some battle-ending hammer-like stroke. Woodlots afforded Longstreet good cover for preparing such a move, although his personal reconnaissance led him to caution Lee. Stuart still had not uncovered Porter's intentions, and there might be great danger to some impetuous assault eastward on the turnpike axis against Sigel, he thought. A "quite disappointed" Lee, observed Longstreet afterward, fretted until Stuart reported the heavy concentration of Federals facing him and threatening the right flank of the army. Lee rode to see for himself and, deciding to reinforce that trouble spot, ordered up Cadmus Wilcox's division from reserve and added it to D. R. Jones's force in that sector. All of this delayed any anticipated Confederate counterstroke that afternoon.[34]

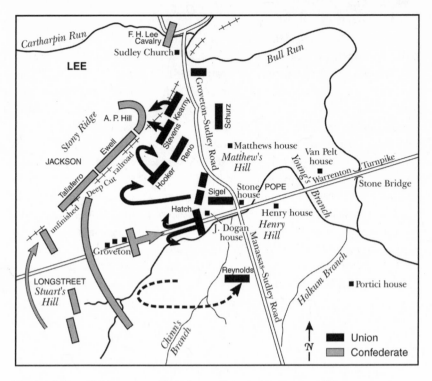

Battle of Second Manassas—Situation 5–8 p.m., August 29, 1862

Unknown to either army commander at the time, their subordinates' movements had effectively checked one another by early afternoon on August 29. Lee's arrival and positioning of Longstreet's corps prevented Pope from enveloping Jackson's right flank via Porter and McDowell. Stuart's masquerade against those two Federal generals as well as Longstreet's prolongation denied accomplishment of the Joint Order. In turn, the presence of Porter and McDowell thwarted Lee's immediate plans for a counterattack that might have swept Sigel, Heintzelman, Reno, and the rest of the Union army off the chessboard completely, possibly repeating First Bull Run's rout. The "noisy-sputter" of battle at midafternoon hid the fact that although Jackson continued to hold the upper hand, Pope retained the initiative and could still fall back behind Bull Run. Every bit as combative as Lee, the Midwesterner chose to merely wait for Fitz John Porter to play the determining role in the battle. Pope would help him with distracting maneuvers against Jackson. Those maneuvers came close to breaching the Confederate line in several places along the unfinished railroad. In the end, however, they devolved into separate, piecemeal attacks, poorly delivered in unsupported fashion that merely killed off combatants, leaving the enemy effectively in place.[35]

The afternoon battle ran its course on August 29. At 3:00 p.m., Cuvier Grover's brigade from Hooker's veteran division delivered a slicing bayonet charge into Thomas's and Gregg's brigades of Dorsey Pender's division in Hill's sector, knocking them back from the rail bed and up the lower slopes of Stony Ridge. Then the attack dissipated. "Men never fought more gallantly or efficiently," Grover said in his after-action report. But unsupported by higher command that saw these matters as merely diversionary to Porter's anticipated assault, Grover's breakthrough failed when willing Confederates rushed to erase the intrusion and then pursued survivors out across the broad killing ground beyond the railroad embankment. At midafternoon Pope sent Reynolds orders to "threaten the enemy's right and rear," ostensibly reinforcing the Porter–McDowell flank assault of Jackson. Reynolds, despite running into Hood earlier, tried again shortly after 3:00 p.m. and, moving forward from the William Lewis house a half-mile south of Groveton, once more ran into heavy opposition and called off the attempt. He and supporting cavalry commander George Bayard sent a staff officer to Pope's command post with information that this messenger had personally counted enemy battle flags and had concluded that the Rebels were in great strength beyond the Yankee left flank. Pope, however, brushed off this news, suggesting that the young staffer was so excited that he had mistaken the enemy for "General Porter's command taking position of the right of the enemy." Yet another sign of Longstreet's presence went unheeded.[36]

Pope decided at around 4:00 p.m. that "a large wood from whence our artillery was annoyed by the enemy's sharpshooters" opposite the Confederate center should be cleared. Col. James Nagle's fifteen-hundred-man brigade from Reno's division of IX Corps received the assignment. The Federal assault knifed into the Confederate position held by parts of Ewell's and Hill's divisions, cracking the line but failing to hold it without support. Once more the Confederates pursued the repulsed attackers back into Union space. That lunge spent itself, in turn, against Federal artillery and infantry led by a reinspired Kearny, shouting "Fall in here you sons of bitches and I'll make major-generals out of everyone of you!" It was all very colorful, if tragically futile. At least it netted merriment for Confederate observers as dozens of captured bluecoats manhandled their own cannon back to Rebel lines, carefully shepherded by their captors. This Confederate willingness to counterattack caused Pope to pull his center northeastward from the Groveton–Sudley road axis to a shorter, more defensible line near the Manassas–Sudley road. The withered Union ranks thus gained better artillery support from Dogan Ridge. The move opened a mile-wide gap, with Reynolds's division posted south of Groveton and assumed by Pope to be serving as a pivot for Porter's assault on Jackson.[37]

Pope now had further tired of Porter's seeming delay. Perhaps McDowell's midafternoon arrival with his foot-sore column (having backtracked to the Manassas–Sudley road to join the main force opposite Jackson) finally convinced Pope that his Joint Order had miscarried. He sent his nephew and aide, Capt. Douglass Pope, to find Porter, with a clearly preemptory rather than discretionary directive. "Your line of march brings you in on the enemy's right flank," Pope told Porter. "I desire you to push forward into action at once on the enemy's flank, and, if possible, on his rear, keeping your right in communication with General Reynolds." Porter was to maintain heavy reserves and use his artillery, "keeping well closed to your right all the time." Pope thought that Jackson's men, "massed in the woods in front of us," could be "shelled out as soon as you engage their flank." Of course, in case Porter should have to fall back, he directed, "Do so to your right and rear, so as to keep you in close communication with the right wing." Just how soon Pope expected Porter to accomplish this feat was uncertain. How long it would take his nephew to even find the corps commander was even more so. In fact the younger Pope delivered his uncle's latest instructions to Porter only sometime after 6:00 p.m. The day was waning, although at 5:30 Pope decided that he would have Heintzelman attack the Confederate left once more, with Kearny conducting the assault.[38]

Few among the Union commanders wanted to face the concentrated enemy fire that had doomed earlier assaults. Only Kearny, although mounting "simply another diversion in favor of Porter," conducted possibly the largest Union effort of the day. Ten regiments (eight in line, two in reserve, perhaps twenty-seven hundred men) under covering fire from six batteries struck Hill's battered battalions. The situation was tense. Both sides were nearly exhausted from the relentless fighting; both were precariously short of ammunition and, more particularly, water to wash lips powder-smeared from tearing paper cartridges all day. Even Jackson sensed the critical moment was near. When informed of Hill's anticipated plight by aide Henry Kyd Douglas, the dour wing commander merely retorted, "Tell him if they attack him again he must beat them." When an anxious Hill confronted his commander in person with the possibility of defeat, Jackson counseled soothingly, "General, your men have done nobly; if you are attacked again you will beat the enemy back." As the Yankee onslaught neared, Hill galloped off to his command, shouting, "Here it comes." Jackson yelled back, "I'll expect you to beat them." Hill did so, although Kearny's men battered their way through his line, thrusting it back from the Groveton–Sudley road. Lacking support, Kearny looked desperately to a brigade from Isaac Ingalls Stevens's nearby division. At the moment of Union success, a rush of Confederate reinforcements appeared instead and drove them back.[39]

Brig. Gen. Jubal Early's reserve brigade (twenty-five hundred fresh soldiers) from Lawton's division crashed into Kearny's weary attackers. The time was about 5:30 p.m. "Thank God, the day is won" was all that Jackson could say when he heard the news. Kearny and Stevens rallied the survivors and rebuffed Early's yelping pursuers. Pope wanted Reno to counterattack in turn, but Reno, in an apparently stormy personal confrontation, prevailed upon him to cancel any further slaughter for the day. When a member of Hill's staff offered his general's compliments and reported the day victorious, Stonewall apparently broke out in a rare grin and replied, "Tell [Hill] I knew he would do it." Although Kearny's attack had come close to success, its failure showed that Pope had expended his strength. The Federals were unwilling and also unable to do anything more against Jackson's decimated defenders. In Texan Campbell's words, the enemy's repeated charges "were met by steady and brave men, who gave not an inch."[40]

Even then, Pope was not finished for the day. Self-deception and misreading of Kearny's near-success worked their wiles at headquarters. A flushed, overheated, and completely unbowed Kearny reported minor success, heavy losses, and bright promise for the morrow. Other reports came in suggesting Rebel traffic on the turnpike—headed west. Pope and his chief of staff, Brig. Gen. George Ruggles, dashed off to a vantage point where they peered at what they thought were Confederate wagons wending their way away from the battlefield. Pope immediately decided that this movement reflected Kearny's success: Jackson was "retreating toward the pike from the direction of Sudley Springs." Ruggles, however, cautioned that these vehicles might merely be ambulances hauling wounded. Pope angrily rejected that notion and fired off another pursuit order that, after a week of such missives, left many subordinates questioning their commander's sanity. Still, Pope transferred his enthusiasm to McDowell, directing him to dispatch a division after the phantom Confederate column. Lacking available cavalry, McDowell sent Hatch's infantry to handle the mission. The problem was that the enemy was not retreating. At that very moment, Lee intended a counterattack.[41]

The two army commanders drew different conclusions from the late-afternoon struggle. Pope thought the enemy was "in wild retreat"; Lee sought to prepare for the battle's "climactic attack." One commander gleaned much from what could be called a second battle of Groveton in the evening twilight on August 29. His opponent would learn nothing from the clash that resulted between Hatch and Hood. At this very moment, the Second Battle of Manassas hung in the balance. Reports reached Lee that Porter was not the threat thought earlier. Stuart wanted to attack, as did Lee, who had chafed at Longstreet's hesitancy all day. But Longstreet prevailed once more, since it was past 5:00 p.m. and the remaining hours of daylight offered little assurance that an attack eastward on the turnpike could prove decisive before nightfall. Postpone the attack until morning, make preparations, and reconnoiter, he urged. Lee agreed reluctantly. Hood's division, with Nathan "Shanks" Evans in support, would make a reconnaissance. Meanwhile, Hatch received word from McDowell that the enemy "is in full retreat along the Warrenton Turnpike, pursue, overtake and attack him." He moved in response.[42]

Supported by artillery, Hatch's two brigades dashed west on the turnpike intending to capture the Rebel wagons and destroy the "retreat." Instead, Hatch plowed into Hood's reconnaissance force just before reaching Groveton. The enemy seemed "rather more combative than we presume retreating forces usually to be," one New Yorker laconically observed later. Indeed, Hood's shouting Texans plus reinforcements doubled Hatch's advance back upon itself as a last-minute melee of fire and maneuver erupted in the gathering darkness. Each side's officers found themselves directing their opponents' formations in the confusion. Nobody could make much sense

of it all, and the fight ended by 8:00 p.m., although cannon fire punc-
tured the darkness and both sides stood within speaking distance
of one another, unaware of their surroundings in the smoky night.
Alabama brigadier Evander Law trapped a last-minute mounted
charge by a squadron of Col. Judson Kilpatrick's Second New York
cavalry; as Capt. John Floyd of the Eighteenth South Carolina assessed
years later, "I don't think that a single horse or man went out alive."
Silence eventually closed over the dead, the dying, and the cheerless
living on the night of August 29. Hood actually stood on the western
slopes of Chinn Ridge across Young's Branch. Hatch rallied back on
Dogan Ridge as the Confederates on Pope's left flank had certainly
not retreated.[43]

Hood's success vindicated Lee and Longstreet's plan. Both generals even considered a night attack to continue the day's success. But
Hood's people were overextended and could not determine the final
Yankee defensive positions in the darkness. Better to await daybreak,
although both Hood and colleagues Evans and Cadmus Wilcox
reported unfavorably even on that idea. Federal resistance seemed
too strong, they told Longstreet. Lee finally canceled all plans, deciding to see if Pope renewed his attacks the next day. At Pope's headquarters, Hatch's rebuff again should have alerted everyone to the
presence of Lee's entire army. Pope, however, clung stubbornly to
the contention noted in his after-action report five months later:
"Every indication during the night of the 29th and up to 10 o'clock
on the morning of the 30th pointed to the retreat of the enemy from
our front." He cited paroled prisoner reports and dubious reconnaissance by McDowell and Heintzelman as evidence. Even when
McDowell finally remembered, at 7:00 p.m., to give Pope Buford's
morning dispatch telling of Longstreet's breakthrough that morning
at Thoroughfare Gap, the army commander merely thought the new
arrivals simply added to Jackson's position, not that they extended
the Rebel battle line overlapping his own. Pope actually appeared
more agitated by what he loudly proclaimed was Porter's intransigence that explained the V Corps commander's lack of supporting
attacks.[44]

Porter sent word to Pope at 6:00 p.m. that he was still unsure as
to the correct course of action. Pope fumed, "I'll arrest him," and
began an order to that effect. McDowell interceded, suggesting that
Porter was not disloyal, merely incompetent, and that the army com-

mander should simply direct him back to the confines of the main army, where he could be supervised more closely. About five hours later, Pope sent a barbed preemptory order to that effect, dispensing much ink on how Porter should acknowledge receipt of the directive and report in person three hours after such reception or after daybreak. Indeed, Porter may have been sloppy in not informing Pope earlier as to what lay directly in front of his advance on the Manassas–Gainesville road. Intelligence historian Edwin Fishel suggests that thanks to McDowell, Porter had read Buford's report about the Thoroughfare breakthrough, had taken prisoners from Longstreet's formations, and thus knew that Lee and Longstreet had joined the action, "holding two or three miles of the front across which Porter was ordered to march."[45]

Despite this, Fishel contends, Porter "sat still and did nothing," not even informing Pope of any reason for such inaction. In a sense, Porter was correct in deferring to McDowell, who ranked him and at some point departed himself to find Pope's headquarters. Moreover, Porter's presence did pin Lee and Longstreet in position for the rest of the afternoon. Yet with his silence and Pope's absolute faith that Jackson's right flank hung in the air and could be rolled up by Porter, McDowell (and even Reynolds) would ultimately exact a price from the V Corps commander for his conduct. He would be court-martialed and cashiered in the aftermath of a campaign where scapegoats and sacrifices would be demanded of the defeated. Perhaps Fishel sensed the ultimate irony: even allowing for the dearth of cavalry for reconnaissance, he concluded, "It seems strange that so large a force as Longstreet's could have been so close at hand and still escaped Pope's observation, but that is what happened."

Pope might have retired to Centreville. Instead, he decided to stand and fight. He had Jackson cornered and battered; he could finish him off the next day, Longstreet or no Longstreet, or so he thought. "We fought a terrific battle here yesterday with the combined forces of the enemy, which lasted with continuous fury from daylight until dark, by which time the enemy was driven from the field, which we now occupy," he wrote Halleck at Washington at 5:00 a.m. on August 30. Blinded by frustration at the day's events, especially Porter's perceived perfidy, yet confident of ultimate success built on Kearny's false sense of achievement, the presence of Porter's men, and the promise of fresh battalions coming from the rest of the

Army of the Potomac at Alexandria, Pope squandered the evening. He hardly recognized that the first day of the battle had been marked by disjointed attacks, heavy losses, and mismanaged battle, largely at his own hands. To him, his opponent, though "still in our front, but badly used up," "is retreating toward the mountains." The battle had been "fought on the identical battle-field of [First] Bull Run, which greatly increased the enthusiasm of our men," despite losses of "not less than 8,000 men killed and wounded." Since the enemy "lost at least two to one," the only option continued to be "to push matters." "I shall do so in the course of the morning," as soon as Porter arrived. Disturbed finally about the lack of resupply from Alexandria and the whereabouts of Franklin's VI Corps, Pope kept Banks's diminished ranks guarding Bristoe Station and the remnant of the rail line against raiders. Pope needed those supplies and should have called them up to bolster his wearied ranks. Overall, the feeling at headquarters that night seemed to be waiting "for the morning to decide upon what should be done."[46]

Meanwhile, McDowell, who had sent Hatch streaming to the bloody rendezvous with Hood, repaired to Henry Hill and his own bivouac after advising Pope about Porter. The army's second in command even summoned one of his scouts, Richard Montgomery, for a second hearing on what that spy had learned from tracking Longstreet for the past week. Montgomery repeated the story that the Rebels expected to whip Pope and send him running back to Washington, which they would not approach frontally, instead "mov[ing] at once up the valley and cross[ing] the Potomac above us." Montgomery claimed that his informant "knew it was the determination of his superior officers to carry the war north of the Potomac." For the moment, McDowell judged the battle at hand to be far more important than this information. A week before, when first informed by Montgomery, McDowell had not conveyed Confederate intentions to his superior. Why do it now? Rightly or wrongly, strategic issues took a back seat to tactical considerations. If Pope had known of Lee's long-range plan, might he have withdrawn to better protect Washington and the Potomac crossings? Or would he still have determined to fight the decisive battle on the Manassas plains?[47]

At the opposite end of the field, Lee too focused on the business at hand. For him, strategic moves also lay dimly ahead in the future. From Stuart's Hill, he dutifully sent word to his superiors in

Richmond. "My dispatches will have informed you of the march of this portion of the army," Lee began his latest message, recounting repulse of enemy attacks, relief of the line of the Rappahannock and Warrenton, and destruction of quantities of captured supplies "for want of transportation." He alluded briefly to wounded Generals Ewell, Trimble, and Taliaferro but moved more surely to operational matters. "My desire has been to avoid a general engagement," he noted, "being the weaker force, & by manoeuvering to relieve the portion of the country referred to." In a passage possibly referring to liberating Maryland (though just as easily applied to the situation in Kentucky and Tennessee or the Shenandoah or even western Virginia), Lee observed, "I think if not overpowered we shall be able to relieve other portions of the country, as it seems to be the purpose of the enemy to collect his strength here." Even in the midst of battle, Lee spoke to larger concerns, such as raising troops, supplies of beef, flour, and forage, and denying the same to the enemy. Finally, Lee told Davis, there was no time to lose: "[We] must make every exertion if we expect to reap advantage."[48]

Lee still faced more than sixty thousand dangerous Federals. Delay in counterattack did not at all indicate his acquiescence to his opponent's moves. Perhaps better to let Pope batter himself against Jackson's resolute defense and then counterstrike at the opportune moment. That was Lee's plan for August 30. Positioned in depth on the right of the line, from Pageland to Lewis lanes, Longstreet's massive corps-size wing was poised to strike via the turnpike. At first Pope's morning inactivity concerned Lee and his generals. "We had hoped we would be attacked," retrospectively noted Lee's chief of staff, Col. Charles Marshall. Jackson optimistically told his subordinates that he did not expect any battle that day and rode over to consult with Lee, Longstreet, and Stuart on a contingency plan. If Pope did not attack again, then the army would wait another night and Jackson would once more sideslip northward to the left. He would cross Bull Run at Sudley ford and take the Gum Springs road to get to the Little River turnpike. Longstreet would hold the Federals in place with a diversion. Once Jackson hit the Little River pike, he would turn right abruptly and make for Pope's retreat route at Germantown or Fairfax Court House to replicate the feat that had brought the two armies to the present circumstance in the first place. Lee's familiar flanking maneuver would afford maximum opportunity to destroy Pope by cutting him off from McClellan. At the least, it could speed Pope's retirement.[49]

Saturday's dawn promised another hot day. The 7:00 a.m. temperature in Washington registered sixty-six degrees. Union scouting parties and captured prisoners suggested Confederate withdrawal and consolidation from the previous evening's encounter between Hood and Hatch. Texan Robert Campbell indicated that at least members of the Eighteenth South Carolina had been out after the evening's fighting, rifling the pockets of the Yankee dead and wounded for watches, wallets, pocket knives, and especially things for the "inner man": bacon and hardtack, which could be borrowed "from our helpless friends." Then they retired to bivouacs nearer their original lines. In any event, Pope, convinced the Rebels were on the run, sent a 5:00 a.m. wire to Halleck noting that the enemy was retreating toward the mountains and enthusiastically recounting the successful bloody action of the day before. The army had "behaved splendidly," although suffering "not less than 8,000 killed and wounded," but he thought the look of the field indicated heavier loss for the enemy. His army was "too much exhausted yet to push matters," said Pope as he awaited Porter's arrival. He also looked for Franklin's, Cox's, and Samuel Sturgis's men with more supplies dispatched from Alexandria to Centreville. In fact that was Pope's battle plan for the day. The specter of Manassas Junction hung over the Army of Virginia. Halleck, in turn, would alert McClellan and the army's chief of ordnance, the chief quartermaster officer at Alexandria, and Banks at Bristoe about Pope's lack of artillery ammunition. By early afternoon he could tell the field commander, "All matters have been attended to." With thirty thousand men marching to reinforce, "Franklin should be with you now and Sumner to-morrow morning." "All will be right soon," Halleck added. Retirement also would be permitted if necessary.[50]

Just what was George B. McClellan doing to help the situation? The Union high command was displeased with Little Mac's sense of purpose, Secretary of War Stanton going so far as to query Halleck on August 28 about the Army of the Potomac commander's promptness in obeying orders to transfer his force back from the Peninsula to cooperate with Pope. Furthermore, Stanton wanted to know if Franklin's corps had responded with all deliberate speed to help the embattled Army of Virginia. Halleck's reply on August 30 hardly inspired confidence when he recited a litany of passed communications, unfulfilled promises, and delays and once again implied an army's senior leadership incapable of prompt reaction to crisis. Halleck's most telling comment, however, was about Franklin's questionable actions: "He knew the importance of opening communication with General Pope's army, and should have acted more promptly" rather than marching only partway to the battlefield. McClellan in fact shouldered the blame for Franklin's dilatory response, citing lack of cavalry to ascertain "what had been officially reported to me from Washington that the enemy in strong force was moving through Vienna in the direction of the Chain Bridge, and had a large force in Vienna." McClellan expanded his comment months later: "It would have been very injudicious to have pushed Franklin's small force beyond Annandale" since "we were cut off from direct communication with General Pope," the enemy was at Manassas in strong force, and Franklin's ten-to eleven-thousand-man corps, "entirely insufficient" in cavalry and artillery, made the situation rather tenuous. At 8:00 p.m. on August 29 he wired Halleck, "It was not safe for Franklin to move beyond Annandale under the circumstances."[51]

Actually, McClellan's position made some sense. With memories of the First Bull Run disaster in mind, Franklin's and Sumner's corps plus odds and ends of garrison troops, cavalry, and rear echelon contingents were all that stood between not only Fitzhugh Lee's raiders, but any Confederate army emerging victorious from combat at Manassas. McClellan complained to wife Mary Ellen on the evening of August 29, "I have no command at present—that is to say I have none of the Army of the Potomac with me & have merely 'turned in' on my own account to straighten out whatever I catch hold of." The next morning he added, "I have sent up every man I have, pushed everything, & am left here on the flat of my back without any command whatever." He could do little more than smoke a cigar and try to get into a better humor, for, McClellan observed, "they have taken *all* my troops from me—I have even sent off all my personal escort & camp guard & am here with a few orderlies & the aides. I have been listening to the distant sound of a great battle in the distance—my men engaged in it & I away! I never felt worse in my life." In truth, McClellan, together with the local quartermasters, may have tripped over rapid reinforcement of Pope. McClellan would telegraph Halleck from Alexandria on August 30 that transport difficulties hampered Franklin and Sumner and their twenty-five thousand men moving to the front, finally noting that everyone but Couch's division had gone forward by afternoon. He observed plaintively, "If it is not deemed best to entrust me with the command even of my own Army I simply ask to be permitted to share their fate on the field [of] battle." Halleck replied feebly the next morning that he could not accede to that request without seeing the president, inasmuch as "General Pope is in command, by his orders, of the department."[52]

In the end, the battle rolled ahead on August 30 beyond the physical capacities of a jammed railroad to convey McClellan, Franklin, and Sumner and massive reinforcement to the front in time to make a difference. Merely highway marching would not have gotten those reinforcements to Manassas in time to count, now that several precious days had been wasted in disembarking, equipping, and moving out the remaining Army of Potomac units. Everything depended on how Pope and his men alone comported themselves against the Army of Northern Virginia on the second day. Frankly, the situation turned on Pope's "sorry reconnaissance" on both flanks. A 7:00 a.m. command council with senior corps commanders on Buck Hill failed to confirm Pope's opinion that Lee had retreated. So Pope ordered a probe of Jackson's position toward Sudley Mill by McDowell, Porter, and Heintzelman. Such a move might build on Kearny's near-success of the previous evening and crack Jackson's line. Ricketts's newly arrived division from Centreville relieved Kearny only to precipitate a nasty firefight with Hill's men that confirmed the Confederates were still in place. Three other reports from different sections of the line did likewise, and Pope's principal staff officer, Colonel Strother, observed cynically that the cigar-smoking army leader seemed content to spend the morning under a tree with McDowell waiting for the enemy to retreat, "evidently solving some problem of contradictory evidence in his mind," his "preconceived opinions and his wishes" having decided him. Pope's command system remained paralyzed by a flood of contradictory reports on the Confederate situation.[53]

Pope's sudden hesitancy also may have resulted from a dispatch from Franklin indicating delay in sending reinforcements and supplies from Alexandria. "It was not until I received this letter that I began to feel discouraged," Pope claimed subsequently. Surprisingly, the dip in Pope's morale was hardly reversed by Porter's personal appearance at Buck Hill at 8:15 a.m., although the V Corps's reappearance itself proved the high point of the Federals' morning activities. Even though some twenty-five hundred men, including Griffin's brigade and two other regiments plus an artillery battery, took the wrong fork at the Gainesville–Sudley–Manassas road intersection and never rejoined the army for the remainder of the battle (spending time resupplying themselves rather than reinforcing their embattled comrades), Porter's eight thousand fresh troops should have been a useful addition. A distrustful and impatient Pope dismissed Porter's repeated suggestion "that there was a very large force on his left, south of the Warrenton Turnpike." Porter contended later, "[Pope] put no confidence in what I said." Reports from Kearny and Ricketts soon underscored Porter's claims. When Reynolds intervened on Porter's behalf, expressing his own fears and observations about a weakened left flank of the army, Pope muttered that he would send cavalry to find out. Porter and Reynolds both left the meeting "bewildered and bereft of good faith in Pope."[54]

Eventually Pope's unswerving commitment to crushing Jackson simply meant that the slaughter would continue for another day. Porter's original instructions to pursue the ostensibly retiring Confederates on the Warrenton turnpike finally changed to a full-scale attack on Jackson in verbal orders Pope sent at 11:30 a.m. Hatch and Reynolds would support Porter. By noon Pope had been persuaded by McDowell and Heintzelman to expand the "pursuit" to include Ricketts and Heintzelman, with McDowell commanding the operation. Pope wanted the army to "press vigorously during the whole day." Perhaps only Reynolds, remaining in position on Lewis lane, sensed that something more stood in front of his units than thin air. In fact, excepting Col. Gouverneur K. Warren's two-regiment Second Brigade of George Sykes's Second Division and corps artillery left behind by Porter on the ridge southeast of Groveton, nothing but Reynolds's Pennsylvanians remained south of the turnpike when Pope's directives shifted everything northward for continued pounding of Jackson. McDowell eventually assessed Reynolds's situation and decided to retire the line at this point back to Chinn Ridge. He did not press Pope on the issue, however, and Warren's tiny command stood unsupported near the Groveton crossroads. Sigel also became apprehensive about an hour later and sent the Fourth New York Cavalry to scout south of the turnpike and eventually persuaded Pope to bolster Reynolds on Chinn Ridge with another brigade. Pope, however, had in mind Henry House Hill and issued orders that misdirected the unit.[55]

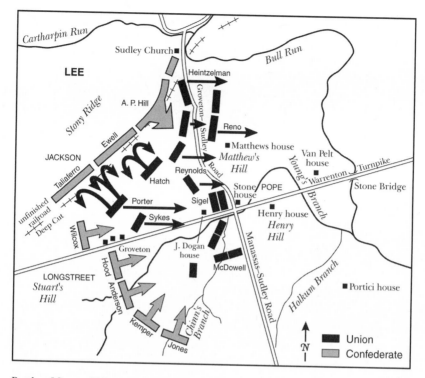

Battle of Second Manassas—Situation 3–5 p.m., August 30, 1862

Porter and Hatch lashed forward at midafternoon with ten thousand fresh Federal troops, angling against Jackson's perceived right flank. The result proved little different from before, no matter how battered the Confederates had been from earlier combat. Stephen Dill Lee's artillery ripped Porter's left flank units, while Jackson's musketry decimated the first waves, pinning them down in a slaughter pen by the rail embankment. When two Rebel brigades ran out of ammunition in the vicinity of a deep cut in that embankment, they resorted to throwing stones at the Yankees in a dramatic, if overrated, incident. True, Jackson's men wavered at one point and their leader sent desperately to Longstreet for support. The latter answered with renewed artillery support. Only the timely arrival of Hill's reinforcement from the other end of Jackson's own line stiffened the butternuts' resolve at the last moment. Porter wisely stopped the carnage before Sykes's regular infantry jumped off in a second-wave assault.

Just then the Army of Virginia's second in command made a critical mistake. Seeing the initial wave's survivors pour back through the rest of Porter's men with Confederates right on their heels, McDowell, from Chinn Ridge a mile or so away, decided that a Rebel counterattack seemed to be threatening the whole army on Dogan Ridge. With Pope at Buck Hill and basically out of touch with Porter's actual combat, McDowell directed Reynolds's whole division to shift to support Porter's embattled units. Only two small and separated commands—Warren in the woods southeast of Groveton and Col. Nathaniel C. McLean's brigade of Schenck's division a half mile behind Warren on Chinn Ridge—protected the Union left flank.[56]

The situation was perfect for Longstreet's counterstroke. Lee directed Longstreet to advance on Chinn Ridge at 5:00 p.m. to relieve pressure on Jackson and allow the "foot cavalry" to disengage and begin the flank march by dark. Porter's 3:00 p.m. assault changed the timing, however, as his "grand display of well organized attack, thoroughly concentrated and operating cleverly," forced Lee and Longstreet to help the beleaguered Jackson earlier than planned. Old Pete wisely chose not to send any infantry but merely to apply concentrated artillery fire, saving his strength for the attack. Forty-five minutes later, Jackson signaled Lee that the Union attack had spent itself. Lee could now send Longstreet forward, directed at Henry House Hill, a half-mile farther east of Chinn Ridge. In fact, Longstreet, anticipating the decisiveness of the moment as he watched Porter's retirement, prepared his twenty-eight-thousand-man wing to crash forward on the axis of the Warrenton turnpike. Pope, watching from Buck Hill, could sense little of the impending blow except that McDowell occasionally apprised him of disintegrating Federal fortunes in the waning afternoon. McDowell, not Pope, orchestrated events on the field. By 4:30 p.m., Longstreet's men advanced across Lewis lane and upper Young's Branch, carrying everything before them en route to Chinn Ridge and beyond.[57]

It was now McDowell's fight, not Pope's battle, as he realized the error of pulling Reynolds off Chinn Ridge to reinforce Porter. McDowell desperately sought reinforcements, but only random brigades and artillery batteries were close at hand. Longstreet, of course, thought only of striking a retiring Yankee flank, not an almost empty void between the attackers and the high ground objectives. What transpired would be nothing short of brutal. Hood's Texans in the van struck the red-legged Fifth New York (Duryee's Zouaves) and the

Tenth New York (National Zouaves) supporting Lt. Charles Hazlett's Battery D, Fifth United States Artillery, on a knoll just south of the turnpike near Groveton. In combined ferocity of close-in musketry and bayonet attack, the Confederates destroyed this body of Federals in about ten minutes. Scarcely 10 percent of Duryee's 560-man contingent rallied two hours later on Henry Hill. It was a scene "which my feeble pen cannot portray," Texan Robert Campbell remembered years later. Another Confederate said it reminded him of a flowered hillside back home in springtime, with all the red and blue uniformed dead and wounded lying in the maize-colored field. One New Yorker declared forty-five years later, when veterans dedicated a monument on the spot, "That day was the very vortex of Hell."[58]

Sacrifice of the New York Zouaves at least allowed Hazlett to withdraw his six guns to Dogan Ridge. That was only the beginning of the final Union ordeal of the afternoon. Pope may have begun to sense impending disaster by this point as he began sliding units piecemeal south of Warrenton turnpike in a futile effort to stem the threat to his left flank. McDowell perhaps best recognized the indispensability of Henry Hill to Union survival. After all, that was the terrain feature where he had met his own defeat the year before. Chinn Ridge, five hundred yards or so east of Henry Hill as well as Bald Hill closer in, offered advanced locations for blunting Longstreet's juggernaut. All the high ground was of roughly the same elevation, although Chinn Branch afforded a seventy-foot gully or ravine to slow the attackers. That feature hardly stopped the determined onslaught by victory-intoxicated Rebels, however. Moreover, only Nathaniel McLean's four Ohio regiments plus Capt. Michael Wiedrich's battery from Sigel's corps stood guard on the ridge itself, and they were not even supposed to have been there, according to Pope's battle plan. McDowell tried desperately to recall Reynolds but could secure only Capt. Mark Kerns's battery and Col. Martin Hardin's Pennsylvania Reserve brigade as a stopgap measure. This scratch force had to buy time at the Benjamin Chinn house and the ridgeline just to the north. As the fighting soon swarmed around the Hooe family's ancestral cemetery nearby, Hood's yelling Texans overwhelmed Kerns before pressing on to dispatch Hardin and Wiedrich. Kerns served his four ten-pounder rifled guns to the last, firing final shots from each before falling wounded and muttering to his captors, "I have promised to drive you back or die under my guns and I have kept my word." Meanwhile other Federal cannon on Dogan Ridge swung around to enfilade Longstreet's attackers. Old Pete lost control of his five division, two-mile front, and the battle devolved upon various subordinates and bands of soldiers, attacking en echelon between Hood's division near the turnpike and D. R. Jones's on the extreme right flank. The "task was desperate," remembered Robert Campbell.[59]

Jackson's help in the struggle became imperative. Despite Lee's two direct orders to him to "look out for and protect" Longstreet's advance and to "advance and drive off the batteries" on Dogan Ridge, Old Blue Light stolidly maintained his position for two hours between 6:00 and 8:00 p.m. In fact, his men were so played out by two continuous days of stopping enemy onslaught that there remained little or no offensive power left in his wing of the army. Longstreet was largely on his own as McDowell began to draw Federal reinforcements from other parts of the battle. The Union general delivered the equivalent of a division to the cauldron that swirled about the northern end of Chinn Ridge and toward Bald Hill. The Confederates prevailed in this area by 6:00 p.m. but could not sustain the momentum. Pope reacted to events by transferring his command post from Buck Hill to Henry Hill and assumed direct responsibility for establishing a defensive position running along the Sudley road from that eminence, across the Warrenton turnpike and onto the high ground of Matthews Hill and Dogan Ridge. Longstreet's drive slowly but steadily pressed the Union lines back from Chinn Ridge and Bald Hill toward the Stone House crossroads of the turnpike and Sudley road. The waning daylight saw the mortal wounding of Second Bull Run's most prominent casualty: Col. Fletcher Webster, son of the noted politician and statesman Daniel Webster. Mounted, with sword in hand before a wavering Twelfth Massachusetts, he only that morning had written his wife, "This may be my last letter, dear love." Captured as his men withdrew, Webster died from chest wounds an hour later. Countless others, like Texan Robert Campbell and Virginian John Wotring with Jackson's Stonewall Brigade, were also wounded during this phase of Second Manassas, Campbell taking shelter below a three-foot pile of fence rails as bullets whistled about his head and hit the ground nearby. The bitter combat of winning and losing flags and cannon in the final ninety-minute struggle of charge and countercharge climaxed the action about a mile from Longstreet's original starting point.[60]

The intensity of the conflict caused brigadier Robert Milroy to theatrically mount a dead horse on Henry Hill while yelling at nearby artillerymen and waving his sword to rally the faint of heart. "The crises [*sic*] of the nation was on hand, and . . . the happiness of unborn millions and the progress of the world depended upon our success," Milroy later wrote his wife. Observers around him at the time thought his conduct "demented." Alas, success did not ride with Milroy or any other Federal that evening, despite hard-fought action and Rebel exhaustion. The picture might have been different had Reynolds's entire veteran division been present on Chinn Ridge at the outset. But war, like all else in history, is the story of might-have-beens. By early evening it was patently clear that Pope and his army were badly beaten. Only a last-ditch stand on Henry Hill stood between the Confederates and repetition of the previous year's rout. Concerned now about a fall-back position at Centreville, Pope sent word to Franklin (who at last had made it forward to that village) to collect his command and all other available troops, "put them in the fortifications and other strong positions" about the place, and "hold those positions to the last extremity." He also tried to ensure that his remaining supplies were out of harm's way by directing Banks at 6:30 p.m. to destroy all public property at Bristoe Station and withdraw to Centreville or through Brentsville.[61]

Pope and his staff formed a final line of defense facing west and almost at a right angle to his earlier actions of August 29 and 30, when he had concentrated on hammering Jackson. From Matthews Hill on the right to the vicinity of the Conrad house near the Sudley road crossing of the old Warrenton–Alexandria–Washington road closer to Manassas Junction, Pope's tattered bluecoats stood fast to ensure the orderly retreat of the army. Ricketts, Stevens, Schenck, Reynolds, Milroy, even Kearny provided the infantry while Bayard's and John Beardsley's cavalry guarded the Stone Bridge crossing of Bull Run and Buford's horsemen protected the ford behind Francis Lewis's Portici farmhouse. Pope turned the battle over to McDowell, issued formal retreat orders at 8:00 p.m., and rode off to rally his army's remnants with Franklin at Centreville. Franklin's tardy arrival would become part of the postbattle analysis and controversy. Had McClellan and his corps commanders Sumner and Franklin done their utmost to help an embattled John Pope and his army?[62]

Lee and Longstreet, not content to rest on a half-victory and unaware of just how costly the Chinn Ridge success had been (both in time and casualties), sent three fresh brigades to the waning combat. D. R. Jones, Cadmus Wilcox, and R. H. Anderson cracked Pope's final defensive position after 7:00 p.m. and gained control of much of Henry Hill. Yet they could not administer a coup de grace, as the Federals stopped Robert Toombs's final assault. Even the arrival of Longstreet and Stuart personally on the front lines could do little to maintain the momentum. McDowell and the last defenders retired with honor and order as a late-day cavalry fight between Buford and Beverly Robertson engulfed the Portici plantation and salvaged some of the Federal cavalrymen's self-respect. Buford probably thwarted Robertson's chance to cut off the remaining Federal line of retreat on the Warrenton turnpike in the gathering darkness. Stuart admitted his inability to coordinate a maneuver that would have made that possible.[63]

Jackson finally advanced north of the turnpike when Longstreet's attack drew off Federal units from that sector. But the move was belated and measured. Stabilization of Pope's final defense as well as the onset of darkness thwarted further success in this area. Moreover, Jackson had those earlier marching orders for further flank movement. They did not preclude destroying Pope, although historian David Martin concludes that the Union troops were demoralized, "their higher command was in shambles," but they nevertheless apparently had sufficient numbers to deny Jackson any final success. In the end, nightfall shut down the battle, with Pope a defeated man and the elated Confederates in possession of the field with war trophies as well as all the attendant debris of dead, wounded, stragglers, broken equipment, and shattered landscape. The Confederates could not prevent the Union Army of Virginia from clearing the venerable Stone Bridge crossing over Bull Run by 11:00 p.m. or reaching Centreville's defenses by early morning. Second Manassas was no Napoleonic Austerlitz victory for Robert E. Lee. Once at Centerville, Pope's dejected Federals endured taunts from Franklin's waiting Potomac army veterans about taking a "new road to Richmond." To Pvt. Charles Walcott of the Twenty-first Massachusetts, these indignities reflected all "the arrogance, jealousy, and hatred" that was the "curse of the Union armies in Virginia." Cavalryman Bayard wrote his father about being badly beaten and enduring heavy losses, adding, "I hope to God this will give us McClellan." One might wonder just who the Federal soldiery thought to be the true enemy: their battered butternut opponents or the rival army in blue? Even Pope seemed unfocused when he sent Halleck a 9:45 p.m. telegram merely recounting "a terrific battle again to-day" in which a reinforced enemy had assaulted and driven his army from its positions.[64]

Pope implied that a two-day lack of food for men and horses as well as enemy numbers had told the tale at Second Bull Run. He said nothing about being out-generaled or his army out-fought at Manassas. The withdrawal had been in good order, "the troops are in good heart" and marched off the field "without the least hurry or confusion," and their conduct had been "very fine." The furious combat had caused both sides' heavy casualties, but "the enemy is badly crippled, and we shall do well enough," he thought. Do not be uneasy, he counseled his superiors, we "will hold our own here" in Centreville. Sounding very tired, Pope wrote that the labors and hardships of his army over the past two or three weeks "have been beyond description," but "we have delayed the enemy as long as possible without losing the army." Lee had been damaged heavily and Pope genuinely felt that his army was "entitled to the gratitude of the country." So "be easy; everything will go well, we have lost nothing; neither guns nor wagons," he concluded disingenuously, although not yet aware of the precise condition through unit recount. Fifteen minutes later and five miles away at Groveton, Pope's opponent sounded a different tone in his telegram to Richmond. Lee spoke of repulsing the enemy, the gallant dead, the "valour of our troops," and gratitude to the Almighty for what he termed "a signal victory over combined forces of Genls McClellan and Pope." To the very last, the two combatants entertained different understandings of virtually everything about the campaign for northern Virginia.[65]

Pope and Jackson had played hide and seek, culminating in a smoldering Manassas Junction supply depot on the night of August 27–28. Jackson eventually collected his forces near the old battlefield of First Manassas and brought on the decisive battle between Lee and Pope. Content that he had found Jackson at last and confident that he could destroy him before reinforcements arrived, Pope then launched two days of bloody but unsuccessful assaults on Jackson's wing until Lee and Longstreet arrived with the rest of the Army of

Northern Virginia and administered a slashing attack on their opponent. Conflicting orders, arrogant confidence, and inadequate reconnaissance coupled with questionable implementation of his plans as key elements in Pope's humiliating defeat. He had not been helped by delays in resupply and reinforcement as well as the Washington merry-go-round of Lincoln, Halleck, and McClellan. In part, Pope and the Union helped their own defeat. On the other hand, Second Manassas may have been Lee's greatest battle. The result was the same: 13,830 Federal casualties and 8,350 fallen Confederates in the two-day affair. Though Second Bull Run (Manassas) failed to replicate the rout of First Bull Run, it once more brought the Union face-to-face with disaster. It certainly impacted Lincoln's plans on emancipation, although that may have been the furthest thing from his mind in the crisis of the moment. The battle certainly uncovered Washington to potential Confederate assault and capture.

Could Lee seize that opportunity? Victory spawned a sense of invincibility among the Confederates, especially Stonewall Jackson's men. "We whipped the Yankees worse this time than they ever was whipped before," noted one Mississippian. What would prevent them from taking Washington and now invading the North, young Col. Harry Burgwyn wrote his father. The northern people had to see that today they were further from subjugating the South than they had ever been before, he decided. Three hundred thousand slain "must be a strong peace argument," he reckoned. Lucy Buck, living at Belle Air in Front Royal, Warren County, Virginia, was even more contemplative. The battle was a glorious victory, and "we felt very hopeful and cheerful for our cause," she wrote in her diary. To think how much circumstances had changed over the previous six months.[66]

There had been nothing but disaster and destruction in the winter and spring, Buck wrote. We had lost our stronghold and permitted the enemy to reach the vitals of the country, with his "desolating armies, laying waste the land with fire and sword." Enemy ironclads swarmed the coasts, and port after port, city after city had been occupied by the ruffian vandals while they drained the whole South of substance. Nothing but starvation and ruin beckoned, and Richmond had been menaced by "a vast army of exultant and victory flushed foes." Confederate arms had melted away or were within the coils of a mighty serpent about to crush them, Buck waxed eloquent. "Oh, it was all disheartening enough," and she wondered how they had struggled through it all. But true to the times, Buck saw the silver lining in God's will, for he "arrested the tide of Union successes and nerved and inspired our men to such deeds of daring heroism." Events like Second Manassas reflected the Almighty's work to Southerners like Lucy Buck. May they never forget to whom they owed such salvation, she hoped. Many in Lee's ranks would have echoed a loud "Amen."

⇥ 5 ⇤

In the Rain at Chantilly

AUGUST 30, 1862, was not a good day for Federal arms. Telegraph wires to Washington hummed with bad news from Bull Run as well as distant Kentucky. Out in the Bluegrass, a scratch force had been pulled together by Maj. Gen. William "Bull" Nelson to contest Confederate Gen. Edward Kirby Smith's northward movement from Knoxville, Tennessee. It was destroyed by the advancing Rebels that day near Richmond, Kentucky. Some 5,263 Federals were lost to only six hundred Confederates. Maj. Gen. Don Carlos Buell's Army of the Ohio was too far south to block an even more robust Confederate column moving into Kentucky under Lt. Gen. Braxton Bragg. Therefore, Union General in Chief Henry Halleck, already suffering greatly from hemorrhoids, had to contend not only with John Pope's fiasco at Manassas but also disintegrating conditions beyond the Appalachians. Little wonder that he told George B. McClellan that he was worn out and needed help. Count Adam Gurowski, an irascible Polish exile who occasionally advised Secretary of War William Seward (but who mostly kept a vitriolic personal diary registering irritation with nearly everything he witnessed in the capital), noted that the intrigues and insubordination of McClellan's subordinates "have almost exclusively brought about the disasters at Manassas and at Bull Run, and brought the country to the verge of the grave."[1]

Such pessimism obviously did not attend the Richmond scene. War clerk diarist John B. Jones captured the exhilaration at such success. Gen. Robert E. Lee's official dispatch announcing a "signal victory" by God's blessing "is glory enough for a week," he piped. Where was that braggart Pope now, he asked rhetorically. Few newsmen had been with the Army of Northern Virginia, and their communiqués would take weeks to get into print. But the informal news grapevine spread the word so that South Carolina gentlewoman and nurse Ada W. Bacot might note how her Charlottesville, Virginia, hospital sewing circle fairly buzzed with intelligence "that our army was within ten miles of Alexandria, and would be in today." God grant it might be so, she jotted in her diary. Soon Pope's famous saddle and dress uniform as well as captured Yankee battle flags went on display as trophies in downtown Richmond. Casualty lists might drop spirits as usual, but such rapid change in Confederate fortunes "dispelled the gloom" that had previously hidden brilliant prospects of future success, recalled Sally Putnam.[2]

At this time, Lee's men retained possession of the ground where "engagements on the plains of Manassas" had taken place. As after Seven Days and Cedar Mountain, the men in gray had the same unenviable task of cleaning up the charnel house. Between 15 and 17 percent of the Army of Northern Virginia and over 20 percent of their opponents littered the landscape to the west of Bull Run. It had been the bloodiest single contest in the eastern theater thus far and second only to Shiloh in the war overall. Lee estimated that some seven thousand prisoners and two thousand wounded were taken from the shattered Federals as well as thirty pieces of artillery and upwards of twenty thousand stand of small arms, not to mention quantities of stores even beyond those seized by Jackson at Manassas Junction. Little could be done about the battered landscape, war correspondent Peter W. Alexander lamented; military operations left a veritable desert of much of central and northern Virginia. This barely concerned exhausted and hungry Rebel soldiers, who simply sank to the ground on the night of August 30, snatching sleep among the dead and moaning injured. Could their resilience carry them forward to finally destroy Pope on the morrow and then capture Washington? Their commanders pondered the question.[3]

The worn, thinned ranks certainly offset the elixir of Lee's success. Direct assault of Pope's decimated legions regrouping at Centreville seemed out of the question. A determined push eastward on the

Warrenton turnpike that evening, followed by an immediate night assault, could have worked against the beaten and disorganized Federals. By morning it was too late. Rain-swollen Bull Run and its tributaries as well as muddy roads made forward movement difficult. Then too Col. Asbury Coward of the Fifth South Carolina wrote, "[In the] grayish light we got a view of Centreville Heights, bristling with cannon of the heaviest caliber." The Federals had massed batteries outside the works so that they could sweep three points of a compass. The battered bluecoats had taken refuge in the old Confederate works and cabins left at the village from the previous winter. Maj. Gen. Fitz John Porter wrote to his friend and patron McClellan that the men were "without heart, but will fight when cornered." He doubted that Lee would attack but rather "get in our rear, and compel us to attack him in a well-selected place." Sharp skirmishing soon proved the defeated Federals were not sapped of fight.[4]

Lee was personally not at his peak despite the victory. He suffered from badly sprained wrists and small broken bones in his hands, incurred when his horse Traveller had bolted at the sudden sight of Yankee prisoners. Elusive destruction of the despised foe might still take place, he thought. Pope might be rooted out of Centreville and forced into the open once more, where he could still be destroyed and Washington besieged. Lee knew his army needed rest and resupply; Loudon County to the west offered that haven. First, everything depended on Jackson's foot cavalry swinging past Sudley, gaining the Little River turnpike at Pleasant Valley and then marching rapidly eastward to the intersection of Little River and Warrenton turnpikes at a place called Germantown between Centreville and Fairfax Court House. J. E. B. Stuart's horsemen would screen the march, and Longstreet's wing would be only a half-day's march behind Jackson. It would be the previous two weeks all over again. Lee ordered the move on the morning of August 31. This time, however, Jackson and his men could not replicate their earlier feat. They were too worn down by that march, the sacking of Manassas Junction, and mostly the battle, first at Brawner's farm and then for two days between Groveton and Sudley Church. Hunger and fatigue reduced their vaunted "fifty-four miles in thirty-six hours five days before" to a pace that scarcely covered ten miles in eight hours. Jackson recognized the problem, at one point ordering A. P. Hill to reduce his division's pace—a most uncharacteristic gesture on Jackson's part. So a slow, silent march all day August 31 continued well after dark, when the wing commander allowed his troops to slump into makeshift bivouacs at the Pleasant Valley church. Pope might mount some counterstroke, but the men needed more rest. Jackson's map maker, Jedediah Hotchkiss, noted that some of them broke off and went "stealing everything they could lay their hands on" after trying to purchase it. Most of the men merely dropped into slumber, unbothered by lack of food, water, shelter, their whereabouts, or even intermittent rain.[5]

Longstreet's command remained behind to police the battlefield. It was not a pretty task, although dead Federals' haversacks and pockets yielded their bounty of food, uniforms could be stripped from lifeless bodies, and resupply of first-rate firearms such as the occasional British Enfield musket made the task less onerous. Still, the stench of dead men and animals was overpowering. Meanwhile Stuart's cavalry discovered Germantown only lightly defended by a security force from Maj. Gen. William B. Franklin's VI Corps. They quickly captured a screening squadron of the Second U.S. Cavalry between Pleasant Valley and Chantilly before moving farther east beyond Ox Hill to a ridge overlooking Difficult Run, where they ill-advisedly shelled a Union wagon train on the distant Warrenton turnpike. Subsequently, encamping back at Ox Hill for the night, Stuart hardly realized that his actions had not only stirred consternation among the teamsters and the wagons but also alerted the Federals to Confederate presence in their rear. The bold cavalier rode off with his staff for an evening of music and cheer with old friends about six miles from Chantilly. He failed to report his activities to Jackson. Still, Pope (who had exhausted his own mounted arm in the campaign) had little awareness of any impending danger. His after-battle despondency of the morning resulting from fatigue and depression found relief in a 10:45 a.m. dispatch to Halleck that a "much used-up and worn-out" army could still give an enemy "as desperate a fight as I can force our men to stand up to." "Should this army be destroyed," Pope added, Halleck "must judge what is to be done, having in view the safety of the capital." He said nothing about any Confederate flank threat.[6]

The disarray left in the wake of the shattered campaign extended to the nation's capital. Before noon that Sunday, General in Chief Henry Halleck responded to Pope's defeat with the enjoinder, "You have done nobly, don't yield another inch if you can avoid it." He promised help as he asked, "With Franklin and Sumner, who must now be with you, can't you renew the attack?" By this point Halleck surely had McClellan's 3:30 a.m. dispatch announcing that that general's aide, Maj. Herbert Hammerstein, had returned from the front with news of a "badly beaten" army, very heavy losses, and some of the individual corps "entirely broken up into stragglers," to which McClellan had added the dire fact that lack of reserves in Washington precluded reinforcing Pope. Privately the general wrote wife Mary Ellen that Hammerstein had claimed, "We were badly whipped." Yet, he added, it was also probable that the enemy was too much fatigued to renew the attack, so that time might permit "our people" to make such arrangements as would enable them to hold their own. He passed none of those thoughts to his superiors, rather spending time in self-pity that he could not go in person to lead his own men without presidential permission. "I feel like a fool here," he told his wife, "sucking my thumbs and doing nothing but what ought to be done by junior officers." He had been brought to earth by an order "defining commands," leaving him only "that part of the Army of the Potomac *not* sent to Pope"—in effect "left in command of *nothing*," a command "[I am] fully competent to exercise, and which I can do full justice." Then Halleck telegraphed at 10:07 p.m.: McClellan would retain the command of "everything in this vicinity not temporarily belonging to Pope's army in the field." He added revealingly, "I beg of you to assist me in this crisis with your ability and experience," as "I am utterly tired out."[7]

McClellan replied within minutes: "[I wish] to afford you every assistance in my power, but you will readily perceive how difficult an undefined position such as I now hold must be." An hour later, he sent field intelligence to Halleck that underscored Pope's exposed flank at Centreville, how the Confederates had undoubtedly taken Fairfax Court House and cut Pope off entirely, and how all possible reserves should be concentrated for the close-in defense of the Virginia approaches to the capital. "There appears to be a total absence of brains," he added, fearing total destruction of the army. "The occasion is grave and demands grave measures," McClellan informed Halleck, the question being "the salvation of the country." Nonetheless the general in chief would not be stampeded. At 1:30 a.m. he replied that he wanted more definitive information before he could order a retreat, "as the falling back on the line of works must necessarily be directed in case of a serious disaster." As for the overall situation, he added irritably, "I am fully aware of the gravity of the crisis and have been for weeks." The pair would remain in communication overnight, trying to get a grip on reality. McClellan and Halleck both anticipated that "the decisive battle will be fought today near Fairfax C.H."[8]

While Halleck and McClellan passed communiqués, Pope tried to clear the fog of war. Coupling what intelligence he had with the counsel of senior commanders, mostly from the Army of the Potomac, not his old Army of Virginia, Pope concluded that the strength of the Centreville position shielded the army from direct attack. Arrayed from south to north around the hamlet were Banks, Sigel, Franklin, and Porter, with Heintzelman and Reno supporting from the rear. Sumner would extend the perimeter from Centreville to Chantilly when he arrived from Alexandria. Pope's counselors—John Reynolds, Samuel Heintzelman, William Franklin, Edwin Sumner, even Fitz John Porter—however, concluded that the Confederates would most likely move north and east either into Maryland or against the army's line of communications with Washington. This suggested immediate withdrawal to the city, possibly presaging McClellan's return to overall command.

Porter particularly deplored Pope's decision to stand and fight, "as I expect to hear hourly of our rear being cut and our supplies and trains at Fairfax Station (scarcely guarded) being destroyed," he hinted to his friend McClellan. Sudden arrival of Halleck's 11:00 a.m. telegram emboldened Pope; he informed subordinates that the army would prepare for a renewed offensive. Porter described the decision as "foolish if not criminal." Some contemporaries as well as subsequent commentators thought that Pope feared dismissal if he retreated to the capital without further combat and even spun "a carefully woven tale of shaded truth" to cover his intended actions. In any case, Pope replied to Halleck that he appreciated his superior's "considerate commendation" and would use it to whip the army back into fighting condition. While "the plan of the enemy will undoubtedly be to turn my flank," said enemy would have his hands full, for "my troops are in good heart."[9]

Pope issued orders to bring up food and ammunition and retire the excess wagons with the remaining wounded. Rejuvenated, he toured troop positions and finally relocated headquarters several miles to the east of Centreville, indicating some equivocation about his next

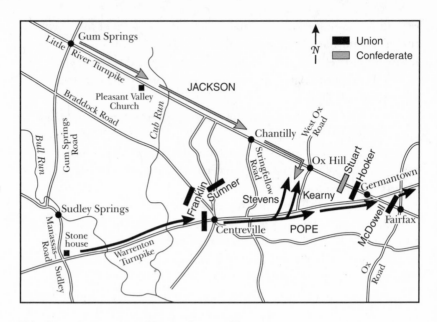

Situation—August 31 and September 1, 1862

move. He anticipated either being closer to the maximum point of danger from a rebel flank move or further retreat of a dispirited and battered army. The general's mood swings sent mixed signals all day. He could not have been heartened by his firsthand view of makeshift field hospitals or waterlogged bivouacs. Maj. Gen. Joseph Hooker spoke for virtually all the army's senior leaders when he told Pope that his division was in no condition to meet the enemy; one staff officer despaired of ever reaching Washington in safety. Before noon several cavalrymen reported seeing a large body of Confederate infantry, cavalry, and artillery moving east on the Little River turnpike. Yet Pope responded only tentatively to such outflanking indicators. He ordered Sumner to scout the Little River turnpike at daybreak with one or two brigades to be "pushed not less than 5 miles" on a reconnaissance designed only to determine whether "there is any considerable movement of the enemy's infantry toward our right and rear." Lee might make a move toward Germantown and Fairfax Court House. If he did so, Pope wished to avoid any engagement in that direction. The situation remained fluid when the first day of September dawned bright and warm.[10]

Pope sought more guidance from Washington. He again wired

Halleck that the army was recuperating but that lack of forage and broken-down cavalry dictated that infantry conduct reconnaissance and rear-echelon security, although "even then it is difficult to keep the enemy's cavalry off the roads." "I shall attack again tomorrow if I can't the next day certainly," he rhapsodized. John Pope seemed mostly concerned about bad relations among his subordinates. "The unsoldierly and dangerous conduct of many brigade and some division commanders of the forces sent here from the Peninsula" rubbed raw. Their every word and act and intention was "calculated to break down the spirits of the men and produce disaster." Their constant talk, "indulged in publicly and in promiscuous company," held that the Army of the Potomac had been demoralized by the administration's order to withdraw from the Peninsula, then its subordination to an inferior Army of Virginia and its incompetent leadership, and accordingly simply would not fight. The influence of such malcontents "was pernicious" as "these men are mere tools or parasites" whose example "is producing and must necessarily produce, very disastrous results." Only Halleck could stop the cancer, said Pope, for "when there is no heart in their leaders, and every disposition to hang back, much cannot be expected from the men." The War Department had best "draw back this army to the entrenchments in front of Washington and set to work in that secure place to reorganize and rearrange it," concluded the beaten general. "You may avoid great disaster by doing so."[11]

Pope's concern formed the basis for a morning meeting where Halleck, Lincoln, and Stanton confronted McClellan on the accusations. In fact the meeting undoubtedly caused McClellan to send a 5:30 p.m. dispatch directly to Porter, asking "of you for my sake, that of the country, and of the old Army of the Potomac, that you and all my friends will lend the fullest and most cordial co-operation to General Pope in all the operations now going on." The destinies of the country and honor of our arms are at stake, waxed Little Mac dramatically, "and all depends now upon the cheerful co-operation of all in the field" since "this week is the crisis of our fate." Meanwhile Pope again promised Washington on September 1 that he would attack Lee "as soon as his movement is sufficiently developed." Then he injected a new note: "I have nothing like the force you undoubtedly suppose, so the fight will be necessarily desperate." Apparently sixty-two thousand men was not enough and he hoped that authorities "will make all preparations to make a vigorous defense of the entrenchments around Washington." Finally Pope received what he may have wanted all along: the withdrawal authorization from Halleck. Apprised that the Confederates were working their way to Pope's rear, the general in chief suggested that should any such new threat produce battle "without a decisive victory," Pope should begin "a gradual drawing in of your army to Fairfax Court-House, Annandale, or, if necessary farther south, toward Alexandria."[12]

In the meantime, Pope responded to continuing reports of escalating Confederate activity in his rear by trying to reinforce Col. Alfred T. Torbert's cavalry brigades at Germantown. "Send back word immediately to Alexandria to hurry up Couch's division and all other troops coming from Washington," he instructed the cavalryman. They were needed by early afternoon, certainly by that night. If the enemy advanced, then Torbert should hold on to that road junction to the last, for the whole army would move to join him. Pope also sent Irvin McDowell's III Corps of the Army of Virginia and subsequently gave Hooker responsibility for what appeared to be a developing situation at the junction of Little River and Warrenton turnpikes. He sent additional orders to Heintzelman, Franz Sigel, Jesse Reno, Porter, and Sumner by early afternoon to "begin to draw slowly to their right in the direction of Fairfax Court-House until they come closely in contact with each other." Heintzelman recalled that the inclusive phrase "as soon after daylight as possible" implied the next day or September 2. Pope still straddled the question of retreat or advance, although a telltale phrase ended his general order: "For the present the general headquarters will be established at Fairfax Court-House." Perhaps Halleck's enjoinder to "look out well for your right, and don't let the enemy turn it and get between you and [Washington's] forts" had had a salutary effect after all.[13]

Pope's canvass of subordinates away from his original Centreville headquarters at Grigsby's house produced differing advice. Sumner and Heintzelman remained adamant about immediate withdrawal; Banks, on the other hand, said nothing. Displeased with a week of exile from the Army of Virginia and missing the main battle, the Massachusetts political general now had the task of merely guiding army trains back to Fairfax Station on the still operational portion of the Orange and Alexandria Railroad. Remarkably Pope suddenly found common cause with Porter. Both men identified Washington and Halleck as the true villains in the piece. The wily Porter urged Pope not to permit the government to control army movements. Best to leave Centreville, Porter suggested, as they had waited too long anyway. By afternoon it was enemy action that forced Pope's hand. Not that Lee, moving with Longstreet's column two hours behind Jackson on the circuitous Gum Springs–Chantilly route, was in any better touch with the situation. Lee had instructed Jackson not to attack the Federals unless he was certain of victory. Yet Lee could not guarantee compliance. Subordinates would dictate events in the direction of Germantown that afternoon.[14]

Pope seemed to tarry at Centreville. Possibly he still sought an opportunity to strike the flank of an evolving new Confederate movement. Heintzelman recalled in his official report, having hardly begun preparations for the next morning's evacuation, that another order came to immediately "get my corps under arms." At 3:30 p.m., Pope further directed that he fall back two and a half miles on the Fairfax road and face to the left in order to aid Reno's IX Corps in driving back enemy forces between the Little River and Warrenton turnpikes. Brig. Gen. Philip Kearny's division moved out a half-hour later. By this point, IX Corps units, led by Brig. Gen. Isaac Ingalls Stevens, already had begun to move on intersecting paths with Jackson's advance. This virtually dictated some pivotal engagement in the vicinity of Chantilly or Ox Hill west of Germantown. Moreover Hooker's supervision of the blocking force comprising the infantry divisions of James Ricketts and Marsena Patrick, supported by Torbert's horsemen, had effectively stymied lead elements of Jackson's advance at Difficult Run. Pope's shift strengthened his Germantown position in advance of Jackson's arrival.[15]

Sumner's reconnaissance finally uncovered Jackson's movement in the rolling countryside of woodland and farms. Col. Oliver Otis Howard's brigade provoked a sharp little skirmish with Confederate brigadier Beverly Robertson's cavalry on the Centreville–Chantilly (Stringfellow) road at about 11:00 a.m., although Pope could only guess at its meaning. Jackson, who lingered at Chantilly crossroads awaiting Longstreet to close up, found himself unable to energize his marchers. He accordingly lost the element of surprise. He struck out for Germantown after the noon hour as Robertson remained engaged with the enemy and Jackson's own infantrymen quickly slowed their pace and sent out skirmishers to guard their right flank against

Federal intrusion. The Ox road indeed provided a perfect avenue for such surprise, and Stevens's men groped for that passage under glowering storm clouds by late afternoon. The weather soon turned quite nasty with heavy thunderstorms. Chilly winds whipped Stevens's column as guides led the men in blue through dense woods on a little-used woodland path in search of the Ox road. They crossed the same unfinished railroad bed that had caused so much carnage miles to the west behind Groveton, marched past the well-tended Millan farm, and then discovered a farm lane leading to a large clearing of prime cropland: the Reid farm, or Fruitwood as it was known locally because of a lush orchard near the main house. John Ballard owned the farm but an aged couple named Heath tenanted the place. The Federals could see shadowy forms of the enemy along a wood line in the distance beyond the farmhouse.[16]

Jackson's men were just as surprised by the sudden appearance of their foe. Altogether they were only about a quarter mile south of the Little River turnpike, where the rattle of musketry suggested that Hooker effectively disputed the Difficult Run passage. By 5:30 p.m., Stevens had deployed for attack and Reno had arrived in person with his third brigade. In poor health, Reno deferred to his subordinate's battle plan, while expressing skepticism as to result. Jackson meanwhile moved all of his command into a curving battle line shielding the turnpike. Just then thunder, rain, and lightning broke over the embattled soldiery. Powder smoke and the storm engulfed the cornfield, meadow, orchard, and farm buildings where, but moments before, two companies of hungry "Highlanders" of Stevens's own Seventy-ninth New York had been more intent on shaking loose apples from the trees than killing Rebels. Pelting rain and Confederate fire brought down the fruit on the hapless bluecoats. Porter had communicated to McClellan earlier, "I think we shall have a fight before night." He was proven right.[17]

The battle of Ox Hill (Chantilly) took place in the wildest weather, according to participants. It prevented both sides from knowing just what opposed them. Jackson brought to bear approximately fifteen thousand troops; the Federals numbered possibly only six thousand. Stevens's brigades lost their way and, becoming entangled with one another, slogged through an attack. In a fit of ill-advised audacity, Stevens personally seized the regimental colors of his old regiment and led the men forward, only to go down with a bullet in the brain.

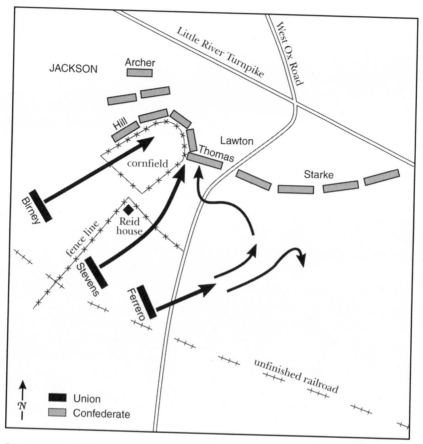

Battle of Chantilly (Ox Hill)—September 1, 1862

Twenty-yard visibility, sheets of rain, and forward momentum propelled the Federals momentarily through Jackson's line. But, as at Second Manassas, success proved temporary. Within minutes, the rain-soaked attackers receded from the Reid cornfield, while east of the Ox road volleys from Isaac Trimble's Rebels ground down Col. Edward Ferraro's three-regiment brigade of Federals. Arrival of Kearny's division began a new phase of the action after 5:30 p.m., with no gain to the Federals.[18]

Stevens had sent a staff officer back to the Warrenton turnpike seeking reinforcements from Heintzelman's passing column. Only the ardent, one-armed Kearny responded, and his action would cost him his life, just like Stevens. Seeking to lead both Stevens's battered line of battle and his own men, Kearny rode out boldly to scout the

Confederate position. He ventured too far and received a challenge from the Forty-ninth Georgia. Hoping to escape, Kearny slipped away quietly, leaning low over his horse, but the suspicious Georgians sent a volley after him, mortally wounding this valiant fighter. Nobody quite realized just who he was in the gloom. The climax of the fighting came in the Reid cornfield by 6:15 p.m., when a Confederate counterattack pushed back the Federals. The two sides then disengaged, with the chastened Rebels holding on to the battlefield. Longstreet, riding through a host of stragglers behind Jackson, quipped to his fellow corps commander, "General, your men don't appear to work well today." A dour Jackson rejoined, "No, but I hope it will prove a victory in the morning." Dorsey Pender, one of Hill's brigade commanders, wrote his wife that nobody "seemed anxious for the fight" or did any credit to themselves.[19]

Heavy cloud cover and a pall of powder smoke hung over the battlefield at nightfall. The ceaseless moans of the wounded, random flashes of late musketry, and the shadowy figures of ever-present scavengers and men seeking comrades identified the Reid farm. Aid stations and a hastily established field hospital at the Millan house treated Federal casualties. The Confederate wounded fared less well, as their medical personnel and supplies lay far to the rear. Just about everybody was hungry. The bodies of Stevens and Kearny were identified, leading Jackson to exclaim in anguish when seeing the latter's body, "My God, boys, you know who you have killed? You have shot the most gallant officer in the United States Army." Hill soon added sadly, "Poor Kearny, he deserved a better death than that!" The next day, Lee, headquartered in a stone farmhouse a mile or so west of Ox Hill on the Little River turnpike, ensured that Kearny's body (and later his possessions, stripped by Rebel robbers) would be sent through the lines. Lee added his condolences to the general's widow. In addition to the two Yankee generals, the sharp little contest claimed five hundred to thirteen hundred Federal casualties, the Confederates five hundred to eight hundred. Battle chronicler David Welker calculates a Federal loss rate of 11.3 percent for numbers engaged to only 3.4 percent for Jackson's command. Chantilly battle historian Paul Taylor notes that some regiments "suffered higher losses than in the entire three days at Second Manassas." Jackson's corps of fourteen brigades clearly had outnumbered their opponent by better than two to one. So while Lee, Jackson, and Longstreet prepared to renew the conflict the next day, the Federals departed after midnight. None of the Confederate generals had calculated on such rapid recovery of Pope's army for a standup fight as just concluded.[20]

The battle of Chantilly (Ox Hill) proved most significant. What Lee later reported as an "obstinately maintained" engagement confirmed that Pope's army could not be destroyed despite its defeat two days before. Military historian Edward J. Stackpole decided nearly a century later that Stevens and Kearny had stopped Jackson "in his tracks," thereby preventing Lee from "achieving the crowning success" to Second Manassas as "a final humiliation" for the despised Pope. More recently Professor Joseph Harsh termed it "the Chantilly Fumble," a phrase applicable to both sides in the rainy combat. No doubt the battle cost the Union two of its best fighting generals. Still, Pope used the time gained by the fighting to strengthen a defensive position near Germantown, thus "relieving the Confederate pressure on Fairfax" (in historian David Martin's view) and turning aside Lee's latest ploy to outflank him. Government historian John Hennessy suggests that Chantilly "amounted to a bloody exclamation point to a campaign substantially completed." In the end, the battle capped Lee's intent to threaten Washington. As participant Lt. Horatio Belcher of the Eighth Michigan saw it, "Had we been defeated again here our army would have been annihilated and Washington taken."[21]

Pope, unaware of specifics of the battle with Jackson, sent word to McDowell at 4:00 p.m. that sounds of combat nearby should cause his advance "to the north, keeping in touch with both Reno and Hooker." Then the heavy rain and evening's events elsewhere led to confusion, further army fragmentation, and, ultimately, retreat. Participants never forgot the cold, wet night march from Centreville to Fairfax Court House. Those shivering Federals left out on the Ox road would be the last to leave, despairing of saving any more of their wounded or recovering the dead. The Fifty-fifth New York's commanding officer recalled how disorder prevailed on the Warrenton turnpike, officers' orders mingling with teamsters' oaths, shouts from the soldiers, and the rumbling thunder overhead. "All of this produced a deafening tumult," he said, and made it difficult to recognize one another so that "we could not free ourselves without leaving behind us a larger number of stragglers." Retirement from Chantilly was hardly the rout of First Bull Run or even the overheated retreat from the second battle. Still, it was yet another disorganized withdrawal. Pope would eventually find makeshift accommodations with a local Fairfax Court House Unionist. His army marched past en route to Alexandria, Washington, or temporary roadside bivouacs, while out on the Little River turnpike Lee suffered too much from his still-throbbing hands and wrists to respond to his enemy's plight. His bedraggled soldiers too huddled in the rain, unable to do more that night.[22]

In Washington Pope's situation continued to be unclear. Initial fragmentary reports from Manassas had sounded like victory, made sweeter since they offset the previous year's disaster at the place. The Treasury Department's public bulletin board showed a dispatch from Pope about not only a "terrific battle" but also casualties far in excess of any suffered during the first three days of the Seven Days' combat. Lincoln's personal secretary, John Hay, jotted in his diary how "well and hilarious" things seemed to go that Saturday, August 30, and how he had gone to bed that night expecting "glad tidings at sunrise." Instead, a dark and rainy Sunday brought with it dire news of Pope's disaster. McClellan chafed at not being able to personally share the fate of his comrades, while Halleck pushed forward reinforcements with the indefatigable railroader Henry Haupt rebuilding bridges and moving supply trains as quickly as possible. One trainload of volunteer male nurses struck out for the battlefront; they never made it past the bottles of liquor medicinally intended for the wounded. Haupt swore never to convey such inebriates again. More successfully, he got a train through with 5,134 boxes of artillery and small arms ammunition.[23]

Evacuation of casualties from Second Bull Run and Chantilly proved embarrassing to the Federal government. Pope had not retained sufficient ambulances for his needs. By dawn on Sunday, September 1, overburdened field hospitals and a drastic shortage of surgeons, provisions, and hospital stores clogged the rear areas behind the army. Refugees and escaped slaves brought back lurid tales of "a surreal landscape of shell fragments, wrecked gun carriages, shattered caissons and wagons, piles of dead horses, and human corpses strewn everywhere, and emitting a putrefying gas." Hundreds still lay on the battlefield unattended; the Centreville facilities were overwhelmed with others. Another humanitarian expedition with carriages, wagons, hacks—virtually any available vehicle in the capital—had departed Saturday night, gotten lost in the rain and dark, and wound

up back at Alexandria, its members also having become too fortified with spirits to make their way on to Fairfax and Centreville. The
War Department then sent medical inspector Richard Coolidge out
to Centreville, and by Sunday he started moving all the wounded
and field hospital teams to Fairfax Station, from which Haupt could
transport the casualties to Washington. More personnel and supplies
were needed, and the indomitable Clara Barton once more arrived
to offer aid.[24]

Barton, with three assistants, had boxes and barrels of supplies in
a freight car headed out to Fairfax by 7:30 a.m. that Sunday. They
alighted from the train to a scene of incredible suffering and ghastly
conditions: a hillside covered with three thousand wounded lying
helpless in a misty drizzle. More wounded kept pouring in as Barton
again moved to assist Dr. James L. Dunn, just as she had done after
Cedar Mountain. This time, however, a sense of urgency pervaded
the scene as the threat of Rebel cavalry and guerrillas lurked on the
fringes. Dunn was overjoyed that she had arrived to "supply us with
bandages, brandy, wine, prepared soup, jellies, meals and every article that could be thought of." They labored all that day and the next
among the wounded and dying, battling time and driving winds and
rain until Haupt could ensure safe evacuation. Despite Secretary of
War Edwin M. Stanton's ban on female nurses, somehow Barton and
her team established their credentials at Fairfax Station. The army's
rear guard passed through the station on Tuesday just as Barton,
Dunn, and the other medics got the last survivors on the train ahead
of Confederate horsemen appearing on the tracks. At 10:00 p.m.,
waiting civilians in Alexandria greeted this last train from Fairfax
Station with food and beverages. Barton returned to her lodgings
in Washington and slept solidly for twenty-four hours, the first rest
she had had in the past forty-eight. The next day she returned to her
hospital duties while Surgeon General William Hammond pleaded
with Halleck for an independent ambulance corps capable of faster
battlefield evacuation. Old Brains demurred; the system run by the
Quartermaster Department seemed sufficient.[25]

The mood in Washington shifted with every dispatch and rumor
from Centreville and Fairfax. A warship stood ready at the navy yard
to evacuate arsenal stores, the president and his cabinet, or both if
necessary. The military governor of the city closed liquor stores in
anticipation of riots. "The military believe a great and decisive battle

is to be fought in front of the city," Secretary of the Navy Gideon Welles penned in his diary, adding, "but I do not anticipate it." As he saw it, "We are prepared and fortified with both army and navy to meet them." Still, Pope was now utterly useless as a commander, convinced that "as soon as the enemy brings up his forces again he will again turn me." "You had best at once decide what is to be done," a whipped Pope told Halleck. Look to the north beyond the Potomac, he warned, "every movement shows that [Lee] means to make trouble in Maryland." He desired Halleck to "come out and see the troops" as "there is an intense idea among them that they must get behind the entrenchments." Pope wanted to attack, but "the troops are absolutely unable" to do so. Indeed, Army of the Potomac veteran Warren Lee Goss recalled after the war that some of the men, for the first time, "began to regard our cause as a losing one" and that "the Confederate armies were more ably commanded than our own." Others in the ranks overwhelmingly supported McClellan's restoration to command them. Corps commander Samuel Heintzelman explained in his journal, "If we are attacked under Pope we fear another defeat," whereas "McClellan would restore confidence to officers and men and he would be received with enthusiasm by the whole Army."[26]

In the end, Lincoln and Halleck made just that move. At first they had confined McClellan's position to merely commanding Washington's defenses: forts, cannon, and perhaps thirty thousand men (on paper—most were untried in battle). Thus he would prepare the refuge for Pope's army. Then, meeting personally with the precocious general and against the advice of cabinet members like Stanton, the president and his principal general admitted that McClellan alone could best overcome "the troubles now impending." With much false modesty, Little Mac told his wife that he thus accepted "the thankless task" fraught with "many difficulties and immense responsibilities" for his country's sake and "with the humble hope that God has called me to it." Vintage McClellan in tone, these words suggest why so many in high office despised the man. But the army believed in him, as did much of the populace, and there was the immediate question of finding a winner. Quite likely McClellan believed sincerely, "My conscience is clear and I trust in God." Decisively and succinctly Halleck then told Pope, "Bring your forces as best you can within or near the line of fortification." McClellan would command all of the defenses, and Pope "will consider any direction, and disposition of the troops as they arrive, given by him as coming from me," directed the general in chief. Pope replied meekly from the Fairfax Court House that he would obey "at once." His future remained unclear.[27]

It might have been a bitter pill for Pope but altogether necessary. In truth the fate of the Union hung in the balance. Lincoln had spent much of the previous week at the War Department telegraph office next to the White House and had become acutely aware that his latest protégé was an abject failure. His army had fallen apart because of battlefield defeat as well as internal schism. Even in retreat Pope and his chief supporter, McDowell, found themselves vilified by the marching soldiery. Only McClellan had the leadership skills to rally the troops and prepare them for the ordeal that many anticipated: a Confederate assault on the capital. Lincoln openly admitted to his cabinet that McClellan was slow and "good for nothing" offensively. But he enjoyed the army's confidence. Stanton tried to counter with a signed petition of the group's majority expressing no confidence in the general. He and Secretary of the Treasury Salmon P. Chase had been collecting cabinet signatures since Friday in order to forestall McClellan's reinstatement. "[Stanton] has long believed and so have I," jotted Chase in his diary, "that Genl. McClellan ought not to be trusted with the command of any army of the Union." In fact, Stanton's longer crusade to sack the general was now largely thwarted by naval secretary Welles. He would not sign any petition, even though agreeing in principle. The president deftly parried Stanton's move, declaring bluntly that reinstatement was his decision alone and that he would stand behind it. Besides, the arrangement applied only for "command of the fortifications of Washington, and of all the troops for the defense of the Capital." He and Halleck viewed it as administrative, not necessarily restoring McClellan to field command. The order went out over Halleck's signature. Lincoln's role remained skillfully muted.[28]

So McClellan, not Halleck, rode out to "pick up the Army of the Potomac," as Little Mac phrased it to his wife. He came across as victor over a competitor when, appearing well-dressed and sporting dress sword with yellow sash, he encountered Pope's campaign-begrimed entourage near Munson's Hill and the outer defense perimeter of the capital at 4:00 p.m. on September 2. Greeting his friend and supporter Brig. Gen. Jacob D. Cox, the reinvigorated McClellan saluted, saying, "Well General, I am in command again." His subsequent exchange with Pope was strained and brief, devoted strictly to matters of troop disposition. Cockiness always accompanied McClellan and it showed with abandon now. Pope-hater John Hatch helped out, beckoning to passing soldiers, "Boys, McClellan is in command of the army again! Three cheers!" Hurrahs and tossing of headgear into the air "moved like a wind along Pope's column" to become part of army lore. Even Cox admitted that it seemed like "an unnecessary affront." Pope merely doffed his hat and passed into history. McClellan wrote in his memoirs twenty years later, "I have never since seen Pope."[29]

Pope informed Halleck by early evening that he had arrived safely at Ball's crossroads and that "within an hour" or by the next morning the various commands would be encamped "within the entrenchments." They were weary but otherwise in fit condition. Passage had been "without molestation," just some artillery firing on the road through Vienna to Chain Bridge—Stuart's activity after the Ox Hill fight. He thought that the enemy "still continue to beat around to the north." "I await your orders," Pope ended expectantly. He, however, was now an afterthought. McClellan had already begun the task of reconstituting the fighting force. The president and his advisers had all seen through the intransigence and disloyalty, and John Hay sensed the president was "in a singularly defiant tone of mind." The general "has acted badly in this matter," the chief executive explained to Hay at the end of the week. No doubt McClellan wanted Pope to fail, "but we must use what tools we have." However unpardonable his recent actions, the American Napoleon was "too useful just now to sacrifice."[30]

Pope and McDowell became supernumeraries; they would be sacrificed to the public demand for scapegoats. Pope, in fact, spent the following week writing an after-action report blasting the McClellan clique in words so singularly ill tempered and vituperative that an embarrassed president quietly set them aside. Looming autumn elections and outcry from Capitol Hill suggested the need to hustle the beaten general out of the way. An Indian uprising in Minnesota provided the pretext and opened a slot for Pope in exile. Even then, Pope complained to Halleck about "the machinations of McClellan and his parasites" and "the praetorian faction in the Army of the Potomac" for "neglect and abandonment of the Army of Virginia." The defeated general even berated Halleck personally for not supporting him as well as allowing public scorn and defamation for his conduct and actions in Virginia. Porter, Franklin, and Charles Griffin would face courts of inquiry as Pope preferred charges against them prior to departure for St. Paul. The immediate limelight after Second Bull Run necessarily focused on McClellan as savior of capital and nation. Critics like the ever-grumbling Adam Gurowski viewed the general as a manipulator of Lincoln par excellence. Even Jacob Cox snarled that "the only one who had fought like a soldier and maneuvered like a general" was dispatched to watch Indian tribes, "carrying the burden of others' sins into the wilderness." He described "Mr. Lincoln's sacrifice of his sense of justice" to expediency in "the terrible crisis" as "sublime." When Halleck eventually acceded to McClellan's request to reinstate Franklin, Sumner, and Griffin, Cox added caustically, "If the country was to be saved, confidence and power could not be bestowed by halves."[31]

No matter the intrigue and duplicity, the contradictions or plain confusion in crisis management, certain themes began to emerge that crucial first week in September. Only Lincoln appeared outwardly calm, although Hay and others reported his extreme anxiety of the previous days. Halleck reflected Lincoln's feelings, writing his wife, "We are doing all in our power to secure Washington." The general in chief confidently rationalized, "Everybody now admits that if I had not brought McClellan's army here when I did, we should have been lost." As Lincoln repeatedly told Hay, there was no one else in the army "who can man these fortifications and lick these troops of ours into shape half as well as [McClellan]." McClellan might not fight well himself, but he "excels in making others ready to fight." As the commander in chief told his naval secretary, "McClellan has the army with him." Apparently that alone was the administration's intent for the reinstated Army of the Potomac leader at the moment. The crisis deflected McClellan's well-known distaste for Pope's turning the army into vandals and thieves against the citizenry and even his thinly disguised desire to see the Westerner fail, possibly helping him do so. McClellan had won back his former control of affairs in the eastern theater by default.[32]

McClellan enthusiastically turned to the task of building a single force from the two defeated armies. First he assessed the state of the capital's defenses. "Rather a volunteer affair—not exactly my business but you know that I have a way of attending to most other things than my own affairs," he admitted to his wife. Accompanied by his former chief engineer, Brig. Gen. John Gross Barnard, McClellan poured over the details of the fort line south of the Potomac (conceivably the most threatened approach). He strengthened cavalry patrols upriver. Newly arriving units like the 117th New York were cut up and thrust into sensitive sectors around the city's perimeter. Most of all, McClellan studied the strength figures, which reflected that nearly thirty thousand men were available strictly for the district and defenses of Washington in August. Barnard claimed a lack of men to sufficiently garrison the southern lines and that most of the 10,026 in this sector were raw regiments newly arrived in the capital. They lacked expertise in handling the heavy fortress artillery, and the forts themselves were isolated works not linked by any continuous line of infantry entrenchments. Barnard had designed them himself the previous year to serve as anchors from which a field army could launch attacks against a besieging enemy. Here alone had been reason to save Pope's force. When Alexandria post commander Brig. Gen. John P. Slough wired Stanton at 3:15 p.m. on September 1 about the "army" of survivors streaming in from Centreville and Fairfax and how they would impact his "new troops, convalescents and stragglers—part fit for the field, part not," he underscored the need for reconstituting a field army to defend Mr. Lincoln's city.[33]

McClellan no longer despaired as he had on August 29, when he suggested to his wife that he had "no means to act with, no authority, yet determined, if possible to save the country and the capital." Heartsick with "the folly and ignorance" around him, he had not known whether he would "be permitted to save the capital or not." Now he knew. He had the authority and the responsibility, although others would also have to help. Welles had earlier tasked the North Atlantic Blockade Squadron commander at Norfolk to dispatch Commodore Charles Wilkes with five warships and six mortar boats to help defend Washington. Six additional mortar craft would go to Baltimore. Maj. Gen. Ambrose Burnside had wanted some of those vessels to protect closure of the Aquia Creek base, but Halleck peremptorily told him to accelerate his transfer of his troops to Alexandria and leave behind a token guard for property protection, or simply burn that property. Even then, Haupt would later complain, destruction of 75,000 dollars' worth of U.S. Military Railroad plus the burning of wharf, buildings, and bridges was "unnecessary and highly censurable." More praiseworthy, railroad superintendent W. W. Wright reported evacuation of Unionist refugees and ten thousand fleeing slaves from the greater Fredericksburg area. In Washington, military governor James Wadsworth organized male public servants into military companies with arms and ammunition. Surgeon General Hammond shifted wounded north, out of the potential fighting zone, while a panicky Stanton ordered the Washington arsenal to ship all ordnance supplies to New York, before Halleck and McClellan interceded to ensure that the rebuilding field army as well as the expanding fort system had sufficient stores to defend the city.[34]

Altogether, the units that fought at Second Bull Run retained most of their integrity, although Slough received permission to use one of the forts as a rendezvous point for reorganizing stragglers into combat teams. Occupants of houses "in front of and near" the fortifications were ordered to clear out; at Robert E. Lee's former dwelling, Arlington House, Brig. Gen. A. W. Whipple prepared to "burn any houses that may afford cover to the enemy or intercept the line of fire from our troops." Meanwhile Pope chirped from the background, "We ought not to lose a moment in pushing forward the fresh troops to confront the enemy." "We must strike again with fresh men while the enemy is weakened and broken down," he believed, and was personally "ready to advance again to the front with the fresh troops now here." Pope angrily lashed out at how his enemies preferred "that the country should be ruined rather than he should triumph." But matters had moved beyond that issue. The administration had to remind Pope of who was now in charge. That person had his hands full, particularly with the numerous new regiments arriving in response to Lincoln's July 2 request for three hundred thousand men from the loyal states. Large in strength, enthusiastic in spirit, they lacked sufficient training and experience for immediate field operations. McClellan had little choice, however; he needed every available man for whatever beckoned.[35]

Washington continued to be "full of exciting, vague and absurd rumors," said Welles. He thought Halleck and Stanton unduly apprehensive about the danger. Always dismissive of such remote possibilities, the naval executive agreed, "There will be serious trouble but not such as to endanger the Capital." Perhaps by retreating inside the fortifications, "our own generals and managers" had inspired the enemy "to be more daring," even venturing across the upper Potomac to strike at Baltimore, "our railroad communications, or both." They would not besiege the capital, he assayed emphatically. In fact, McClellan (to whom Welles imparted no direct credit) recalled that by dawn on September 3 his troops were all in position to repulse an attack. Washington was safe. He positioned his old corps and divisions at strategic locations in connection with the southern line of fortifications. Porter set up well forward at Upton's Hill with McDowell nearby. Franklin's command stood in front of the Alexandria sector with Heintzelman in support. Couch took position around Fort Corcoran, protecting the aqueduct bridge to Georgetown while also screening upriver toward Chain Bridge. Sumner lay in reserve from Fort Albany (commanding Long Bridge approaches) down to Alexandria. Anxiety, even panic waned in the city proper as citizens and the administration reflected Heintzelman's explanation that confidence in McClellan had erased "fear of another defeat." Naturally nobody could be sure of Lee's intentions, and the initiative still lay with the intrepid southern leader and his army. No one in the capital could be sure, as Welles, Pope, Porter, and others contended, that the Confederates would cross upriver. If they did, they might descend upon Washington from the north, via the relatively underprotected back door, as had the British in 1814.[36]

By early September, Lee was able to dictate two dispatches to his own commander in chief in Richmond. The first letter, written at Chantilly on September 2, merely informed President Jefferson Davis about the recent victories, underscoring that "the great advantage of the advance of the army is the withdrawal of the enemy from our territory, and the hurling back upon their capital their two great armies from the banks of the James and Rappahannock Rivers." Liberated Virginia citizenry had welcomed the departure of both armies, what with destruction of crops, land, and other property. Lee had achieved this goal by his late summer counteroffensive. But what should be done next? Over a century of analysis since has led to the speculation that the president and his main battle chieftain had been synchronized for some time on Jackson's long-held belief in opportunities north of the Potomac. Those opportunities had seemed remote until after Second Manassas. So the opening sentence of Lee's second message to Davis, written farther north at Dranesville on September 3, read simply, "The present seems to be the most propitious time since the commencement of the war for the Confederate Army to enter Maryland." The Old Line State, southern by geography and slaveholding by economics, had been held in the Union by Lincoln's coercion, went the reasoning, and "if it is ever desired to give material aid to Maryland and afford her an opportunity of throwing off the oppression to which she is now subject, this would seem the most favorable." In Lee's view it was that simple. Tacitly admitting that he had not been able to annihilate the enemy, who had disappeared from Fairfax Court House and environs, he wrote, "I did not think it would be advantageous to follow him farther," as "I had no intention of attacking him in his fortifications, and am not prepared to invest them."[37]

Perhaps the Confederacy's Great Captain was merely paving the way for Richmond to accept what he had already determined to do and was confident would enjoy his government's approval. Yet Lee hinted that the reason for not deploying in front of Washington was a lack of munitions and provisions. He intended drawing off into crop-rich Loudoun County and threatening Washington from that quarter. His army badly needed forage and provisions, shoes, ammunition, and rest. Capture of Winchester in the valley on September 3 netted another cache of ammunition, firearms, camp equipment, and medical stores. But was it enough? And how soon could such matériel reach Lee's army? Meanwhile, from Loudon they could menace Yankee control of the Shenandoah, "and, if found practicable," cross into Maryland. The "two grand armies" of the United States operating in Virginia were "much weakened and demoralized," and sixty thousand new Union levies for replacements "are not yet organized and will take some time to prepare for the field." So Lee anticipated virtual free rein for a while. What better time for some grand offensive? Such a move, even "if discovered, will have the effect of carrying the enemy north of the Potomac." If prevented, it would not "result in much evil" were Lee's rather humble words. His army, he reiterated, "is not properly equipped for an invasion of an enemy's territory" and "lacks much of the material of war, is feeble in transportation, the animals being much reduced, and the men are poorly provided with clothes, and in thousands of instances are destitute of shoes." Yet "we cannot afford to be idle," he pronounced. Though weaker in men and equipment than the Federals, we "must endeavor to harass, if we cannot destroy them." An offensive would help defend Richmond, and should affairs west of the Appalachians permit, Lee welcomed Bragg's reinforcement from that quarter.[38]

Dispatches from Richmond confirmed the government's elation with Lee's success while promising to spur a diversion in the Kanawha region of western Virginia from which the Army of Northern Virginia might draw reinforcements. Lee continued to brief Davis over the next two days as he slipped off to Leesburg in Loudoun County. "I am more fully persuaded of the benefits that would result from an expedition into Maryland" and would proceed accordingly "unless you should signify your disapprobation," he wrote Davis on September 4, knowing well that he would be across the Potomac before any reply might reach him. Again he underlined that the only two subjects giving him "any uneasiness are my supplies of ammunition and subsistence." The latter could be collected in Maryland, where he sought "the services of some one known to the people and acquainted with the resources of the country" to ease such procurement. Apparently Lee had in mind former Maryland governor Enoch Lowe from Frederick County and had already contacted him in this regard. Newspaper reports from Baltimore and Washington suggested that Pope and McClellan were bottled up in the capital and that Winchester's evacuation left the Shenandoah "entirely free" of the enemy. So a confident Lee told Davis, "Should the results of the expedition justify it, I propose to enter Pennsylvania" unless, once again, "you should deem it unadvisable upon political or other grounds." By September 5 Lee's daily letter to his chief said simply, "As I have already had the honor to inform you, this army is about entering Maryland, with a view of affording the people of that State an opportunity of liberating themselves." Whatever "success may attend that effort," he continued, "I hope at any rate to annoy and harass the enemy." The die was already cast. Portions of Lee's army had begun crossing the Potomac the previous day.[39]

Thus a new direction to the war appeared within the week following Second Bull Run. Pope had regrouped his beaten army behind the protective ramparts of old Confederate fortifications at Centreville. Lee continued his successful stratagem of sending Jackson off on yet another flank movement to gain the Federal rear and force either battle or another enemy retreat. Jackson's men marched badly, showing the effects of hard campaigning despite the recent victories. Pope sensed the danger and, relinquishing all hope of some counterstroke of his own, parried successfully Jackson's moving column. The result was the fiercely contested action at Chantilly (Ox Hill). Two Federal generals were killed and the contest ended in a draw, with Union forces leaving the field. Still, Jackson had been stopped, and the strategically important battle enabled Pope to retire intact through Fairfax Court House to Alexandria and Washington. Lee realized that he could not annihilate Pope short of reunion with McClellan and the sheltering forts of the capital. Not wishing to risk his fragile army any further, Lee drew off to Loudon County to recuperate.

Had Lee known how broken was the Federal retreat, he might well have pressed an assault. But the remains of Pope's Army of Virginia (and attached Potomac army contingents) found sanctuary before Washington. Pope bore responsibility for the defeat and was relieved of command, and McClellan was reinstated by Lincoln and Halleck to defend the city. Lincoln felt he had little choice. McClellan had no peer in reconstituting and administering a fighting army. He enjoyed overwhelming popularity with the ranks. Conveniently and for practical reasons, Lincoln and the high command brushed aside Little Mac's lack of cooperation with Pope during the late campaign in the interest of saving the capital. Deferred once again was Lincoln's cherished desire for a military victory to enable issue of an emancipation proclamation. Moreover Lincoln, the political leader of the nation, needed battlefield victory before the fall midterm elections. Most immediately, however, he had to save Washington.

By contrast, Lee and his army emerged gloriously from the campaign that stretched from his Seven Days' victories to the banks of the Potomac. The contests at Cedar Mountain and Chantilly paled in comparison with what arguably could be styled his greatest victory at Second Manassas. Certainly the Confederacy stood near its peak moment of success by early fall 1862. Although violating his own precept to "avoid a general engagement, being the weaker force," by maneuvering to relieve the portion of the country seriously threatened by Pope's advance, Lee had actually succeeded in moving the war from the outskirts of the Confederate capital to those of his opponent through daring and superior generalship. Above all Lee's success had reversed the tide of the war in the east. It further developed the leadership team of Lee, Jackson, and Longstreet and opened the door for still larger achievements to come—possibly on Yankee territory. Unfortunately for Lee, his army was too weakened by victory to consummate the war by taking the enemy capital. He drew off after Chantilly with no intention of trying for the final prize. He still believed, however, that a continuing string of successes could sap northern will and resolve before superior resources simply over-whelmed the youthful Confederacy.

Pope's ill-fated campaign left behind a legacy of torn landscape and human debris. Central Virginia groaned beneath the weight of wounded and trampled fields and woods. Requisition of homes and structures from Warrenton and Culpeper to Charlottesville and Richmond attested to the impact of ceaseless warfare. Some twenty-two thousand Union casualties clogged fifty churches and public buildings in Washington DC. Exiled Judith McGuire confided in her diary from Lynchburg about the Manassas and Chantilly combat: "In those fights I had eight nephews! Are they all safe? I have heard from two, who fought gallantly, and are unscathed. It is said that our army is to go to Maryland." In upcountry Front Royal, Warren County, Lucy Buck deplored the wasteland of war and blamed Lincoln and Union authorities for seizing property, exclaiming, "Oh, I'm so tired of tyranny." At least her beloved graycoats had reclaimed the neighborhood and now seemed to be moving north to wreak similar havoc on northern soil. That was Lee's intention by early September. He sought to resupply his ranks and reprovision from a landscape untouched by passing armies, possibly induce rebellion in Maryland, and liberate that southern state from Yankee oppression. Above all he hoped to draw the Army of the Potomac into the open field and destroy it.[40]

A resurgent Confederacy was on the march from the Mississippi and Kentucky to the Chesapeake. The battle for border slave states had begun. Cries of northern abolitionists mingled with a swelling anti-war feeling, complicating the fortunes of the Union. Native American unrest in the upper Midwest needed attention, and beyond the broad Atlantic, European nations worried about the carnage in America and sought some sign asking for their intervention to end the struggle. A turning point loomed for the Union and the Confederacy as bedraggled but happy Rebels splashed across sparkling Potomac waters, lustily singing the stirring Rebel anthem, "Maryland, My Maryland."

Robert E. Lee. Prints and Photographs Division, Library of Congress.

Thomas Jonathan Jackson. Prints and Photographs Division, Library of Congress.

Nathaniel Banks. Prints and Photographs Division, Library of Congress.

John Pope. Prints and Photographs Division, Library of Congress.

George and Mary Ellen McClellan. Prints and Photographs Division, Library of Congress.

Cedar Mountain Battlefield. Prints and Photographs Division,
Library of Congress.

Attack by Sykes's division at Railroad Embankment, Second Manassas. From
cyclorama painting by Theophile Poilpot. Prints and Photographs Division,
Library of Congress.

Railroad bridge at Harpers Ferry. Prints and Photographs Division,
Library of Congress.

Lower (Burnside's) Bridge at Antietam. Prints and Photographs Division,
Library of Congress.

⇝6⇜

Maryland, My Maryland

D. H. HILL'S MEN led the vanguard of Robert E. Lee's army across the Potomac River near Leesburg, Virginia, in column of fours, "well closed up, shouting, laughing, singing," with a brass band in front playing "Maryland, My Maryland." The early September move was unopposed; the Union army was still roughly twenty miles distant at Washington. "An inspiriting scene," declared Stonewall Jackson's young aide, Henry Kyd Douglas, himself a native Marylander. Other loyal sons in the ranks were "especially wild with enthusiasm," and Capt. E. V. "Lige" White, who lived near the crossing, embraced a covey of female relatives and friends as he emerged dripping from the stream. One old local watched the troops crossing at White's ford and remarked, "Goodness gracious, look at the Seceshes." Worried for his family, he added, "I've been to shows and circuses and theaters and all them things, but I never seen such a sight'n all my life." Eventually he hosted a meal for some dozen Rebels, reluctantly charging them twenty-five cents apiece in Confederate money. Noted Douglas, there was a "surfeit of enthusiasm all about us, except for enlisting."[1]

Other omens portended ill. When one "patriotic citizen" presented Jackson with a strong sinewy gray mare to replace his temporarily misplaced Little Sorrel, the new steed displayed an innate skepticism about strangers. Old Jack applied spurs to her and she reared "with distended nostrils and flashing eyes," throwing her rider senseless to the ground. Jackson lay there stunned for a full half-hour before he could be moved. He declared himself unwilling to mount the gray horse ever again. As Douglas wrote years later, Lee and Jackson both entered Maryland in ambulances. Other Confederates met similar disappointment. J. B. Polley of Hood's Texas brigade recalled that a colleague exclaimed, "Darned if I don't believe all the ice houses in western Maryland were emptied into this river last night." Polley later added that the water's coldness was more than equaled by the "frigidity of welcome extended" by Marylanders. Not even "the dulcet strains" of the state anthem "aroused the enthusiasm of the people; no arms opened to receive, no fires blazed to warm, and no feast waited to feed us, as wet, shivering and hungry" they set foot on the soil of the Old Line State. In many ways, the first fortnight told the tale.[2]

Yet Capt. Greenlee Davidson of Virginia wrote his father on September 8 from near Frederick, Maryland, "The people seemed rejoiced to see us." Capt. William G. Morris of the Thirty-seventh North Carolina agreed, claiming, "We find More & better friends heare than in Va." Nonetheless, many civilians seemed afraid of Union retaliation since they anticipated only "a raid of Jackson's" and that the Confederates would soon withdraw back to Virginia. Frederick, a small city of seven or eight thousand residents founded by German settlers a century before, provided a hospital center for Federal wounded from Shenandoah Valley operations and now displayed mixed feelings toward the invaders. It had hosted the state legislature the previous spring and summer in spacious Kemp Hall, rented from the Evangelical Reformed Church. Politicians, carefully monitored by Union bayonets, had deliberated secession until the Lincoln government unceremoniously arrested many of them in blatant violation of their civil liberties. The nagging question to local Frederick historians Paul and Rita Gordon remains whether Maryland would have seceded if the legislative session had not been interrupted by force.[3]

In September 1862, a few merchants kept their stores open and received Confederate money without hesitation. Davidson at least was confident that once convinced that "we intend to occupy the state permanently," Marylanders would "come out openly and go heart and hand for the South." Certainly voters among her 687,049 residents in 1860, which also counted 83,942 free and 87,189 enslaved blacks, had roundly thumped Lincoln Republicanism and implied abolitionism in the national election. They had preferred Kentuckian John C. Breckinridge and other Democratic contenders as the former vice president, subsequently a Confederate major general, took a razor-thin 0.6 percent of the popular vote to garner the state's electoral count. In fact, Maryland's subsequent flirtation with secession cockades had been strong in the winter and spring of 1860–61. The feeling had passed by the time Lee responded over a year later.[4]

How to explain Maryland's change of course? One chronicler of the state's history, Robert J. Brugger, has observed that Marylanders generally had wanted "both to uphold Southern rights and to hold the Union together." The oldest border state, a state of "middle temperament," Maryland embraced ironies, contradictions, and compromises. Amid the typical storm of rhetoric and fist waving that secession winter and spring, the Old Line State awaited Virginia's lead out of perceived long-standing filial and economic ties. Tempered too by ill will between state legislature and Governor Thomas Hicks, who seemed as irresolute as the outgoing U.S. president, James Buchanan, Marylanders desired compromise and detachment from the impending fray. When Fort Sumter shattered that illusion, the state's physical location alone proved untenable for Kentucky-like neutrality, much less secession. The *Baltimore Sun* captured the dilemma: "If we look for an instant to our geographical position, we cannot fail to realize how impracticable is a demonstrative policy at our hands adverse to the general government." Like Kentucky, Maryland teetered until other forces plotted her course.[5]

Marylanders ultimately bowed to stern reality: an indefensible northern border and economic ties north and west. Few citizens wanted their soil to be sullied by sectional bloodshed. That surely would have been the case had the state become the Confederacy's eastern frontier with the Union. Just as important, increasing east–west commercial ties could be found in the very name of the state's premier railroad, the Baltimore and Ohio, as well as the older Chesapeake and Ohio Canal. Similar rail links between the state's principal city and the Northeast solidified an economic alliance. Agricultural products and coal for the port of Baltimore honed the focus, while awaiting Virginia's lead simply proved fatal to the hopes of secession advocates. When the Old Dominion herself finally went out on April 17, 1861, she tipped Maryland's fate, but not as Maryland separationists had intended. Lincoln's installation in the White House the previous month hinted that the new national government would never let its capital be separated from its northern political base by hostile territory. Without question, Lincoln would prevent Maryland from leaving the Union. Thus his unprecedented action with regard to the Frederick legislature meeting and subsequent application of power and the trampling of citizens' rights by the federal government.

Maryland secessionists at the time, then Maryland exiles subsequently and neo-Confederate Marylanders since, decried the Lincolnite tactics. But as the president informed three members of the state legislature sent to protest his government's actions, necessity and self-preservation of the Union overrode any state claim to sovereignty. And he enforced that interpretation at the point of the bayonet. The abiding question of what might have happened if Maryland had joined the Confederacy and surrounded Washington with secessionist territory remains moot. Perhaps the state might even have pursued a course like western Virginia, split apart with Frederick, Washington, Allegheny, and Cecil, perhaps even Harford and Carroll counties moving to create two or more new states or affiliate with Delaware and Pennsylvania. In fact, nothing of the kind occurred, and a tepidly Unionist governor and a largely pro-secessionist but irresolute legislature together with a somewhat noncommittal populace found themselves courting an issue that "involved procedure that bogged down revolution." Like Brugger, a student of secessionist movements in the middle states, William C. Wright, has decided that such a move failed in Maryland simply because of a lack of a state convention forum, inadequate secessionist leadership, and a variety of institutional and intellectual reasons. Among the latter were an aversion to becoming a killing ground, the inadequacy of state forces to resist northern invasion, but most of all the redirection of economic fortunes, especially after bloody spring riots in Baltimore caused a commercial shutdown in the city in the spring of 1861.[6]

Perhaps no section of the state lacked some support for secession, but did so hoping for peaceful separation, not war. Civil unrest broke out in April 1861, when northern militia volunteers transited Baltimore, the nation's third largest city and the South's major manufacturing center. Commercial deadlock occurred, and Marylanders realized that the Federal Union through blockade and coercion could always blight the city and state if Maryland joined her southern sisters in the Confederacy. Still, Wright observes that Marylanders' irresolution "created a vacuum in which the Union Army and the authority of the federal government balanced the scales in their favor." The Towsontown *Baltimore County American* trumpeted shrilly on Saturday evening, April 20, "Civil War is in our midst!" The paper decried how unarmed men "have fallen beneath the musket shots of soldiers from another state." A Federal crackdown throughout the Chesapeake region by Benjamin F. Butler, Nathaniel Banks, and John A. Dix, themselves all citizen-soldiers not given to waltzing with rebellious Southerners, helped with the further rush to save Washington by soldiery from other northern states. Military force and raw assertion of national governmental power solved the Maryland issue by midsummer and fall 1861.[7]

National authorities firmly controlled the state, slapping a lid on virulent Baltimore secessionism and ethnic unrest so as to guard transit and logistical lifelines, suppress civil dissidence, and incarcerate the treasonous along with innocent native sons sans habeas corpus. Mayor George Brown of Baltimore, for example, had been one of those jailed despite his professed Unionism and attempt to quell violence in his city. Something of a diaspora of secessionist Marylanders then headed south, where they became an exile community among distant relatives or friends while pilloried by Virginians for spineless ineptitude at conveying their state over to the Confederacy. One contemporary ditty told the story:

> We've left our homes in Maryland
> our Friends in Baltimore
> To take up arms for the gallant South
> on Old Virginia's shore.

Such exiles, however, dreamed of returning under liberating Confederate colors. They created a false hope among their new comrades, including leaders like President Jefferson Davis and Generals Lee and Jackson, that Marylanders back home awaited deliverance.[8]

The plight of exiled Maryland Confederates spawned the most incendiary poem of the time when James Ryder Randall penned his manifesto of liberty, "Maryland, My Maryland" (almost a century and a half later still a controversial state song). In between stanzas repeating the poem's storied line, Randall ranted against a despot's heel, burning torches threatening sacred shrines, and the gory Baltimore riots. Indeed, eight additional verses spoke to a distant son's appeal for life or death, for Randall actually wrote the piece from New Orleans. The poet alluded to the state's peerless chivalry, evoked heightened emotions, and appealed to citizens' memories of fighting in the Mexican War. The lyrics fairly rang with protecting Maryland's creeks and countryside against the "vandal toll" and "not to crook to his control."

> I hear the distant thunder-hum,
> Maryland, My Maryland!
> The Old Line's bugle, fife, and drum,
> Maryland, My Maryland!
> She is not dead, nor deaf, nor dumb—
> Huzza! she spurns the Northern scum!
> She breathes! She burns! she'll come! she'll come!
> Maryland! my Maryland!

When set to the music of the ancient German Christmas air "O Tannenbaum"—something of an irony since Maryland Germans were uniformly pro-Union—the work became a stirring Rebel marching song. One Kentuckian tried to appropriate the ode for his version of "Kentucky! O Kentucky!," yet identification remained clearly with Randall's original Maryland version.[9]

Many young Maryland swains hastened to join Virginia units and then found themselves denied transfer to what they wanted to style their own "Maryland Line" in the tradition of Continental Army units of their Revolutionary War forefathers. George Washington himself had bestowed the nickname Old Line State after Maryland's sons had held off the British at the battle of Long Island in August 1776, allowing his fleeing army to escape destruction. The phrase implied reliability, and Confederate Marylanders paraded it proudly. Eventually, despite the state's reluctance to secede, they formed their own battalions, with native leaders and native banners, and proved as valorous (perhaps vainglorious) as any scion of the First Families of Virginia. As such, they badgered Confederate authorities for support and optimistically promised to garner renewed support for secession if sent north of the Potomac. Clamoring to be heard were Arnold Elzey and George H. Steuart, colonels of the First Maryland (CSA); Talbot County naval officer Franklin Buchanan, who commanded the CSS *Virginia* (*Merrimac*); and Frederick Countian Bradley Johnson, a lawyer and grandson of the state's first governor and signer of the

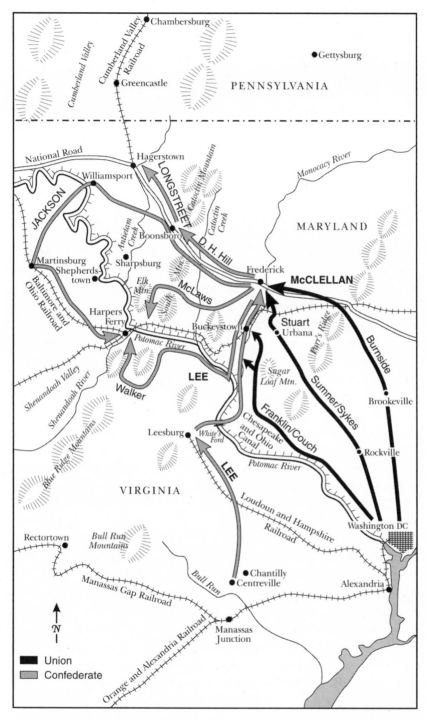

Movements—September 3–13, 1862

Declaration of Independence, appropriately. Like Kentuckian John Hunt Morgan, Marylanders misled the Richmond government into thinking that a mere whiff of gunpowder might cause border states to add stars for rebel banners.[10]

At the same time, absent rebellious rabble-rousers, Maryland Unionism asserted itself under the watchful eye of Washington. A more avowedly loyal Augustus Bradford replaced Governor Hicks during the federally supervised autumn 1861 elections. The working classes rallied to blue-uniformed Maryland regiments that often relied on multicounty recruitment but used traditional militia designations like the Baltimore-based Fifth Infantry. They supplied volunteer regiments to national expeditionary forces in Virginia while also providing neighborhood protection north of the river as Potomac Home Brigade contingents. They helped suppress civil disobedience and rewarded loyalism. Astute farmers and businessmen, unswayed now by southern promises, began capturing the brisk wartime trade. John Garrett's umbilical Baltimore and Ohio Railroad traversed a sort of no man's land on the upper Potomac, thus incurring constant depredations by both Union and Confederate military. He courted Washington and profited from military as well as transportation needs of both state and nation. Acquiescence to federal authority outpaced the folly of open opposition when incarceration in Fort McHenry resulted. Excessive force, unnecessary violation of civil rights, and overzealous enforcement of national government dicta most certainly attended Maryland's experience. On the other hand, such measures achieved Lincoln's aim. Moreover, they met favorable response elsewhere in the Union, comforted hometown Unionists in the Old Line State, and assured that Virginia, not Maryland, would become the dark and bloody ground in the East.[11]

In a sense, then, Lee's invasion seemed doomed from the start. If intended as liberation and redemption (implied by words in the general's proclamation upon entering the state that September), it had little chance of success, if judged by its trajectory. Geography dictated movement, and lacking naval support Lee necessarily chose the incorrect entry point. Had he been able to cross the lower Potomac or the Chesapeake Bay into the Eastern Shore section of Maryland, he could have tapped more ardently secessionist sections of the state. But such possibilities had been effectively squelched the previous year after First Manassas and subsequent lack of Confederate naval resources. At that time President Davis had reputedly sent word to southern Marylanders to avoid insurrection and keep Baltimore quiet for the present. In ten days he would command the Potomac and cross between Mathias Point and Aquia Creek into Charles and St. Mary's counties, where "they are all friends," before marching on Annapolis. Once he possessed the two approaches to Washington, "Let Baltimore rise and burn the bridges." The movements on the upper Potomac were only feints, he proclaimed. Federal response quickly ended Davis's intentions.[12]

Quick imposition of the U.S. Navy's newly formed Potomac Flotilla, plus the Confederacy's own incapacity to find sufficient boats to carry such an invasion force to the Maryland shore, produced stalemate in that quarter. There could be no succor for Maryland secessionists as Mr. Davis's army settled into what has been styled a "blockade" of the nation's capital during the fall and winter. Federal forces spread out through both upper and lower counties of the state. Their presence consolidated defense of Maryland's maritime frontier and imposed national control over citizens' hearts and minds, particularly in the southern counties. Capt. Fleet Cox, a southern Marylander who joined the Fortieth Virginia, wrote his fiancée back home that he anticipated fifty thousand Virginia and Georgia troops, proving "to the Yankees that Maryland is part of the sunny South and shall be free." But his hope to drill his Potomac Rifles in hometown Port Tobacco came to naught. Confederate authorities resorted to emplacing heavy batteries on the Virginia shore from the Occoquan River to Quantico and interdicting commerce with Washington. They guarded the Old Dominion but could mount no offensive into southern Maryland. There only a brooding rebellion, a nettlesome and oppressive Yankee presence, and a brisk contraband trade in goods, mail, and recruitment resulted.[13]

Had Lee even turned eastward toward Washington and Baltimore after crossing the Potomac in September 1862 his army might have tapped the latent support of Montgomery, Howard, and Prince George's counties as well as the greater Baltimore region and thereby effected links to southern and eastern shore Maryland. Of course, living off rich Maryland farmland anywhere would offset being logistically cut off from Virginia supply bases. Similarly, he might have effectively besieged the nation's capital on its least protected northern side. A rapidly moving expedition might even have liberated Baltimore, giving Lee a superb base of operations for state occupation. That city was poorly defended, and even most of Washington's garrison plus its field army remained south of the river when Lee crossed. An incomplete defense line—roughly forty-five independent forts, only partially improved and meagerly supplemented by field batteries and rifle entrenchments—would have stood between Lee's victorious veterans and the inviting target of the national capital. Ironically, it would be this weaker northern sector of Washington's defenses that received the Confederacy's most serious threat two summers later, blunted only in the eleventh hour at a fort on the Seventh Street road. There Lincoln himself, the only sitting president in U.S. history to experience enemy fire, would nearly be shot nine months before his assassination by Marylander John Wilkes Booth. Lee stood on Old Line soil in 1862 and moved, not on Washington or Baltimore, but rather to Frederick County, in strongly Unionist western Maryland. At least from there the Confederates could cut the east–west canal and railroad lines, rejuvenate themselves, and stir the state's avowed secessionists to uprising and secession by their proximity. Western Maryland also fit Lee's idea of advancing into Pennsylvania as his ultimate destination.[14]

If Lee intended a more permanent presence for establishing a Confederate Maryland in the first place, certainly his subsequent words and actions suggested otherwise. Nevertheless, he no doubt spoiled for a fight—but on his terms, not his enemy's. This meant luring a battered Army of the Potomac away from Washington and even to the distant Cumberland Valley of western Maryland and central Pennsylvania. For that matter, he might have won a decisive battle east of the mountains. In the end, however, revictualing his army remained Lee's foremost goal, as a *Richmond Examiner* article implied on September 12. The true cause of the Confederate northward move, surmised the writer, resulted from exhaustion of the crop-and-livestock-producing country, which stretched from the Potomac at Harpers Ferry all the way to Memphis, Tennessee. Southern armies had "consumed everything in the central portion of it," while the joint armies of the belligerents "have consumed the supplies of the extremes." Thus Lee's focus was feeding ill-provisioned troops, if not continuing farther into Pennsylvania. Interpreters since have chosen that explanation as most plausible. And for a while it was. Then, suddenly, events near Frederick City sped Lee and his army on what may already have been their predetermined destiny. His strategic plan, whether military, political, economic, or diplomatic (combat, secession, resupply, European intervention, or even to impact on northern politics—all at one or another time entered Lee's dispatches), came unglued at one stroke. On September 10, his legions would turn west, not east or north, and take up the line of march away from, not toward, either the national capital or the supposedly still-seething seedbed of Maryland's rebellion on the Chesapeake.[15]

Circumstances coalesced as Lee's army encamped on the banks of the Monocacy River just south of Frederick. By September 7, Lee and his staff had established headquarters in a pleasant grove of oak trees on a farm just off the Washington turnpike adjacent to the Monocacy River and the Frederick railroad junction. Lee opted not to disturb the tenanting Best family, who occupied premises that Victoire de la Vincendiere's family had built when they emigrated to the area after the Santo Domingo slave revolt toward the end of the previous century. The courtly Confederate general still suffered from his earlier injuries. He occupied a government-provided tent notwithstanding the inviting atmosphere of the French Caribbean–style structures on the property. The 748-acre spread, originally one of the largest slaveholding operations in both Frederick County and the state, provided ample water and shade for much of his resting army. Lee's bivouac soon became a focal point for local sightseers and secessionists, although he took great trouble to ration his time for more important military business, some of which concerned Richmond. In fact, Lee wrote his president that day that virtually all of his army was across the Potomac and that he had found "plenty of provisions and forage in this country, and the community have received us with kindness." Yet despite individual expressions of support "and the general sympathy in the success of the Confederate States," Maryland's positioning between the warring parties caused Lee to "not anticipate any general rising of the people in our behalf." Some additions to the army's ranks and subsistence levels would be all.[16]

Lee had prepared his army well for the quasi-political task at hand. Three days before, he had issued general orders forbidding straggling and directing that pillagers would be summarily punished. There would be no southern version of John Pope's infamous war on the populace. "This army is about to engage in most important operations where any excesses committed will exasperate the people, lead to disastrous results, and enlist the populace on the side of the Federal forces in hostility to our own," were Lee's words. Quartermasters and commissaries should "make all arrangements for purchase of supplies needed by our army." He wished to avoid confiscation, although a dearth of hard currency handicapped the logistical effort. Lee subsequently told Richmond that border state citizens seemed reluctant to accept Confederate specie and so the Army of Northern Virginia had to give "certificates of indebtedness of the Confederates states for future adjustment." Actually this differed little from what Federal military authorities were doing in Dixie. Lee also informed Davis that, based on experience, "some general arrangement should be made for liquidating the debts that may be incurred to the satisfaction of the people of Maryland, in order that they may willingly furnish us what is wanted." These observations suggest why Lee wanted the state's ex-governor Enoch Lowe to join him "with a view of expediting these and other arrangements necessary to the success of our army in this State." Lowe came from the Frederick area; he had been a popular executive and people would respect his assurances. Lee twice assured Davis that "every outrage upon the feelings and property" of unpersuaded Marylanders would be checked. Temporarily freed of any immediate threat from McClellan, Lee could afford the luxury of venturing beyond his purely military role when he wrote Davis the next day concerning Confederate independence itself.[17]

More than a year of hostilities had devastated both North and South, Lee advised the president, yet without signal success in "advancing the objects which our enemies proposed to themselves in beginning the contest." The present state of affairs, therefore, enabled the Confederate government "with propriety" to propose "recognition of our independence" to the U.S. government. In no manner would this be "suing for peace." Rather, such a proposition would indicate to the world that the Confederacy's sole object was establishment of independence and attainment of an honorable peace at such a time "when it is in our power to inflict injury upon our adversary." Rejection of the proposition would transfer the onus to the Lincoln regime for continuing the contest. The peace proposal would also enable the people of the United States to determine in the fall elections whether they would support those who favored a prolongation of the war or those who wished to terminate it, and "can but be productive of good to both parties without affecting the honor of either,"

Lee claimed. With his Maryland dispatches, Lee moved beyond his primary responsibilities as field commander or even military adviser to the president. Success in battle, however, gave him confidence for projecting the interlocking nature of war and grand strategy to his superiors. That success suggested how his particular army might be the purveyor of peace as well as diplomatic initiative.[18]

That same day, September 8, Lee independently issued a proclamation to the people of Maryland penned by his aide Col. Charles Marshall. Explaining that citizens had a right to know why his army was present in their state, the proclamation stated that the Confederate people had long viewed with deepest sympathy "the wrongs and outrages that have been inflicted upon the citizens of a commonwealth allied to the States of the South by the strongest social, political, and commercial ties." They had indignantly watched Marylanders deprived of "every right and reduced to the condition of a conquered province." Under the pretense of supporting the Constitution (but really violating most of its valuable provisions), said Lee, the Federal government had arrested and imprisoned Maryland citizens without charge and "contrary to all forms of law." Scorn and contempt had been heaped upon secessionist Marylanders, the principal city of the state occupied "by armed strangers," the state legislature dissolved by unlawful arrest of its members, and "freedom of the press and of speech suppressed." "Words have been declared offenses by an arbitrary decree of the Federal executive, and citizens ordered to be tried by a military commission for what they may dare to speak." So, "believing that the people of Maryland possessed a spirit too lofty to submit to such a government, the people of the South have long wished to aid you in throwing off this foreign yoke." Marylanders could again "enjoy the inalienable rights of freemen, and restore independence and sovereignty to your State." It was "in obedience to this wish" that the Army of Northern Virginia had come, prepared to assist with the power of arms in "regaining the rights" of which Maryland had been deprived. Southerners would welcome Marylanders "to your natural position among them," but only if the border state itself chose to join. "It is for you to decide your destiny freely and without constraint," Lee pronounced of self-determination.[19]

Curiously an even more brazen proclamation went forth that same day. Arguably the most prominent Marylander in Lee's ranks at that moment because he too came from Frederick County, Col. Bradley

Johnson penned his own invitation to Marylanders to embrace the Confederacy. Far more incendiary than Lee's mild rhetoric, Johnson spoke to the semantics of tyranny and despotism. Empowered to recruit for companies and regiments of Marylanders, he called on his fellow citizens to remember the cells and dungeons of Yankee forts McHenry, Lafayette, and Warren, where innocent Maryland men had been imprisoned, as well as "the insults to your Wives and Daughters and the midnight searches of your houses!" Bring only "a stout pair of Shoes, a good Blanket and a Tin Cup," he directed, citing that "Jackson's men have no Baggage." The victorious southern army would provide for the rest of their needs. "Remember these your wrongs, and rise at once in arms and strike for Liberty and Right," Johnson enjoined. Perhaps the season was simply ripe for writing such proclamations. In Richmond President Davis and his advisers prepared their own pronouncement, addressing border state concerns of Kentuckians as well as Marylanders. Lee's trusted lieutenant James Longstreet later suggested that Davis "from the head of his victorious army would call for recognition," possibly even from a Pennsylvania location.[20]

Davis and his advisers wanted Lee, as well as Smith and Bragg in Kentucky, to announce "the motives and purposes of your presence among them at the head of an invading army." That the Davis proclamation was generic rather than specific to either state could be seen in eight general points reflecting a rather stiff, even constitutionalist viewpoint that only tangentially reflected appreciation of local conditions that might be encountered by respective Confederate field commanders. The eight points started with the predictable note that the Confederate government "is waging this war solely for self-defense," with no design of conquest "or any other purpose than to secure peace and the abandonment by the United States of their pretensions to govern a people who have never been their subjects, and who prefer self-government to a union with them." They continued with recitation of peace initiatives scorned in Washington, the question of free navigation of western rivers, "the simple demand that the people of the United States should cease to war upon us, and permit us to pursue our own path to happiness, while they in peace pursue theirs." The Davis document trumpeted, "We are driven to protect our own country by transferring the seat of war to that of an enemy who pursues us with a relentless and, apparently, aimless hostility," laying waste to fields, killing people, and desecrating homes "together with ravaging Confederate frontiers through rapine and murder."

Then came an interesting seventh provision in Davis's proclamation. Somewhat contrary to Lee's words to Marylanders, the Confederate leader had the Confederate army coming "to occupy the territory of their enemies, and to make it the theater of hostilities," thereby enabling states like Maryland and Kentucky and possibly others to use their own state government "in exercise of its sovereignty" to secure "immunity from the desolating effects of warfare" on its own soil "by a separate treaty of peace," which the Confederacy promised to conclude "on the most just and liberal basis." The eighth and final point, like Lee's words, suggested, "The responsibility thus rests on the people of [a blank occurred at this point in the text, permitting insertion of Maryland, Kentucky, or some other territory] of continuing an unjust and oppressive warfare upon the Confederate States—a warfare which can never end in any other manner than that now proposed." The people had "the option of preserving the blessings of peace by the simple abandonment of the design of subjugating a people over whom no right of dominion has ever been conferred, either by God or man," were Davis's final words.[21]

Davis no doubt intended leading a triumphal procession with Lee north of the Potomac. His summer had been an anxious one, first from McClellan's threat, then from the continuing capture of southern territory on the coasts and in the hinterland (including raids on Davis's family plantations on the Mississippi) as well as the tribulations of governance generally. So an opportunity to take to the field like some conquering hero beckoned with Lee across the Potomac. Accompanied by Lowe, he left Richmond on the morning of September 7, intending a conference with his field commander at Leesburg. Obviously Lee had gone on ahead; he wrote the president on September 9, from "near Fredericktown," squelching the move by noting the dangers of traveling along a route through devastated northern Virginia as well as possible enemy interception of the chief executive. By this time Lee intended changing his own line of communications from Leesburg back through Culpeper and Gordonsville. Destruction of the railroad north of Culpeper as well as an unprotected logistical lifeline so close to Washington dictated such a move. He sought the more secure Shenandoah Valley for enabling a longer stay in Maryland and possible operations into Pennsylvania.

Intent on developing a forward base at Winchester, Lee would move "in the direction I originally intended, towards Hagerstown and Chambersburg, for the purpose of opening our line of communication through the Valley, in order to procure sufficient supplies of flour." Three days later, from Hagerstown, he would again tell the president point-blank, "Before crossing the Potomac I considered the advantages of entering Maryland east or west of the Blue Ridge," and "in either case it was my intention to march upon this town." By this point, Davis and Lowe had turned back, getting only to Warrenton by September 8, when ill health forced their return to the capital.[22]

Marylanders' tepid reception only served to speed Lee on his way west. A delayed harvest, a lukewarm response from local farmers and millers, the reluctance of Frederick merchants to readily open their stores to the Rebels, and a decidedly meager yield of recruits conditioned Lee's actions. Returning to Virginia to meet up with the president would only be an inconvenience. Alerted perhaps that the president planned to upstage Lee's presence north of the Potomac, the general would forward a copy of his proclamation to Davis on September 13, penitently asking that should there be anything in it needing correction, the general would certainly comply, knowing full well that it was already in the hands of Marylanders and that Davis could do little about it anyway at this juncture. The matter became moot when Davis and Lowe turned back at Warrenton, Virginia. Lee could comfortably return to his primary concerns: his army, supplies and stragglers, and the enemy.

Poorly clad and shod soldiers, a great number of stragglers among that soldiery, and shortages of various types of munitions and arms plagued Lee at this juncture. Then suddenly his situation changed dramatically thanks to the unanticipated promptness of the Federal advance from Washington and a refusal of Union garrisons at Harpers Ferry and Martinsburg to fade before the Rebel approach. Just as Federal bayonets had decided Maryland's ultimate political choice a year before, they now determined Lee's actions. Contrary to the Great Captain's expectations, the Army of the Potomac had amalgamated Army of Virginia contingents and refused to react as Lee had anticipated. The men in blue had grown restive merely guarding the capital. Flavius Bellamy of the Nineteenth Indiana wrote home, "I wish Washington was burned and thus our army would be marched out to do something beside protect and lay around that sink of iniquity." There were fortifications enough "to protect it against the world." Mr. Lincoln's army had regained confidence and composure for renewed campaigning. Maj. Gen. George B. McClellan undoubtedly provided the cause of this renaissance. As Pulitzer prize–winning author Margaret Leech noted of the week after Second Bull Run, "That week, McClellan performed something very like a miracle." "When McClellan spoke the word, it was an army once again." But did McClellan have confidence in himself or that he could shape events and exploit opportunity?[23]

Whether or not General in Chief Henry Halleck and the administration "capitulated to McClellan," as Halleck's latest biographer, John F. Marszalek, implies, McClellan's inspiriting presence and organizational talents accomplished what Lincoln intended by his reappointment to command. The sentiments the general expressed to wife Mary Ellen on September 8 were typical: "You don't know what a task has been imposed on me! I have been obliged to do the best I could with the broken & discouraged fragments of two armies defeated by no fault of mine." Only a desire to do his duty had induced him to accept such a burden, as "no one else *could save* the country," so he had not shrunk from "the terrible task." True, the man spent too much time writing unguarded comments to his wife and political friends in the North that later disclosed a troubling side of his personality to historians. Trepidations about his agenda, his ethics, even his loyalty soured Washington against him even at the time, however. Restored by the president against the advice of others, he not only had to reform the army but win back respect and support from the administration. It hardly helped that Halleck barraged him ceaselessly about the government's paranoia for the capital's defense. Then alarmed state officials and citizens in Pennsylvania as well as a railroad president and a departmental commander in Baltimore vied for his help against the Rebel threat. Above all, could he lead this reorganized army to victory against Lee?[24]

At first, McClellan's mandate from Lincoln had simply been army reorganization, not command of any field force. In fact, the president had directed Halleck on September 2 to "immediately commence, and proceed with all possible dispatch, to organize an army for active operations, from all the material within and coming within his control, independent of the forces he may deem necessary for the defense of Washington, when such active army shall take the field."

This directive was quite normal, the responsibility of the senior uniformed official, and nothing in it specifically charged Halleck with taking command of the force. So, working manfully on Halleck's orders, McClellan mustered some seventy-three thousand men with 120 field pieces and five hundred fortress guns—fully half the available manpower and one-quarter to one-third larger than Lee's force—solely for defense of the capital. He re-formed Pope's shattered units and melded them with the Army of the Potomac and absorbed new arrivals from another round of manpower mobilization. By September 5 he had a nucleus field army of six corps in which well over half were new men and units from other commands, or at least thirty-six newly organized regiments by one count. Biographer Stephen Sears contends that they were "strangers to his battlefield leadership," but his catalyzing effect had returned Union arms in the East from the degradation of defeat. He also managed to convince the government to reinstate Fitz John Porter, William B. Franklin, and Charles Griffin, all three generals facing courts-martial or courts of inquiry at Pope's request for malfeasance during the late operations in northern Virginia. McClellan could not restore his old subordinate Charles P. Stone, recently released from confinement for supposed disloyalty the previous fall with regard to the operation that had produced Ball's Bluff.[25]

No matter, McClellan's young staff officers and unit commanders swept stragglers from Washington's hotels, barrooms, and brothels, tamed unruly teamsters whose wagon trains blocked city streets, and checked the reckless and senseless galloping about of orderlies and other horsemen, who terrorized pedestrians. In two days' time they restored order in a panicky city "full of exciting, vague and absurd rumors," according to Secretary of the Navy Gideon Welles. Years of speculation since had Halleck or even Ambrose Burnside destined to lead the new army out once more against Lee. Burnside, however, deferred to his friend Mac, and it may well have been that Old Brains realized that there was no one else but McClellan who could inspire this army to battle. He worded his follow-up directive to the general not only to prepare the army but also to position him for its field command. Again some of Lincoln's cabinet tried to block the move and even wrest matters from the president's own hands. That move foundered, leaving everyone in Washington, in the words of soldier-historian Edward Stackpole, "to acquiesce passively."[26]

War Department orders on September 2 and 5 formalized the situation that evolved from a personal meeting between Lincoln, Halleck, and McClellan. The president verbally told McClellan, "You will take command of the forces in the field." Then, issuing no written directive, Lincoln seemingly disavowed his own decision when, immediately upon leaving the meeting, he offered the command once more to Burnside, only to be turned down a second time. Lincoln let Halleck take responsibility for naming McClellan expeditionary leader, according to Secretary Welles, although Halleck later attributed the decision to the commander in chief when appearing before a Radical-dominated congressional committee. McClellan himself thought that it was "one of those things that grew into shape itself— when the time came I went out." Whatever the truth, ducking responsibility at highest levels smoothed over anti-McClellan sentiment all over town. Moreover, guarding the capital remained on the table, so an influx of reserve and training regiments as well as retention of Franz Sigel's ineffective corps, Samuel Heintzelman's battered III Corps, and Porter's men, together with the city's own garrison, left Nathaniel Banks with seventy-two thousand soldiers for the administration and defense of Washington. Once designated field commander, McClellan quickly shifted more of his army to the northern side of the city in response to Lee's moving across the Potomac. Late in the afternoon of September 7, before Lee ever expected it, McClellan began a fan-shaped, measured advance toward western Maryland. He could search for the Confederates as well as cover Washington and Baltimore. To historian Stephen Sears, "George McClellan's skill as a military administrator never shone more brightly."[27]

McClellan's return to command thrilled the soldiers. For two days his boys in blue marched through the streets of the city, shifting northward toward the developing new threat. Many of them went past McClellan's headquarters on Lafayette Square, not past the White House. Their shouts and cheers for the general could be heard for blocks. The ever-theatrical general also left calling cards with Halleck and Stanton bearing his name and a French military phrase indicating departure on campaign—a Napoleonic touch, inviting comparison between the two soldiers. Benignly he wrote his wife that he felt the government was now with him, and so he left "with God's blessing, to justify the great confidence they now repose in me & will bury the past in oblivion." Encountering Secretary Welles and his son

Edgar as McClellan and his staff rode along Pennsylvania Avenue that Sunday evening, September 7, the general received the friendly greeting, "Well *onward* General is now the word—the country will expect you to go *forward.*" He intended doing so, McClellan replied, dashing off into the dusk. Just how such intent would translate into victory over Lee was another matter. Many people continued to ascribe his motives to a desire to become an American Cromwell. The ever-caustic Adam Gurowski groused, "Mr. Lincoln, with McClellan, Seward, Blair, Halleck, and scores of such, are as able to cope with this crisis as to stop the revolution of our planet." Stanton alone "is inspired by a national patriotic idea." Yet, with "no unity, no harmony between the people and the leaders; this discord must generate disasters," he feared.[28]

Welles possibly best diagnosed the situation. The War Department was bewildered, he noted on September 6, "knows but little, does nothing, proposes nothing." He dismissed Stanton's and Halleck's apprehension for the city's safety. The day after the battle of Chantilly Welles had concluded that Lee would cross upriver to strike at Baltimore or "our railroad communications or both," but certainly not against Washington. Moreover, the Connecticut Yankee discerned the crucial problem of army leadership: it "has no head." Halleck was a military director, not a general, whose scholastic attainments did not equate with soldierly capacity. McClellan was "an intelligent engineer and officer," but "to fight is not his forte." The secretary did not doubt his loyalty but wondered if his heart was really in the cause, for "the study of military operations interests and amuses him." To Welles, McClellan liked "show, parade, and power," as he "wishes to outgeneral the rebels, but not to kill and destroy him." On September 9, Welles told Treasury Secretary Salmon P. Chase, "He has military acquirements and capacity, dash, but has not audacity, lacks decision, delays, hesitates, vacillates," and would "persist in delays and inaction and do nothing affirmative." Certainly McClellan "has a great opportunity," and as Welles recognized, only he could gather the army together, so "let's give him credit when he deserves it."[29]

McClellan was a "soldier's soldier," at least in the eyes of the eastern army. He understood the needs and capabilities of his men. They were like his children to him; he would not place them unduly in harm's way. This idea fit nicely with his own risk-averse style of war. Faced with the situation of an enemy now across the Potomac and on loyal soil, he might have returned to a campaign to dislodge that enemy by threatening Richmond. But combining the condition of his army (which, ironically, both he and Pope had nearly destroyed by their earlier actions and which desperately needed rehabilitation in his eyes), his own tenuous hold on command with which to effect a conciliatory "way of war" (that was as much a fight against northern radicalism and abolitionism as it was against the Confederacy), and the fact that Halleck and Lincoln had already indicated the object of McClellan's new mission (Lee's army, not the Rebel capital), Little Mac's approach becomes understandable. No matter that Lee might well have been recalled to Virginia by the Davis government, as fearful of its capital as Lincoln was of his. McClellan was predisposed and now chained to the safe school of maneuver warfare. Risk would be left to the future, to someone like "Fighting Joe" Hooker the following year, who proposed to advance on Richmond when Lee once more was across the Potomac. Even then, Lincoln would veto such boldness.

In passing from protection of the city to field offensive as his mission, McClellan quickly shifted gears as to form and purpose. As he explained retrospectively in his memoirs, because Lee maintained the offensive in crossing the upper Potomac "to threaten or invade Pennsylvania, it became necessary to meet him at any cost, notwithstanding the condition of the troops; to put a stop to the invasion, save Baltimore and Washington, and throw him back across the Potomac." There was nothing in those words indicating understanding of Lincoln's wish for the total defeat and annihilation of Lee and his army. "The purpose of advancing from Washington," McClellan continued, "was simply to meet the necessities of the moment by frustrating Lee's invasion of the Northern States, and, when that was accomplished, to push with the utmost rapidity the work of reorganization and supply, so that a new campaign might be promptly inaugurated with the army in condition to prosecute it to a successful termination without intermission." Here was McClellan's whole philosophy of war: methodical preparation and execution by measured step that would resolve the immediate problem rather than eradicating the cause of that problem. Frankly conscious that he might lose the war by singular misstep and hence his concept of restoration of the old Union, he would do nothing rash, would move strictly in communication with and through Halleck, his military superior, and wrest the initiative back from his opponent before returning to war making on his own terms. How better to explain what would transpire over the next fortnight and beyond?[30]

Meanwhile, alerted to developments upstream by a new cavalry chief, Brig. Gen. Alfred Pleasonton, McClellan's army plodded forward into the countryside. The army projected a formidable array of some ninety-five thousand officers and men, sixty-three batteries of artillery, and a division of cavalry. Ensconced the first evening out in the sturdy brick Rockville residence of a Miss Beall ("an old maid of strong Union sentiment," who would take no recompense for their lodging), the general and his staff shifted headquarters with the weight and pace of the army's advance. Rockville impressed one *Philadelphia Inquirer* reporter as "a small and dilapidated looking town of four or five hundred inhabitants" and little different from "the generality of small villages in the interior of Maryland." Cavalry clashed soon after Pleasonton began probing Confederate outposts in the upper reaches of Montgomery County. Poolesville on September 8 and Monocacy Church (Beallsville) the next day witnessed heavy skirmishing as Pleasonton's units tested J. E. B. Stuart's screen of horsemen strung out from the Potomac northward to New Market on the National road between Frederick and Baltimore. Advancing Federals pushed Confederate signalmen off nearby seven-hundred-foot-high Sugarloaf Mountain by September 11 and could better scout Lee's main force encamped in the Monocacy River valley. Still, Pleasonton relied too much on hearsay from captured prisoners and country folk, who invariably inflated enemy strength. His estimates of the enemy approached 120,000, a figure that spooked McClellan, so that the army advanced no more than five to ten miles a day for fear of being overwhelmed in detail. Pleasonton did prove that Confederate forces had not advanced to the important Parr's Ridge, running north of Darnesville and east of Fredrick, which could have provided a formidable obstacle had Lee chosen to make it his line of defense or even Stuart's forward screening position. Stuart merely masked "the line of the Monocacy," as Lee reported to Davis on September 7.[31]

The heat, humidity, and dusty roads, plus McClellan's solicitation for his soldiers' recovery from the grueling Virginia ordeal, made for a slow march. His army's fan-shaped advance marched by stages, first to Seneca Creek, then to Parr's Ridge, and eventually to the line of the Monocacy River. Such maneuvering permitted recoil to defensive positions should any prong of the advance meet determined resistance. In this fashion, McClellan complied with instructions to cover approaches to Washington and Baltimore as well as freeing available roads for the marching columns. One wing of the army, William B. Franklin's VI Corps in advance and Darius Couch's division in reserve, moved through Offutt's Crossroads (modern Potomac), across Muddy Branch, and past the previous winter's encampments of Charles P. Stone's "Army of Observation" en route to Darnestown, Dawsonville, Poolesville, and Barnesville. It anchored the army's left flank on the Potomac River and adjacent Chesapeake and Ohio Canal. The center wing, Edwin Sumner's II Corps with George Sykes's division from the V Corps in reserve and accompanied by McClellan and his staff, took the direct Frederick road from Rockville through Gaithersburg, Clarksburg, and Hyattstown toward Urbana.

Brig. Gen. Alpheus S. Williams's XII Corps (part of Sumner's "wing") split to the right at Middlebrook on September 10 and 11, passing through Damascus en route to Ijamsville and the Monocacy crossing of the National turnpike east of Frederick. Such a move coordinated with Ambrose Burnside's third wing of the army as Hooker's I Corps and Jesse Reno's IX Corps tramped the Brookeville turnpike from Silver Spring through Mechanicsville (modern Olney), headed to Cookeville and the line of both the National turnpike and the Baltimore and Ohio Railroad running west from Baltimore. A portion of this column broke off at Brookeville to close with Williams by passing through Cracklintown (Laytonsville), Goshen, and Seneca Bridge. The advance overall represented a balanced movement of cohesion and strength.[32]

In contrast to Lee's disciplined advance into Maryland, however, McClellan's men foraged freely when they encountered frowns and animosity among random secessionist sympathizers of Montgomery County. Two miles north of Brookeville, the Yankee soldiers passed Elton, near Sunshine, home to one of Maryland's most prominent Confederate heroes, Ridgely Brown, then serving with and later to command the First Maryland Cavalry (CSA). In fact, another future commander, Gustavus Dorsey, was a native of the Brookeville area. With soldiers encountering such mixed sympathy—loyalist and secessionist all within a given locale—little wonder that chicken coops, barns, and livestock became fair prey to looting, despite officer prohibitions. Even some violence occurred when citizens attempted to protect their property. Unionist Rockville residents Judge Richard J. Bowie, John England, and James T. Henning actually petitioned Military District of Washington commander Nathaniel Banks for provost protection. They failed to secure help at the time, guards appearing later as much to harass neighborhood dissidents as to protect private property. In the eyes of most northern soldiery, especially newcomers to McClellan's ranks, Maryland lay south of the Mason-Dixon line, hence was disloyal territory and open to heavy-handed treatment.[33]

The campaign quickened suddenly during the second week of September. Two events portended the change; interestingly, they occurred within five miles of one another. One took place at the crossroads hamlet of Urbana, the other on a farm near Frederick Junction. The first episode at Urbana involved cavalryman Stuart's proverbial infatuation with the fair sex. It reflected his inattention to tactical mission and involved the charm of young Maryland ladies. The second event, on the Best farm, suggested another security breakdown and in fact a changing strategic direction. Both episodes represented Confederate miscues and both accelerated passing the initiative from Lee to McClellan, although the latter has been criticized for failing to exploit either opportunity through speedy reaction. The event at Urbana breached the cavalry screen of Lee's activities. The episode near Frederick Junction compromised Lee's plans and involved a package of cigars, the wrapping for which was a copy of Confederate marching orders that transferred operations west of the mountains to the Shenandoah–Great Valley axis to Pennsylvania. Delivered to McClellan, this Lost Order would alert McClellan to Lee's changing movements and intentions. As vignettes, these events provided color and drama to the moment. As quirks of fate, they gave unwanted anxiety to the final stages of the Confederate invasion. Navy Secretary Welles recorded in his diary that the week brought "less sensation and fewer rumors" to the Union capital. Events in upper Maryland, however, increased the suspense.[34]

In a sense, Stuart and his merry band of followers could hardly be faulted for seeking a lighter moment amid the rigors of campaign and horrors of battle. Bivouacked on Sebastian Cockey's farm at Urbana, the cavalier jumped at the idea of using a nearby academy for a dance. The white frame building, an old tobacco warehouse that had been transported from Rappahannock County, Virginia, in the previous century, seemed well suited for this purpose. As Stuart told his trusty adjutant, Prussian soldier-of-fortune Maj. Heros von Borcke, "What a capital place for us to give a ball in honor of our arrival in Maryland!" The womenfolk within hearing applauded in delight as Stuart promised to provide the music, von Borcke vowed to decorate the hall, and everything was set in motion for the evening of September 8. Anne Cockey, an attractive family member visiting from New York, caught Stuart's eye as the favorite "New York relative," and von Borcke styled her the "New York Rebel." That evening roses and candlelight cast an air of glamour in the flag-festooned hall. Carriages and buggies brought the guests, while the cavalrymen unbuckled sabers in hallways and fastened their horses nearby in case of need. The band of the Eighteenth Mississippi struck up "Dixie," polkas, and quadrilles. Suddenly the alert sounded as Yankee horsemen broke through Stuart's picket line a short distance away at Hyattstown and advanced rapidly. The ball broke up hastily, with Stuart's crowd rushing off into the night while conveyances took some of the belles home. But the disturbance subsided just as quickly, and soldiers and ladies returned to frolic until arriving wounded brought a sober note to the festivities. Stuart's and von Borcke's "sabers and roses" ball ended at daybreak, with exhausted revelers collapsing with fatigue.[35]

Moonlight, flowers, and gallantry offered momentary romantic relief. But they hid the realities of a rapidly changing situation. Stuart and his entourage continued to enjoy the hospitality of the Cockey family while his picket line continued to disintegrate. Stuart and von Borcke lingered on in such company on September 9. Even when at last moving out under orders from Lee the next day, terpsichorean-intoxicated knights of the South wiled away more time, courting and dancing with other ladies just outside Frederick. Stuart's headquarters remained so intent on merrymaking that Union success at Hyattstown, Poolesville, and Barnesville passed without serious note. As historian Joseph Harsh observes, nothing indicated that Lee's cavalry chief "perceived the Army of the Potomac to be pressing in a menacing way," hence it was likely that reports "from such an indolent headquarters" led Lee to think that his army "could spare three days" to secure its line of communications through the Shenandoah. As at Chantilly, where Stuart took leave to socialize with nearby friends, thus failing to alert Jackson and Lee of Federal presence, once again social matters at Urbana intruded on the serious duty entrusted to the cavalryman. Confederate overconfidence that the Army of the Potomac must still be close to Washington nearly proved fatal. Indeed, while Sumner stood only at Middlebrook, Franklin had advanced to Darnestown and Burnside to Cracklintown, about halfway from Washington to Frederick. More shocking, however, lead elements of the bluecoat army on the left at Barnesville and the far northern or right flank on the National Pike at Ridgeville were only about ten miles from Confederate camps on the Monocacy. On September 9, Lee decided to divide his army and go after Harpers Ferry, while shifting logistically to the valley.[36]

In some ways the people of Maryland themselves most affected Lee's timetable. Their response to liberation had been perplexing. However, the Federal military response had also proved unanticipated. Not only had McClellan and his men pursued more quickly, but more important, Union commanders had not evacuated their respective positions at Harpers Ferry and Martinsburg in the Shenandoah, as Lee had expected. He could not know that Halleck had decreed that they remain there. Their presence affected Lee's freedom of movement and establishment of the new line of communications based in Winchester. Lee needed to resolve this problem before undertaking additional operations north of the Potomac. He started to do so sometime on the afternoon of July 9. Just as Halleck remained confident that Col. Dixon Miles and Brig. Gen. Julius White could hold their positions in the lower Shenandoah Valley until relieved by McClellan, so Lee believed that his own subordinates easily could take Harpers Ferry, having imprecise knowledge of the number of Federals actually in garrison there. Longstreet might balk at Lee's risky division of the army to do so, but Jackson did not, and his foot cavalry received the mission of reducing the Harpers Ferry obstacle. After directing that no officers or men would pay Frederick any further visits except on army business, Lee further ordered his aide, Maj. Walter Taylor, to return to Leesburg and shift the army's sick and straggler returnees to Winchester, "being the general depot of the army" for the foreseeable future. The Army of Northern Virginia would then once more take to the road, move through Frederick and out the National pike, and head west. The stage was set for the Confederates' next miscue.[37]

Special Order 191, dated September 9, 1862, detailed Lee's plan. Everyone would march the next morning. Jackson's men would branch off to Sharpsburg from Boonsborough, having passed through Middletown and over South Mountain. They would recross the Potomac "and by Friday morning" capture the Baltimore and Ohio Railroad and Martinsburg "and intercept such [of the enemy] as may attempt to escape from Harper's Ferry." Longstreet, meanwhile, following Jackson west on the National pike, would halt briefly at Boonsborough together with the army's reserve, supply, and baggage trains. McLaws and Anderson, following Longstreet on the march route, would diverge at Middletown to besiege Harpers Ferry from the overlooking pinnacle of Maryland Heights. Brig. Gen. John G. Walker's recently arrived contingents would destroy the Chesapeake and Ohio Canal aqueduct at the mouth of the Monocacy (much as other Confederate troops would do at the Monocacy railroad bridge crossing near Frederick Junction) before continuing across the Potomac to slip around to lay siege to Harpers Ferry from Loudoun Heights. Maj. Gen. Daniel Harvey Hill's division would shepherd the reserve artillery, ordnance, and supply trains. Stuart, having detached units to work with Longstreet, Jackson, and McLaws, would "cover the route of the army, bringing up all stragglers that may have been left behind." When their missions had been completed successfully, Jackson, McLaws, and Walker would rejoin the main army at either Boonsborough or Hagerstown. Lee's timetable rested on his own army's celerity of movement as well as anticipated enemy slowness. Then, unexpectedly, and unbeknown to Lee and the others at the time, a copy of these orders fell into Federal hands.[38]

How could such a thing happen? Like so much about the Civil War, the so-called Lost Order eventually prompted controversy as well as mystery. A field of clover on the Best farm or perhaps the grove of trees that had hosted Lee's headquarters tents supposedly provided the discovery site. Several Union soldiers from the Twenty-seventh Indiana, entering the old Rebel campsite on September 13, would stumble across three cigars wrapped in a copy of the order. No Confederate ever admitted losing them. They were destined for D. H. Hill and may have been mislaid, missent, or otherwise misplaced. Years afterward, even the Yankees who found them would bicker over who should be credited with their discovery. In any event, they had the good sense to pass the papers up their chain of command, and corps commander Alpheus Williams sent them on to McClellan with the comment, "It is a document of interest and is also thought genuine." "The Lost Order represented an opportunity of a lifetime," claims McClellan biographer Stephen Sears. Army of the Potomac chronicler Jeffrey Wert agreed that its discovery "has been regarded as one of the most significant intelligence finds in American military history." McClellan's receipt of the order might have immediately set off a footrace with Lee. To Sears, however, not even this good fortune would cause Little Mac to depart from "his deliberate habits." Therein lies the rub.[39]

At the moment, convinced that the Rebel army of "120,000 men or more" intended "to attempt penetrating Pennsylvania," McClellan expended great effort trying to dissuade Halleck from defending Washington. He needed all available manpower and employed the same old lines: "There is but little probability of the enemy being in much force south of the Potomac," and while not "undervaluing the importance of holding Washington," as "it is of great consequence, but upon the success of this army the fate of the nation depends." He also battled Halleck about the Harpers Ferry garrison, doubting that Miles could hold out against Lee's numbers and might be more useful if evacuated to the main Army of the Potomac. The numbers question remained uppermost. McClellan's refrain dated to the Peninsula: "I have the mass of their troops to contend with, and they outnumber me when united." Special Order 191 yielded no clue as to Lee's actual strength in that regard. McClellan neither doubted the authenticity of the find nor other intelligence from the field corroborating its contents. But his meticulous approach, determination to verify through Pleasonton's reconnaissance, and continuing concern that Lee might spring a trap on an overly ambitious pursuit competed with an innate feeling that the Army of the Potomac had not fully recovered from Pope's mishandling and possibly lacked the discipline, the leadership, "or the legs to outrun the Army of Northern Virginia."[40]

Four days elapsed between the Lost Order's distribution and its discovery by the Federals. Had the situation changed? McClellan did not know, and so, for the moment, on September 13, he awaited more conclusive information. Of course, Lee had no knowledge yet that his order had been compromised. In fact, viewed in retrospect, more important at this point was what he did know. If Lee had been foiled at Chantilly from destroying his opponent, McClellan's rapid recovery now threatened Lee's very survival. True, the Federal response produced what the Gray Fox sought in part: drawing the Army of the Potomac into the field and away from Washington's forts so that it might be beaten and destroyed in the open. Still, the Frederick area seemed too close to that sanctuary. So Lee moved west, principally for logistical reasons, it seems, and in order to continue with plans to move on to Pennsylvania, but also to pull McClellan still further from his own logistical base at the capital. In the process, other Federals would not play to Lee's plan, particularly those at Martinsburg and Harpers Ferry.

A risk taker, Lee divided his army in anticipation that it could eradicate quickly those annoying roadblocks and reunite before McClellan's columns could pin him down to decisive battle. The Federals' movements of the past few days had shut down Lee's option of moving up the eastern side of the Catoctin/South Mountain range into Pennsylvania. McClellan's feat of raising phoenixlike an army of "a crippled nation's *defenders*" (to quote one of the army's brigadiers) and then maneuver fanlike into central Maryland effectively channeled Lee's options. In McClellan's view, he had effectively protected Washington and Baltimore as well as Pennsylvania. Those fourteen thousand scattered troops guarding the Baltimore and Ohio Railroad on the upper Potomac and lower Shenandoah threatened Lee's change of line of communications, although McClellan thought they should evacuate their exposed posts and move to better block the Cumberland Valley route to Pennsylvania, or even reinforce his outnumbered army against Lee. Halleck vetoed both ideas, demanding that the garrisons stand fast in the face of Lee's movements. The general in chief viewed Miles and White as insurance against Lee's dispatching flying columns down the Virginia side of the Potomac to strike at Washington. His stubbornness in fact forced Lee to blunder, thus affording McClellan the chance to strike a dangerously divided Army of Northern Virginia.[41]

Set against the larger unfolding panorama of Confederate counteroffensive from the Potomac to the Mississippi, Lee's political failure to raise dissident Marylanders and his decision to shift his line of communications when faced with McClellan's resurgent army loom important. Could Lee accomplish the daring task of eliminating Martinsburg and Harpers Ferry defenders and reunite his army before McClellan gave battle? Discovery of Special Order 191 cast doubt on the wisdom of his stratagem. But for that matter, could

McClellan successfully exploit his stroke of luck? Uncertain about his army's condition for prolonged heavy campaigning and desperate fighting, especially from an organizational and logistical standpoint, the Army of the Potomac commander deliberately chose to methodically measure the unfolding situation. Worried about Lee's strength, if not his larger intent (whether or not he intended a stand in Maryland, a march into Pennsylvania, or even a return to Virginia), Little Mac truly could not afford to react rashly to Lee's Lost Orders. Even if divided and on the move, McClellan knew, Lee was still dangerous. For his part, Lee still hoped to end the war by defeating his enemy "in their own backyard." Thus far, he had partially succeeded, and confident that his men could outrace the Yankees, he pressed forward with his base shift to the Shenandoah axis. Without knowing it, both sides had reached the possible tipping point of the campaign and perhaps the war. As of mid-September, the result hung in the balance.[42]

Many in Federal blue seemed unaware of the full ramifications of events at this time. Surgeon John B. Bashler of the Eighty-First Pennsylvania had written a cousin from a temporary camp on the march near Rockville, Maryland, the same day Lee's Order 191 had been written. They had been moving since mid-August, said Bashler, but without the aid of his diary (lost in transit), he could not remember "from what point, proclivity, swamp or period," he had written. They were covering anywhere from three to twenty-four miles per day, subsisting and pursuing "the same irregularity," with green peaches, apples, and berries together with a part of a government-provided biscuit, even a confiscated turkey on occasion for breakfast. "Like the pendulum of a clock, or the ever rattling tongue of woman (some) or in illustration of perpetual motion," he thought, "we have been going—moving," on "hardtack and salt horse, through a heavy rain and desperate roads," while "my fatigue baffles all description." Still, Bashler remained alert to the background picture unfolding around him.[43]

The surgeon then launched into a harangue about the war's bigger picture. "From what I can learn, our friends in the North cannot realize anything but defeat in our late movements," he bemoaned. However, let us look at it for a moment, he added quickly. "Here were perhaps 60,000 efficient men on the Peninsula, safe from allmost [sic] any imaginable army that could be brot [sic] against them," unlining his penciled handwriting, "*perfectly secure but what could we accomplish*[?]" "Holding a perfectly desolate country, with scarcely [any] other vegetation than scrub oak or pines, in a most demoralizing region for an army of mercurial men and nothing to win or lose," Bashler observed. "Wisdom and fool hardiness combined pushed Bully Pope into Va," and *you know the results*, he once more underlined. McClellan for a short while "suffered martyrdom in all the nobleness of greatness," thought Bashler. It was he after all "the depreciation by Northern fanatical envious demagogues, who care more for self aggrandizement than for our beloved country," who "had to move forward and relieve Pope from his perilous position." "Ah," Bashler sighed, "the rejoicing of his forces, the fullness of hearts on the reception of his full reinstatement was worth more than a months leave of absence to those who compose his invincible army," pronounced Bashler. The camps abounded in song, he noted, quoting the words of one popular ditty of the moment, "McClellan's our leader, he's gallant and strong, for God and our Country, we are marching along." Again, he underlined; *"History will only record his worth, God Bless our brave little Mac and his Army."*

But Bashler had not finished. "We have withdrawn from one of the most barren, devastated countries—you or those at home cannot imagine the wretchedness and misery that follows the track of war." We avoid "transportation of subsistence, our posts are reduced to small camps, we live and breathe in pure country air, where productions of the soil once more greet and cheer us when nature turns us to her God and makes us thankful for his goodness" and where "we veterans can recruit both in number and health in close communication with our friends and a hundred other salutary considerations."

Besides, "we may draw Jackson this side of the Potomac where his fate is sealed," Bashler promised, "never will those who rashly cross return. It was so written, he thought, "and will be accomplished," he decided. Fear not, he told his cousin, "our prospects were never better for a speedy solution of this infamous unholy Rebellion and the army never enjoyed a better spirit." "Exultant in hope," Bashler signed his letter and moved on with his gallant leader and comrades in arms toward their rendezvous with destiny in the hills of western Maryland.

⇾ 7 ⇽

South Mountain and Harpers Ferry

THE ARMY OF NORTHERN VIRGINIA evacuated its Monocacy camps on the morning of September 10, taking up the line of march west through Frederick. Possibly seventy thousand to seventy-five thousand would pass through the town in the process. The Confederates left behind few supporters among the populace but did not harm Unionist houses or barns. In fact only John W. Garrett's railroad bridge across the Monocacy and adjacent company property were targeted. The railroad president wired McClellan at 10:00 p.m. the next day that the bridge was totally gone, with even the masonry piers and abutments greatly damaged. Yet he felt the structure could be put back in operation within four days and trains could be gotten to the eastern side from Washington in five hours. If Harpers Ferry could be held, said Garrett, "and the enemy driven from the intermediate line, the road through can be used with but little delay." This was important logistically for McClellan, but even more so for maintaining ties with the Ohio Valley. Still, Sgt. Benjamin D. Hirst of the Fourteenth Connecticut expressed shock when crossing the Monocacy River: "The first signs of active war, the Depot and railroad was a heap of ruins, and the stench of dead horses and men was very disagreeable."[1]

Lee's men took nearly two days transiting Frederick. A photographer memorialized one contingent halted in front of Rosenstock's dry goods and clothing store on Market Street. A more muted reception attended their departure than their arrival the week before. Their novelty had worn off even among secessionists. A few people stood at curbside receiving cheers and jeers from the passing troops, and a reputedly inebriated Maj. Gen. Howell Cobb (former U.S treasury secretary and speaker of the House) led his Georgians past scowling onlookers with a challenge to the ladies to take the names of recalcitrant menfolk and he would attend to them upon his return. Three days later, Cobb would be beating a fast retreat off Crampton's Gap on South Mountain, his vow never to be fulfilled. Capt. William Blackford, one of J. E. B. Stuart's aides, netted a plum pudding from an admirer as he rode through town. Most of the residents merely bade the Rebels good riddance, largely due to their appearance.[2]

Lee's soldiers were "the dirtiest men I ever saw," commented Leighton Parks, "a most ragged, lean, and hungry set of wolves." Dr. Lewis H. Steiner, a resident who had been assisting the U.S. Sanitary Commission in the city before the visitors' arrival, declared, "A dirtier, filthier, a more unsavory set of human beings never strolled through a town." These were "the deliverers of Maryland from Lincoln's oppressive yoke," he scoffed. Steiner, for one, could not contain his joy when George B. McClellan and his crisp-looking Union staff rode into town on September 13, received "on all sides with the most unlimited expressions of delight." Mothers held their babies toward the general "as their deliverer from a foreign army," he recounted. Young women pressed close, with little flags for McClellan's horse Dan's bridle and bunches of flowers for his rider. The general was overwhelmed, although one wonders if these same young women might not have been equally emotional earlier with Lee, Jackson, and Stuart. The Army of Northern Virginia's departure occasioned an anonymous Unionist wag to counter James Randall with an "Answer to My Maryland." Between the refrains came stanzas like the following:

> The rebel feet are on our shore,
> I smell 'em half a mile or more;
> Their sockless hordes are at my door,
> their drunken generals on my floor;
> What now can sweet Baltimore?
> Maryland, My Maryland!

And finally,

> To get thee clean—'tis truth I speak—
> Would dirty every stream and creek,
> From Potomac to Chesapeake,
> Maryland, My Maryland.[3]

No, most Marylanders hardly regretted Lee's departure. Lt. George Wilson Booth of the First Maryland (CSA) admitted later that the appearance of "our men was not conducive to the inspiring of confidence." Southern pundits tried to put a good face on the adventure north of the Potomac. *Charleston Daily Courier* correspondent Felix Gregory De Fontaine, traveling with the army and writing as "PERSONNE," estimated that secessionist sympathy in Frederick stood at about 50 percent. True, Confederate money had been shunned and some thievery had occurred despite Lee's orders. Still, Marylanders should not complain about rape, pillage, or burning as the army left town, he observed. De Fontaine and others failed to mention a few tense moments, such as the famous Barbara Frietchie (or Fritchie) incident. As Jackson's column reputedly crossed Carroll Creek on West Patrick Street, the men spotted a small brick bungalow at water's edge sporting the Stars and Stripes. One of the city's oldest residents, Frietchie had braved Rebel ire with her banner. Apparently many of her neighbors in town had been doing so too. Mrs. Mary Quantrell several blocks away also numbered among the invaders' tormentors. But it was Dame Barbara who subsequently gained fame in poet John Greenleaf Whittier's testament to her heroics with the well-publicized line, "Shoot if you must, this old gray head, but spare your country's flag." After Frietchie saucily flung her defiance at the passing Stonewall Jackson, Old Blue Light supposedly retreated sheepishly, declaring, "Who touches a hair of yon gray head, dies like a dog! March on!"[4]

Little matter that Jackson was really a street or two away visiting his old friend, the city's Presbyterian minister, the Rev. Dr. Ross, and apparently missed any such encounter with Frietchie. The old woman died in December and the Boston Bard went to his grave believing the story as presented to him. His poetic account of this Frederick woman inspired Yankee spirits at this bleak time of the war as reflecting a loyal Maryland. The ultimate irony may have been that Frietchie undoubtedly waved her flag, not before Jackson and his men, but when liberated the next day by Maj. Gen. Ambrose Burnside's Federals. The flag was a small one, taken from its hiding place in her family Bible. When Brig. Gen. Jesse Reno passed by and heard of her supposed defiance of the enemy, he stopped to meet and salute her. Offering to purchase her flag, which she refused to sell, Reno secured another from her. Placing it in his saddlebag, he rode off to an appointment with death on South Mountain. The truth or fiction of the Frietchie incident notwithstanding, Union soldiers encountered Frederick sidewalks crowded with citizens of "every age, sex, and color" basking in a "wild spontaneous outcry of joy." At Clarksburg, in upper Montgomery County, the general himself shared a moment with a loyal family viewing their carte-de-visite albums. McClellan wrote his wife, "[I] found the Union sentiment much stronger in this region than I had expected," with people "disposed to be very kind & polite to me." They invited him into their homes and offered him meals and generally evidenced "other acts of kindness that were quite unknown in the Peninsula."[5]

Little wonder that McClellan rhapsodized to Ellen about traveling through delightful countryside, broken up "with lovely valleys in all directions and fine mountains in the distance," a tonic for a man of McClellan's temperament. Others, like Lt. Col. Griffin Stedman of the Eleventh Connecticut, concluded that there was "not much to tell of our march through Maryland." In fact, with supply wagons far behind, the famished and fatigued Federals welcomed patriotic locals with their pails of milk and water, pies, cakes, and bread, along with expressions of thanks and loyalty. They also foraged enthusiastically; though not pillaging the vicinity, sufficient drunkenness and impromptu requisitioning from the economy raised many protests in the community. The culprits may have been raw regiments unaccustomed to army regulations. Identified secessionists suffered particular confiscation and abuse, and the pace of McClellan's advance slowed noticeably from such deviation. Once the Monocacy had been crossed, a Confederate rear guard contested their entry into Frederick City. Skirmishing took place all the way from the renowned "Jug" bridge on the National road east of town (where Wade Hampton's gray-clad brigade failed to destroy the structure with explosives), through the center of the city (a firefight left a number of dead horses as well as fallen troopers in the streets), and then west to Catoctin Mountain. By that point, Frederick diarist Jacob Engelbrecht noted approvingly, bluecoats came "flocking into town from nearly every point of the compass."[6]

McClellan enjoyed the flowers and adulation and settled into camp on the Steiner farm just west of town. He had planned for Burnside's wing together with Pleasonton's horsemen to immediately push ahead into Middletown Valley between the Catoctin and South mountains. Soon he was socializing with his old friend Burnside and other senior army commanders. A citizens' delegation from Frederick appeared just about the time that brigadier Alpheus Williams arrived with Lee's Lost Order. Not wishing to disclose details to prying civilian eyes, McClellan exclaimed emphatically, "Now I know what to do." But did he? No doubt "the finding of this paper was a piece of rare good fortune," suggested veteran Union officer and historian Francis Winthrop Palfrey. However, exploitation still depended on Federal response. "Tomorrow we will pitch into his center," Little Mac told his commanders that evening, according to Brig. Gen. John Gibbon. "If you people will only do two good hard days' marching I will put Lee in a position he will find hard to get out of." Gibbon promptly volunteered that his command would do its part. Time would tell, as Gibbon rode back to his bivouac in far better spirits than he had been in a month. As events would prove, it could not be said that McClellan "did not act with considerable energy," commented Palfrey, "but he did not act with sufficient [energy]." Maybe it was Palfrey who first pointed out that opportunity lay within reach, "such an opportunity as hardly ever presented itself." And, he added, McClellan "almost grasped it, but not quite." Such criticism could only partially account for the subsequent turn of events.[7]

Lee had the jump on his opponent time-wise as his subordinates promptly disappeared over the Catoctin range to the west of Frederick. Perhaps "Johnny Reb" truly could march faster and fight harder than "Billy Yank." Jackson even practiced a bit of deception when leaving Frederick by ostentatiously seeking maps of Chambersburg, Pennsylvania, as if to indicate that was his destination. Unionists quickly spread that news to both military and public sectors, and panic gripped the Cumberland Valley. Perhaps the icy reception among Unionists west of Frederick spurred the marching Rebels to a faster pace. When the army passed through Middletown, Capt. Greenlee Davidson of Virginia described the people "as valid as those of any village in Massachusetts or Vermont," since the town held the reputation "of being the bitterest abolition hole in the state." Stores and houses were shuttered and the men had departed, leaving only young women with red, white, and blue ribbons to taunt the marchers. The Rebels ordered Nancy Crouse and Effie Titlow to turn over their Stars and Stripes hanging from their upstairs window, but like Barbara Frietchie in Frederick, they resisted. This incident spawned a local verse about a "Valley maid" who, "beneath the porch of her humble house," had "boldly defied the men in gray." Jackson merely muttered, "We evidently have no friends in this town." Despite the countryside being in the highest state of cultivation, with magnificent barns and roomy smokehouses, according to Davidson, the Confederates failed to secure so much as "a pound of meat or a bushel of corn." The people almost without exception "are soul and body Union shriekers," thought Davidson. "If we stay in this portion of Maryland we will soon starve," unless "the system of impressments is resorted to."[8]

Jackson hurried along, intent on meeting Lee's deadline of noon on September 12, when he and Maj. Gen. Lafayette McLaws should capture or disperse Federal garrisons at Martinsburg and Harpers Ferry. Jackson might have moved more quickly via the Old Sharpsburg road west of Middletown but for an unexpected encounter with Federal outriders in Boonsboro just over South Mountain. That encounter spooked the general into selecting a more westerly direction to the Potomac via Williamsport, thus incurring delay. Nonetheless, his foot cavalry covered the twenty-five miles to the crossing by late the next afternoon. Stonewall dispatched a division to corner Brig. Gen. Julius White's Federals at Martinsburg only to discover that his quarry had joined Col. Dixon Miles at Harpers Ferry. Jackson followed dutifully so that the two sides soon confronted each other on Bolivar Heights, just outside the arsenal town, on September 12. Jackson then awaited word from McLaws and Maj. Gen. John G. Walker, who were supposed to surround the defenders from commanding positions on Maryland Heights and Loudoun Heights. McLaws had marched through Burkittsville, across South Mountain at Crampton's Gap, and gained Pleasant Valley before trekking up Elk Ridge (which became Maryland Heights at its southern extremity). Walker appeared at about the same time across the river, having failed to destroy the Chesapeake and Ohio Canal locks on the Maryland side while taking a circuitous route from Frederick to Point of Rocks and thence via

Hillsboro. Together the trio sealed the fate of Harpers Ferry, commented Palfrey later, but did not meet Lee's deadline for capture.[9]

If the town lay at the mercy of the enemy, why did its garrison stand in place rather than evacuate? At first, McClellan, like Lee, anticipated that lower valley garrisons might leave upon the Confederates' approach. McClellan wanted the Martinsburg and Harpers Ferry contingents to join the main army. He had argued the case with Halleck all the previous week, but to no avail. Just as he and Halleck could never agree on the importance of or the method for defending Washington, so the pair never found accord concerning the use of Miles and White, until the very day that Jackson and his colleagues completed their investment. McClellan had humored Halleck by slowing the forward movements of Franklin and Darius Couch close by the Potomac so as to provide cover for Washington. But he never backed off his contention: "Even if Washington should be taken while these armies are confronting each other, this would not, in my judgment, bear comparison with the ruin and disasters which would follow a signal defeat of this Army." Halleck constantly rejoined, "You attach too little importance to the capital," while assuring his principal field marshal, "The capture of this place will throw us back six months, if it should not destroy us." Halleck hamstrung McClellan by viewing Harpers Ferry as affecting that defense of Washington as well as posing a major problem for Lee. He retained Miles and White possibly too long in position, denying them any real freedom of action that might help McClellan or, for that matter, other threatened areas like Pennsylvania. On the other hand, neither Miles nor White might have done much with those missions. At the very least, McClellan and Halleck expected the pair to fight, and their defense of Harpers Ferry would pose serious problems for Lee's plans.[10]

McClellan viewed Miles and White, along with at least twenty-five thousand veteran troops from the Virginia campaigns as well as those in Washington garrisons, as reinforcement necessary to even his odds with Lee. Maj. Gen. John Wool, department commander at Baltimore, offered to transfer the Harpers Ferry garrison to McClellan's use, but Halleck balked, claiming that Miles's "only chance is to defend his works till [McClellan] can open communication with him," and then a transfer might be accomplished. The top Union general very reluctantly reempowered Fitz John Porter to march to McClellan's aid with twenty-one thousand men from Washington, acceding to President

Lincoln's wishes sent to McClellan at 6:00 p.m. on September 11: "I am for sending you all that can be spared, and I hope others can follow Porter very soon." On the other hand, McClellan also felt pressure directly from Baltimore and Ohio Railroad officials and Pennsylvania governor Andrew G. Curtin, all clamoring for protection. Inconclusive intelligence reports from Pleasonton's reconnaissance and citizenry only further inflated enemy strength and location, although the cavalryman eventually confirmed that Lee's army seemed to be moving as the Lost Order directed.[11]

In the meantime, Lee would not become apprised of the Federal occupation of Frederick for another twenty-four hours. By early afternoon on September 12, Jackson informed his chief of delay in finishing the task at Harpers Ferry. At this point, Longstreet's corps had closed on Hagerstown (rumored to possess quantities of flour, necessary to the army's well-being), where Lee pitched his headquarters tent. D. H. Hill had taken position at Boonsboro covering the National pike crossing of South Mountain. Stuart screened the army's rear west of Frederick, skirmishing with McClellan's advance coming over Catoctin Mountain, and sent news of that progress through Hill for transmittal to headquarters. Lee spent the day writing President Davis that his dispersed army still had time to complete its various missions and reconcentrate for new endeavors. He reiterated his original intent to concentrate at Hagerstown from the onset of the Potomac crossing and thus free the northern Virginia frontier of enemy presence and implied threat to Richmond. Lee admitted assuming that the Federals would retire altogether from the Shenandoah. He also acknowledged a better reception in Hagerstown (compared with the Frederick region), where his quartermasters purchased much-needed flour but not beef and bacon or shoes for his ill-shod men. He alluded to drawing McClellan even farther from his Washington base and finally remembered to tell Davis about his proclamation to the people of Maryland.[12]

Then, by nightfall on September 13, a Frederick citizen slipped a note to Stuart, who sent it on to Lee, alerting the army commander to the fact that Special Order 191 had been compromised. Perhaps more alarming to Lee was the realization that, indeed, McClellan's pursuit had reached Frederick and was moving "more rapidly than convenient." In fact, the Federals reached the eastern foot of South Mountain by that evening. Lee thought that McClellan would move directly to raise any investment of Harpers Ferry. Still, he knew instinctively that he had to draw his forces together to blunt the Federal advance. Longstreet advised dong so at Sharpsburg. Lee ducked the decision in order to first permit Jackson, McLaws, and Walker to complete their mission. He wrote several anxious messages specifically to McLaws in that regard. Once successful, McLaws was to move to Sharpsburg. D. H. Hill and Stuart, meanwhile, would have to defend the South Mountain passes, while Longstreet moved back to Boonsboro to support that effort. Longstreet protested that such heavy marching would tire his foot-sore men and make them of little help in the event of battle. But he obeyed. To historian Joseph Harsh, Lee lost the initiative because "he underestimated the rate and character of the advance of the Federal army" and "attempted to accomplish too much with the limited resources available"—not because McClellan had possession of the Lost Order.[13]

No doubt, as McClellan informed Halleck one month and two major battles later, he had "confidently expected that [Harpers Ferry] would hold out until we had carried the mountains and were in a position to make a detachment for its relief." When sufficient intelligence had been gleaned, the Federal commander directed two principal pursuit columns forward over Catoctin and South mountains. One would go through Jefferson to Burkittsville and Crampton's Gap, directed toward freeing Harpers Ferry. The second column would head straight west from Frederick on the National road via Middletown and over Turner's Gap to Boonsboro to fix and fight Lee's main army. As McClellan told VI Corps commander Maj. Gen. William B. Franklin, he planned to cut the enemy in two and beat him in detail. McClellan would accompany that part of the army taking the National road, indicating that Lee's army, not Harpers Ferry, dictated his main effort. To date, McClellan had not imposed tough marches on his army, as the necessity of refitting campaign-weary troops preyed on his mind. Precisely why he let slip those critical hours of the afternoon and evening of September 13 before exploiting the captured orders has prompted wonder. Ever fearful of ambush, he awaited Pleasonton's critical scouting reports, focusing merely on paperwork and basking in the rosy afterglow of Frederick's friendly reception, ever confident that he had Lee in a box. Letters to wife Mary Ellen, to Adj. Gen. Lorenzo Thomas about reorganizing and reinforcing his regular artillery batteries, and to Pennsylvania governor Curtin concerning transferring Brig. Gen. John Reynolds from Hooker's corps to bolster Keystone State defenses suggested a certain focus, if not purpose. Finally piecing together reports from Pleasonton about sounds of gunfire from Harpers Ferry and signal station reports from Sugarloaf Mountain, McClellan began dictating movement orders at 6:00 p.m. on September 13. Celerity of movement would be subordinates' responsibility.[14]

McClellan did not issue orders to Franklin to move his troops forward until 6:20 p.m. Those orders, somewhat florid in detail, called for the VI Corps to march the next morning from its bivouacs far back at Buckeystown on the Monocacy to Crampton's Gap and thence to relief of Harpers Ferry—a long, time-consuming trek by any standard. After disclosing what he knew of Lee's plans and ordering a designated early start for Pleasonton and Hooker, followed by other corps toward Turner's Gap, McClellan enumerated what he wanted Franklin to accomplish. Apparently it did not include the VI Corps marching in the cooler night air to make up the distance from the rear at Buckeystown. McClellan particularly indicated that Franklin should not wait for Darius Couch's division to close up but was to move at daybreak via Jefferson and Burkittsville on the road to Rohrersville beyond Crampton's Gap. He should seize that pass as soon as practicable if undefended, but if occupied by the enemy, then Franklin should deploy and commence the attack "about half an hour after you hear severe firing at the pass on the Hagerstown pike, where the main body will attack." Franklin's responsibility "will be first to cut off, destroy, or capture McLaws['s] command," presumably so focused on its Harpers Ferry mission that it would not protect its rear, "and relieve Colonel Miles."

That done, and McClellan had no way of knowing how long it might take, Franklin and Miles (having destroyed the Harpers Ferry bridges and leaving a small contingent to prevent the rebels "from passing the ford" upriver at Shepherdstown) would march together for Rohrersville if Burnside and Hooker had failed to breach Turner's Gap. If the attacks by Burnside and Hooker on South Mountain to the north proved successful, then Franklin and Miles were to move to Sharpsburg and Williamsport to cut off Hill and Longstreet or prevent Jackson's repassage of the Potomac. Perhaps the army commander included too much information before concluding, "I have sufficiently explained my intentions." McClellan asked his friend

Franklin "at this important moment" to apply "all of your intellect & utmost activity that a general can exercise." But McClellan also offered an escape to the VI Corps commander: "Knowing my views and intentions you are fully authorized to change any of the details of this order as circumstances may change, provided the purpose is carried out."

McClellan probably expected too much from the languid Franklin. "Force your Colonels to prevent straggling & bring every available man into action," he advised. Perhaps he also underestimated the determination of Confederate resistance at Crampton's Gap. That he did not send Franklin to Harpers Ferry via the turnpike through Knoxville came from information that the enemy "were anticipating our approach in that direction, and had established batteries on the south side of the Potomac." In McClellan's view, the road through Crampton's into Pleasant Valley in the rear of Maryland Heights "was the only one which afforded any reasonable prospect of carrying that formidable position." But McClellan's real reason could be ascertained when he further observed, "At the same time, the troops upon that road were in better relation to the main body of the forces." He wanted all his subordinates within close supporting distance of one another so as not to be surprised and beaten in detail. Franklin claimed at 10:00 p.m. that he received and understood his orders: "[I] will do my best to carry them out." His command would begin the effort at 5:30 a.m. on September 14.[15]

The situation at South Mountain and Harpers Ferry assumed center stage for both armies. McLaws ran into delays gaining Maryland Heights on September 12 as Walker and Jackson took position across the Potomac investing Harpers Ferry. All of these maneuvers consumed precious time on the schedule prescribed by Special Order 191. McLaws eventually blocked Miles's downriver escape route at Weverton below Sandy Hook, while Walker and Jackson similarly sealed the Virginia egress for the garrison over the next two days. Apparently nobody closed a road across the river to Antietam Forge, however. Two brigades of McLaws's infantry had to drag themselves across the stony, wooded, and almost trackless slopes from Solomon's Gap and up into position on Elk Ridge as it fused with Maryland Heights. They soon engaged Yankee skirmishers sent to dispute their progress. The defenders' abatis and musketry and the terrain itself hampered the Confederate effort. Nonetheless, the contested control of Maryland Heights sealed the fate of Miles's command. The fifteen-hundred-foot elevation commanded all else in the area. McClellan and others had argued that the place should be a last-ditch redoubt "until it could be relieved by the Army of the Potomac."[16]

Brigade commander Col. Thomas H. Ford of the Thirty-second Ohio had responsibility for defending Maryland Heights. A prewar politician, Ford suffered from a chronic abscess on his buttocks yet remained on duty when reporting with White's command from Winchester and Martinsburg. Miles sent him across to command heavy artillery batteries that had been emplaced on Maryland Heights to provide distance fire for defending the town, Bolivar Heights, and Camp Hill to the west. Those guns pointed in the wrong direction for countering McLaws's approach. Ford's troops did occupy two lines of abatis entanglements and a breastwork known as the "Lookout," although all were inadequate for contesting any determined assault in strength from the north. Much depended on Ford and his men, as well as the rest of Miles's defenders on the ridgeline west of Bolivar. Thomas Jefferson had once claimed the picturesque Ferry site worth crossing the Atlantic to see, and Union veteran Palfrey would echo the sentiment years later by asserting that a man might "travel far and wide in America without coming upon a lovelier spot than the heights above Harper's Ferry." Yet in 1862 the arsenal town possessed no particular attractions and had largely been shut down or otherwise made destitute by the war. Granted, the place had symbolic and strategic meaning, as three years before John Brown's incendiary raid to incite slave rebellion in Virginia had essentially started the conflict at this spot. But above all, the confluence of the Shenandoah River with the Potomac and a branch rail line to Winchester geographically opened the Shenandoah Valley. For that reason Harpers Ferry had to be defended at all cost.[17]

It appeared that the Federals might do just that for a time on September 13. Then success suddenly slipped from their grasp in the late afternoon as a raw New York regiment crumbled before McLaws's pressure on Maryland Heights. "My God, Colonel Ford is evacuating his position, we must stop it," Miles exclaimed when he witnessed the tired and beaten Federals dribbling down the mountainside at 4:00 p.m. He rushed across to rally the men, shouting to Ford, "You will and you must hold out." It was too late, as a young lieutenant had started the collapse by merely waving his hat, indicating withdrawal.

The Federals spiked the heavy naval guns and retired across to town before joining the main force about to confront Jackson beyond Bolivar. An unhappy Miles had no choice now but to grimly hang on pending relief as the Confederates completed their encirclement by moving artillery onto Maryland and Loudon heights to pound the besieged into submission. McLaws experienced great trouble bringing four Parrott guns to the summit of Maryland Heights to effectively join Jackson and Walker with long-range bombardment. Yet once McLaws's and Walker's guns opened up and Jackson edged his infantry ever closer to Federal lines, it was simply a matter of time before the contest reached a conclusion. Miles's own actions soon determined the course.[18]

Indeed, much of the story of those fateful autumn days at Harpers Ferry centered on Col. Dixon Miles. The fifty-eight-year-old regular officer counted forty years in uniform, with service on the western frontier and in the Mexican War. In 1862, the native Marylander labored under a double cloud: his doubted loyalty and a liking for liquor. In fact, allegations of drunkenness in an altercation with Col. Israel Richardson the previous year at the battle of First Bull Run further clouded his reputation. Accordingly he was exiled to guarding John Garrett's Baltimore and Ohio Railroad in western Maryland. Irascibility, the reputation for intoxication, and a stubbornness born of age and fatigue, stagnancy in rank, and frustration with his present assignment combined with ambition for redemption by the time Jackson's column appeared. Still, Miles's departmental commander at Baltimore (himself the oldest officer to exercise active command on either side during the war) felt his subordinate was the best officer in his command and urged him to hold his position. Wool and Miles had exchanged numerous dispatches earlier concerning the indefensibility of Harpers Ferry and what to do about it. Wool had inspected the place in August and had suggested improvements to the defense of Maryland Heights. Miles either shelved or only partially heeded Wool's admonitions. He especially disregarded subordinates' protestations about Harpers Ferry's weakness once Lee had crossed into Maryland and undertook no aggressive reconnaissance that might have aided McClellan. He hunkered down, and Ford's collapse on September 13 made defense virtually impossible. White, Miles's superior in rank, deferred to Miles, who disdained all requests from subordinates to evacuate along the base of Maryland Heights to Antietam Forge. Meanwhile the Confederate noose closed around him.[19]

Following the loss of Maryland Heights, the critical point of action temporarily shifted to the South Mountain passes. A bright Sunday morning, September 14, greeted McClellan's troops snaking their way across Middletown Valley toward the three prominent passageways over South Mountain. Reveille had sounded for many of them at 4:00 a.m., sunrise came at 5:49, and a Frederick recording station noted the 7:00 a.m. temperature at a very pleasant fifty-eight degrees, just right for rapid marching. John Gibbon's men could make out the city's spires and church bells behind them that beautiful morning, although there seemed to be something like the sound of thunder to the southwest from the direction of Harpers Ferry. Throughout the army, as soldiers stretched, wheezed, and completed their toilets before venturing back on the road, the universal feeling was We have got a general now, and we will show the country what we can do. That general, McClellan, remained at Frederick, wiring Washington at 9:00 a.m. that he had received a critical message from Miles at Harpers Ferry noting the loss of Maryland Heights. Miles thought he could hold perhaps two days longer, said McClellan: "If he holds out today I can probably save him." The whole Army of the Potomac was moving as rapidly as possible, he contended. He also wrote his wife sometime that morning that he was "off to try to relieve Harper's Ferry" and anticipated "a serious engagement today & perhaps a general battle for if we have one at all during the operation it ought to be today or tomorrow." Reflecting the same faith that drove Lee, the Federal leader added, "I feel as reasonably confident of success as any one well can who trusts in an higher power & does not know what its decision will be." He enclosed a little flag that an enthusiastic Frederick matron had thrust into Dan's bridle.[20]

Leaving Frederick, McClellan and his large staff established a command post in a hilltop field west of Middletown to watch the action unfold at Turner's Gap. Pleasonton's horsemen had moved to the foot of the mountain the previous evening, and Cox's newly arrived Kanawha division of Reno's IX Corps had moved out early on the National pike. Both parties soon received the opening rounds from Confederate guns in the pass. The day before, the cavalry chief had fanned his squadrons westward to find the elusive Rebels while sending Col. A. T. McReynolds's fourth brigade and a section of artillery northward toward Gettysburg, across the state line in Pennsylvania, in response to reports of Rebels in that direction. Likewise, he separated out Col. R. H. Rush and his lancer regiment to operate with Franklin to the south at Crampton's Gap. Mainly, however, Col. John Farnsworth's brigade had steadily pushed J. E. B. Stuart's rear guard back from Hagan's Gap in Catoctin Mountain through Middletown and on up into Turner's Gap, discovering the defensive strength of the defile in the process. One hastily gathered force of Yankees had only narrowed missed uncovering how weakly held was Crampton's Gap. Overall, Pleasonton discovered passes north and south of Turner's that offered opportunities to outflank any stubborn resistance in that principal gap.

The skirmishing had been so crisp that Pleasonton contentedly let McClellan's infantry assume principal responsibility for whatever battle might develop on September 14. Eventually the Federals advancing on Turner's Gap would receive support from Jesse Reno's IX Corps while Gibbon's veteran Midwesterners would advance straight ahead toward Turner's Gap. Reno's people filed off to the south via the Old Sharpsburg road to outflank the Confederates through Fox's Gap. It was here that British Maj. Gen. Edward Braddock's ill-fated column had passed toward the Ohio country over a century before, although probably none of those present on September 14 knew or cared. Eventually more Federals under Fighting Joe Hooker would try the same flanking maneuver to the north via Mt. Tabor Church and Frosttown, converging at the Mountain House tavern in the gap's saddle. McClellan assumed that Franklin would rapidly march from Buckeystown to Burkittsville and assault Crampton's Gap, six miles distant from Fox's and Turner's, in coordination with Reno and Hooker.[21]

Few on the Federal side could be sure what precisely awaited them in any of the South Mountain passes. Cox, for instance, encountered a paroled Union colonel, Augustus Moor, just outside Bolivar, who greeted him with the cryptic comment, "My God! Be careful," indicating that the Rebels were in force up on the mountain. Because much of the Army of the Potomac had encamped so far back in the Frederick and Buckeystown area, it would take most of the day to march over hill and dale to get to South Mountain in sufficient numbers. If truly rested, as their commander intended, the blue-coated soldiers should have made the distance in short order. Once in position, however, they would still encounter daunting obstacles. The defenders occupied tangled ravines and hollows, as well as steep, heavily wooded slopes only intermittently broken by hard-scrabble, cultivated fields surrounded by stone and wooden fences erected by intrepid yeomen farmers like Daniel Wise and his family at Fox's Gap. Alert to surprise on unfamiliar roads, the Army of the Potomac felt its way forward gingerly. Besides, Miles's holding situation at Harpers Ferry, Lee's presumed numerical superiority, and the absence of any specific reference to defending South Mountain in Special Order 191 weighed on McClellan's mind. Reports referring to enemy movement back across the Potomac indicated a possible dash down the south side of the river to Washington. Above all, the general focused on what was immediately in front at Turner's and Fox's gaps. Crampton's Gap and Harpers Ferry were Franklin's responsibility.[22]

Confederate Daniel Harvey Hill had the unenviable task of covering a lot of ground in the face of the main Union advance. The situation was this: brigadier Samuel Garland's men faced Reno's advance at Fox's Gap; Col. Alfred Holt Colquitt stood before Gibbon's advance at Turner's pass; and Brig. Gen. Robert Rodes moved to hold Frosttown Gap to the north. Fortunately, a wood road connected Turner's and Fox's gaps to aid his defense. Still, there were three avenues of approach, and Colquitt had told Hill about the impressive array of enemy campfires spread before him across the Middletown Valley the night before. Hill rode up the mountain to see for himself and located only Col. Thomas L. Rosser with two hundred cavalrymen and an artillery battery posted to dispute passage. Stuart had vacated the place, thinking the real threat might be against McLaws's rear at Crampton's Gap. With Yankee movements clearly discernable before him, Hill called up G. B. Anderson's brigade to reinforce Colquitt's eleven-hundred-man Georgia–Alabama brigade set squarely behind a stone fence beside the National pike. They would hold this position later in the day against Gibbon's Iron Brigade, relentlessly clambering their way up into the pass through rock-strewn and tangled ravines.[23]

By 9:00 a.m. Cox's division made contact with Garland's thinly spread brigade at Fox's Gap, and the fight for South Mountain was on. It would continue all day, spurred by the Ohioan's initial success. In fact, Cox's Kanawhans simply blustered their way up the Old Sharpsburg road, killed Garland, and routed his command back on Colquitt and Hill at Turner's Gap by late morning. Then Confederate artillery fire found its mark among the victors and the Federals with-

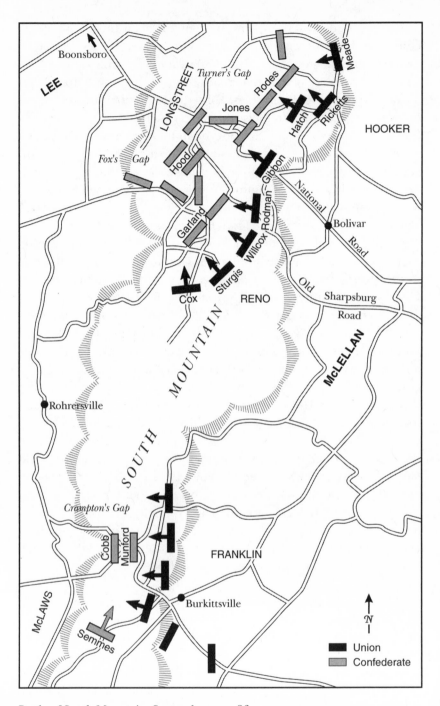

Battle of South Mountain, September 14, 1862

drew, their ammunition low and the men fatigued by hand-to-hand fighting. Cox paused, awaiting reinforcement, as the rest of the IX Corps lay out of immediate supporting range. A lull descended over that part of the battlefield by noon, as if by mutual consent an unspoken truce had been declared until both contestants should receive reinforcements to enable them to again close with one another. By this time Franklin had finally gotten to Burkittsville and McClellan had begun a spate of dispatches designed to spur matters along. Suddenly evidencing great anxiety about the Harpers Ferry relief column, he wrote Franklin near noon, reiterating Miles's predicament (but not the colonel's confidence at holding out) and how matters were going at the other gaps. "Please lose no time in driving the rebel cavalry out of Burkeadsville [*sic*]," McClellan enjoined, and taking Crampton's Gap. He wanted to be kept informed of "everything transpiring at the pass before you," especially the enemy's strength and position. Franklin did so forty-five minutes later, noting the defenders' artillery support and adding, "We may have a heavy fight to get the pass."[24]

McClellan replied in turn at 2:00 p.m. instructing the corps commander to hurry Couch's IV Corps division, mass troops, "and carry Burkittsville at any cost." Everyone now faced strong opposition at all the South Mountain passes, he observed. If Franklin found the enemy "in very great force at the pass," McClellan ordered, "amuse them as best you can so to retain them there" (an odd turn of phrase considering the need to break through at Crampton's and lift the Harpers Ferry siege). McClellan would throw the mass of the army at the other passes: "If I carry that it will clear the way for you, and you must then follow the enemy as rapidly as possible." Such instructions gave the normally cautious Franklin even more excuse to "amuse" his opposition all afternoon while awaiting Couch and dithering about some well-posted but flankable Rebels behind a stone fence on the lower slopes just outside the village. Of course, Franklin still had the previous night's instruction that told him to commence his own attack "about a half an hour after you hear severe firing at the pass on the Hagerstown pike." In any case, McClellan sent a 1:00 p.m. dispatch to Miles at Harpers Ferry enumerating efforts at relief then under way. "You may count on our making every effort to relieve you— you may count upon my accomplishing that object," he promised. Reoccupying Maryland Heights, if possible, Miles should hold out to the last, were McClellan's final words as he sent three separate civil-

ian dispatch riders of detective Allan Pinkerton's intelligence operation to carry the message to Miles. Unfortunately not one would get
through.[25]

Timing proved critical once more. Jackson and the others spent
most of the day at Harpers Ferry moving artillery into position and
attempting to coordinate their efforts by signal. By afternoon they
had begun bombardment and probing attacks that kept Miles's
defenders pinned in place and unable to make any attempt to retake
Maryland Heights. Afternoon temperatures climbed into the seventies and battle smoke enshrouded the gaps of South Mountain to the
northeast as Federal commanders tried to pummel their way through.
Delays in arriving at all three gaps plagued Federal efforts and particularly bought time for Hill and his colleagues at Crampton's Gap.
Finally Federal right wing commander Ambrose Burnside and Reno
met in brief conference (soon joined by McClellan) and reinforced
Cox with the remaining IX Corps divisions of Samuel Sturgis and
Isaac Rodman to help at Fox's Gap. Burnside asserted that no further
attacks would occur until Hooker's I Corps was on the field. That
delayed serious action until 5:00 p.m. By this time Longstreet had
also thrown reinforcements onto the mountain, including John B.
Hood's brigade (with its commander reinstated personally by Lee
from a post-Manassas arrest stemming from an incident with Brig.
Gen. Nathan "Shanks" Evans over captured Federal ambulances).
The contest at Fox's Gap culminated at the Wise hilltop farm, where
the Old Sharpsburg, Mountain, and Ridge roads intersected. Daniel
Wise's stone fences became battlements, his cultivated fields slaughter pens for dead and wounded, and his modest log cabin served as
haven for the wounded. After the battle his well became the tomb for
many Rebel dead. It was near here that the gallant and popular Jesse
Reno suffered a mortal wound. Cox took charge of the corps and
launched another ferocious offensive that drove within a half-mile of
the Mountain House at Turner's Gap. By this time, Hooker's corps
had moved, using the Old Hagerstown road via Mt. Tabor Church
and Frosttown to angle in on Turner's Gap from the north side. The
beleaguered Confederate line would be sorely tested in the gathering darkness.[26]

The fighting between Hooker and Rodes proved as desperate
as that at Wise's farm. The Federals possessed overwhelming odds
against Rodes's thousand-man brigade. The divisions of George

Gordon Meade and John Hatch advanced directly up the road, James B. Ricketts's division moving in reserve. Meade first, then Hatch managed to turn the Confederate flanks as the confusing battle virtually ended in a cornfield just below the summit. Meade held fast to Frosttown Gap, and Hatch's people were within fifteen hundred feet of Turner's Gap. Gibbon's men meanwhile had driven straight at a strong defensive line in the gorge on the National road, only to be stopped by withering fire from Southerners positioned behind a stone wall. With their flanks enfiladed by other Rebels concealed in the woods, the "Black Hatters" finally drove the defenders back on Colquitt's main body. The retiring Rebels were heard to cry out, "O, you damned Yanks, we gave you hell again at Bull Run!" The Federals yelled in return, "Never mind Johnny, it's not McDowell after you now. Little Mac and Johnny Gibbon are after you now." The Confederate line at Turner's Gap barely held as darkness ended the major fighting. The weary contestants on both sides merely slumped to the ground among the dead and wounded as relentless picket firing kept up all night. McClellan would write Halleck, "After a very serious engagement, the corps of Hooker and Reno have carried the heights commanding the Hagerstown Road. The troops behaved magnificently. They never fought better." The next day, poet Walt Whitman's brother George, a lieutenant in the Fifty-first New York, walked past heaps of fallen at Fox's Gap: "In a road for nearly a quarter of a mile they lay so thick that I had to pick my way carefully to avoid stepping on them." This was "war without romance": dead men with heads shattered, bowels protruding, limbs missing. Sgt. Benjamin Hirst of the Fourteenth Connecticut wrote, "I hoped to God never to see such another sight again."[27]

By day's end two additional Federal corps (Sumner's and Mansfield's) reached the eastern base of South Mountain and bivouacked. The Army of the Potomac was now fully concentrated. Little wonder that Longstreet appeared in person to conduct the final defense at Turner's Gap. He subsequently joined Hill and Hood at Lee's makeshift command post on the eastern edge of Boonsboro, where they argued for immediate withdrawal. All three generals told their chief that the passes of South Mountain could not be held. Their men were exhausted, their commands disorganized, the Federals now enfiladed the mountaintop positions. A combative Lee first thought of renewing the Turner's Gap fighting until news of Sumner's arrival reached him. Any defensive stand in the Boonsboro area now seemed fruitless. Retirement to the Potomac via Sharpsburg seemed the best prospect, although it meant abandoning the Maryland campaign. Dispatches went to Longstreet and Hill to retire to Sharpsburg, and McLaws and Jackson received word to break off their efforts and rejoin the main army. Lee's words to McLaws may have paralleled those to Old Jack: "The day has gone against us and this army will go by Sharpsburg and cross the river." Lee remained calm and still had no knowledge of the results at Crampton's Gap. There Col. Thomas T. Munford's thousand-man mixed cavalry and artillery force incredibly had held at bay Franklin's twelve-thousand-man reinforced corps for most of the day.[28]

Munford essentially covered McLaws's rear on Maryland Heights. That morning Stuart had passed through, concerned that McClellan intended making relief of Harpers Ferry his priority via Crampton's or other nearby passes. Sensing that not to be the case, yet failing to properly reconnoiter Franklin's advance east of Burkittsville, Stuart rode on to confer with McLaws. The division commander had left three infantry brigades in the vicinity of the Brownsville and Burkittsville gaps, with two more closing the Weverton aperture from Harpers Ferry, so he felt comfortable that his rear was well protected. Still, Franklin never realized that the odds stood so heavily in his favor at Crampton's Gap. In fact, contrary to McClellan's orders, the VI Corps commander waited at Jefferson for the arrival of Couch's reserve division of the IV Corps. Meanwhile, at Burkittsville, Munford dug in nicely behind stone walls along Mountain Church road. When Franklin finally arrived at about noon, the Federals wasted four hours laboriously making preparations. When the final assault rolled forward, a simple outflanking by the divisions of Major Generals William Smith and Henry Slocum quickly dislodged the defenders.

Together they drove Munford helter-skelter back up the mountain. The defenders finally disintegrated completely near the crest, and only the timely arrival of the infantry brigades of Paul Semmes and Howell Cobb temporarily stabilized a new defense line at the top. Even that could not stem the Union momentum. The entire force, including original defenders and reinforcements sent by McLaws, plunged in disorder down the western side of the mountain into Pleasant Valley. Once off the mountain, Munford split to the north at Rohrersville; the disorganized infantry peeled in the opposite direction to reunite with McLaws's main body. McLaws, accompanied by Stuart, arrived too late to stem the disaster, although they were able to establish a thin defense from the fugitives. Seven hundred prisoners from seventeen separate Confederate units plus their arms and equipment, three stands of colors, and an artillery piece fell into Franklin's hands. It was the Army of Northern Virginia's largest cumulative loss by capture up to that time, claims historian Dennis E. Frye.[29]

All told, the fighting on September 14 proved a disaster for Confederate arms. On South Mountain, approximately thirty-six thousand Federals had inflicted twenty-three hundred casualties upon perhaps eighteen thousand Confederates at a cost of 2,325 killed and wounded to themselves. Could the Federals exploit their success? Harpers Ferry remained besieged. Franklin mused plaintively to McClellan at 5:20 p.m., "I have been severely engaged with the enemy for the last hour." Because that enemy proved "too great for us to take the pass to night," Franklin asked for orders. Barring such, he promised to attack again in the morning. His men subsequently proved him wrong, accomplishing a striking victory. Franklin had his opportunity to move quickly to relieve Harpers Ferry, or even threaten the rear of Lee's remaining forces at Boonsboro. Instead, he chose to regroup atop the mountain while inexplicably returning personally to his prebattle headquarters east of Crampton's Gap. He delayed until daylight to complete the task assigned by McClellan: destroying McLaws and relieving Miles. As military historian Edward Stackpole uncharitably observed later, "In view of McClellan's own habit of vastly overestimating his opposition, Franklin was simply following the leader's example." On the other hand, McClellan dictated fairly straightforward directions to Franklin at 1:00 a.m. on September 15 that would place the VI Corps in a perfect position on the road between Rohrersville and Harpers Ferry, thus separating McLaws from the rest of the Army of Northern Virginia. Franklin was to try to establish communication with Miles, tell the latter to break out of the encirclement (spiking guns and destroying public property), and together the pair should rejoin the Army of the Potomac at Boonsboro, where McClellan still expected Lee to make a stand. "Should you find, however, that the enemy have retreated from Boonsborough toward Sharpsburg," concluded McClellan, "you will endeavor to fall upon him and cut off his retreat."[30]

An unsuspecting McClellan never knew of the lost opportunity.

Lamely he telegraphed Halleck at 9:40 p.m. that Franklin had been hotly engaged, but "I do not know the result." Franklin finally accomplished the first part of his mission the next morning. He ensured that one brigade and a battery from Couch's late-arriving division occupied Rohrersville. Then he discovered the unpleasant fact that notwithstanding Lee's withdrawal orders, McLaws had rallied his command overnight and positioned two strong battle lines on a traversing ridge across Pleasant Valley just north of Brownsville. There he confronted Franklin during the pleasant morning hours of September 15. Franklin saw this fact as soon as he rode again over the gap to scout the Rebel position. At 8:50 a.m. and again at 11:00 a.m. the VI Corps commander wrote to McClellan about needing reinforcements before tackling an enemy that "outnumber[s] me two to one." Franklin spent the morning fretting about McLaws rather than attacking and dispersing what truly were fewer than half his numbers. He failed to exploit a reconnaissance made by the Sixth Maine and part of the Fourth Vermont supported by an artillery section to the Brownsville Pass that would have enabled the Federals to gain the rear of the Confederate position if Franklin had followed through with a major thrust. Remarkably, Franklin could not grasp the impact of his resounding victory the day before, in which his men had killed or wounded eight hundred of Lee's finest soldiers and captured additional hundreds, at a cost of but 533 Federals. On the other hand, examination of the terrain around Brownsville even today suggests that Franklin might have been prudent in not pressing an attack. At any rate, McLaws became alert to the Brownsville Pass danger and retired in the afternoon just south of the town, anchoring his line on another traversing ridge at St. Luke's Episcopal Church. McLaws admitted later that sounds of a battle on the morning of September 15 would have kept Miles from so willingly serving up his twelve thousand Federals to Jackson. As one of his aides jotted in his diary, "Surprise that the enemy do not attack—thought they were trying to follow to the Mt."[31]

Franklin's first dispatch of the day to McClellan contained the telltale phrase "If Harper's Ferry has fallen—and the cessation of firing makes me fear that it has. . . ." Indeed, Miles had surrendered nearly an hour before Franklin's communiqué. Franklin had clearly not used "the utmost activity that a general can exercise," as his commander had requested of him. McClellan rationalized in his campaign report that the close of action on the night of September 14 found Franklin's advance in Pleasant Valley "within 3½ miles of the point on Maryland Heights, where he might, on the same night or on the morning of the 15th, have formed a junction with the garrison of Harper's Ferry had it not been previously withdrawn from Maryland Heights, and within 6 miles of Harper's Ferry itself." Franklin had sufficient guidance from McClellan that Miles anticipated holding his position until Monday evening. Until experiencing McLaws's superb charade that morning, the VI Corps commander may well have thought he had sufficient time to relieve the garrison. McClellan had implicit faith in his subordinate. Lee's main army focused his attention at Boonsboro. Of course, Miles had no accurate way of knowing how close Franklin was that morning, although McClellan had instructed Pleasonton as early as September 13 to "fire occasionally a few artillery shots (even though no enemy be in your front to fire at)" to assure Miles "that our troops are near him." Jackson's artillery barrages may have drowned out noise from Franklin's efforts at Crampton's Gap. To Paul Teetor, a student of the Harpers Ferry event, Franklin's decision to give his victorious soldiers a Sunday night breather just six miles short of Harpers Ferry was "fatal to a garrison which Miles seems to have intended to surrender and in any event *did* surrender on Monday morning."[32]

Neither McClellan's headquarters nor Washington had such knowledge available to them. Officials in the city focused on ensuring that the city's defenses on the south side remained on alert and that the unguarded crossings of the Potomac received additional cover. They busily pushed forward reinforcements and supplies to the army. McClellan's morning dispatches to Washington on September 15 fairly glowed with news of progress at all three gaps, Lee routed, prisoners taken, troops well in hand, and confidence for the morrow. His 9:40 p.m. wire the night before had boasted, "The troops behaved magnificently" and had "never fought better." He regretted the gallant and able Reno's death, but "it has been a glorious victory." Uncertain whether the enemy would retreat or appear in increased force in the morning, he wrote, "I am hurrying up everything from the rear to be prepared for any eventuality." Even at 8:00 a.m. the next morning Little Mac waxed, "On all parts of the line the troops, old and new, behaved with the utmost steadiness and gallantry," and "the *morale* of our men is now restored." Oddly, he even took to writing old Winfield Scott, in retirement at West Point, of his victory. Little wonder then that President Lincoln sent that congratulatory note to McClellan at midafternoon enjoining total destruction of the enemy. To the state governor in Springfield, Illinois, an old political friend, the president wired, "I consider it safe to say that Gen. McClellan has gained a great victory over the great rebel army in Maryland between Fredericktown and Hagerstown. He is now pursuing the flying foe." Governor Richard Yates replied that such news "has filled our people with the wildest joy," and "salutes are being fired & our citizens are relieved from a fearful state of suspense." Such euphoria would have been less profound had the truth been known about events at Harpers Ferry that day.[33]

The Confederate artillery bombardment of Sunday afternoon, though inaccurate, nevertheless softened Miles's garrison. Federal soldiers scurried for shelter in cellars, houses, trenches, and ravines and their own counterbattery fire availed them little beyond expending long-range ammunition. Jackson sent A. P. Hill's Light Division to occupy critical Bull's Hill, where it enfiladed the Union flank above Bolivar at a thousand-yard distance. A feeble Union response suggested demoralized defenders, even though Miles, White, and their officers constantly urged the shell-shocked troops not to yield but to fight to the end. Jackson wrote Lee at 8:15 p.m., "Through God's blessing, the advance had been successful" and "I look to Him for complete success to-morrow." By contrast, Miles could only complain bitterly to an aide, "Oh, where is McClellan and his army?" Defeat and surrender now supplanted any idea of defiance in the aging soldier's mind. He seemed ready to wave the white flag when convening various command councils that evening. Some of his subordinates were not, in particular Lt. Col. Benjamin Grimes Davis of the Eighth New York cavalry. His fifteen hundred horsemen had been underemployed and restless to get away. Determined personally to escape what appeared to be certain capture, Davis (a native Mississippian but loyal to the Union) asked his commander's permission to sortie out from the trap. When Miles wavered, Grimes told him that his five units would leave anyway.[34]

As an inky black night settled over Harper's Ferry, Davis and his column departed at 8:00 p.m. via a pontoon bridge across the Potomac. Led by a local guide, they made the twelve-mile ride undetected to Antietam Forge and on to Sharpsburg. Then, moving directly behind

Lee's concentrating army, at that moment still largely located to the east beyond Antietam Creek toward Keedysville and Boonsboro, the column made good its escape. Informed of a large enemy concentration near Hagerstown, Davis turned westward, struck the Williamsport–Hagerstown road, and, finding Lee's passing wagon train, utilized his southern accent to effect its capture. Shocked Rebel teamsters realized that Yankee cavalry (who should not have been there in the first place) had snagged them as Davis and his men cut out some forty-five wagons of ammunition and commissary stores, burned five, and then crossed unscathed into Pennsylvania at Greencastle the next morning. Lee's larger reserve ordnance train and the rest of the wagons eluded Davis. Riding with Davis at the time was Maj. Henry Cole, commanding the Maryland home brigade local defense corps, who had returned to Harpers Ferry just before the escape with a critical dispatch from McClellan to Miles. This was McClellan's "Hold out to the last extremity" message. Cole conveyed it, Miles pocketed it, and nobody else in the garrison knew about it at that time. Miles never destroyed the pontoon bridge to the Maryland shore to deny Confederate entry once McLaws commanded Maryland Heights. Such a move led to questions of whether Dixon Miles was guilty of treason or disobedience of orders. Fortunately for Davis, Miles's actions had enabled the cavalry's escape.[35]

In any event, a morning mist burned away quickly that Monday September 15. The Confederate guns, at least fifty in number, blasted away once more. By 8:00 a.m. Federal gunners had exhausted their long-range ammunition and Miles readied a white flag. Jackson penned a note to Lee: "Through God's blessing, Harper's Ferry and its garrison are to be surrendered." Yet consternation reigned at lower echelons on the Federal side. "For God's sake, Colonel, don't surrender us," implored Captain Philo D. Phillips of the 126th New York. Let us cut our way out, and join the relief column, he demanded. Miles merely answered that the enemy "would blow us out of this [place] in half an hour." In fact, one of the final shots before parley (possibly from Walker's gunners on Loudoun Heights, maybe even friendly fire) seriously wounded Miles in the leg. His lifeblood ebbing away, the old regular told his aide, "We have done our duty, but where can McClellan be?" Hidden in his pocket was the missive from McClellan conveyed by Cole. Many Union soldiers, learning later of its existence, blessed Miles's death that day on the plain above Harpers Ferry. Ignorant of McClellan's instructions, White and the garrison's senior leadership acquiesced to Miles's decision, and White and Powell Hill negotiated terms. Miles died, resigned to his fate but regretting that his subordinates, especially White, would not get full credit for the defense. He lived long enough to curse the government for being too slow in sending help. Miles held the ignominious distinction of effecting the largest surrender of U.S. forces until World War II: seventy-three guns, thirteen thousand small arms, two hundred wagons, fifteen hundred much-needed horses, and an estimated 12,500 prisoners of war. Jackson had killed or wounded 219 Federals at a cost of possibly 286 of his own men. The Federals had been cleared at last from Lee's access to the Shenandoah Valley.[36]

News of Harpers Ferry's surrender certainly heartened the hard-pressed Confederates. Capt. Henry Lord Page King of McLaws's staff recorded, "Thank God! Whatever the result of our battle we are not cut in two." The loss of South Mountain the night before had caused Lee great anxiety, and he had halted the army's retirement at Keedysville to cover the contingency that McLaws might be cut off by Franklin's actions in the morning. Not until noon would Jackson's victory message make its way to headquarters. Lee was loath to end the campaign in Maryland and sought desperately for some way to fight, first in the vicinity of Boonsboro on Beaver Creek, then subsequently at Keedysville, where he hoped that McLaws might rejoin the army. Slowly those options faded as McClellan advanced through the gaps and army engineers explained to Lee the poor tactical ground at both Boonsboro and Keedysville. He then instructed the elderly artillerist clergyman-turned-soldier Brig. Gen. William Pendleton to guard the crossings at Williamsport, Falling Waters, and Sheperdstown with guns and infantry. He also wanted stragglers, ammunition, cannon, and provisions rushed forward to his back-peddling army. Could he regroup, move upriver on the Virginia side, and resume a northward movement into Pennsylvania? In historian Joseph Harsh's view, "Lee had taken fate-defying risks a half-dozen times, and each time fate had winked at his contempt—until now." Everything threatened to now come undone as McClellan's South Mountain victories nonplussed Lee.[37]

Suddenly fate again intervened, enabling Lee to possibly snatch victory from uncertainty. Reaching Keedysville at 5:00 a.m., Lee spent less than an hour there. His forces too scattered on divergent lines from fourteen miles west to Williamsport and eleven miles southwest to Shepherdstown as well as at Harpers Ferry, Lee realized his army was neither in good shape nor well in hand. While awaiting definite word concerning Harpers Ferry's fate and having in hand cavalryman Munford's information that McLaws might escape only by crossing the Potomac to rejoin Walker and Jackson, Lee concluded to press on another three miles or so to Sharpsburg and recross the Potomac at Boteler's ford. Just before passing Antietam Creek about sunrise, possibly on the farm of Philip and Elizabeth Cost Pry, Lee had his ambulance driven onto a high meadow overlooking the stream and the heights beyond at Sharpsburg. Peering eastward to South Mountain, he could see the Union pursuit just then breaking into view, while to the south nothing could be gleaned about Harpers Ferry. Turning to the view across the creek toward Sharpsburg, Lee spotted the high ground he needed to stop his pursuers. A hot cup of coffee supplied by some local farm wife, or the previous day's message from Jackson promising success this day, suddenly inspired Lee to a determined stand against the Federal army. He and his entourage then joined the stream of bedraggled troops crossing the Middle Bridge over the Antietam and hiking up the three-quarter-mile rise to enter sleepy Sharpsburg at a prominence that locals called Cemetery Hill. Here he could survey even better the intended killing ground. It was about 8:00 a.m. on a balmy Monday morning when Lee set up headquarters at this location.[38]

Units of the exhausted Army of Northern Virginia began to fill the landscape during the day on September 15. Longstreet, D. H. Hill, and others edged northward out the Hagerstown road from town to the site of a small plain-sect German Baptist Brethren meetinghouse termed the Dunker Church. They also assumed positions on high ground south of Sharpsburg, toward another of the picturesque gray limestone bridges that arched the Antietam. It was called the Lower Bridge. Behind Lee stood his line of retreat and resupply via Boteler's ford. In front lay the Antietam, and beyond, an enemy coming on fast behind his own rear guard. As if to inspire the passing soldiery, Lee announced, "We will make our stand on these hills." Perhaps the men cheered him; history has not so indicated. Yet shouting across the creek by afternoon indicated that McClellan and his generals had reached the front. His soldiers' wild enthusiasm always inspired Little Mac, and even his horse, Dan Webster, seemed to pick up the pace with this "one continuous cheering." Ironically, McClellan and his large entourage quickly rode to the same high meadow where Lee had alighted in the morning, and Confederate artillerists soon found them an inviting target. The victory-expectant Union leader, joined by Sumner, Hooker, Burnside, Cox, and the newly arrived Fitz John Porter, became preoccupied with how to get across the creek and assault the Confederates. Just hours before he had written Mary Ellen that he was pushing everything after the enemy "with the greatest rapidity & expect to gain great results." He thanked God "most humbly for his great mercy." "How glad I am for my country that it is delivered from immediate peril," he enthused. On the banks of the Antietam, McClellan's pursuit of Lee was about to end.[39]

Here execution once more haunted this Union Napoleon. As brigadier Jacob Cox said later, "The examination of the enemy's position and the discussion of it continued till near the close of the day." Still anticipating that Lee's army would remain dispersed, McClellan's directives suggested that he wanted to concentrate his six corps plus Pleasonton's cavalry (excepting Morell's division and Humphrey's division of green troops not yet in from Frederick) before giving battle. That was only part of the issue. McClellan had used his South Mountain victories to order rapid pursuit in a fashion that could have caught Lee's retreating force on the march. The Southerners, however, marched all night; the Federals did not. Notwithstanding McClellan's orders that Burnside travel fast and light, his friend allowed his wing of the army to enjoy breakfast, thus impeding Porter's V Corps movement. When the Federals did step out early the next morning Sumner, followed by Hooker and Mansfield, marched directly from Turner's Gap to Boonsboro and thence to Keedysville, where they were joined by Burnside and Porter coming from Fox's Gap via the Old Sharpsburg road. Notwithstanding McClellan's expectations, the pursuit bogged down in the merger of marching columns at the Keedysville choke point. McClellan and Burnside would remain estranged for the next few days over Burnside's slowness. Yet even Sumner and Hooker had taken their time to close with the army's commander at the middle bridge over the Antietam. Then the army's own commander wasted more time selecting artillery positions and designating bivouac areas for the army rather than acting while his opponent was off-guard and outnumbered more than four to one. McClellan would begin his first communiqué the next morning to Halleck simply: "When our troops arrived in sufficient force it was too late in the day to attack."[40]

In fact, one corps would not be up at all. Franklin remained stationary in Pleasant Valley all day, even when McLaws retired southward to Harpers Ferry and reunion with Walker and Jackson. True, the VI Corps provided rear area security to the Army of the Potomac, as Jackson and McLaws had notions of threatening McClellan from this quarter until reminded that they needed to help a beleaguered Lee. McLaws's rapidly disappearing Rebels prompted only token pursuit by Franklin, and he missed an opportunity to overtake Lee's marching columns via the little road west from Brownsville to Sharpsburg. Franklin simply awaited instructions all day, and McClellan's eventual round of dispatches suggested a reinforcing role for the VI Corps later rather than sooner in the impending action. Despite the changed situation from morning and early afternoon that Franklin failed to clarify sufficiently for headquarters, McClellan's 9:00 p.m. dispatch tepidly told Franklin "to send out to-night a squadron of cavalry to picket the Frederick pike," while recounting how the enemy "was found in position in considerable force this afternoon" and how "the troops have not been able to come up sufficiently to-day to enable us to attack the enemy." A "reconnaissance will be made at daylight, and if he is found to be in position, he will be attacked," said the army commander. Franklin apparently would play no immediate role other than that of army reserve in the rear.[41]

Why did not McClellan attack immediately with whatever troops he had on hand late on the afternoon of September 15? Such an assault by upwards of seventy thousand Federals might well have bested Lee's poorly disposed eighteen thousand (absent Jackson's column—although even with them, the depleted army might have counted scarcely more than forty thousand muskets). The pace of the day's events yields the answer. Morning scouting reports had placed the Rebels on high ground just beyond Keedysville overlooking Little Antietam Creek and ready for battle. McClellan had already thought of such a contingency. "If the enemy were overtaken on the march they should be attacked at once," he claimed later in his memoirs, but "if found in heavy force and in position, the corps in advance should be placed in position for attack and await my arrival." Maj. Gen. Edwin V. Sumner, ranking general of the advance, had asked at 3:00 p.m. whether he should make dispositions for an attack and actually go forward even without specific orders. He admitted that he did not know the enemy's strength, as it was impossible to estimate their "*entire* force." This communiqué brought McClellan forward in haste through all the stalled but cheering throngs of soldiers. By that time Lee's rear guard had retired over the main Antietam to the outskirts of Sharpsburg, occupying about a mile and a half on the forward slope of a long, low ridge just to the east, according to both Sumner and a young staff officer, Capt. George Armstrong Custer. To attack at that stage, given such uncertainty, was not McClellan's way. Until reconnaissance found crossings above and below the Middle Bridge, a frontal assault up the long slope and toward Sharpsburg seemed ill conceived.[42]

McClellan adhered to the dictum expressed later in his memoirs, "that the true course was "to make no movement until the preparations are as complete as circumstances permit," and never to fight a battle "without some definite object worth the probable loss." The ground beyond the Antietam was terra incognita in the general's mind. Lee no doubt held unseen units in reserve and in strength, thus preventing achievement of some definite objective. Daylight was waning, his full force not on the scene as yet. Where was Jackson? There was a distinct possibility—at least to McClellan—that he faced Lee's whole army. Caution ruled that September evening. With Harpers Ferry gone, why rush to major battle when careful preparation, dawn scouting reports, and proper operational planning could ensure decisive victory on the morrow? Perhaps that was what McClellan and Porter talked about as they stared across the creek from the ridge near Philip Pry's house. McClellan and his staff then rode back to headquarters at a church just outside Keedysville to prepare for the next day's events. Across the Antietam, his opponent awaited the decision, anxious to have the remainder of his army available for what now seemed an inevitable fight.[43]

Uncertain of Lee's strategy or true strength, McClellan had led his restored Army of the Potomac from Washington to the banks of the Antietam. Caution and order had dictated his every move. He always feared ambush by a superior enemy. He had helped ease Lee out of Frederick and unexpectedly secured a copy of the Confederate's operational plan. With this prized Lost Order in hand, McClellan more confidently pursued Lee's divided army, intending to defeat it in detail. Franklin's VI Corps would interpose between Harpers

Ferry and the Confederate "main body" at Boonsboro and relieve the twelve-thousand-man Harpers Ferry garrison, which General in Chief Henry Halleck had refused to release from its tenuous but strategically important location. Lee, on the other hand, had found little support in central and western Maryland; not knowing that his campaign plan had been compromised, he divided his army in order to establish a new line of communications back through the Shenandoah Valley for further campaigning north of the Potomac. Dispersing his forces to capture Federal garrisons at Martinsburg and Harpers Ferry incurred risk, but Lee felt those tasks could be accomplished before his pursuers could bring him to battle. Then Union victories in three South Mountain passes on September 14 seriously threatened Lee's plans. True, Franklin's failure to exploit his success at Crampton's Gap ensured the fall of Harpers Ferry to Stonewall Jackson the next morning. But the Army of Northern Virginia remained dangerously dispersed in the face of a determined opponent.

Lee moved quickly to reconcentrate his forces, first at Keedysville and then behind more formidable Antietam Creek at Sharpsburg. Anticipating retirement to Virginia but intending to stop McClellan until the Harpers Ferry victors could rejoin the main army, Lee faced overwhelming odds as the Army of the Potomac slowly reacted to its South Mountain victories and eventually collected in the vicinity of Keedysville, just east of the Antietam. By late on September 15, McClellan realized that his subordinates' pursuit of the fleeing Confederates had not matched his goals. Clogged roads and unsure subordinates meant that Lee had escaped to the high ground around Sharpsburg and awaited the Federals on ground of his own choosing. McClellan counted on the corps of Sumner, Hooker, and Porter with two divisions already well forward and in position to attack the next morning. McClellan hesitated, determined to thoroughly scout and plan his battle before launching his army forward. A pivotal moment was lost, although the stage remained set for the culminating action of the Maryland campaign. Much depended on speed at sunrise on September 16.[44]

8

The Bridges of the Antietam

IN 1910, MARYLAND AUTHOR Helen Ashe Hays wrote about a gentle stream flowing through Washington County, Maryland, "whose name will be famous as long as America endures, the placid Antietam." To her, writing long after the bloody events of 1862, "it is a beautiful, wide stream, meandering slowly through a country of great beauty and interest." Sycamores lean across it, water willows mark its course, "with soft masses of grayish foliage while they hide it from view." Tangles of blackberries and wild roses, papaws and hazel bushes, elder and poison ivy fringe its banks. Its waters do not sparkle, as often they carry sediment, "which gives the stream a thick and turgid appearance." Still, this gifted observer decided, the Antietam "is peacefully beautiful, and flows through one of the richest farming lands in America." Its beauty did not dictate its fame in mid-September 1862.[1]

In fact, Southerners would remember these environs by another name, Sharpsburg, taken from the nearby town occupied by their army. Ultimately both names became synonymous with the bloodiest single day of the war, a day that spread horror across rocky slopes and rills, corn and wheat fields, into farm lanes and beneath rail and stone fences. More than twenty-two thousand Americans would fall killed or wounded between sunrise and sunset in that autumn harvest of destruction. The result would mean different things to different people. Recalling the words of one participant, historian Stephen W. Sears termed it a "landscape turned red," while Professor James McPherson used the phrase "crossroads of freedom," suggesting a different take for "the battle that changed the course of the Civil War." Above all it was truly "America's Deadliest Day." Not that bloodshed was necessarily new to western Maryland. German and English settlers had hacked their living from among the limestone ridges between North and South mountains. There had been Indian fights and later duels over whiskey and commercial matters by these back-country people. Then the National road between Baltimore and the Ohio country had brought a calming influence. Local and national government had partnered to construct thirteen arched crossings of the Antietam to enhance the community's profitability. In September 1862 those bridges dictated how a great battle would be fought between George B. McClellan and Robert E. Lee.[2]

True, the story encompassed more than just bridges and a creek. Sharpsburg itself lay in a convenient crook of the Potomac between the river and the Antietam's egress near an old iron furnace. More than thirteen hundred residents of the town related their calling to surrounding farmland. McClellan himself would later declare that farmland to be "well adapted to defensive warfare," with its wooded knolls and hollows, ridges, and stone outcroppings interspersed among cornfields. The crossroads town posed something of a choke point for an army's transiting to Virginia as well as an impediment to any attacker. Four stone bridges and perhaps five farm fords controlled access to the Sharpsburg pocket from the east. Such crossings also would channel attackers into killing grounds for defenders using the town as a backstop. These bridges, from south to north, included the one at the Iron Works (dating to 1832) that carried the road from Sharpsburg to Harpers Ferry; the Rohrbach or Lower Bridge (constructed in 1836) just outside town to the southeast; the Orndorff or Middle Bridge (built in 1824) on the main Sharpsburg-to-Boonsboro turnpike; and the Hitt or Upper Bridge (added in 1830), which handled the Keedysville thoroughfare to Williamsport. These structures offered easy passage to either side of the stream. Meanwhile sleepy Sharpsburg sat behind a high ridge protecting southern and eastern approaches but less protected by the more rolling terrain on the Hagerstown road to the north. Lee's army occupied this ground on September 15. With McClellan's pursuit only a half-dozen miles behind them across the Antietam, the impending battle was inevitable.[3]

What was not visible to McClellan from his observation point on the eastern bank of the Antietam required investigation. So he necessarily lost time to this task late on September 15. Praising the general and his army for their South Mountain victory, President Lincoln had specifically called for destroying the enemy "if possible." That opportunity lay within McClellan's grasp that afternoon and evening. But once more, opportunity slipped by. Moving an army never proved easy during the Civil War, especially for someone of McClellan's cautious nature. Meticulous preparation always attended his approach, pointing to a set-piece, well-organized battle. Of course, the general considered the fact that destructive, unpredictable combat might even be unnecessary. Lee could be pressured to merely retire from Maryland and northern soil. Altogether, as he reported later, "the corps were not all in their positions until the next morning after sunrise," which was partially true. Frankly there was only so much that McClellan could do to prod his commanders to press ahead in the ebbing daylight of mid-September. Questions of Lee's strength and ability to spring surprise most assuredly bothered McClellan. The enemy could be destroyed on the morrow.[4]

Heavy fog shrouded the area at dawn the next day, further delaying any scouting effort or even formulation of a battle plan. At least that was what McClellan wired Halleck at 7:00 a.m. on September 16, noting Dixon Miles's surrender of Harpers Ferry and adding gratuitously, "Had he held the Maryland heights he would inevitably have been saved." More to the point, the general hinted that he hoped the ground across the Antietam might be devoid of the enemy. If some remained there, the Army of the Potomac "will attack as soon as situation of the enemy is developed." Meanwhile the time lost to the fog "is being occupied in getting up supplies, for the want of which many of our men are suffering." Certainly McClellan was wise in "hurrying up the ammunition and supply trains, which had been delayed by the rapid march of the troops over the few practicable approaches from Frederick." Artillery, cavalry, and infantry had commanded the roads so that "many of the troops were out of rations on the previous day, and a good deal of their ammunition had been expended in the severe action on the fourteenth." Pursuit, not combat, had been his self-assigned mission to date. No doubt McClellan anticipated his actions changing from pursuit to battle when he also penned an early-hour note to his wife boasting that he and his men "have no doubt delivered Penna & Maryland." Nonetheless both missions proved difficult that September morn.[5]

McClellan repeated the fog problem, the anticipated absence of the enemy, and his intention to attack "this morning" when he wrote VI Corps commander William B. Franklin at 7:45 a.m. Still pinned to his previous assignment regarding Confederate Gen. Lafayette McLaws in Pleasant Valley, Franklin shielded the army's flank and rear. Little Mac told wife Ellen that morning that he awaited movement to the sound of the guns: "We shall not have much fighting, for I believe the enemy has crossed the river." In fact everyone from the Antietam to Washington had anticipated Lee's abject withdrawal overnight. Halleck wired back to McClellan just after noon, "[You] will find that the whole force of the enemy in your front has crossed the river." Now the general in chief feared more than ever that they would recross at Harpers Ferry or below and "turn your left, thus cutting you off from Washington." This seemed to Halleck "to be a part of their plan," hence his never-ending anxiety about the capital's safety. One can anticipate everybody's surprise when the fog lifted to reveal a fully arrayed Confederate army awaiting McClellan's advance.[6]

The gunners of both armies resumed their desultory artillery fire of the day, with Lee recording that it actually intensified as the day wore on. McClellan engaged in distractedly shifting his own batteries and trying to determine the precise positions of an enemy apparently arrayed on the crest of every hill and ridge. He became preoccupied with the possibility that Sharpsburg's undulating terrain might hide massive enemy reserves so that his adversary could "maneuver unobserved by our army, and, from the shortness of their line, could rapidly re-enforce any point threatened by our attack." He also worried about the speed with which Ambrose Burnside and the IX Corps could move to the vicinity of the Lower (Rohrbach) Bridge both to protect the army's left flank but also to be in position to assail Lee's own right flank on the Sharpsburg–Harpers Ferry road. Later McClellan would declare that position "one of the strongest to be found in this region of country." His opponents later marveled about the Federals' lost opportunity. To Lt. George Wilson Booth of Maryland, "Had the attack been made at once and in force, the result could not have failed but to have been disastrous to the confederate arms by reason of the meager force at hand for battle."[7]

Just why Brig. Gen. Alfred Pleasonton's cavalry could not have better scouted beyond the Antietam has never been explained satisfactorily. Indeed, they were busy finding crossing points for the main army. He claimed, "My cavalry was engaged in reconnaissances, escorts, and supports to batteries." Such dispersal of resources, however, affected that army's getting quickly across the Antietam and precisely finding the enemy's position. The bridge crossing near the old forge or even intermediate farm fords upstream toward the Rohrbach Bridge offered alternative ways to accomplish that task. True, such crossings would have stretched McClellan's battle line but also could have led to much earlier movement via the Harpers Ferry road into town. Prying Lee out of his strong position without a bloodbath fit McClellan's inherent nature. Here was a chance to achieve that goal. Earlier exploitation of the lower end of the battle sector might well have had better effect. Nevertheless McClellan apparently intended his principal attack to occur against Lee's other flank, north of town on the Hagerstown pike. The ground seemed flatter and could accomplish the same result: dislodging and forcing Lee to continue retiring through Sharpsburg to the Potomac. Burnside's role would then come into play—unless, of course, the Confederates were too strong or if they had already retreated to the Potomac.[8]

McClellan recorded in his campaign report a year later and in postwar memoirs as well, "My plan for the impending general engagement was to attack the enemy's left with the corps of Hooker and Mansfield, supported by Sumner's and, if necessary, by Franklin's and, as soon as matters looked favorably there, to move the corps of Burnside against the enemy's extreme right, upon the ridge running to the south and rear of Sharpsburg." Having carried that position, Little Mac intended pressing "along the crest toward our right, and, whenever either of these flank movements should be successful, to advance our center with all the forces then disposable." Something of the quintessential double envelopment of the Cannae model, the actual battle would unfold more in the fashion of a disjointed ripple from north to south. Adequate perhaps for inducing the Confederates to withdraw to Virginia, but certainly not annihilation, the battle plan depended on timing and properly monitored coordination lest it disintegrate into the customary series of piecemeal attacks so indicative of most Civil War battles. Such assaults could be bloodily repulsed by an enemy inferior in numbers but tactically well positioned. At no point between his arrival on September 15 and dispatch of a small force across the Middle Bridge as reconnaissance did McClellan contemplate the major attack being launched from the Boonsboro road across the creek and against the center of Lee's right on the heights called Cemetery Hill.[9]

Without knowing it the Army of the Potomac held numerical superiority on September 16. A head count would have shown some forty-five thousand Federals present for battle, compared with Lee's twenty-five thousand in position. Yet neither side had its full complement of men and weapons, and McClellan poorly clarified what he wanted done by his subordinates. Lee subsequently claimed that the Federals had offered battle before he was ready. That assertion obscures the fact that McClellan's own timetable had broken down, notwithstanding historian Ethan Rafuse's conclusion that the Federal commander wished to retain maximum flexibility and avoid committing himself prematurely "to a course of action that circumstances might prove unwise." By midafternoon he was actually as unready to commence the action as his opponent. The morning fog may have been the culprit, although McClellan and his corps commanders simply began moving too late in the day for much accomplishment. Orders went to Hooker between 1:00 and 2:00 p.m. to cross the Upper (Hitt) Bridge as well as nearby Pry ford. Fighting Joe did so at 2:00 p.m. and then rode back to find his chief at Keedysville for further instructions. Recalling later, "I was at liberty to call for reinforcements if I should need them" and that they would be placed under his command, Hooker returned to his column and found it angling away from the intended southwesterly advance. McClellan and his staff soon joined him "to see how we were progressing." According to Iron Brigade leader John Gibbon, Little Mac "was received with great enthusiasm by the troops," his own men having just filled their pockets and haversacks with apples from intervening orchards, hardly in preparation for an attack. The ever-combative Hooker complained to McClellan that his small corps (twelve thousand to thirteen thousand men, but reduced by the South Mountain casualties) had been sent "across the river to attack the whole rebel army." If reinforcement did not come quickly or if Burnside's attack did not occur simultaneously, he said, "the rebels would eat me up."[10]

In fact, McClellan had just as much trouble placing Burnside as Hooker that afternoon. "Old Burn" continued his dilatory movement as after South Mountain. The army commander had ridden personally to the Rohrbach Bridge sector during the day, and various couriers and staffers were unable to get the IX Corps commander to promptly position his men, much less undertake his role in the double envelopment. To the north, Hooker's attackers eventually turned in the right direction by about 4:00 p.m. and engaged Confederate pickets and skirmishers in their front. As they advanced over the farms in large numbers west of the Upper Bridge, tearing down fences to make way for their advance and trampling crops indiscriminately, J. E. B. Stuart's Confederate pickets reported the Yankee presence to Lee's headquarters. McClellan lost whatever element of surprise he had intended thanks to the daylong delay and his subordinates' lack of speed in implementing their assignments. On the other hand, Hooker's noisy presence pinned Lee in place and rather effectively closed Lee's escape route to Hagerstown. A brisk firefight developed at dusk while McClellan himself retired back across the Antietam to establish a new headquarters in the Pry house yard atop the bluffs overlooking what promised to be the next day's main battle. Meanwhile Lee too had spent the day planning his next move while awaiting the return of Jackson and the men sent to take Harpers Ferry. Above all, however, the Confederate leader hesitated relinquishing the offensive.[11]

Lee pondered his options: retreat, receive McClellan's assault in place, or reclaim the offensive. He also passed time reporting events since leaving Frederick to President Davis and then, like McClellan, restlessly roaming the field, positioning batteries and ordering cavalry reconnaissance up the Potomac to find possible escape routes via Williamsport and Hagerstown. The Confederate leader seemed determined to keep his options open, personally regaining a measure of flexibility when he transferred from ambulance back to his legendary mount Traveller. Confident of his opponent's slowness but also aware that he needed another twenty-four-hour respite to permit escape from the Sharpsburg pocket, Lee's spirits rose once again with Jackson's long-awaited arrival. The senior leaders—Lee, Longstreet, and Jackson—went into immediate consultation over local maps and charts while their army awaited its destiny. Everyone remained optimistic until Hooker's late-afternoon foray hinted that the Federal presence across the Antietam might close the Hagerstown escape option and that the main Union effort would drive south on the Hagerstown

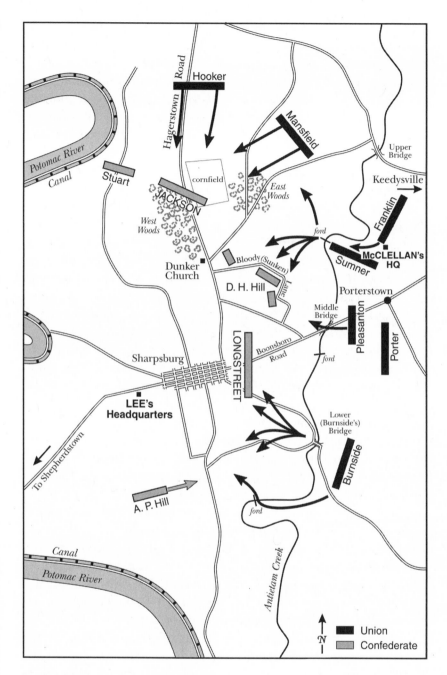

Battle of Antietam, September 17, 1862

road. Lee suspected from picket reports that his right flank at the Rohrbach Bridge might also be endangered. Still, Hooker posed the immediate threat. Springing into action, Lee and his lieutenants recalled ammunition wagons and Jackson's men marched to extend the north end of the line threatened by Hooker. As a regimental band whipped up "Dixie" to inspire jaded rankers, Jackson personally led the vanguard up the Hagerstown road and into the vicinity of the little whitewashed Dunker Church. Meanwhile, Alexander R. Lawton's division (Richard S. Ewell's old command until his wounding at Groveton) moved to bolster positions south of town.[12]

The battle of Antietam actually opened late on September 16, when John Bell Hood's division counterattacked Hooker's advancing units. In a locale to be made more famous the next day—the D. R. Miller cornfield, the East Woods, and the junction of Hagerstown and Smoketown roads—perhaps a half-dozen Rebel regiments brought the Federal advance to a standstill in gathering darkness. Both sides then settled into restless confrontation within sight and hearing of one another. McClellan forbade fires in an unrealistic presumption of security; the news of Yankee presence was manifest by this time to all in Lee's ranks. Rainy drizzle added a dismal air, as nothing could be more sobering, claimed Rufus Dawes of the Sixth Wisconsin, than a period of "silent waiting for the summons to battle." Back at Lee's headquarters, moved to a grove adjacent to the Shepherdstown road on the west end of town, the general sent dispatches to hasten McLaws and Powell Hill back from Harpers Ferry. He directed artillerist William Pendleton and army engineers to improve Boteler's ford as well as passage of the Chesapeake and Ohio Canal for ease of movement in bringing forward ammunition and drawing off wounded, or, if need be, the whole army in retreat. For some reason Lee did not order the return of outlying artillery at Williamsport or even in reserve closer to Sharpsburg. Either he felt no immediate need for such reinforcement or he continued to anticipate reentry into Maryland after temporary retirement across the Potomac. Each passing hour offered Lee options as well as danger.[13]

McClellan also adjusted to events. Mansfield and the small XII Corps would cross the upper passages during the night and join Hooker's effort. Burnside would complete his deployment downstream. Franklin, no longer needed for the liberation of Harpers Ferry or to screen McLaws, would close on Keedysville. The VI Corps together with Porter's V Corps would constitute a reserve for containing any Rebel counter-thrust from Sharpsburg heights via the Middle (Orndorff) Bridge. Memories of Lee and the Seven Days as well as what Pope had told Little Mac about Second Manassas caused him anxiety and hesitancy concerning retention of a strong reserve. Less charitably, later historians portrayed the Federal commander's strategy and action as lacking cohesion, unity of command, and well-defined objective. In fact, still wary of his cornered prey, McClellan would pull his punches. By 9:00 p.m. ominous random gunfire and sounds of moving troops portended a busy morrow. From a command post at the Joseph Poffenberger barn, Hooker wrote a message asking for even more reinforcements from his chief. He grumbled, "If they had let us start earlier, we might have finished tonight." Still, he would confidently reinitiate the first phase of the Antietam battle at daybreak.[14]

Roused from impromptu bivouacs at 2:00 a.m., the men in blue piled their knapsacks in regimental heaps, drew eighty to ninety rounds of ammunition apiece, and prepared for combat. Once again it would be a soldier's fight, waged by separate units with all too meager direction from above. Advancing southward on a two-division front, with a third in reserve, Hooker's target lay about three-quarters of a mile distant at Dunker Church. In turn, Jackson's people calmly awaited the attackers with massed infantry and artillery, supported on their left flank by John Pelham's intrepid horse artillery and other batteries atop high ground on the Nicodemus farm. The lead Federal brigades swung easily from ten-rank column into standard two-rank-deep line of battle, skirmishers in front. As the battle warmed, reserve brigades moved forward to build up the firing line and extend the flanks until Hooker's entire corps engaged the enemy. Cannon to Hooker's rear as well as the army's reserve artillery, including twenty-pounder Parrotts on the high ground east of Antietam Creek, provided fire support. Soon the more accurate Union fire claimed its toll of waiting Southerners in what the latter would dub an "artillery hell." Overall the early-morning combat degenerated into a simple slug-fest between crushing lines of infantrymen. Postwar accounts would recall the gory details of D. R. Miller's infamous "Corn Field."[15]

The three divisions of brigadiers Abner Doubleday, George Gordon Meade, and James Ricketts slammed forward between 6:00 and 7:30 a.m. in a bitter attempt to wrest control of terrain from the Confederates. Hood once more counterattacked ferociously, causing Hooker to seek reinforcement from Mansfield, who allocated Alpheus Williams's and Joseph Greene's divisions to the fray. In turn, charge and countercharge marked the action in the thirty-acre cornfield and nearby fields and woodlots. Canister and musketry sheared the stalks of corn "as closely as could have been done with a knife," Hooker noted later, while the "slain lay in rows precisely as they had stood in their ranks a few moments before." "It was never my fortune to witness a more bloody, dismal battle-field," he reported. "There was no resisting this torrent of death-dealing missives." The combat seesawed until at least 9:00 a.m., with Ricketts losing about one-third of his combatants while Hood's old Texas brigade (now led by Col. William Tatum Wofford) suffered 64 percent casualties. The First Texas alone lost over 82 percent of its 226 men, the highest of any single unit during the entire war. And the day's action had just begun.[16]

The ferocious struggle soon engulfed an "iron triangle" between the North and East Woods and the Hagerstown pike, a bloody half-square mile from Dunker Church to the North Woods. Confederate batteries from Nicodemus Heights on the west to a plateau east of Dunker Church rained death and destruction. The fighting chewed up both Hooker's and Mansfield's corps by about midmorning, wounding Hooker and killing Mansfield in the process. New leaders lost the momentum, although by this point McClellan finally responded to Hooker's need for reinforcement by dispatching Sumner's II Corps across the Antietam and into battle on the I Corps's left. Somewhat dubious of the snowy-haired Sumner's abilities, McClellan cautioned him to be very careful in his advance, as "our right is suffering." So it became Sumner's turn to lead his men across the Pry ford and, while guiding on the Smoketown road, watch as two of his fresh divisions led by John Sedgwick and William B. French plowed across the fields toward Samuel Mumma's now burning farm buildings.

It was "like wheeling a wheelbarrow over a mile of heaped up cobblestones," observed one Philadelphia Brigade veteran. Anxious to accomplish something positive, Sumner impetuously organized his attack force into a column stack of three brigades, one behind the other, roughly sixty or seventy yards apart, that limited both firepower and tactical maneuver. He failed to post skirmishers in front. Sedgwick's men marched forward, stepping over human debris from earlier fighting before rushing headlong into the West Woods beyond the Hagerstown pike. Sumner rode freely over the scene trying to discern terrain and enemy positions through residual battle smoke hanging over the undulating ground. Few organized Confederates could be seen at first as the hills and swales proved deceptive in this regard. The sixty-five-year-old Indian War fighter's failure to employ skirmishers and Sedgwick's open flanks quickly proved disastrous.[17]

Stuart further posted a line of guns along Hauser's Ridge, running south from Nicodemus Hill, and enfiladed Sedgwick's line as it moved south, guiding on the Hagerstown pike. Only Jubal Early and other shattered contingents from Jackson's wing were available to hold the line until Lee could aid them. Together with McLaws and Walker, they caught Sedgwick's six thousand men unaware in the West Woods. The closely packed Federals suffered greatly as their formations disintegrated in this ambush. Firing wildly into one another rather than the enemy, Sedgwick's men soon streamed back in abject disorder, leaving twenty-two hundred of their number writhing on the ground or dead. James Wright of the First Minnesota recalled how wounded and crazed cattle ran "here and there bellowing" in the Nicodemus farmyard. Sedgwick had never been routed before, and Sumner personally tried to stem the tide, although he was rather dazed by the sudden turn of events. Division commanders Williams and Sedgwick finally rallied along a long line of strong post-and-rail fences that provided impromptu breastworks near the East Woods and "an incessant storm of shot and shell, grape and canister" the elated Confederates sent back to the sheltering West Woods. Greene's division of Mansfield's corps stolidly clung near Dunker Church until noon, when it too had to withdraw to the main Union line. The battle on Lee's left had about spent itself. Both sides had been badly bloodied; even cavalryman Stuart helped manhandle artillery pieces when gunners, equipment, and horses were cut down by more accurate, long-range Federal fire. Terrain and hard fighting together with the arrival of Confederate reinforcements produced a stalemate north of Sharpsburg. Lee's northern flank had held.[18]

Two days later, Orderly Sgt. James Wright and Corp. Horatio N. Barber would venture onto the ground where Hood's Texans had fought so bitterly. Between what had been a cornfield on one side of the Hagerstown pike and a stubble field "with its aftergrowth of weeds" on the other side, two fences, one a board and the other a post-and-rail variety, had flanked the road itself. Both of them "were perforated and splintered" in a fashion that showed that they had afforded little protection to those using them as such. The Federals had huddled behind one, the Confederates the other, and Wright could recall "no other place in the open where there were so many dead in so small a space." Barber decided, "It was a sight that never could be forgotten." Nor would nurse Clara Barton's presence at the northern end of the Antietam battlefield ever be forgotten. Here the indefatigable nurse once more attended the wounded. Out from Washington as she had been after Second Bull Run, Barton and her team had braved the sights and sounds of South Mountain fighting before encamping with Burnside's IX Corps on the banks of the Antietam. Gunfire from Hooker's sector drew her to Sam Poffenberger's farm, just northeast of the Cornfield and East Woods. There she and her collages worked all day and long into the night, dispensing supplies to the surgeons, preparing food, and even assisting in bullet extraction. Her familiar bonnet, red bow, and dark skirt could be seen moving ceaselessly among the injured; when it grew dark she added lanterns from her wagon kit to light the farmhouse and barn surgeries. Her old friend and comrade Dr. James Dunn remarked, "In my feeble estimation, General McClellan, with all his laurels, sinks into insignificance beside the true heroine of the age, the angel of the battlefield."[19]

The fighting drifted southeastward as the morning progressed and entered yet another phase. Sumner's other division (French) lost track of Sedgwick and consequently fed into the cauldron by veering left, leaving Greene as the plug between corps. Greene's original insertion as part of Mansfield's effort had caused this misalignment in the first place. It was too late now to correct, what with Hooker, Sedgwick, and other leaders wounded, Mansfield dead, and Sumner and Williams taken aback with the slaughter west of Antietam Creek. In fact, "Bull" Sumner (a nickname attributable to a prewar quip that musket balls bounced off his impregnable skull) proved unwilling to resume the bloodshed when Franklin arrived with portions of his VI Corps and immediately wanted to attack. Greene was finally driven from the Dunker Church plateau, and Sumner relied on Franklin's arrival to bolster his "shaky" line. One brigade under Col. William Irwin brushed too close to the woods surrounding the structure and paid for the indiscretion with a quarter of its men as casualties.

Veterans of the morning were content to regroup, stare at the unbelievable windrows of the fallen in a sort of no-man's land, and allow the battle to blossom elsewhere. The Federals had lost 30 percent of their men in the morning fight, the Confederates 23.7 percent. Nonetheless, McClellan remained in high spirits at the Pry house, declaring to staff officer Col. David Strother that it was the grandest battle he had ever witnessed: "If we whip them today it will wipe out Bull Run forever." He paraded with Porter along the adjacent ridgeline, looking soldierly as he peered into the battle smoke across the Antietam.[20]

The actions of French and Richardson now took center stage as they successively assaulted another strong and compact Confederate position, a well-worn, sunken lane on the William Roulette farm. Here, in this depressed roadbed, the Federals encountered stiff resistance from additional elements of D. H. Hill's division. Close to the hinge in Lee's battle line, the Federals had slid southward rather than striking west. They found Robert Rodes's Alabamians, George B. Anderson's North Carolinians, and Alfred H. Colquitt's Georgians bolstered by R. H. Anderson's division (fresh in from Harpers Ferry in reserve) ready to dispute what amounted to the eastern side of the Dunker Church plateau. The farm lane and bordering fences provided an almost natural defense line. Braving both enemy fire and an irate swarm of domesticated bees (their hive upset by all the activity near the Roulette farmhouse), French's Federals closed to within some eighty to one hundred yards of the sunken lane. Both sides slugged it out at that interval with alternating volleys, bayonet charges, and pure obstinacy as color bearers, officers, and men were shot down indiscriminately. The action assumed all the earlier pathos and valor of the Cornfield, West Woods, and Dunker Church fighting with Delawareans, Marylanders, and New Yorkers in French's ranks sacrificing easily 30 percent of their numbers. The bluecoats could look across the road, filling with Confederate bodies. Later an elderly Sharpsburg resident would immortalize the place as "the bloody lane."[21]

Richardson essentially repeated French's experience from about 10:30 to noon, pushing the Rebels out of the sunken lane but falling mortally wounded in the process. Gallant and popularized action of the so-called Irish Brigade also marked this phase. One New Hampshire man witnessed "Irish Molly," a large muscular woman who had accompanied her husband into battle, "jumping up and down swinging her sun-bonnet around her head, as she cheered the Paddy's on." The heavy fighting also took its toll of Confederate commanders, with R. H. Anderson and John B. Gordon cut down (the latter reputedly struck five times by bullets), and the mounting casualties and disintegrating Confederate position threatened to collapse Lee's lines by the noon hour. Rodes's contingents retired as Col. Francis Barlow's New Yorkers surged across the upper reaches of the Roulette lane, overlapping the Confederate right and delivering an enfilading fire on the rest of the defenders, who fled, leaving dead, wounded, and three hundred captives to the foe. As the victorious Federals moved onto the Piper farm to the south, Longstreet wheeled four guns of the Washington Artillery into line and pressed his own staff to serve the pieces when Union sharpshooters shot down their regular crews. These cannon, barely supported by rallying infantry, poured such a pelting storm that each explosion seemed like a "rushing mighty wind and driving hail" to observers. D. H. Hill personally picked up a musket and took his place in the ranks of the defenders. The Federals quickly went to ground in Piper's cornfield, and "it was not surprising how readily they stuck their noses in the dirt." Unable to sustain themselves against such fire, they eventually retired to the Roulette lane, closely pursued by whatever yelping Rebels Hill could rake together for a counterattack.[22]

In truth, the Federals made it all the way to the Piper orchard near the Hagerstown pike. They had broken the hinge in Lee's line. But like Hooker, Mansfield, and Sumner earlier, they could not sustain momentum for breaching the final line of defenders. Both sides eventually settled on the ground overlooking body-filled Roulette's sunken lane, and the fighting subsided here much as it had to the north. Sergeant Hirst of the Fourteenth Connecticut remembered everyone lying prone to escape the continuing enemy fire, although some colleagues were wounded anyway. By this time McClellan had ordered Brig. Gen. Winfield Scott Hancock to go and "command the center of our forces," following Richardson's wounding. Hold the position, he was told, so Hancock, "too weak to make an attack," let the battle subside accordingly. Could McClellan have won the battle of Antietam at this stage? Historian James Murfin argued years later, "Never before had a battle come so close to ending, a war so close to a conclusion, and the victor not realized it." Three of McClellan's corps had been shattered, but so too had the preponderance of Lee's fighting strength. Even Longstreet later contended that at 1:00 p.m. that afternoon, ten thousand fresh Federals put into the fight would have been able to sweep the Confederates off the field. Indeed, McClellan still had at least sixteen thousand such troops close at hand "to renew the contest against the weak and shattered wings of Jackson and Longstreet," according to historian James Cannan. Franklin's VI Corps sans one brigade (ten thousand) and Porter's V Corps (sixty-six hundred) were available from the army reserve. Possibly at no time before or thereafter, suggests Cannan, did the Federals have such an opportunity to crush Lee and his army. With the sun only at its daily zenith, the Army of Northern Virginia faced a crisis of survival.[23]

Both Lee and McClellan needed to take stock of the situation after a morning of bloody conflict. Apparently unwilling to concede the field to the tattered Federals north of Sharpsburg and no matter his own army's condition, Lee looked to counterattack and batter his way north to Hagerstown. At 1:00 p.m. he queried Jackson about such a move, and together they decided that Stonewall would press the dismantled Union right while Stuart with horse and artillery would circle the Yankee flank and menace his rear. Once again, Lee clearly sought a flanking movement to reintroduce maneuver room. Stuart's move misfired when by midafternoon he tested Federal lines with his artillery and received a hail of return fire, thus eclipsing notions of further action in that sector. This left the Federal commander to seek some other solution to the day's stalemate. McClellan might have inserted Franklin or even Porter to achieve a decision. The VI Corps leader had regained his fighting spirit since the standoff with McLaws in Pleasant Valley. In response to Sumner's plight, he led two divisions of nearly nine thousand fresh troops across the Antietam. Despite Irwin's unfortunate experience in the West Woods and Sumner's warning that there would be no reserve in the northern sector but for the VI Corps, the younger general wanted to push ahead into the waning fray.[24]

McClellan conducted a personal inspection of the still-smoking Hagerstown pike sector and by midafternoon conferred with the two corps commanders in the East Woods. The breakdown of both physical and mental willpower of the army wing to resume the attacks, according to Sumner, played to McClellan's typical hesitancy about pressing the issue. Franklin no longer expressed the same ardor for renewed attack as he had earlier with Sumner. Might the army commander have surmised the same devastating effect of combat on the other side of the lines? Jackson had refashioned a defense of sorts, yet the Federals might have broken his position with renewed assaults. McClellan told Sumner and Franklin that he was afraid to risk the day by another attack on the right at that time since "things had gone so well on the other parts of the field" (alluding perhaps to Burnside's success at the Lower Bridge?). Franklin wanted to risk it but was overruled. In his own rather tepid public words later he wrote, "The commanding general came to the position and decided that it would not be prudent to make the attacks, our position on the right being then considerably in advance of what it had been in the morning." Privately he wrote his wife after the battle that his command "laid down and stood shelling the remainder of the day," drawing solace from the fact that his own batteries eventually silenced those of the enemy. McClellan did tell Franklin during their meeting that given reinforcements anticipated to arrive overnight, he could make his attack the next morning.[25]

The upshot was that McClellan effectively changed his battle plan when he suspended further attacks in the north. No longer would there be simultaneous attacks on Lee's flanks or uniform pressure along the whole battlefront. Aid would not be sent to Burnside either, although his actions now became the army's primary effort. McClellan earlier had anticipated exploiting what French and Richardson seemed to be accomplishing (and similarly relieve pressure on Sumner) by reinforcement through the Orndorff (Middle) Bridge corridor, but he did so against Porter's counsel. Pleasonton went across with some horsemen, four batteries of artillery, and a regular army infantry battalion in support shortly before noon. But Lee had effectively sealed the middle approach by massing cannon on the town's Cemetery Hill. Pleasonton judiciously ignored suggestions for some full-blown cavalry charge. With "no infantry to spare," McClellan soon realized the futility of advancing across clear fields of fire against high ground, not only at the cemetery but also toward the Roulette and Piper farms. Pleasonton secured a resupply of ammunition and further reinforcement from Brig. Gen. George Sykes's division of the V Corps by early afternoon and requested permission to attack. Such a decision was not forthcoming, so the guns banged away at great distance and able lieutenants like Charles Francis Adams Jr. wiled away the hours watching shells pass monotonously overhead, to the point that he and his comrades simply fell asleep waiting for something more momentous to take place. Faint hearts lost the initiative, yet witnessing the destruction of whole fighting units in the morning battles, who could blame senior Federal commanders for not risking annihilation of the only Union field army that could lose the war in an afternoon?[26]

That army alone defended Maryland and Pennsylvania as well as the national capital. Respect for, even apprehension of Lee's ability to counterattack held McClellan hostage. So he further occupied his time with tangential matters. He plaintively asked Brig. Gen. A. A. Humphreys (at the time marching from Frederick with seven thousand additional but very raw troops gleaned from Washington's protection), "Come on as soon as possible, and hurry up with all haste," indeed, "force your march." He sent for more twenty-pounder Parrott ammunition from the ordnance chief in the capital. As Richardson battled at the Roulette farm, Little Mac fired off a wire to Halleck at 1:25 p.m.: "We are in the midst of the most terrible battle of the war, perhaps of history." Terrific losses notwithstanding, the army had gained much ground, he claimed. He divulged his intentions quite clearly by declaring, "I have thrown the mass of the army on their left flank." Burnside "is now attacking their right & I hold my small reserve consisting of Porters (Fifth) corps ready to attack the center as soon as the flank movements are developed." He crossed out two sentences—"It will be either a great defeat or a most glorious victory. I think and hope that God will give us the latter"—substituting more positively the hope "that God will give us a glorious victory." Twenty minutes later he wrote his wife assuring her of his safety and how they were "in the midst of the most terrible battle of the age." Despite "many variations," it wasn't over, and, similar to his words to Halleck, he told her, "I trust that God will smile upon our cause."[27]

Lee and his generals also hoped that same God would grant them ultimate success—or, at the very least, survival. Battered to the breaking point, both Lee and Jackson sought some bold stroke like the one that had gained the day at Second Manassas. Only this time a counterattack would lack the punch of Longstreet's action in that battle. Jackson, undismayed by a report from a young private who had scrambled up a hickory tree to see that "oceans" of Yankees were still out there, doggedly tried to muster a maneuver element of some four thousand to five thousand men so that Stuart might strike

McClellan's beleaguered right flank. Old Jack's own bluster shone as he trumpeted, "We shall drive McClellan into the Potomac." Brig. Gen. John Walker awaited the signal that never came. Stuart's reconnaissance repeated the error of Chantilly when he engaged in unnecessary artillery exchange, and Jackson muttered something about the "great pity" of a lost opportunity. The forces of Mars truly had spent themselves in the combat north of Sharpsburg. Neither side could do more than preside over a scene of death and destruction while awaiting events even then transpiring elsewhere. The battle of Antietam would move now to a third and final phase below Sharpsburg.[28]

Lee's right flank, not McClellan's, became the point of greatest danger on the afternoon of September 17. The action had begun in the morning at the Rohrbach (Lower) Bridge, where McClellan had been prodding his friend Burnside to make a crossing. Storm the bridge and the heights beyond and get into Sharpsburg on Lee's line of retreat, read a series of directives that McClellan sent Burnside from 7:00 a.m. on. Hardly a simple task, as it turned out; the triple-arched bridge itself was narrow, angular, and completely dominated by Confederates on a bluff opposite. Moreover the succession of very high ground all the way into town favored the defenders. Nonetheless, Burnside's wing counted 12,500 bayonets despite Fox's Gap losses and subtraction of Hooker's I Corps for the fight in the northern sector at Antietam. Part of the problem lay with command: Burnside still considered himself wing commander; Jacob Cox acted as corps leader. McClellan–Burnside amity had cooled noticeably over the previous two days, and there would be much postwar debate as to whether McClellan intended the IX Corps merely as a diversion on Lee's right flank or as an all-out simultaneous attack with Hooker, Mansfield, and Sumner. At the time it was very much a matter of timing—of McClellan's orders to Burnside and, like everything else on the Federal side, coordination of actual performance of those orders. Reliance on dispatch riders amid the heat of battle proved a poor substitute for clarity beforehand. Protective staff officers later rationalized for both their generals, with Burnside's clique convinced that McClellan jealously remembered how Lincoln twice had offered him command of the army, hence their general was to be a sacrifice to Little Mac's vanity. McClellan's protectors blamed "Old Burn" for the lost opportunity at Antietam.[29]

Still, it was up to Burnside, Cox, and the IX Corps as a body to snatch victory from stalemate or even defeat for the Army of the Potomac. They faced an admittedly daunting task. The Lower Bridge had been the graceful creation of engineer-cum-artist John Weaver. Locals named the span after nearby farmer Henry Rohrbach, whose ancestors had fled wars and persecution in the German states to settle in and work the fertile soil of the Antietam valley. The Rohrbach family had always worshipped at Dunker Church, ripped earlier that day in the Hagerstown pike fighting. Nobody was at home now at the modest two-story Rohrbach house. The terrain at their bridge differed from elsewhere on the field as the Rohrersville road angled in over a slight rise before crossing the 125-foot span and then progressing for about two hundred yards beneath the bluff. From there into Sharpsburg the road ran steadily upward past the Otto and Sherrick farms and a stone house and mill tucked into a hollow just before entering the town. The bridge itself could accommodate only about four fully equipped attackers storming abreast. Even the smallest number of defenders atop the bluff ensured a funnel of death. Several small farm fords on the Snavely property as well as the Antietam forge bridge lower down afforded other crossing points. Yet, above all, the bluff above the Rohrbach bridge truly held the key to the sector—that and the Confederates guarding the sector.[30]

The divisions of D. R. Jones and John Walker had originally defended the sector until mostly called to the morning fight. By afternoon only about three thousand men held the whole Confederate line from Cemetery Hill on the Boonsboro pike southward to the Harpers Ferry road below town. But Brig. Gen. Robert Toombs, a Georgia political general who would later contend that the Confederacy died of too many West Pointers in leadership positions, had his five-hundred-man brigade well dug in at the Rohrbach bridge, using coaling pits just beneath the bluff's crest with supporting artillery on top. These miniforts peppered the crossings with point-blank fire for five hours as three brigade-size Yankee assaults washed unsuccessfully against the eastern entry to the bridge. Little wonder that historian Phillip Tucker vehemently declares, "These Georgians were truly Spartans in gray, who fought against impossible odds to achieve the Thermopylae of the Civil War." By this time, an impatient McClellan sent pointed communiqués demanding either the crossing or Burnside's relief for noncompliance. The possibility that the Federals could have merely waded across the stream and outflanked the bastion has always added controversy to the story of Lower Bridge fighting. No matter, Cox supervised various misdirected attempts to brave the gauntlet of Confederate fire while a search proceeded for alternative fords upstream and down. Crossing via the forge bridge downstream apparently never entered the picture, although such a move would have quickly placed the Federals on the Harpers Ferry road for a straight shot into Sharpsburg. Finally, at 1:00 p.m., "twin 51st" regiments from Pennsylvania and New York dashed across the Lower Bridge crossing, spurred by Col. Edward Ferrero's promise of whiskey as well as "Remember Reno" yells in honor of their fallen commander at Fox's Gap. At about the same time, a two-hour search for alternative crossings stumbled across a Snavely farm ford and Brig. Gen. Isaac Rodman's bluecoats outflanked and routed Toombs's beleaguered defenders. Union perseverance in the end cost five hundred men in the bridge assaults.[31]

Still, the IX Corps finally crossed the Antietam by early afternoon and stood ready to roll up Lee's right flank. McClellan received the news enthusiastically at headquarters. Yet even then, tricky terrain and temporary rallying points like a forty-acre cornfield some 650 yards west of the bridge bought time for Toombs and his principal subordinate, Col. Henry Benning. Still, no reserves could be found, and even Pvt. Alexander Hunter of the Seventeenth Virginia told his regimental commander after a scout from a church steeple lookout in town that he could not see a single additional man running to support the last-ditch defense line along the Harpers Ferry road in the vicinity of the Magraw house. Then Burnside's men hesitated. Exhausted from the Rohrbach Bridge ordeal, low on ammunition, hungry, and facing a tough uphill climb toward the final enemy positions, their division commanders, such as Samuel Sturgis, allowed momentum to dissipate while wagons rolled across the narrow bridge with supplies. For some reason Burnside permitted infantry and vehicular traffic to simultaneously clog the passage, and the young bluecoats stopped to build fires for coffee despite taking continuing enemy fire. Commissary Sgt. and future president William McKinley moved among his Twenty-third Ohio, dispensing food and water to thirsty comrades who had gone into battle that day without breakfast. What could have been a relatively rapid and direct passage up the road into Sharpsburg devolved into a two-hour delay from 1:00 to 3:00 p.m. That interval proved a Godsend to their opponents awaiting Hill's arrival from Harpers Ferry.[32]

When Cox finally renewed the offensive at 3:00 p.m. his mile-and-a-half battle line (from just north of the Rohersville road to the Snavely crossing) made only slow headway against Jones's over-stretched defenders. Close fighting surged over the hills, ravines, and valleys south of town, past the Sherrick and Otto farms, with the embattled Confederates fading uphill toward the key Harpers Ferry road. One of Sykes's regiments along the Boonsboro road and two of Orlando Willcox's brigades immediately to their south drove their foe from Cemetery Hill and back into Sharpsburg's streets. A portion of the town itself fell to the attackers, and Confederate batteries retired from the hill under intense artillery fire from across the Antietam. Just as Burnside's wing stood minutes from "gaining Lee's rear," Jones ordered the ever-feisty Toombs to vigorously counterattack. Helped by artillery support, the Georgian stemmed the Union advance. Nonetheless, historian Bruce Catton suggested, "The last desperate hour of the Confederate Army [was] visibly at hand.[33]

What better time for relief to then appear in the person of A. P. Hill. Either a Jackson–Stuart turning movement (which by this point had fizzled) or Hill's arrival from Harpers Ferry provided the hope of saving the day for Lee. When the red-shirted Hill rode up breathlessly to Lee's command post at the western end of Sharpsburg at 2:30 p.m., Lee greeted him with "General Hill, I was never so glad to see you." Lee urged the newcomer, "Put your force in on the right as soon as they come up." Still the minutes ticked away. By 4:00 p.m. it appeared that the town would be lost, hence the retreat route to Shepherdstown also gone. Just then a staff officer with telescope confirmed that arriving formations indeed carried the cross-barred Confederate battle flag. Why Hill had followed the circuitous march via Halltown and Shepherdstown rather than a more direct, shorter route that had carried Grimes Davis and his escaping Federal cavalry through Sharpsburg several days before simply resulted from Jackson's consolidated march route. Hill might have come in on Burnside's left flank and imperiled McClellan's whole army. Hill possibly feared that route might risk Federal interception, so better to be tardy in reaching Lee than "to not [get] there at all." He appeared just as the Federals stood on the cusp of victory.[34]

Hill's people took their place on the threatened line, and South Carolinian Maxey Gregg's five-regiment, thousand-man brigade pitched into the untested Sixteenth Connecticut on Rodman's left.

Enjoying less than a month in active service and having fired their muskets for the first time only the day before, the greenhorns crumpled embarrassingly. Trying to maneuver in the middle of a cornfield from which they could not see their assailants, the Nutmeggers doubled up adjacent units and Rodman went down with a mortal wound. "Things began to look rather squally," poet Walt Whitman's brother George wrote their mother later. The momentum of fresh Confederates, many clad in blue uniforms captured at Harpers Ferry, pushed the quickly tiring Federal line back down the slopes in bitter attack and counterattack. By dusk Burnside withdrew Cox's weary soldiers back to the Rohrbach Bridge area, carefully monitored by their successful opponents. Rodman and Confederate brigadier Lawrence O'Brien Branch would also count among the 16 percent casualties suffered by the Federals and 18 percent by their opponents in this fight. The colorfully attired Ninth New York "Hawkins Zouaves" incurred a 63 percent loss chanting "Zoo-zoo-zoo" when cracking the Rebel line of battle before Hill's men drove them back. The bloody but unbowed Rebels dug makeshift defensive works along the Harpers Ferry road while Burnside and Cox rallied their men closer to the creek. Darkness enveloped what henceforth would be styled Burnside's, not Rohrbach's, bridge. In the end Jones, Toombs, Gregg, and Hill had stopped the IX Corps and saved the Army of Northern Virginia.[35]

McClellan, who had been promising reinforcements all day, now barked out to a courier, "Tell General Burnside this is the battle of the war—he must hold his ground till dark at any cost," adding, "Tell him if he *cannot* hold his ground, then the bridge, to the last man!— always the bridge! If the bridge is lost, all is lost!" But he steadfastly refused to send any reinforcements to his friend. Content that "Old Burn" could hold his position, McClellan always feared Confederate counterattack. He was also deterred by Porter when about to dispatch the V Corps slashing across the Orndorff (Middle) Bridge, since such troops "are the only reserves of the army; they cannot be spared." An oppressive, sticky night closed over the battlefield's southern sector just as north of town. The temperature hovered around seventy degrees at 9:00 p.m. over in Frederick. Smoke and stench hung low over the landscape, the smoldering ground belonging more to the casualties than the combatants. Charles W. Rouse of the Eleventh Connecticut recorded, "Along the whole line the burning buildings and hay stacks made a splendid sight." According to National Park Service statistics, in twelve hours approximately eighty-two thousand men in blue and gray had sacrificed 22,728 of their number (about 27 percent) for a slice of ground counting less than a thousand acres. Six one-and two-star generals were killed or mortally wounded. Something like 12,400 of 56,000 Federals and 10,300 of 37,400 Confederates (25 percent of McClellan's army and 31 percent of Lee's force) accounted for the killed, wounded, and missing.[36]

To what could be attributed this result, this bloody rebuff Lee handed McClellan? Was it tactical error, the collapse of the Sixteenth Connecticut, or the deadly ambush of Sedgwick, Stuart's premature bombardment, or even Hooker's stillborn attack on September 16? Most certainly the absence of Jackson's force denied Lee his normal aggressive freedom of action. Perhaps the loss of key leaders like Mansfield and Hooker or a collapse of willpower when Sumner, Franklin, and even McClellan saw firsthand the wreckage of once-proud fighting units contributed to the malaise. Burnside's inexplicable slowness, the pause to brew coffee and feed the troops once across the Lower Bridge, or simply the sudden appearance of Hill's men turning the tide denied decisive result. Could it have been simply Lee's luck that offset his questionable decision to stand at Sharpsburg in the first place? Surely he might have consolidated his army south of the Potomac, slipped to Williamsport, and recrossed for a move northward in the Cumberland Valley before McClellan secured a blocking position. Thus a battle might have been averted or at least delayed until a more propitious time for the Confederates. In any event, one day's combat at Antietam (Sharpsburg) caused more casualties than the War of 1812, the Mexican War, and the Spanish-American War combined. Twenty Medals of Honor went to Federal soldiers. "It was possibly the hardest fought field of the war," remembered Maryland Confederate Lt. George Wilson Booth. Like Second Manassas, Antietam stood as a tribute to the triumph of modern weapons lethality. Was the human cost worth it?[37]

What all of this meant "time can only show when the smoke and dust shall have been blown away," commented McClellan's staff officer David Strother. For the moment, McClellan and Lee had "met face to face in a grand pitched battle on a fair field." Neither side "can make excuses or complain of disadvantages," he continued. "We beat them with great slaughter and heavy loss to ourselves." It was as simple as that. Strother and his comrades rode back to headquarters camp at Keedysville, "where a good supper and a good night's rest closed the day of the great battle." They neither witnessed nor suffered the frightful night on the other side of the Antietam, where Dante's Inferno held sway. Shrieks of wounded men and animals spread across field, forest, and valley while the shadowy shapes of ghoulish scavengers braved trigger-happy pickets to strip the fallen of treasures, ammunition, and food. Recovery crews were out there too, searching for wounded comrades or deceased kinsmen. In Sharpsburg Lee and his commanders weighed their options. Food and ammunition had been depleted for prolonged combat. Yet Lee, ever the risk taker, announced solemnly, "Gentlemen, we will not cross the Potomac to-night." If McClellan "wants to fight in the morning I will give him battle again." With that, the army's leadership departed to reconstitute their units and gird for more fighting. Perhaps Lee lacked time to reorganize the army for retreat or he still dreamed of breaking out of the Sharpsburg pocket to resume his campaign from Hagerstown. Unwilling to admit defeat of his proud army, Lee never felt the need to explain his decision. "We awaited without apprehension the renewal of the attack," Lee claimed in his after-action report to Richmond.[38]

Lee's lieutenants did not share his confidence. Stuart particularly worried about relinquishing Nicodemus Heights, especially when Lee constricted his battle line rearward to Reel house ridge that night, leaving most of the Hagerstown road battleground in a sort of no-man's land of dead, wounded, and destruction. Few on the field looked to renew combat after dark. Lt. Elisha Hunt Rhodes of the Second Rhode Island jotted in his diary, "I have never in my soldier life seen such a sight," as "the dead and wounded covered the ground." Many would have agreed with Captain William H. Edwards of the Seventeenth South Carolina, who said later that his side regarded the battle as a draw game or "dog fall." The Federals had attacked "and it was a plain case that they had got enough and were tired of the job." The anti-McClellan *New York Tribune* recounted later how an obviously exhilarated McClellan had ridden the lines that afternoon and greeted one old friend, a Massachusetts colonel whose regiment had been badly handled in the fight: "Collect them at once, we must fight tonight and fight tomorrow." If they could not whip the enemy in this golden opportunity, McClellan said, "We may just as well all die upon the field." Such ardor did not abate that night, although the men generally had little stomach for renewed battle and their frontline leaders implored McClellan not to do so.

Still, the field general expected to renew Franklin's attack, looking to gain Andrew Humphreys's arriving division of fresh troops and John F. Reynolds to hasten his Pennsylvania militia forward to Keedysville. After consulting Burnside, McClellan also ordered George Morrell's division to support the IX Corps. Both McClellan and Lee looked to renewal of conflict on the morrow.[39]

Uncharitable observers such as Francis Palfrey subsequently asserted that the "fault was in the man" when September 18 brought only equivocation on the Union side of the lines. For a time, however, McClellan projected the spark of victory. His telegrams to Halleck and his wife the next morning spoke of the battle as a "masterpiece of art," heavy losses, and trust in the Almighty's judgment. They also contained one telling phrase: "The battle will probably be renewed today." An hour later McClellan released Franklin to attack Nicodemus Heights. He really wanted to await arrival of Humphrey and Couch and Reynolds's militia (who, ironically, eventually refused to cross the Maryland border). McClellan anticipated thirty thousand fresh troops (counting also those V and VI Corps units that had seen little or no combat the day before). But most of the reinforcements arrived too fatigued from all-night marches. Moreover, McClellan thought he needed artillery ammunition. Brig. Gen. James Ripley, the chief of ordnance, directed 1,014 wagonloads of field and small arms ammunition to Frederick by midmonth. But the circuitous route eventually taken by twenty-five hundred rounds of twenty-pounder Parrott shells through Pennsylvania due to the blown Monocacy bridge on the Baltimore and Ohio Railroad meant that McClellan could not depend on sufficient quantities of that commodity for at least several days following Antietam. Logistical historian James Huston contended, "Neither army was prepared to renew the attack on the 18th, but the ammunition was there for the Army of the Potomac if it had been needed." In his view, "This would suggest that with a little better organization McClellan could have had the means at hand to renew the attack for a decisive victory." In truth, traffic snarls at Hagerstown for the artillery ammunition and Frederick for the musket ammunition lay beyond the army commander's control. He most certainly could not have had them on hand for any battle renewal on September 18. A reluctant army commander eventually postponed Franklin's offensive for the time being.[40]

Put bluntly, McClellan as usual found a reason to pause while he took stock of the situation after the battle. "After a night of anxious deliberation, and a full and careful survey of the situation and condition of our army, the strength and position of the enemy, I concluded that the success of an attack on the 18th was not certain," he reported subsequently. Palfrey pithily observed, "It is hardly worth while to state his reasons." Suffering from an old gastrointestinal malady that dated to the Mexican War, which he cited as "the want of rest & anxiety" but may be more accurately attributed to the tension and excitement of the battle, McClellan took counsel of his fear that "at that moment," with Virginia lost, Washington menaced, and Maryland invaded, "the national cause could afford no risks of defeat." Nowhere east of the Alleghenies "was there another organized force able to arrest" the Rebels' march if the Army of the Potomac was destroyed by another attack at Antietam. Why he thought Lee had emerged any better from the terrible combat seems odd, but, in McClellan's view, he alone was the Savior of the Union and could not risk the Army of the Potomac. In the end McClellan's physical condition the next morning stifled Union initiative. Confined to his tent by a painful neuralgia attack and chronic dysentery, only later would he ride about in an ambulance. On the advice of Porter, Burnside, Sumner, and others, battle would not be renewed. Even Franklin thought the veteran regiments "too tired and too diminished in numbers" for more combat. Only at 5:45 p.m. on September 18 would McClellan at least reissue orders for Franklin to take Nicodemus Heights—early the next morning. One brigade only would make the assault, supported by a reinforced VI Corps with I and IX Corps moving forward pickets in their sectors—hardly an overwhelming offensive.[41]

As the day after Antietam dragged by inactively, both armies relaxed in place, gathered up dead and wounded, and nervously awaited developments. Lee, on the other hand, spent the day plotting escape while delaying retreat. He sought to mass fifty guns and smash through on the Hagerstown pike. Mustering that number of cannon and requisite fresh infantrymen for a determined assault on Franklin's fifteen-thousand-strong VI Corps with supporting artillery from I, II, VI, and XII Corps appeared beyond the ability of either Jackson or artillerist Col. Stephen D. Lee (who had performed so brilliantly in that capacity for Longstreet at Second Manassas). So advised and crestfallen, the commander of the Army of Northern Virginia next turned to ensuring retirement via Boteler's ford and whatever other crossings might be available. In Joseph Harsh's view, by not retiring on September 18 at least and threatening Franklin's attack, McClellan "exerted enough pressure to thwart Lee's last attempt to stay in Maryland."[42]

Crossing to Shepherdstown and thence marching upriver to Martinsburg before recrossing at Williamsport to move on Hagerstown and farther north had always been an option. Lee sent Stuart ahead with fifteen hundred troopers, five hundred infantry, and fourteen cannon to set up a new bridgehead at the Maryland town. With roads turned soupy by an afternoon thunderstorm, the Confederate army gathered together and began the horrendously difficult job of disengagement from the enemy and transiting murky Boteler's ford with men, wagons, and artillery. They successfully retired unmolested, so that by 10:00 a.m. on September 19, the Army of Northern Virginia had returned to the Old Dominion. "Carry Me Back to Old Virginia" replaced "Maryland, My Maryland" as the army's marching song. Parting shots discouraged the sparsely advancing Union skirmishers and Pleasonton's hesitant pursuit. Sadly, Lee left many wounded to the mercy of the victors. But he and his army had escaped. Although Federal pickets knew that the Rebels had evacuated their lines by dawn on September 19, McClellan issued no general order for some sweeping pursuit aimed at a Napoleonic coup de grace. He did direct repositioning of all the army corps for a studied, methodical advance and sent Williams to secure the Harpers Ferry flank and Couch and Franklin to cover the other flank upriver toward Williamsport. "The enemy is driven back into Virginia. Maryland and Pennsylvania are now safe," McClellan simply wired the War Department and counted his action a success. Nonetheless, the Maryland campaign had its coda.[43]

McClellan finally ordered Porter forward with two divisions behind Pleasonton's horsemen. He had instructions not to cross the Potomac. The reconnaissance merely confirmed Lee's withdrawal and that artillery commanded the Boteler's ford crossing from the south bank. McClellan, riding in an ambulance, communicated to Pleasonton the essence of this thinking at the end of the bloody week. The cavalry commander would pursue only if he saw "a splendid opportunity to inflict great damage upon the enemy without loss to yourself." Sparring with Lee remained a game of numbers; more casualties could only lengthen Union odds for success. Even Halleck's late-arriving wires continued to exude fears in the capital that "there is much danger of a movement below your left," as a "part of Lee's original plan to draw you as far as possible up the Potomac, and then move between you and Washington." Actually Lee continued to concentrate on attacking the opposite Federal flank even after returning to Virginia. Six days later, he would write Davis, "When I withdrew from Sharpsburg into Virginia, it was my intention to recross the Potomac at Williamsport, and move upon Hagerstown." By that time, however, Lee's plans would change as "the condition of the army prevented, nor is it yet strong enough to advance advantageously." Somehow, from the Pry house to the White House, nobody on the Union side figured all that out after Antietam. Concern for Lee's residual striking power conditioned McClellan's response, helped, ironically, by a series of little affairs at Shepherdstown from September 19 to 20.[44]

Here Lee's rearguard under the Episcopal priest turned soldier William Pendleton got into a mismanaged scrape with McClellan's token pursuit under Pleasonton and Porter, losing cannon and much face. McClellan, Porter, and Pleasonton planned to push the success until word of Confederate activity at Williamsport caused a diversion of Franklin's corps. An alerted Jackson responded to Pendleton's mishap by dispatching A. P. Hill back to take control and whip the Federals. The subsequent one-hour battle cost Pleasonton and Porter about 10 percent of their three-thousand-man reconnaissance while Hill's four thousand suffered the loss of only 261 men. The 118th Pennsylvania "Corn Exchange" regiment was all but destroyed in the action when its muskets malfunctioned and the Confederates slaughtered the men as they tried to recross the river. Hill said in his official report, "This was a wholesome lesson to the enemy, and taught them to know that it may be dangerous sometimes to press a retreating army." Col. Thomas H. Mann of the ill-fated Eighteenth Connecticut observed, "This little affair" proved "amusing as an interesting episode of history, thrilling to every participant, and terribly disastrous, particularly to the 118th Pennsylvania."[45]

The Shepherdstown episode suggested to Lee that his opponent finally had started in pursuit, but that his own battered army could still defeat its foe. Similarly, McClellan concluded that the enemy remained dangerous. However, Stuart's experience that same day at Williamsport put a nail in the coffin of Confederate hopes for Maryland. His cavalrymen proved incapable of sustaining a new bridgehead across the Potomac when McClellan countered with fully half of Pleasonton's mounted force plus Couch's division and two of Franklin's divisions. The stronger Federal force ushered Stuart back across the river with young Elisha Hunt Rhodes wondering, "Oh, why did we not attack them and drive them into the river?" He confided to his pocket diary that he did not understand such things, "but then I am only a boy." Taken together, Shepherdstown and Williamsport confirmed to Lee that his army was now too broken to indulge its leader's strategic whims. What he had begun three weeks before at White's ford could no longer be sustained. Like worn-out gladiators the two sides eyed each other from a distance, separated basically by the line of the Potomac. McClellan denied Confederate reentry into Maryland; Lee stymied immediate Federal return to the Old Dominion. What had begun on the Virginia Peninsula in late June concluded two months later on the upper Potomac. As Lee told the Confederate War Department in his official report, "The condition of our troops now demanded repose." Little Mac wrote his superiors the same thing: "The entire army had been greatly exhausted by unavoidable overwork, fatiguing marches, hunger, and want of sleep and rest previous to the last battle." In effect, both men had wrecked their armies fighting at Antietam. The Maryland campaign was over.[46]

If McClellan clearly lost yet another golden opportunity to destroy Lee in the two days after Antietam, he failed to admit that fact. He and the Army of the Potomac had nearly caught Lee's dispersed legions after South Mountain. His plan was good, his subordinates' execution less so. Franklin's inability to capitalize on the Crampton's Gap success corresponded with Miles's inept performance trying to defend Harpers Ferry. Lee rallied the rest of his army on solid defensive ground around Sharpsburg and used the advantage of terrain as he and McClellan prepared for a showdown. Little Mac retained the initiative that he had held since leaving Frederick, enjoying overwhelming numbers and the elixir of recent victories in the mountain passes. Still, he failed to translate planning into dynamic action and lost the immediate chance to destroy his enemy on September 16. The decisive confrontation that would decide the fate of the campaign, Maryland's allegiance, and perhaps the survival of the Union took place the next day, Wednesday, September 17, 1862. Even then McClellan's intentions had been telegraphed to the enemy by Hooker's pulled punch across the creek toward the Hagerstown road the evening before. Lee's diminished legions had no freedom of maneuver absent Jackson and the victors of Harpers Ferry. But they held the edge of terrain and compactness.

McClellan's intended coordinated assaults over the Antietam

devolved into an almost classic case of how not to fight a battle. Three virtually separate phases took place, from north of Sharpsburg on the Hagerstown pike to the rugged hilly terrain south of town. Picturesque sites like the Cornfield, West Woods, Dunker Church, Roulette farm lane, and Burnside's Bridge became indelibly etched into American legend as bloody touchstones of the nation's past. Lee held, McClellan's attacks disintegrated at the hands of concentrated rifle and artillery fire, and neither army could annihilate the other although more than twenty-two thousand young Americans fell in the carnage. Like Second Manassas, Antietam again proved the impossibility of annihilative victory for either contestant. When it ended, both armies took stock on September 18. The corpse-strewn, twelve-mile-square battlefield provided no inducement for further bloodshed on either's part. Lee remained combative, but McClellan declined to attack anew. Burying the dead and tending the wounded provided a substitute. Lee withdrew to Virginia that night, leaving behind his fallen and an impression of Union victory. In a way, McClellan secured his objective.

Antietam was a pyrrhic success at best for McClellan. It culminated an almost miraculous three-week renaissance of his army, the well-orchestrated pursuit that maneuvered his opponent away from his original intent and induced strategic risks on the part of Lee. Yet in the end McClellan permitted the badly damaged Army of Northern Virginia to escape intact. Incapable of aggressive or even daring action, McClellan and his army failed to destroy Lee as intended by the president and administration. True, the Union army, just as battered as the Confederate, barred Lee's reentry north of the Potomac in the days after the battle. Yet the politicians and the country hoped for something more. What had begun months before as a dream in Confederate eyes and had survived through the long hot summer of Cedar Mountain, Second Manassas, and Chantilly had indeed foundered in the gaps of South Mountain and along the banks of the Antietam. George B. McClellan and his army had saved the Old Line State, the nation's capital, and, in his eyes at least, the Union. His words to wife Ellen betrayed his real intent. "Our victory was complete," he declared, feeling "some little pride in having with a beaten and demoralized army defeated Lee so utterly, & saved the North so completely." McClellan thought that he could do no more.[47]

⇥ 9 ⇤

Opportunities Found and Lost

AUTUMN HAD JUST BEGUN its colorful ritual along the Antietam. But after the battle the forests and fields were scorched and bleak. Orderly Sgt. James A. Wright of the First Minnesota remembered buildings riddled by shot and shell, harvested crops singed by exploding projectiles, fences broken or scattered, and the fields "trampled by hurrying battalions until they looked as if swept by a tornado." Leafless trees stood as stark as at midwinter, if not split apart by the holocaust. "The green sward had been stained with a brighter crimson than nature gives to the dying leaves," he noted years later. The human toll equaled that of nature. Statistics hardly told the whole story. Shepherdstown resident Mary Bedinger Mitchell, daughter of a former minister to Denmark, recalled the noise, confusion, dust, throngs of stragglers, horsemen galloping about, wagons blocking one another, and teamsters wrangling—a continual din of shouting, swearing, and rumbling. Most of all she remembered the overflow of wounded: "Wherever four walls and a roof were found together," with "every inch of space" filled with suffering, "and yet the cry was for room." "An ever present sense of anguish, dread, pity, and, I fear, hatred" constituted her recollections of Antietam. On Samuel Poffenberger's farm north of Sharpsburg, nurse Clara Barton helped load the vanguard of thousands of Union wounded for an overland trek to Frederick hospitals and beyond. There could be no rest, said her assistant, Cornelius Welles: "All around us were dying men, calling for water, for friends, for God to deliver them from their miseries."[1]

Once the burial parties had done their job and the armies moved on, other angels of the battlefield would hew to reconstruction. Sightseers traveled great distances to view the scenes atop South Mountain or, like Otho Nesbitt from Clear Spring, Maryland, gaped at the sight of Confederate dead at Antietam. "I suppose a mile long or more," nearly "all lying on their backs as if they hadn't even made a struggle," he observed before leaving for home, "having satisfied myself in regard to falling humanity." Slowly, frightened local citizenry emerged from hiding places in cellars and the Killiansburg Cave along the Chesapeake and Ohio Canal about two miles from town. Little Theresa Kretzer remembered how everything at the end of the day of the battle seemed painted in red: haze from the sunset, the brick of the church, "red, red, red." "Too afraid to cry," she recalled. "It was a red stew," and the smell of death hung over the region for weeks, even months. Sergeant Wright recalled how arriving soldiery had found "an old-fashioned country neighborhood—almost ideal for the times," with the people living in peace and enjoying undisturbed life on farms where most had been born. "But, we left it with homes, fields, and forests, marred, shattered, devastated, and ruined." Little wonder that "the inhabitants were as glad that we were going as we were to go." The only gain for Sharpsburg, he observed, "was its 4,000 or more new-made graves, and people are not generally desirous of gain in that direction."[2]

The basic facts about the battle were known in Washington within hours, in Richmond somewhat later. Copies of the *Philadelphia Examiner* reputedly spread news of South Mountain and Sharpsburg to the Confederate capital "like a thunderclap out of a rainbow." President Abraham Lincoln told an associate that while Antietam had been fought on a Wednesday, Lee had not pulled back before Friday, so that he could not find out until Saturday, September 20, "whether we had really won a victory or not." Government censorship shrouded the details in the South, although Felix G. de Fontaine of the *Charleston Daily Courier* and Peter Wellington Alexander, another reporter, recounted the heroic gallantry and general excitement of combat along with a fair share of dubious facts on numbers, casualties, and details of combat. George E. Smalley of the *New York Tribune* and Charles Coffin of the *Boston Journal* supplied similar stories for northern readers. Smalley's account of Antietam, written in the dim light of a swaying oil lamp on the night train to New York, observes historian J. Cutler Andrews, "was finer than any other writing of the kind during the whole four years of the conflict." Southern commentators proved more charitable toward Lee and his retreat than one *Tribune* correspondent, who deplored "the clean leisurely escape of the foe," a staple complaint of Union editors in the weeks after the contest. More indicative, the refugee *Memphis Appeal* not so worshipfully observed, "Maryland has a few noble patriots in her limits, but as a state, she resembles Ephraim—she is tied to her idol, the g-l-o-u-r-i-o-u-s Union, and ought to be let alone." Nurse Ada W. Bacot, the South Carolina plantation widow working hospital wards in Charlottesville, Virginia, agreed. On Sunday night, September 21, she noted in her diary, "Maryland is not going to come to our relief." God help us, she wrote, "we can do nothing of ourselves." By October a New York City exhibition of ninety-five glass plate views of the Antietam battlefield by photographers Alexander Gardner and James F. Gibson would convey another dimension of battlefield horrors to that city's populace, just as many northern voters began to demand peace.[3]

Whatever the immediate impact of the September battles for the general public, these events provided opportunities that opened and then closed for both sides. Contemporaries as well as historians keyed on Union commander George B. McClellan's failure to follow up his victories while glossing over the fact that both armies had suffered so much at Antietam that neither could renew major combat. Lee's men could not recross the Potomac to exploit Yankee crop harvests or continue any advance into Pennsylvania. Other Confederate counteroffensives in Kentucky and west Tennessee equally recoiled by October, counting for something on political and diplomatic fronts. McClellan set his own marker by wiring the War Department at 1:30 p.m. on September 19, "I have the honor to report that Maryland is entirely freed from the presence of the enemy, who has been driven across the Potomac. No fears need now be entertained for the safety of Pennsylvania." That same incomplete definition of success also came from Don Carlos Buell in Kentucky, a kindred spirit with Little Mac, that mere rejection of enemy armies from loyal soil constituted sufficiency instead of Washington's desire for annihilative victory. Officials understood the need for more manpower to achieve that kind of victory. Soon Maryland governor A. W. Bradford and his

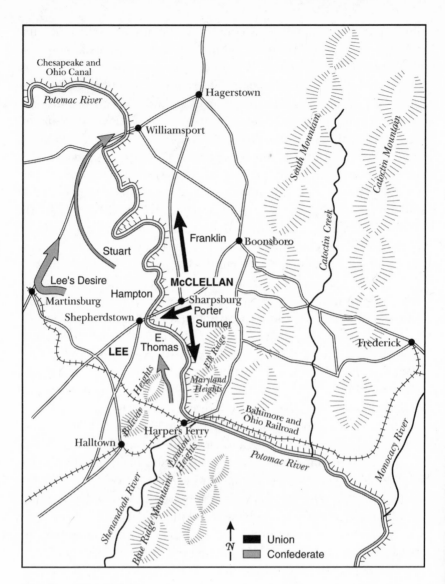

Situation—Post-Antietam

Keystone State counterpart, Andrew G. Curtin, faced violent resistance to the process of enrollment for Federal military service in that new war and eventually had to ask Washington for aid in suppressing citizen interference with the process. More draft resistance would soon occur in the Midwest as Lincoln issued two executive proclamations the week after Antietam that exacerbated the discontent.[4]

Although Antietam had not been the signature victory sought by the president, he decided to utilize this event to expedite slave emancipation. Only five days after the battle, Lincoln publicly promulgated a preliminary Emancipation Proclamation. On January 1, 1863, he decreed, "All persons held as slaves within any state, or designated part of a state, the people where of shall then be in rebellion against the United States shall be then, thenceforward, and forever free." The executive government of the United States (including military and naval authority) would recognize and maintain freedom of such persons without acting to repress them "in any efforts they may make for their actual freedom." These provisions were subsumed by his opening statement: "Hereafter, as heretofore, the war will be prosecuted for the object of practically restoring the constitutional relation between the United States and each of the states and the people therefore, in which States that relation is or may be suspended or disturbed." Earlier notions of compensated emancipation and voluntary colonization of freed slaves remained on the table for discussion with Congress. Key clauses of the March article of war and the Second Confiscation Act were attached to this expansion of the confiscation process. Still troubled with issuing any decree as long as Confederate arms remained on northern soil, as well as what to do with massive numbers of freedmen, Lincoln finally announced to his noon cabinet meeting on September 22, "I determined, as soon as [the Rebel army] should be driven out of Maryland, to issue a Proclamation of Emancipation such as I thought most likely to be useful." The enemy had been driven out, "and I am going to fulfill that promise." Later recalling that he had made up his mind when Lee was in Frederick and hinting at his change of heart in a meeting with midwestern church leaders the day before South Mountain, it was Antietam that caused him to go public.[5]

In short, the preliminary emancipation reflected Lincoln's own willingness to use his commander in chief's powers to underscore "a practical war measure" aimed at Southerners using that property for rebellion. Two days later, Lincoln also struck hard at internal dissent in the North whereby persons countenancing evasion of militia call-ups, discouraging voluntary enlistments, "or guilty of any disloyal practice, affording aid and comfort to Rebels against the authority of the United States" would be subject to martial law and trial and punishment by military courts and commissions. The writ of habeas corpus would be suspended for "all persons arrested, or who are now, or hereafter during the rebellion shall be, imprisoned in any fort, camp, arsenal, military prison, or other place of confinement by any military authority or by the sentence of any Court Martial or Military Commission." Army of the Potomac corps artillery commander Charles Wainwright viewed the habeas corpus suspension as an action simply to "return some of the many men absent at home without leave, and who are really deserters," not as any demonstrable action against citizens' rights. But this move, like that of emancipation, came at risk to the chief executive. McClellan, for his part, deplored both presidential pronouncements, and he wielded some influence. Lincoln, however, viewed his own actions as critical to saving the Union. They also appeared vital for parrying centrifugal forces buffeting the administration: the Radicals on Capitol Hill as well as a distinctly political threat from the McClellan–Buell faction of army leadership and the conservative public. Lincoln's perceived attack on civil liberties possibly garnered more notoriety than emancipation at the time. Several scholars suggest that the habeas corpus action dampened public and press dissent for fear of imprisonment and created a dangerous image of Lincoln as dictator.[6]

Scholars understandably accorded more significance to the battle of Antietam and the Emancipation Proclamation. "A revolution in the affairs of the Republic," comments Stephen Sears, while Alan C. Guelzo underscores the proclamation as "the most revolutionary pronouncement ever signed by an American president." Possibly "no consequence of Antietam was more momentous than this one," states James McPherson, whose book on Antietam carries the subtitle *Crossroads of Freedom* to underscore the connection. Earlier students, such as Edward Stackpole, proclaimed that the bloodiest day "was made the vehicle whereby the war between the states was transformed from a family dispute into a crusade for human freedom," and James Murfin thought that with a few pen strokes and the "thin thread" of recent victory, Lincoln changed the war from one of "economics and politics" into a struggle for the abolition of slavery, thus automatically making Lee's Maryland campaign and the battle of Antietam "one of the most decisive of the war." Daniel E. Sutherland ends his terse study *The Emergence of Total War* with the assertion that the preliminary Emancipation Proclamation was a calculated blow at southern morale "and a subtle means of maintaining a policy of total war." However much the document was merely another emancipation way station, building on the confiscation acts and destined to gather momentum only over time with constitutional amendments and civil rights legislation a century later to enhance compliance, it reflected the president's "concentric legal and political grasp of issues," according to jurist Frank Williams, requiring "boldness and considerable risk taking" not to be taken for granted. Most important, as Henry Halleck explained to western army general Ulysses S. Grant at the end of March 1863, "there is now no possible hope of reconciliation" for "we must conquer the rebels or be conquered by them," as "every slave withdrawn from the enemy is the equivalent of a white man put *hors de combat.*"[7]

Would Lincoln's contemporaries have seen this fact at the time of its issue after Antietam? It took until December's annual congressional message for Lincoln to tell that body, "In giving freedom to the *slave* we *assure* freedom to the *free*," but it was a hard sell for many Northerners. Lincoln's cabinet had little more say in the September decision than in the summer. Postmaster General Montgomery Blair again offered objections based on fears about border slave-state response; his sister Elizabeth Blair Lee recorded in her diary, "It is really felt to be a paper pronunciamento and of no practical result." Secretary of the Treasury Salmon P. Chase patronizingly told his chief, "What you have said, Mr. President, fully satisfies me that you have given to every proposition which has been made, a kind and candid consideration." But Secretary of the Navy Gideon Welles despaired, "It is a step in the progress of this war which will extend into the distant future," rendering a favorable termination to the struggle "more remote with every moment." Others wondered about the document's impact on fall elections. Fifteen thousand printed copies of the proclamation went out for distribution to ensure army and navy compliance.[8]

Still, abolitionists praised the move as the dawning of a new day and predicted an imminent end to the rebellion. Radicals begrudgingly conceded the high ground to Lincoln's initiative, and conservatives decried usurpation of the Constitution. The Democratic *New York World* claimed that Lincoln and his government were "adrift on the current of radical fanaticism." A small-town newspaper in the Cumberland Valley of central Pennsylvania feared Lincoln's act would unify the South as never before. The ever-acidic Baltimore caricaturist Adalbert Volck drew a bitter cartoon depicting Lincoln dipping his pen in the devil's inkwell to write the document, a view of the Santo Domingo slave uprising replete with rape, murder, and other atrocities hanging on the wall behind him. Jefferson Davis called the proclamation "the most execrable measure recorded in the history of guilty man," and the Confederate Congress demanded raising the black flag of no quarter. Richmond clerk John B. Jones thought many northern newspapers seemed "to dissent from the policy of Lincoln's emancipation" hoping that evil consequences might not grow from it. Virginia slaveholders, skeptical of Yankee enforcement, began "running the Negroes" by foot, rail, and, in the words of Danville slave Lorenzo Ivy, "shipped them South like cattle."[9]

Staunton, Virginia, diarist Joseph Waddell deplored that "the war must come to this" with no end in sight, civil liberty gone from both North and South, and a military despotism in prospect. Without European intervention the war "must go on interminally [sic]," exhaustion "must soon come," and a state of guerrilla warfare with it. War-weary Americans, he thought, would be ready to accept any authority that might restore peace. Northern Virginia refugee Judith McGuire caustically noted, "Abolition papers are in ecstasies, as if they did not know that it can only be carried out *within their* lines, and there they have been practically free from the moment we were invaded." Similarly, Boston Brahmin Robert Gould Shaw, soon to personally lead the African American Fifty-fourth Massachusetts to death and glory, wrote his mother shortly after Antietam and Lincoln's action, "I can't see what *practical* good it can do now." To Shaw, wherever the army had gone "there remain no slaves, and the proclamation won't free them where we don't go." And the army knew it.[10]

McClellan was aghast at Lincoln's deed, although the president surely understood better the need to offer the people persuasive humanitarian or moralistic meaning to their sacrifices rather than appeasement of the enemy. As historian Michael C. C. Adams discerns, he simply sought desperate measures giving new impetus "to apparently jaded soldiers afflicted with a chronic slowness." Soldiers from Owen County, Indiana, might continue "united in allegiance," but no longer in purpose. However, Col. Rufus Dawes of Wisconsin told a Marietta, Ohio, audience while on furlough after Antietam, "We like the Emancipation Proclamation because it is right, and because it is the edict of our Commander in Chief, the President of the United States." Thus reaction proved predictably mixed. Pennsylvania brigadier John Geary (lately returned to service after wounding at Cedar Mountain) told his wife that the president's dictum "is the most important public document ever issued by an officer of our Government," although he still feared the consequences for the country "on the verge of anarchy and despotism." God save us, he exhorted, "from the treason which surrounds us on every hand."[11]

To loyal Virginian David Strother at McClellan's headquarters, "Father Abraham's paper wads" were as unserviceable as blank cartridges: such "wild blows show that the revolution is progressing to its grand denouement." To him, "violent and senseless proclamations" (both the emancipation and habeas corpus documents) merely tried to counter the great military triumphs of the other side and thus were "a giving way of strength and self-confidence." They were unnecessary, indicating "cowardice in the government in addition to other weaknesses." Artillery colonel Wainwright agreed. He heard little talk about the proclamation in the army, "but all think it unadvised at this time; even those most anti-slavery." Corp. Thomas H. Mann of the Eighteenth Connecticut had hoped for gradual emancipation rather than the anticipated misery of a wholesale freeing of a people "who could not take care of themselves." Still, affairs had arrived at a point where the proclamation "is absolutely necessary for the country's salvation." After the war, Minnesotan James Wright recalled that discussion of the proclamation in Army of the Potomac camps had shown "a diversity of personal views and some talk about the rights of private property." Greeting the proclamation strictly as a war measure, "there were none at that time but believed that a successful ending of the war . . . meant the end of slavery." Besides, he contended, "our minds were turned to more personal matters."[12]

At first Lincoln worried that his proclamation met such mixed response. When Vice President Hannibal Hamlin wrote him expressing thanks for "the great act of the age," wise in statesmanship and patriotic purpose, the president replied soberly that on face value, his move did not seem very satisfactory. Stocks had declined and troops came forward more slowly than ever. Fewer troops were actually in the field at the end of six days following his announcement than at the beginning, for attrition among the old outnumbered new additions. "The North responds to the proclamation sufficiently in breath; but breath alone kills no rebels," he concluded dejectedly.

Of course, Lincoln also aimed his action at a European audience. The issue of mediation or outright intervention had simmered all summer, hung up on some "sign" of Confederate success. Rebel victories from the Seven Days through Second Manassas, followed by Lee's invasion of Maryland, might have seemed sufficient. Yet the European political picture stayed cloudy, with elements in Great Britain and France ostensibly pro-Confederate or at least neutral but not overwhelmingly interventionist. Queen Victoria sanctioned a unified response from the continent and her own government. Prussia and Russia would not oblige, playing make-weight against the more headstrong French emperor Napoleon III as well as most members of Viscount Henry John Temple Palmerston's British cabinet. Timing remained critical, what with a ten-day transatlantic transmission time confusing the meaning of North American events. Neither the news of Antietam nor the proclamation had the immediate impact desired by Lincoln.

In fact, diplomatic historian Howard Jones advances that the Union's rather narrow success at bloody Antietam actually increased British interest in intervening "before the fighting spun completely out of control." Although no one knew for sure, the fact may have been, as he suggests, that the Confederacy was actually closer to winning European *mediation* after Second Manassas but then became becalmed anticipating that Lee's offensive would cause outright *intervention.* When word of both Antietam and Lincoln's proclamation finally reached Europe in late September, the latter drew significance away from the former, which fit Lincoln's own intent that "emancipation would help us in Europe and convince them that we are incited by something more than ambition." Still, initial reactions from London and the continent equated his words with an unleashing of a people's war: carnage on the battlefield as well as a massive African American uprising such as seen decades earlier in Santo Domingo. To Jones, Europe at first saw emancipation by the sword or race war and Antietam as "catalysts to intervention."[13]

On the day of the South Mountain battle, Palmerston told Lord Russell, the foreign secretary, that the "very complete smashing" the Federals had received at Second Bull Run suggested that additional, even greater disasters awaited them and that possibly Washington or Baltimore would fall to the Confederates. In that case, "would it not be time for us to consider whether . . . England and France might not address the contending parties and recommend an arrangement upon the basis of separation?" Russell certainly thought so, replying, "We ought ourselves to recognize the Southern States as an independent State." Later, on the day after Lincoln's emancipation announcement (but obviously still not privy to its existence), the prime minister informed Russell that the outcome of the Maryland campaign "must have a great effect on the state of affairs." If Lee emerged victorious, then the Federals might be ready for mediation. If the opposite occurred, "we may wait awhile and see what may follow." Thus, until news from America clarified matters, Confederate European envoys James Mason and John Sliddell had every reason to believe that Anglo-French mediation was "very close at hand." After all, Chancellor of the Exchequer William Gladstone had declared in a much publicized address at Newcastle-on-Tyne that Jefferson Davis had made an army, was doing the same for a navy, and, what is more important than either, "they have made a nation."

Reality struck publicly only when the London *Times* marveled at "the exceedingly remarkable" turnaround of the Army of the Potomac at Antietam. Palmerston advised Russell early in October that South Mountain and Antietam "have rather set the North up again." The whole matter was "full of difficulty, and can only be cleared up by some more decided events between the contending armies." Other members of the British cabinet, such as the Earl of Granville, George Gower, lord president of the Queen's Council, fretted that Great Britain could not avoid "drifting" into the American war, not merely mediate the warring parties. U.S. Minister Charles Francis Adams in London told his superiors in Washington that Antietam had "done a good deal to restore our drooping credit here" as "less and less appears to be thought of mediation and intervention." He saw little adverse effect from the proclamation. Neither a major battle nor a presidential edict could resolve the dilemma for Europe—or America—as yet.[14]

European concern about America's carnage competed with self-interest. Unsettled conditions in central Europe demanded the Great Powers' attention, while some British statesmen feared that an increasingly powerful United States might take Canada. Gower and especially the British secretary for war, Sir George Cornewall Lewis, presented a compelling challenge to intervention to Russell and the prime minister. The mild-mannered Lewis suggested that any premature move would perceptively identify Europe with the slaveholding South, thus ensuring conflict with the more formidable industrializing North. Moreover, significant logistical difficulties would accompany British military coercion, especially with the impending winter months. England could also find herself drafting peace terms that required not merely Union and Confederate acquiescence but also European sanction. Lacking that, "England might stand alone." By October 22, even Palmerston would tell Russell, "We must continue merely to be lookers-on till the war shall have taken a more decided turn." Napoleon III might advance a proposal for asking the warring sides for a six months' armistice with accompanying lifting of the blockade, renewal of cotton exports, and commencement of peace negotiations. But Russia would not concur, and Gladstone wrote his wife by November 11, "The United States affair has ended and not well." Minister Adams concluded that the Union had passed through the crisis of its fate in the wake of Antietam. In the end, however, British pragmatism and the fact that fall elections still showed northern public support for Lincoln and the Union may have been just as important.[15]

Meanwhile the proclamation's impact at home blended with growing northern unease about the government's handling of the war generally and politicization within the eastern field army concerning its commander. Gideon Welles felt Lincoln's action "less exciting than I had apprehended," causing "but little jubilation on one hand, nor much angry outbreak on the other." Time was passing, the end of the rebellion no closer, and the administration's major headache after Antietam as it was before seemed the general who had engineered a kind of victory in Maryland but failed to exploit it to the fullest. Welles further confided to his diary on September 26 that it had been "almost a fortnight" since Antietam, "but our army is doing nothing." To be sure, McClellan had been hard at work trying to rid himself of Stanton and Halleck. His letters to Mary Ellen sound almost childlike: "I have shown that I can fight battles & *win* them!" He complained about Lincoln's hardening war policy. Yet William H. Aspinwall, McClellan's old patron, an anti-administration Democratic New York businessman and financier, quickly snuffed out the general's inclination to publicly announce his opinions by visiting army headquarters and telling him flatly that it was "my duty to submit to the Presdt's proclamation & quietly continue doing my duty as a soldier," although "the nation cannot stand the burdens of the war much longer & that a speedy solution is necessary." Little support came from army friends Ambrose Burnside, Jacob Cox, or John Cochrane. A northern governor's conference, unhappy with Lincoln yet distracted by the implications of his proclamations, vetoed any support for McClellan. Postmaster General Blair too counseled that a soldier should toe the line in civil-military relations.[16]

McClellan returned to brooding, much as he had after Malvern Hill, seeing renewed persecution by his enemies and resentful of those in higher authority. He talked of retirement after one more success. He jealously protected his beloved Army of the Potomac, the enthusiasm of which "surpasses anything you ever imagined," he told his wife. He doubted "Napoleon even ever possessed the love & confidence of his men more fully than I do of mine." He spoke of reorganizing a battered field force, moving to retake Harpers Ferry prior to advancing across the Potomac toward the Shenandoah Valley while shielding the nation's capital downriver and regaining control over supply problems. In fact, dialogue between the Army of the Potomac commander and General in Chief Henry Halleck relapsed into an all-too-familiar pattern concerning enemy intentions ("a renewal of the attempt in Maryland" versus threatening "both your army and the capital"), the necessary strength to accomplish missions ("retain in Washington merely the force necessary to garrison it and send everything else available to reinforce this Army"), and McClellan's adamant contention that the army was not ready to undertake another campaign or to bring on another battle, "unless great advantages are offered by some mistake of the enemy or pressing military exigencies render it necessary." He promised that if reinforced as requested and "allowed to take my own course, I will hold myself responsible for the safety of Washington." McClellan's refrain had not changed much since the spring. When he complained now about insufficient horses for his cavalry, Lincoln shot back caustically, "Will you pardon me for asking what the horses of your army have done since the battle of Antietam that fatigue anything."[17]

At this point, the commander in chief again traveled to McClellan's headquarters. Corps commander William B. Franklin had it right when he decided the president's intent was "to hurry us on again," although he added uncharitably, "or as I begin to think it is, a desire for more blood." Protesting his army's unreadiness, McClellan told

Ellen, "I incline to think that the real purpose is to push me into a premature advance into Virginia." Claiming great victory merely by saving Maryland and Pennsylvania could not help a political leader facing off-year elections, however. The president had wired the general immediately after South Mountain, "Can't you beat them some more before they get off?" Apparently not, and there had been nasty post-Antietam rumors about McClellan's lackluster performance and conciliationist sentiments. The wounded Joe Hooker did not help, undercutting his superior's reputation and actively plumbing his chances of succeeding Little Mac in command. Boarding one of Baltimore and Ohio president John Garrett's trains, the chief executive and a small party journeyed to Harpers Ferry to personally see the situation. A somewhat nonplussed McClellan greeted them at noon on October 1. They proceeded to visit army camps and hospitals, and Lincoln saw for himself the army's condition and morale, despite some unflattering comments from the ranks about a seemingly disinterested commander in chief. Most of all, Lincoln wanted to chat with McClellan. The leader of the embattled nation wondered if his principal field commander was up to his old tricks. The president had just cashiered one War Department officer who had asserted openly that common army knowledge held the object of the late campaign to be "that neither army shall get much advantage of the other; that both shall be kept in the field till they are exhausted, when we will make a compromise and save slavery." That incident alone had prompted Blair to advise McClellan against meddling in presidential policies.[18]

The meeting between Lincoln and McClellan proved cordial, although some observers considered the president boorish, rude, unkempt, and disrespectful of the soldiery. The official party, accompanied by Burnside, Franklin, Edwin V. Sumner, and John Reynolds, reviewed the troops and toured the battlefields of Antietam and South Mountain. The president appeared uncomfortable with all the military pomp, seeming to duck appearances before the troops on several occasions. Brigadier Geary thought the president appeared "quite careworn," but McClellan found him affable and "very kind personally," especially since "he was convinced I was the best general in the country." A harsher view came from artillerist Charles Wainwright: "Not a word of approval, not even a smile of approbation; for that matter the army has not received the smallest official acknowledge-

ment from Washington for their late victories." He added gratuitously, "Mr. Lincoln [is] not only the ugliest man I ever saw, but the
most uncouth and gawky in his manners and appearance." The lanky
Lincoln would have chuckled at a member of the Ninth New York
Zouaves' observation, "Ain't the old bugger lean? Why he wouldn't
pay for skinning." Erstwhile corps commander Alpheus Williams told
his daughter that he had talked with the president "sitting on a pile
of logs," finding him "unaffected, simple-minded, honest, and frank"
but perhaps lacking firmness "amongst the multitude of advisers and
advice." One Minnesotan suspected that because "the newspapers
began to criticize the conduct of the war" and "to misstate conditions
and misconstrue actions," the president's visit "seemed to indicate an
early movement."[19]

Yet neither Lincoln nor McClellan could quite get the measure
of the other. McClellan came away convinced that the president
"departed with a more vivid idea of the great difficulty of the task we
had accomplished." Lincoln left McClellan's headquarters perplexed
about his general's procrastination. He apparently told one of his
companions during the visit that it was not the Army of the Potomac
that they beheld from a hilltop near camp, but simply "McClellan's
bodyguard." Lincoln did gain an appreciation of manpower now available to McClellan:88,095, more than enough to move out smartly
against Lee's battered army. Had he understood McClellan's constant refrain of how ill-prepared the army was for renewed offensive?
The chief executive informed McClellan that he would be "a ruined
man" if McClellan did not move forward rapidly and effectively. Did
such a short visit truly show the ill-shod, ill-clothed, and meagerly
provisioned army that had fought the deadly battle at Antietam?
Could a short visit to a gory battlefield several weeks after the bodies
had been buried and dead horses burned really tell the president of
the psychological as well as physical toll exacted from the army? Or
was McClellan using all that merely as an excuse, a stalling tactic to
prevent radicalization of the conduct of the war? When McClellan
escorted Lincoln to South Mountain on the return to Frederick to
catch his train, were the pair as one in their understanding of the
need for rapid follow-up by the Army of the Potomac in an election
year? Or were the two men as far apart as ever and time fast drawing
nigh on their relationship?[20]

The president certainly had plenty of time to reflect on what he had seen as his party retraced its journey back to Frederick. They stopped in Burkittsville for a humble supper embellished by homemade pie and fresh cream but sobered by repeated hospital visits and a subsequent brief stop at the Ramsey house behind the Frederick courthouse to cheer wounded brigadier George I. Hartsuff. Lincoln's departure from the train station at 5:20 p.m. on October 4 took place amid high winds and drenching rain as a small partisan crowd heard him graciously thank soldiers and civilians alike for "their devotion to our glorious cause." In camp, *Springfield Republican* correspondent "Dunn Browne" (Samuel Wheelock Fiske, a Congregational minister and officer) wrote home that "the tremendous army of McClellan" still lay "in its tracks" in "the most precious part" of the campaigning season and seemed to be repeating "its masterly inactivity of the last year over again with utmost precision." Agitation had to be suppressed, incendiary opinions "promptly choked down," while the grand Army of the Potomac "is safe and so are its enemies." In Washington a grumpy Salmon P. Chase penned in his diary the day before that he expected little good from the president's visit to McClellan; his naval colleague Welles observed that the "reticent, vexed, disappointed" war secretary Edwin Stanton and the ineffective general in chief Henry Halleck could do little to move McClellan, "sadly afflicted with what the President calls the 'slows.'" Elizabeth Blair Lee also noted that McClellan gave the enemy time "to breathe and rally—too slow—that's his besetting Sin," when writing her naval captain husband Samuel Phillips Lee at sea. Lincoln, for his part, expressed no opinion "as to Generalship, nor of results of McClellan and the battle of Antietam" at the next cabinet meeting. To Welles, however, "The army is quiet, reposing in camp," while "the country groans, but nothing is done." Confidence had to be giving way under "this fatuous inaction."[21]

Once back at his desk at the White House, however, the president moved to ensure that McClellan clearly understood the purpose of his visit. He sent special instructions through Stanton and Halleck that McClellan was to "cross the Potomac and give battle to the enemy or drive him south." He should move "while the roads are good," keeping (as always) between the enemy and the capital. Only then could the administration guarantee thirty thousand reinforcements, barely half that amount if McClellan advanced into the Shenandoah Valley (which, incidentally, Lee was hoping he might do and which would clearly uncover Washington). It was the springtime strategic guidance all over again. Lincoln advised all this "but does not order," Halleck iterated on October 6, being "very desirous" that movement start as soon as possible. Yet McClellan's announced plan of patiently preparing bridges and railroads so that Harpers Ferry might serve as the logistical base for his next campaign with Lee in the lower Shenandoah found little favor until the plan of operations had been "positively determined." Brooking no nonsense, the administration wanted an immediate report on the general's campaign plans and schedule and to what point he wished reinforcements dispatched. McClellan proceeded to spend the next three weeks haggling over the details. Seeing no "strategical value" to Lincoln's preferred line of advance, McClellan planned to "fight the enemy if they remain near Winchester, or, failing in that, to force them to abandon the Valley of the Shenandoah, then to adopt a new and decisive line of operations which shall strike at the heart of the rebellion." Such vagueness impressed no one who knew that McClellan's preferred line of advance meant a return to the Virginia Peninsula.[22]

McClellan had some cause for delay. The material requirements of his army were huge. No replacement clothing had been issued since leaving the Peninsula, and apparel remained dirty, greasy, threadbare, and faded in color. Many in the ranks lacked shoes. His cavalry desperately needed remounts. The bloody battles also demanded manpower and munitions replacements. McClellan expended much ink over corrective actions with the quartermasters. Even with such replenishments (which could not arrive before late October, despite the logisticians' promises), McClellan admitted that his own planned "little campaign can't last many days for when it is once fought some other line of operations will have to be taken as the one up here leads to no final result." The whole situation was a struggle of wills between Lincoln and McClellan, each wanting the war conducted in his own way and each with his own ideas regarding defeat of Lee's army. Meanwhile, under great duress, the army commander begrudgingly followed official publication of the preliminary emancipation with a general order on October 7 reminding the men that "armed forces are raised & supported simply to sustain the Civil Authorities and are to be held in strict subordination thereto in all respects." Such authority, "who is charged with the administration of the National affairs," would determine the objects for which armies were to be employed in suppressing rebellion. Discussion of government measures beyond "temperate and respectful expressions of opinion" would be detrimental to the discipline and efficiency of the military, as "the remedy for political error if any are committed is to be found only in the action of the people at the polls." McClellan thought his message reflected well on the comity of the president's visit. Those close to the administration gave it short shrift.[23]

Events began to move past McClellan after Antietam. Lee masked his own army's recuperation by accurately writing President Jefferson Davis that his opponent's force "is apparently quiescent" since its commander "is yet unable to move, and finds a difficulty in procuring provisions more than sufficient from day to day." Lee was much more concerned that somehow McClellan might move on Richmond, "as at present there is no way in which I can endanger his safety." Indeed, Lee might have better exploited William W. Loring's activities in the Kanawha Valley of western Virginia. McClellan placidly acquiesced to War Department orders sending Cox's division back to counter a Confederate resurgence in that sector. But Lee saw Loring merely as a source of reinforcements for his own army and instead looked to his valued cavalry chief J. E. B. Stuart to keep McClellan's Federals off balance. Stuart took his eighteen hundred cavalrymen on another daring raid north of the Potomac from October 10 to 12 designed "to impede and embarrass the military operations of the enemy."[24]

Stuart's latest escapade netted horses, destroyed property, and raised the alarm once more in the Cumberland Valley before the invaders slipped east of the mountains, evaded Pleasonton's pursuit, and passed virtually unscathed back across the Potomac between Harpers Ferry and Washington. It was, observed Baltimore department commander John Wool, "certainly a bold and daring enterprise, in the execution of which the [Rebel] soldiers at Chambersburg [Pennsylvania] changed the rags which covered them for the uniform clothing of the United States, and supplied themselves on their route with 1,000 fresh horses, besides destroying, at Chambersburg, the railroad depot, with all the rolling stock" as well as "ripping up rails of that road and damaging several bridges," thus seriously affecting McClellan's logistics. Sgt. Maj. Elisha Hunt Rhodes of the Second New Hampshire blushed in his diary, "We are very much ashamed that the Rebels were allowed to make their late raid into Pennsylvania," and mortified the more "that we did not catch some of the rebel raiders."[25]

In fact, Stuart's second "ride around McClellan" (replicating a feat of similar notoriety earlier on the Peninsula) proved the pivotal event of the post-Antietam period. One of Stuart's aides, R. Channing Price, lightheartedly described the ride: "It was ludicrous in the extreme to see the old Dutchmen as their horses were taken in every variety of circumstances, from the stable, the threshing machine, wagons etc.," with receipts given "to the effect that the horses were taken for the Army of the Confederate States, to be paid as damage by the U.S. Government." Having executed the action with "prudence and enterprise," Stuart confirmed for Lee that McClellan "has detached no part of his army eastward, but, on the contrary, has been receiving reinforcements," his line stretching from Hagerstown to Rockville with the center at Harpers Ferry. Lee next turned to breaking up the Harpers Ferry–to–Winchester railroad "to increase the obstacles to [Federal] advance up the Shenandoah valley" as well as to provide material for Confederate needs elsewhere. McClellan's response (besides excuses to Washington) saw a somewhat desultory reconnaissance across the Potomac toward Charlestown and Martinsburg that tested Lincoln's waning patience. McClellan apparently could not protect the line of the Potomac and again showed a lack of offensive drive. As the president told Halleck, if the Confederates had more to occupy their attention south of the Potomac they would be less likely to raid north of the river.[26]

On October 13, Old Abe wrote his troubling field commander, "You remember my speaking to you of what I called your overcautiousness." Was McClellan not still so, "when you assume that you cannot do what the enemy is constantly doing?" Brushing aside the general's persistent requests for more wagons and rail capacity, the commander in chief commented that he would be more than pleased to accommodate him, "but it wastes all the remainder of autumn to give it to you, and, in fact ignores the question of time, which cannot and must not be ignored." In a passage that must have galled the general, the president lectured that one of the standard maxims of war was "to operate upon the enemy's communications as much as possible without exposing your own." If Lee were in McClellan's place, Lincoln prodded, "would he not break your communication with Richmond within the next twenty-four hours?" Given the general's focus on Confederates reentering Maryland and going on to Pennsylvania, Lincoln countered, "[Lee] gives up his communications to you absolutely, and you have nothing to do but to follow and ruin him."[27]

Then, shifting to his perennial interest in targeting Richmond, the president proffered that, exclusive of the water route, the Army of the Potomac was already closer to the Confederate capital than "the enemy is by the route that you can and must take." "Why can you not reach there before him," Lincoln goaded, "unless you admit that he is more than your equal on a march?" His is the arc, yours the chord of a circle, and the roads favored either side, Lincoln wrote. Moving east of the Blue Ridge was the correct way: "This would at once menace the enemy's communications, which I would seize if he would permit." If Lee went north, "I would follow him closely, holding his communications." If he moved "to prevent our seizing his communications and move toward Richmond, I would press closely to him; fight him, if a favorable opportunity should present, and at least try to beat him to Richmond on the inside track."

Such thoughts were suggestions, said Lincoln, but "I say 'try,' if we never try we shall never succeed." If Lee makes a stand at Winchester, fight him, "on the idea that if we cannot beat him when he bears the wastage of coming to us, we never can when we bear the wastage of going to him." It was a simple truth, not to be forgotten. "We should not so operate as to merely drive him away" because if the Army of the Potomac could not beat the enemy under present circumstances, then it certainly could not when Lee would retire within the Richmond entrenchments. In Lincoln's mind, the inside track to the James provided a "remarkable facility" for resupply, much like the spokes of a wheel extending from the hub toward the rim, "whether you move directly by the chord or on the inside arc, hugging the Blue Ridge more closely." In possibly too much detail for a civilian strategist to impose on a West Pointer, Lincoln persisted on the chord-line theme. Via hamlets like Aldie, Haymarket, and Fredericksburg, "turnpikes, railroads, and finally the Potomac, by Aquia creek, meet you at all points from Washington." McClellan could sideslip Lee, "disabling him to make an important move without your knowledge, and compelling him to keep his forces together for dread of you."

Seven specific access gaps to the south of Harpers Ferry would enable McClellan to attack should he wish to do so, mentioned Lincoln, warming to the details in his own mind. The Army of the Potomac would be placed between the enemy and both Washington and Richmond for most of the way and thus address the abiding phobia of protecting the capital as it would "enable us to spare you the greatest number of troops from here." If Lee tried to move against Washington, then McClellan should "turn and attack him in the rear." Once more, the idea of shielding Washington lay at the crux of Washington thinking. This scheme had become administration litany, although "I think [the enemy] should be engaged long before such point is reached," Lincoln observed. "It is all easy if our troops march as well as the enemy, and it is unmanly to say they cannot do so," he chided. "This letter is in no sense an order," repeated the president, yet McClellan surely must have understood the message.

Indeed, Washington's direct protection had matured as the city continued to transform from political capital to wartime logistical hub. Lines of entrenchments and military roads crisscrossed the rural suburbs, while the infrastructure of support came from storehouses, convalescent hospitals, barracks, stables, guard posts, and freedmen or contraband villages. Stanton and the city's chief engineer, Maj. Gen. John Gross Barnard, set up a special commission to study the problems of unwieldy cannon, wide gaps between individual works, and the ever-present need for better river protection. Even as McClellan regrouped, the northern defense lines of the city were being improved by sweating garrison troops. Elizabeth Blair Lee described how virgin forests had been destroyed from Fort Massachusetts inside the District of Columbia on the Seventh Street road all the way to the gate of her family's Silver Spring farm at least two miles distant, so as to improve fields of fire for the fort's artillery. By year's end, Barnard's commission would produce a voluminous report, leading to further expenditures of time and money to expand the military defense of the city. Still, generals and politicians somehow could not agree even then that the field army on the offensive and not tied to the defensive provided the proper guard for Mr. Lincoln's city.[28]

The Confederates, in fact, faced a similar problem both before and after the Maryland expedition. Lee's army operated far distant from direct defense of Richmond. Confederate congressmen, newspaper editors, and the public pressured President Davis to withdraw the Army of Northern Virginia closer to the capital. From the lower Shenandoah, Lee only indirectly threatened Washington by counterpoise. His focus remained on the line to central Pennsylvania. Either way, Lee's main difficulties, like McClellan's, lay with resupply, reconstitution of his force, and the perennial bane of stragglers. Federal scouting reports described the whole country from Warrenton to Leesburg alive with sick Rebel soldiers, abandoned by the wayside on the trek north, with three hundred alone convalescing at the latter town. "Many of the [Confederate] sick said they hoped to be captured, to be paroled," reported Col. J. M. Davies, Second New York Cavalry. Stragglers and convalescents eventually would drift back to the army so that by October 10, Lee reported 64,273 officers and men present for duty. Lee personally continued to shield the public and the government from the harsh realities of his ill-fated venture northward. He told Davis two weeks after Antietam, "History records but few examples of a greater amount of labor and fighting than has been done by this army during the present campaign." He praised his soldiers' "indomitable courage" in battle and "cheerful endurance of privation and hardship on the march." Others too thought Sharpsburg had restored fighting spirit in the ranks, although Lafayette McLaws more accurately termed the army "exhausted from hunger, fatigue and exposure and often without ammunition." "The stay of the army in Maryland was so short to prevent our receiving the aid I had expected from that State," Lee admitted (apparently dismissing Marylander George H. Steuart's assertion that "five fine companies of over 500 men" constituted proof of his state's allegiance to the Cause). Most productively, Lee used the lull to reorganize his army from wing into corps formations, with both Jackson and Longstreet named to three-star rank. Little more by way of needed resources accrued to the army's stay on the upper Potomac, however.[29]

Sharpsburg rendered the Army of Northern Virginia unfit for renewed offensive. Yet relations between Davis and Lee remained far superior to those of Lincoln and McClellan, if only because the courtly southern commander readily deferred to (yet adroitly manipulated) his chief compared with the mistrustful relationship on the Federal side. For a time Davis and Lee considered shifting Loring eastward to reinforce the Army of Northern Virginia (while at the same time clearing the Kanawha Valley of Unionists, destroying the Baltimore and Ohio Railroad at Grafton, and looking to the safety of the Virginia and Tennessee Railroad and salt works in southwest Virginia—a totally impossible task). The lateness of the campaign season militated against an even more daring idea that Loring should threaten western Pennsylvania, especially Pittsburgh. That move, coordinated with Lee east of and Bragg west of the mountains, might have produced salutary results if it had been undertaken earlier in the fall. The best that Loring could do by October was to protect the key salt works at Charleston and "keep the enemy out of that country," since "the condition of things [had] so changed." Davis more realistically captured the situation when he told Lee on September 28, "The feverish anxiety to invade the North has been relieved by the counterirritant of apprehension for the safety of the capital in the absence of the army, so long criticized for a 'want of dash,' and the class who so vociferously urged a forward movement, in which they were not personally to be involved, would now be most pleased to welcome the return of that army." Not wanting to diminish his force opposite McClellan, but fearful of "the risk of Richmond being captured for the want of adequate force," placed Lee in a quandary.[30]

Using Stuart's horsemen to screen Pleasonton's suddenly more aggressive reconnaissance as well as pressing regular and irregular operations against the railroads on the upper Potomac, Lee talked to Davis about winter encampment versus bringing on a general battle, "which I do not desire to do so near the enemy's base of operations." By late October, Lee faced Federal movements that ended all Confederate hopes of remaining on the upper Potomac or again striking northward. On October 27, McClellan wired Lincoln, "I commenced crossing the army into Virginia yesterday, and shall push forward as rapidly as possible to endeavor to meet the enemy." Unwittingly, Little Mac had again wrested the initiative from his opponent. The next morning Lee ordered Longstreet, "Put your corps in march to Culpeper Court-House with as little delay as practicable, but without any signs of precipitation." Jackson would remain in the lower Valley for the present. Gustavus Smith, called up from immediate defense of Richmond, would provide an early warning on the line of the Rappahannock from Warrenton. Clearly, the die was cast, even though it took nine days to get the Army of the Potomac moving back to the Old Dominion once Lincoln and the high command had made orders preemptory. From Lee's viewpoint, "About the last of October the Federal army began to incline eastwardly towards Warrenton."[31]

Like Lee, McClellan may have been dubious of any major result from campaigning before winter. But realizing his position as army commander was now in jeopardy, he selected Lincoln's plan of movement east of the mountains. A reinforced XII Corps would guard against further incursions like Stuart's Chambersburg raid and reoccupy the rebuilt Harpers Ferry bastion, termed "a second Gibraltar" by one impressionable recruit. McClellan intended his massive army to pass within ten days from the Harpers Ferry and Berlin supply bases via an advance through Loudoun Valley between the Bull Run and Blue Ridge mountains to the rebuilt Manassas Gap and Orange and Alexandria Railroad line of communications with Alexandria. In his words, "I could either separate their army and beat them in detail, or else force them to concentrate as far back as Gordonsville," thus placing the Army of the Potomac in position either to move forward through Fredericksburg on Richmond, or to be removed to the Peninsula, "if, as I apprehended, it were found impossible to supply it by the Orange and Alexandria railroad beyond Culpeper."[32]

Should Lee suddenly go north, McClellan could operate against the Confederate supply line in the valley. Either way, Lee would be at a disadvantage unless he moved more quickly to concentrate behind the Rappahannock and Rapidan rivers near Culpeper. Nearly 160,000 men would execute McClellan's plan, though execution once more plagued the Union effort. Confederate recovery proved swifter than McClellan had anticipated. Lee's lieutenants, such as Jubal Early, drove their men unmercifully over mountain and stream to get ahead of the Federal army. As one historian decided, "It would be a race to the Rappahannock River, and George McClellan's career would hang in the balance." His need to cover Washington (despite a reported eighty-thousand-man garrison, including the XI Corps, and 433 artillery pieces in the forts) and the ever-present chance that Lee might strike across the Potomac heightened McClellan's worries.

Logistics dogged McClellan's footsteps. Finally resupplied sufficiently to begin the campaign, the marching Federals ostensibly carried ten days' rations with them. Though foraging had been forbidden north of the Potomac, little prevented the Yankee soldiery from returning to that practice in Virginia. Surely Lincoln's various confiscation acts even provided the license. Veteran commentator Francis Palfrey observed, "There was undoubtedly great delay in the arrival of supplies," but it was still tempting to believe that the delays were unnecessary and "would not have existed had headquarters at Washington been, not to say friendly to McClellan, but loyal to the general commanding." For a long time, many in the Army of the

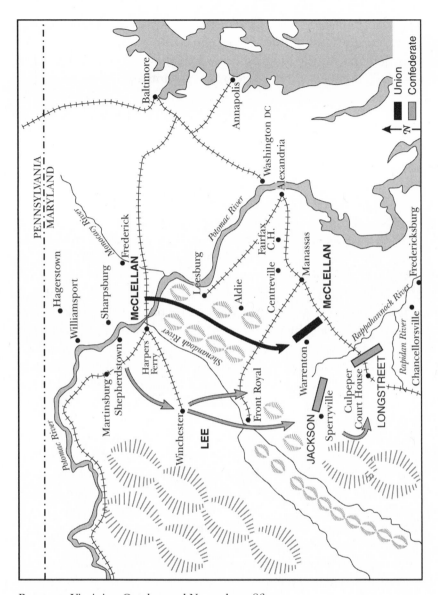

Return to Virginia—October and November 1862

Potomac reflected Palfrey's prejudice, placing the blame for that army's misfortunes on the War Department and the politicians, not their general. In the long run, however, it may have been simply a matter of numbers. Strength returns of October 20 showed 133,433 "present for duty" in the Union ranks from an "aggregate present" number of 159,860. Such statistics promised road congestion and traffic jams, slowed march rates, and aggravated a sorely stretched and inadequate railroad system. Lee, on the other hand, reported 68,033 officers and men present for duty out of an aggregate 79,595. As it turned out, McClellan's more direct line of advance may have unwittingly funneled his larger and more unwieldy force onto a rural road system totally inadequate for rapid marching. No matter, for Lee's foot soldiers again proved superior to their opponents in terms of celerity of movement.[33]

Disintegrating weather conditions hardly helped matters. Still, to McClellan it remained principally a supply issue. He and railroad czar Henry Haupt haggled briefly about restoration of a Washington–Leesburg line, but the railroader quickly rejected that notion since only the Orange and Alexandria and Manassas Gap lines could be made ready in the time available. The general also wanted depot facilities restored in the Aquia Creek area, but Haupt flatly told him that it would take four months to rebuild that base and requested an order of priority from the general: restored rail or reopened base, McClellan could not have both. Moreover, evacuation of the area between Aquia and Fredericksburg prior to Second Bull Run had destroyed the railroad bridges. Meanwhile, McClellan's advance, buffeted by weather that fluctuated daily between warmth and sunshine and slashing winds and icy snow, ate out the countryside, including Unionist Quaker portions of Loudoun County, while their wagon trains chewed up the marginally passable roads. An epidemic of hoof-and-mouth disease further cut down the army's horse supply, although Washington officials really could do little to offset such losses.[34]

Seemingly thwarted by bureaucratic hostility at every turn, McClellan could only ask headquarters plaintively "whether the President desires me to march on the enemy at once, or to await the reception of the new horses, every possible step having been taken to insure their prompt arrival." He complained to his wife about people in Washington intending everything "possible to do me all the harm they can" and bitterly described "the mean and dirty character" of dispatches sent by "men whom I know to be greatly my inferiors socially, intellectually and morally!" He intemperately suggested, "There never was a truer epithet applied to a certain individual than that of the 'Gorilla,'" referring to Lincoln. "Blind and foolish [Washington officials] will continue to the end," he fumed. From the Middleburg area he admitted that lack of direct telegraph linkage plagued the new effort, although "we are in the full tide of success so far as it is or can be successful to advance without a battle." He sent a revealing message from Rectortown at 1:00 p.m. on November 6: "The machine is so huge and complicated that it is slow in its motions." Part of the problem was that Mary Ellen could no longer soften the general's feelings as she had when the pair had been together in camp briefly in mid-October.[35]

Still mindful of the northern elections and their potential for reversing Lincoln's course on hard war, McClellan nonetheless focused on his military obligations by late October. Not surprisingly, his early lead over Lee in the new race back to central Virginia evaporated. Under Lee's orders of October 28, Longstreet's corps left its camps near Winchester and force-marched via Front Royal and Chester Gap for Culpeper, while John Walker's division remained bivouacked as an observer shield near Upperville in Loudoun Valley until Longstreet passed the Blue Ridge. Jackson shifted to Millwood, just west of where the turnpike from Snickersville crossed the Shenandoah River at Castleman's Ferry. One Winchester resident watched A. P. Hill's Light Division march out of town: "Very destitute, many without shoes, all without overcoats or gloves, although the weather was freezing," and their hands "looked so red and cold holding their muskets in the bitter wind." Lee intended for Longstreet to block the Union advance at the Rappahannock while Jackson sought opportunities to knife through intervening gaps in the mountain to strike McClellan's right flank. But McClellan sealed the Blue Ridge gaps and kept the Federal columns within supporting distance of one another.[36]

Stuart's cavalry, meanwhile, actively harassed Union units in the Loudoun Valley so that the last week in October and first few days of November produced an outburst of fighting in Snicker's Gap in the Blue Ridge and cavalry brushes along the stone fences and creek beds of the Piedmont. Pleasonton effectively countered Stuart's probes, prompting McClellan to tell Halleck that his cavalry had achieved parity with, even superiority to, the enemy in efficiency. "So forcibly has this been impressed upon our old Cavalry Regts by repeated successes that the men are fully persuaded that they are equal to twice their number of rebel Cavalry," he boasted on October 21. In fact, by the snowy afternoon of November 7, the general sounded quite upbeat as he began a letter to Ellen suggesting that the return of Sumner and Oliver Howard from their Antietam wounds and the presence of reliable subordinates like Franklin, Darius Couch, and Fitz John Porter more than offset the less palatable reappearance of Franz Sigel with reinforcements from Washington. Each portion of the advancing army was meeting its time and distance requirements as set down by its commander, he claimed. Supply difficulties remained, but Confederate Gen. Gustavus Smith "was yesterday driven out of Warrenton." Then he set aside the uncompleted note for other matters. They would be the final words that Little Mac would pen to his wife as commander of the Army of the Potomac. Late that evening, Brig. Gen. Catharinus P. Buckingham arrived with relief orders from Halleck.[37]

The campaign from the Peninsula to the Antietam had come to an end. The jousting between McClellan and Lee as well as McClellan and the Lincoln administration had reached a conclusion. Perhaps Iron Brigade commander John Gibbon had it right: "There is but one opinion . . . and that is the Government has gone mad." The plain fact was that McClellan had outlived his usefulness to the Lincoln administration. His dispatches about this new operation, however promising, contained key phrases that set the president and his advisers on edge once again. Generally their objections related to logistics, but there were also differences in strategic outlook, all of which implied to Lincoln that McClellan had returned to old habits and was delaying the business of destroying Lee. Perhaps more subtly, McClellan had become as much a political liability as anything else. Much of the general public and the administration had shifted away from tolerating McClellan's habits. Of course, the general also posed a possible political rival, a rallying point for peace Democrats and a potential competitor for the presidency in two years. Given opposition to the general in his cabinet and awareness of continuing dissatisfaction permeating cliques in the army, the chief executive of the country needed change. With some truth, McClellan's own staff felt "that had we marched two weeks ago, Mac would today have been General-in-Chief." By November 7, Lincoln simply did what he had intended doing for some weeks after Antietam. As he told the Republican candidate for New York governor, Gen. James W. Wadsworth, on October 13, doubting that his army commander would move after all and tiring of his excuses, "[I'd] remove him at once but for the elections." Once those elections had passed—and none too favorably for the administration at that—Lincoln had no compelling reason to put up with McClellan any longer. Notwithstanding his personal liking for the man, by November Lincoln did not hesitate to remove him once he learned of Longstreet's reoccupation of Culpeper. The president had privately cited Lee's ability to reinsert his army between McClellan and the Confederate capital as the final litmus test for Little Mac's retention.[38]

McClellan represented a war now past—a conciliatory war of controlled movement and compromise peace. Neither the nature of the conflict itself nor Lincoln's agenda for restoration of the Union any longer permitted this approach. How the war had changed could be found in the observation of one Wisconsin officer: though he did not fathom the effect of Lincoln's Emancipation Proclamation on the South, "There is one thing certain it is just what was wanted and if they don't lay down their arms we will have to annihilate them, niggers, cotton and all." Cabinet member Blair visited the White House the night before McClellan's removal, unknowing of that move, to counsel the president on some convoluted scheme of allowing the general to continue to advance either to victory, which the administration could claim as its own, thus rallying war Democrats and undermining the peace advocates, or defeat, which would discredit Mac with all parties and get him out of the picture. But Lincoln merely observed wryly that he had tried long enough "to bore with an auger too dull to take hold." So Buckingham had gone by train, first to Ambrose Burnside's headquarters near Waterloo, Virginia, to ensure acceptance of command by McClellan's anointed successor. Then, with the reluctant IX Corps commander in tow, the pair rode to Rector's Crossroads to deliver the order. It was 11:00 p.m. that snowy night when they gained admission to McClellan's tent and passed small talk before delivering the document. The transition went smoothly, the army commander stoically accepting his fate. Burnside "feels dreadfully, almost crazy," McClellan commented to his wife.[39]

Now McClellan could finish his note to Ellen. He admitted committing errors, but no great blunders personally: "Our consolation must be that we have tried to do what was right—if we have failed it was not our fault." "Alas for my poor country," he sighed, vowing that his enemies would not enjoy triumph. The sacked general agreed to remain several days to help with an orderly change of command as well as to take honors and salute from the army he had created and identified with personally (and vice versa). He would also silence army rumors about marching on Washington. His final champagne toast to his staff and escort was "To the Army of the Potomac and bless the day when I shall return to it." Emotionally overcome at the final pass-in-review near Warrenton on November 10, McClellan sounded even more Napoleon-like when declaring in his final message to his troops, "As an army you have grown up under my care," and the glory achieved, mutual perils and fatigues endured, "the graves of our comrades fallen in battle and by disease, the broken forms of those whom wounds and sickness have disabled," bonded "the strongest associations which can exist among men," uniting "us still by an indissoluble tie. Farewell!" The spectacle ended. With cheers echoing in his ears, McClellan took the train for Washington on November 11 and exile to Trenton, New Jersey. A closing sentence found its way into the farewell speech at some point: "We shall ever be comrades in supporting the Constitution of our country and the nationality of its people." McClellan would be gone but hardly forgotten.[40]

Relief, disbelief, shock, and confusion all echoed across the country in response to McClellan's dismissal. Secretary of the Navy Welles distanced himself from the political intrigue that had surrounded the general's fall, but opined, "I had expected it might take place earlier, when McClellan seemed testing the forbearance of the Government, and not one good word was said for him." Then the general had started to move on Lee, and Welles was shocked by his removal. The ever-cranky Polish exile Adam Gurowski penned in his diary on November 9, "Great and holy day! McClellan gone overboard! Better late than never. But this belated act of justice to the country cannot atone for all the deadly disasters, will not remove the fearful responsibility from Lincoln—Seward—Blair, for having so long sustained this horrible vampire." New Hampshire soldier James Larkin captured the thoughts of McClellan's soldiers that the ouster had come unexpectedly to the army "and seems to cast a gloom over it." The general had been loved by the men, for they believed in him and trusted him. "The politicians have caused it," Larkin concluded. Talk of a coup vied with other reactions among the soldiery and may have mirrored the split along partisan lines of the popular press. Some veterans may have groused about ousting the politicians, but newcomers in the ranks did not have the same intensity of purpose. On the Confederate side, Lee merely remarked to Longstreet, "I fear they may continue to make these changes till they find some one whom I don't understand." Georgian soldier Gordon Bradwell remembered later that he and his mates welcomed the change, for though McClellan "was overcautious, he always hurt them more than any of the other Union generals when he did fight." Like it or not, McClellan was out, and the war moved on under Lincoln's firm stewardship.[41]

Lincoln's fears about frustrated voters proved uncomfortably true in the fall elections. The citizenry reacted at the polls to languid progress in suppressing the rebellion as well as to the government's draconian curtailment of civil liberties, conscription, and especially the preliminary emancipation. Inflation and escalating taxes also figured in the result. The last of the October–November vote counts came in from New York on November 4 (unbecomingly close to Lincoln's firing McClellan). Possibly not a "near disaster," a "revolution in public sentiment," or even a "great triumph" for the Democrats, as some have concluded, the loss of the New York governorship, both the governorship and the legislative majority in New Jersey, legislative majorities in Illinois and Indiana, and thirty-four seats in the national Congress attested to the power of the opposition. Republican totals dropped even where victorious, yet Lincoln's party held on in Washington by the narrowest of margins as they picked up seven Senate seats and retained their House majority.[42]

Confederate Gen. Lafayette McLaws believed that the northern elections would "open the press, which has been so long muzzled in the North," so that "we will soon learn the true Northern sentiment in regard to the war." Whether for war continuation or peace, however, "I am afraid they will base their hopes on reorganization of the union, which can never be." The message of discontent was strong in the land. To political historian Philip Paludan, "Wartime malaise, dismay at the military situation, and possibly even feelings that the war had not produced revolution enough" closed out the season. Republican voters "may even have been protesting restraint as much as radicalism," he suggested. Even abroad, the election results helped Palmerston and Gladstone to further defer the possibility of

Confederate recognition "with less risk in the spring." Back in January 1862, Lincoln had prophetically suggested, "I cannot imagine that any European power would dare to recognize and aid the Southern Confederacy if it became clear that the Confederacy stands for slavery and the Union for freedom."[43]

Thus the battle of Antietam and the end of the Maryland campaign had far-ranging impact. McClellan and the Union army had prevailed; Lee's Confederates retreated to Virginia. While military exploitation proved impossible, due as much to troop exhaustion as the general condition of the opposing forces, an opportunity came on the political front. Antietam yielded just enough momentum for President Lincoln to issue a preliminary Emancipation Proclamation, effective January 1, 1863. Before, the war had been fought officially to suppress rebellion and preserve the Union under the Constitution. Now the Union added a crusade to free slaves. Lincoln's intent was not preeminently humanitarian but rather to target the Confederacy's economy and society, in short, its ability to conduct war. Lincoln used his presidential war powers to effect change, although slavery would remain unaffected in areas not in rebellion. That would require a constitutional amendment, impossible at this point in the struggle, as the president well understood. Unwittingly Lincoln's action in the wake of the Maryland campaign also worked its will upon the Confederacy and its people. As historian Edward L. Ayers suggests, the preliminary proclamation "may have given some in the North a new sense of purpose and resolve, but it did the same thing for the white South." Lincoln was doing what Southerners had expected of the Republicans and had revolted accordingly in 1860 and 1861. Fears of race war, much less loss of property, steeled Rebel resolve anew, and for the immediate future, claims Ayers, "the Confederacy would not be dissuaded or discouraged by a greater clarity of purpose in the United States." Thus, together with Conservative or Democratic sentiment in the North as of fall 1862, Ayers argues compellingly, "Antietam might have been a turning point against Abraham Lincoln." The president, the Radical Republicans, and the generals and their armies had to "convert the narrow victory in Maryland into the first of a series of victories and across the rest of the South," a goal by no means easily achievable at the time. It was a risky business, and Lincoln, by necessity, took that risk.[44]

Such facts notwithstanding, the war seemed to be lengthening inexorably for citizens and soldiers alike. By October the Confederate Congress would renew a law authorizing suspension of the privilege of the writ of habeas corpus until February 12, 1863. Restrictions on civil liberties and resistance to the highly ineffective and controversial Federal militia draft inflamed northern states at midmonth, reflected quickly in the off-year elections. Republican power survived, but Lincoln and his administration realized that northern will was wavering. Trouble in the eastern anthracite region of Pennsylvania suggested both political and economic difficulties. Draft resistance based on conspiratorial agitation worried Governor Andrew Curtin and could be traced to militant Irish coal miners known as the Molly Maguires (a secret organization and an offshoot of the Ancient Order of Hibernians of the previous two decades). This strife, internal to business–labor relations, had taken on new tones with an antiwar and anticonscription cast over the past year. Production of an energy source vital to northern war production, fueling the blockade navy, and even supply to Europe dipped during the first two years of war; thus it was of concern to Washington as much as to Harrisburg. Violence in the coal fields grabbed headlines and prompted military response; economic ramifications caught the attention of business and political communities. Ironically it was the religious community, namely Bishop James F. Wood of the Philadelphia Roman Catholic Diocese, who restored some degree of calm in the coal fields just about the time that voters throughout the North went to the polls to express their own views on the government's conduct of the war.[45]

And yet, rising above all else at the time, the great Confederate counteroffensives into Maryland, Kentucky, and west Tennessee had failed. Militarily, the Confederacy's best bid to win the war fell short. Whether Sterling Price and Earl Van Dorn in northern Mississippi and west Tennessee or Braxton Bragg and Edmund Kirby Smith in Kentucky or Robert E. Lee in Maryland, the power of Confederate arms to invade loyal territory had been met and thrown back by Federal arms from Corinth and Perryville to Antietam. Soft-war generals like McClellan in the east and Don Carlos Buell in the west, though bringing pyrrhic victories in this regard, became politically expendable; their military caution and delays as well as their conciliatory attitudes toward the South conflicted with new directions determined by the politicians in Washington. Both generals passed into history, although McClellan's flame shone briefly for the presidential election of 1864 and his mantle lingered with the army he so adored. It would always be McClellan's Bodyguard, not Mr. Lincoln's Army, in many minds. Two years and more campaigns would be required before that army truly shook the ghost of Little Mac from its shoulders. For some in the ranks and in command, it never did. But standing above all, Lincoln's formal Emancipation Proclamation took effect at the first of the new year. With the passage of time and development of informed public opinion, this final tribute to the events of September 1862 became the principal legacy of the Maryland campaign, not Little Mac's saving of the Union on the bloodiest single day in American history.[46]

Confederate fortunes arced like a comet in this same period, yet never burned out completely. Lee and his army had traversed one spectacular victory to another before reaching too far strategically and having to fall back upon the realities of stubborn battlefield defense to ensure survival. If Second Manassas arguably provided their finest moment, Antietam suggested their most marginal. Lee's victories erased the sting of earlier defeats in other war theaters. Even the episodes at Harpers Ferry and Shepherdstown offset what Southerners took to be a draw at South Mountain and Sharpsburg. The story of Lee and his army rode on the gallantry and invincibility of the soldiers and sustained hearts and purpose on the home front. "In the space of less than three months," suggests historian Gary Gallagher, "the Confederate people had come to expect good news from the Army of Northern Virginia, investing ever more emotional capital in its leaders and soldiers." Those men and their leaders would return twice more to northern soil in an attempt to swing the tide of victory. They carried with them the hopes and dreams of a young nation seeking independence and a peculiar way of life. As from the Peninsula to the Antietam, so thereafter, Lee the soldier and his devoted followers were a band of brothers who "would be as important as any other factor in lengthening the life of the Confederacy." To Brian Holden Reid, Lee in this period was fast becoming the "icon for a nation," the Southern Confederacy. His aggressiveness and risk taking mirrored that nation, itself a risky endeavor. Yet those attributes ensured heavy casualties that the emerging nation could ill afford.[47]

Lost in the passage of the armies, borderland civilians remained in the backwash of these events. Two women in Winchester, Virginia, especially reflected such shifting fortunes. Pro-Union Julia Chase and Laura Lee, a supporter of the Confederacy, experienced constant uncertainty following the close of the Maryland campaign. Daily military rumors competed with real concern for famine should either army remain over the winter. Food and fuel prices shot up, the presence of wounded and dead from local hospitals seemed unending, and news from the outside proved nil. "Sad and dreary is the prospect before us," Lee wrote in her diary on October 6. An incredulous Chase could not reconcile Lincoln's proclamation on emancipation with his inaugural promise not to interfere with the institution of slavery. She quickly saw it as a measure for undermining the Confederacy's ability to fight a war. By late November she would pen in her diary, "God grant that this winter's campaign may be more successful than the past year has been to the army of Virginia under McClellan." The following week, Lee, apprehensive of the Yankees' return, wrote, "We lead the strangest life of excitement and change which can be imagined." Across the mountains in Washington, Lincoln granted an interview to an English Quaker, Mrs. Eliza P. Gurnsey, on Sunday, October 26. He reportedly told her sadly, "If I had my way, this war would never have been commenced. If I had been allowed my way this war would have been ended before this, but we find it still continues." In truth, the country's trials since summer, the battles from Cedar Mountain through Second Manassas, Chantilly, South Mountain, Antietam, and even for the slaves *had* ended the war—but only for the dead.[48]

Notes

Preface

1. James A. Rawley, *Turning Points of the Civil War* (Lincoln: University of Nebraska Press, 1966), 99–143, especially 100.

2. Charles A. Stevenson, *Warriors and Politicians: U.S. Civil-Military Relations under Stress* (London: Routledge, 2006), chap. 3.

3. Davis's experience can be found in the documents compiled by Lynda Lasswell Crist, ed., *The Papers of Jefferson Davis*: Vol. 8, *1862* (Baton Rouge: Louisiana State University Press, 1995).

4. James M. McPherson, "No Peace without Victory, 1861–1865," *American Historical Review* (February 2004): 159.

5. John Codman Ropes, *The Army under Pope*, vol. 4 of *Campaigns of the Civil War* (New York: Charles Scribner's Sons, 1881); Francis Winthrop Palfrey, *The Antietam and Fredericksburg*, vol. 5 of *Campaigns of the Civil War* (New York: Charles Scribner's Sons, 1881); James M. McPherson, *Crossroads of Freedom: Antietam, the Battle That Changed the Course of the Civil War* (New York: Oxford University Press, 2002), reviewed by Jonathan Yardley as "Antietam's Legacy: 'The Event of the War'?," *Washington Post Book World*, August 22, 2002.

1. Summer Impasse

1. Letter, "John" to Father, July 13, 1862, courtesy of Ron and Marilyn Snyder, Annapolis MD.

2. William B. Styple, ed., *Writing and Fighting the Civil War* (Kearny NJ: Belle Grove, 2000), 87.

3. William J. Cooper Jr., *Jefferson Davis, American* (New York: Knopf, 2000), 403–4, 408–9, 421–22; Joseph L. Harsh, *Confederate Tide Rising: Robert E. Lee and the Making of Southern Strategy, 1861–1862* (Kent OH: Kent State University Press, 1998), chap. 1; Gilbert W. Livingood, *A Different Valor: The Story of General Joseph Johnston, C.S.A.* (Indianapolis: Bobbs-Merrill, 1956), chaps. 7, 8; Craig L. Symonds, *Joseph E. Johnston: A Civil War Biography* (New York: Norton, 1992), chaps. 10, 11; Jeffrey N. Lash, *Destroyer of the Iron Horse: General Joseph E. Johnston and Confederate Transport, 1861–1865* (Kent OH: Kent State University Press, 1991), chap. 1.

4. Judith W. McGuire, *Diary of a Southern Refugee* (1967, rpt. Lincoln: University of Nebraska Press, 1995), 128, 129; Sallie Brock Putnam, *Richmond During the War* (1867, rpt. Lincoln: University of Nebraska Press, 1996), 154; J. Gottfried Lange, "The New Name of the Shoemaker in the Old and the New World," manuscript, Virginia Historical Society, Richmond, n.d., 159.

5. Casualties computed from Francis H. Kennedy, ed., *The Civil War Battlefield Guide* (New York: Houghton Mifflin, 1998), 88–104.

6. Nat S. Turner III, *A Southern Soldier's Letters Home: The Civil War Letters of Samuel A. Burne, Cobb's Georgia Legion, Army of Northern Virginia* (Macon GA: Mercer University Press, 2002), 191; Thomas W. Cutrer and T. Michael Parrish, eds., *Brothers in Gray: The Civil War Letters of the Pierson Family* (Baton Rouge: Louisiana State University Press, 1997), 102; William Nathaniel Wood, *Reminiscences of Big I*, ed. Bell Irvin Wiley (Jackson TN: McCowat-Mercer Press, 1957), 26, 27; U.S. War Department, *The War of the Rebellion: Official Records of Union and Confederate Armies* (Washington DC: U.S. Government Printing Office, 1880–1901), ser. I, vol. 11, pt. 3, pp. 646, 690 (hereafter *ORA*); Ernest B. Ferguson, *Ashes of Glory: Richmond at War* (New York: Knopf, 1996), 150–57; Putman, *Richmond During the War*, 151–52.

7. John B. Jones, *A Rebel War Clerk's Diary* (1866, rpt. New York: Sagamore Press, 1958), 88–91; Ferguson, *Ashes of Glory*, 162; *ORA*, I, 11, pt. 3, 636–37; Edward Porter Alexander, *Fighting for the Confederacy: The Personal Recollections of General Edward Porter Alexander*, ed. Gary W. Gallagher (Chapel Hill: University of North Carolina Press, 1998), 117.

8. *Richmond Dispatch*, July 9, 1862; *ORA*, I, 11, pt. 2, 645; Jay Luvaas, "Lee and the Operational Art: The Right Place, the Right Time," *Parameters: The Journal of the Army War College* (Autumn 1992): 2, 7, 8; Harsh, *Confederate Tide Rising*, 100; Douglas Southall Freeman, *Lee's Lieutenants: A Study in Command* (New York: Scribner's, 1941–44), 2:670–71; James Marten, "A Feeling of Restless Anxiety: Loyalty and Race in the Peninsula Campaign and Beyond," in *The Richmond Campaign of 1862: The Peninsula and the Seven Days*, ed. Gary W. Gallagher (Chapel Hill: University of North Carolina Press, 2000), 121–52; Spencer Glasgow Welch, *A Confederate Surgeon's Letters to His Wife* (1911, rpt. Marietta GA: Continental, 1954), 17; Nicholas A. Davis, *The Campaign from Texas to Maryland* (1863, rpt. Austin TX: Steck, 1961), 64–67; W. N. Wood, *Reminiscences of Big I*, 26; N. S. Turner, *A Soldier's Letters Home*, 186.

9. Harsh, *Confederate Tide Rising*, 105–6, and on Confederate strategic offensive strategy, see 27, 54, 62, 77–79, and James A. Kegel, *North with Lee and Jackson: The Lost Story of Gettysburg* (Mechanicsburg PA: Stackpole, 1996), chaps. 1–11.

10. Clifford W. Dowdey and Louis H. Manarin, eds., *The Wartime Papers of R. E. Lee* (New York: Bramall House, 1961), 182–83; Harsh, *Confederate Tide Rising*, 19.

11. Stephen W. Sears, *To the Gates of Richmond: The Peninsula Campaign* (New York: Ticknor and Fields, 1992), 342–48; Stephen W. Sears, ed., *The Civil War Papers of George B. McClellan: Selected Correspondence 1860–1865* (New York: Ticknor and Fields, 1989), 339; Jeffrey D. Wert, *The Sword of Lincoln: The Army of the Potomac* (New York: Simon and Schuster, 2005), 122–25.

12. Patricia L. Faust, ed., *Historical Times Illustrated Encyclopedia of the Civil War* (New York: Harper and Row, 1986), 519; ORA, I, 11, pt. 3, 349–51, 642–43; Christian G. Samito, ed., *"Fear Was Not in Him": The Civil War Letters of Major General Francis C. Barlow, U.S.A.* (New York: Fordham University Press, 2004), 91, 94; Mark De Wolfe Howe, ed., *Touched with Fire: Civil War Letters and Diary of Oliver Wendell Holmes, Jr. 1861–1864* (Cambridge MA: Harvard University Press, 1947), 60.

13. ORA, I, 11, pt. 3, 281, 282, 287–88, 291–92, 312, 319, 321–22, 329; Roy P. Basler, ed., *The Collected Works of Abraham Lincoln* (New Brunswick NJ: Rutgers University Press, 1953), 5:301, 303, 305–6; Sears, *Civil War Papers of McClellan*, 334–35, 338–41, 354–55; Ethan S. Rafuse, *McClellan's War: The Failure of Moderation in the Struggle for the Union* (Bloomington: Indiana University Press, 2005), 231.

14. Robert Knox Sneden, *Eye of the Storm: A Civil War Odyssey*, ed. Charles F. Bryan Jr. and Nelson D. Lankford (New York: Free Press, 2000), 99–100; Robert Hunt Rhodes, ed., *All for the Union: The Civil War Diary and Letters of Elisha Hunt Rhodes* (1985, rpt. New York: Random House, 1999), 66.

15. Gallagher, *The Richmond Campaign*, x–xi, 3–22; John T. Hubbell, "The Seven Days of George B. McClellan," in Gallagher, The *Richmond Campaign*, 18–30, 39–40; Sears, *Civil War Papers of McClellan*, 345–47; Stephen W. Sears, *George B. McClellan; The Young Napoleon* (New York: Ticknor and Fields, 1988), chap. 10, especially 235–36.

16. T. Harry Williams, *Lincoln and His Generals* (New York: Grosset and Dunlap, 1952), chaps. 4, 5; Curt Anders, *Henry Halleck's War: A Fresh Look at Lincoln's Controversial General-in-Chief* (Carmel IN: Guild Press, 1999), chaps. 2–4; Benjamin Franklin Cooling, *Symbol, Sword and Shield: Defending Washington During the Civil War* (Hamden CT: Archon, 1967), chaps. 1–6; Sears, *Civil War Papers of McClellan*, 304, 334, 344–45; Ethan S. Rafuse, "McClellan, von Clausewitz and the Politics of War," in *The Ongoing Civil War; New Versions of Old Stories*, ed. Herman Hattaway and Ethan S. Rafuse (Columbia: University of Missouri Press, 2004), 40–57.

17. Sears, *Civil War Papers of McClellan*, 348, 362; Sneden, *Eye of the Storm*, 102–3; Wert, *Sword of Lincoln*, 126–27.

18. E. B. Long, *The Civil War Day by Day: An Almanac 1861–1865* (Garden City NY: Doubleday, 1971), 234–35.

19. Mark Grimsley, *The Hard Hand of War: Union Military Policy toward Southern Civilians 1861–1865* (New York: Cambridge University Press, 1995), chaps. 1–3; Steven V. Ash, *When the Yankees Came: Conflict and Chaos in the Occupied South, 1861–1865* (Chapel Hill: University of North Carolina Press, 1995), 50; Mark E. Neely Jr., *The Fate of Liberty: Abraham Lincoln and Civil Liberties* (New York: Oxford University Press, 1991); John Syrett, "The Confiscation Acts: The North Strikes Back," in *An Uncommon Time: The Civil War and the Northern Home Front*, ed. Paul A. Cimballa and Randall M. Miller (New York: Fordham University Press, 2002), 280–325.

20. William A. Blair, "The Seven Days and the Radical Persuasion," in Gallagher,

The Richmond Campaign, 153–54; Grimsley, Hard Hand of War, 67; Ash, When the Yankees Came, 59.

21. William Freehling, The South versus the South (Oxford: Oxford University Press, 2001), 94–95; Arnold Shankman, "For the Union As It Was and the Constitution As It Is: A Copperhead Views the Civil War," in Rank and File: Civil War Essays in Honor of Bell I. Wiley, ed. James I. Robertson and Richard M. McMurry (San Rafael CA: Presidio, 1976), 93–111; Frank J. Williams, "'Doing Less' and 'Doing More': The President and the Proclamation—Legally, Militarily, and Politically," in Harold Holzer, Edna Greene Medford, and Frank J. Williams, The Emancipation Proclamation: Three Views (Baton Rouge: Louisiana State University Press, 2006), 48, 54–62. The confiscation issue receives fullest treatment in John Syrett, The Civil War Confiscation Acts: Failing to Reconstruct the South (New York: Fordham University Press, 2005).

22. Shankman, "For the Union," 99–100; Sneden, Eye of the Storm, 104–6; Ash, When the Yankees Came, 45–48; Letter, "Dear Friend Frank, September 6, 1862," author's collection.

23. ORA, I, 11, pt. 3, 669–70.

24. Sears, Civil War Papers of McClellan, 344–45; Allen C. Guelzo, Lincoln's Emancipation Proclamation: The End of Slavery in America (New York: Simon and Schuster, 2004), 105–6.

25. Guelzo, Lincoln's Emancipation Proclamation, 107–8; Blair, "The Seven Days and the Radical Persuasion," 154–56; Rafuse, McClellan's War, 2–7, 29, 49, 65–66, 83–84, 91.

26. Letter, Gouverneur K. Warren to W. J. Warren, July 20, 1862, Warren Papers, New York State Library, Albany.

27. Blair, "The Seven Days and the Radical Persuasion," 115–16.

28. ORA, I, 11, pt. 3, 331–32; Grimsley, Hard Hand of War, 68–74.

29. Beatty quoted in Gary Gallagher et al., The American Civil War: This Mighty Scourge of War (Oxford: Osprey, 2003), 154; Grimsley, Hard Hand of War, 77–78; Syrett, "The Confiscation Acts," 298–322, especially 321; Syrett, The Civil War Confiscation Acts, chaps. 3, 4.

30. Williams, "'Doing Less' and 'Doing More,'" 59; Blair, "The Seven Days and the Radical Persuasion," 173–74; Robert W. Coakley, The Role of Federal Military Forces in Domestic Disorders 1789–1878 (Washington DC: U.S. Army Center of Military History, 1988), 230.

31. Basler, Collected Works of Lincoln, 5:517–19; McPherson, Crossroads of Freedom, 69–70; Blair, "The Seven Days and the Radical Persuasion," 176; Syrett, "The Confiscation Acts," 322.

32. Francis B. Carpenter, Six Months at the White House with Abraham Lincoln (New York: Hurd and Houghton, 1867), 20–22; Guelzo, Lincoln's Emancipation Proclamation, chap. 3.

33. Sears, Civil War Papers of McClellan, 390, n. 1; Denis B. Mahin, One War at Time: The International Dimensions of the American Civil War (Washington DC: Brassey's, 1999), chap. 9; Howard Jones, Union in Peril: The Crisis over British

Intervention in the Civil War (Chapel Hill: University of North Carolina Press, 1992), chap. 6.

34. Freehling, *South versus South*, 104–6; McPherson, *Crossroads of Freedom*, 73–75.

35. *ORA*, I, 11, pt. 3, 295–97, 306.

36. Jason H. Silverman, Samuel N. Thomas Jr., and Beverly D. Evans IV, "'Shanks': Portrait of a General," *North and South* 3 (March 2000): 38; Charles Minor Blackford, *Letters from Lee's Army, or Memoirs of Life in and out of the Army in Virginia During the War between the States*, ed. Charles Minor Blackford III (New York: Scribner's, 1947), 85–89; Herbert M. Schiller, ed., *A Captain's War: The Letters and Diaries of William H. S. Burgwyn, 1861–1865* (Shippensburg PA: White Mae, 1994), 5–12; Capt. John B. Richard's diary, quoted in "In the Field and on the Town with the Washington Artillery," *Civil War Regiments* 5, no. 1 (1997):106; Cutrer and Parrish, *Brothers in Gray*, 101; Joe Henslee et al., "Unpublished Reminiscence, W. C. Henslee," August 2, 2001, 2, author's files.

37. Harsh, *Confederate Tide Rising*, 114; Ted Tunnell, ed., *Carpetbagger from Vermont: The Autobiography of Marshall Harvey Twitchell* (Baton Rouge: Louisiana State University Press, 1989), 43; Jeffrey D. Marshall, ed., *A War of the People: Vermont Civil War Letters* (Hanover NH: University Press of New England, 1999), 98; Eric J. Wittenberg, ed., *"We Have It Damn Hard Out Here": The Civil War Letters of Sergeant Thomas W. Smith, Sixth Pennsylvania Cavalry* (Kent OH: Kent State University Press, 1999), 52; Alexander, *Fighting for the Confederacy*, 121.

38. Rafuse, *McClellan's War*, 248–50; Stephen W. Sears, ed., *On Campaign with the Army of the Potomac: The Civil War Journal of Theodore Ayrault Dodge* (New York: Cooper Square Press, 2001), 49–83, especially 78; Sears, *McClellan: The Young Napoleon*, 243–44; Sears, *Civil War Papers of McClellan*, 385–87; Harsh, *Confederate Tide Rising*, 115–16; Dowdey and Manarin, *Wartime Papers of Lee*, 246–48.

39. John F. Marszalek, *Commander of All Lincoln's Armies: A Life of General Henry W. Halleck* (Cambridge MA: Belknap Press of Harvard University Press, 2004), 136–38.

40. Anders, *Henry Halleck's War*, 156–60; Sears, *McClellan: The Young Napoleon*, 239–41; Sears, *Civil War Papers of McClellan*, 352, 353; Wittenberg, *"We Have It Damn Hard Out Here*," 51.

41. *ORA*, I, 11, pt. 3, 331–33.

42. Anders, *Henry Halleck's War*, 153–59; Sears, *Civil War Papers of McClellan*, 378, n. 1.

43. Sears, *McClellan: The Young Napoleon*, 243–44; Sears, *Civil War Papers of McClellan*, 357–58, 361, 363, 366, 372, 375, 376, 380–84; Marszalek, *Commander of All Lincoln's Armies*, 138–42; Anders, *Henry Halleck's War*, 159–61.

44. Sears, *McClellan: The Young Napoleon*, 239–40; Sears, *Civil War Papers of McClellan*, 384; George B. McClellan, "From the Peninsula to Antietam," *The Century* 32 (March 1886), reprinted in Robert Underwood Johnson and Clarence Clough Buel, eds., *Battles and Leaders of the Civil War* (New York: Century, 1887–88), 2:548; George B. McClellan, *McClellan's Own Story*, ed. William C. Prime (New York: Charles L. Webster, 1887), 482; *ORA*, I, 11, pt. 3, 310, 353.

45. *ORA*, I, 11, pt. 2, 353–54, 356–58, 361–67, and 12, pt. 3, 578; Rafuse, "McClellan, von Clausewitz, and the Politics of War," 45–46; Rafuse, *McClellan's War*, chaps. 7, 8, 9.

46. *ORA*, I, 11, pt. 3, 367, 375.

47. Crist, *Papers of Jefferson Davis*, 8:293–95.

2. From Tidewater to Cedar Mountain

1. Sneden, *Eye of the Storm*, 111; McGuire, *Diary of a Southern Refugee*, 130; Edwin W. Stone, *Rhode Island in the Rebellion* (Providence RI: George H. Whitney, 1864), 130–35.

2. Sears, *On Campaign*, 77, 79; Rafuse, *McClellan's War*, 251–54; Sneden, *Eye of the Storm*, 112; Rhodes, *All for the Union*, 69.

3. Sneden, *Eye of the Storm*, 113–14; Richard Moe, *The Last Full Measure: The Life and Death of the First Minnesota Volunteers* (St. Paul: Minnesota Historical Society, 1993), 165.

4. Sears, *On Campaign*, 81–83; E. M. Woodward, *Our Campaigns: The Second Regiment Pennsylvania Reserve Volunteers*, ed. Stanley W. Zamonski (Shippensburg PA: Burd Street Press, 1995), 128; E. W. Stone, Rhode Island, 130–31; Rhodes, *All for the Union*, 69–70; William B. Westervelt, *Lights and Shadows of Army Life*, ed. George S. Mahary (Shippensburg PA: White Mane, 1998), 56; Sneden, *Eye of the Storm*, 116–18.

5. Harsh, *Confederate Tide Rising*, 108–9; Charles Wilkes, *Autobiography of Rear Admiral Charles Wilkes, U.S. Navy, 1798–1877*, ed. William James Morgan, David B. Tyler, Joyce L. Leonhart, and Mary F. Loughlin (Washington DC: Department of the Navy, 1978), 885; Sneden, *Eye of the Storm*, 116–18; Sears, *On Campaign*, 79; E. W. Stone, *Rhode Island*, 131, 134.

6. Dowdey and Manarin, *Wartime Papers of Lee*, 245–55; *ORA*, I, 12, pt. 3, 916; Alfred Hoyt Bill, *The Beleaguered City: Richmond, 1861–1865* (New York: Knopf, 1946), 147; Ferguson, *Ashes of Glory*, 159–68; Jones, *A Rebel War Clerk's Diary*, 91; Sara Emma Edmonds, *Memoirs of a Soldier, Nurse and Spy* (1867, rpt. DeKalb: Northern Illinois University Press, 1999), 140–41.

7. For problems of Lincoln and command, see classic treatments by T. H. Williams, *Lincoln and His Generals*, chaps. 4–6; Kenneth P. Williams, *Lincoln Finds a General: A Military Study of the Civil War* (New York: Macmillan, 1952), chaps. 4–8; W. A. Croffut, ed., *Fifty Years in Camp and Field: Diary of Ethan Allan Hitchcock* (New York: Putnam's Sons, 1909), 443–44; Stephen W. Sears, "Lincoln and McClellan," in *Lincoln's Generals*, ed. Gabor S. Boritt (New York: Oxford University Press, 1994), chap. 1; essays in Gary W. Gallagher, ed., *The Shenandoah Valley Campaign of 1862* (Chapel Hill: University of North Carolina Press, 2003), including Gallagher, "You Must Either Attack Richmond or Give Up the Job and Come to the Defence of Washington: Abraham Lincoln and the 1862 Shenandoah Valley Campaign," 3–23, William J. Miller, "Such Men as Shields: Banks and Fremont, Federal Command in Western Virginia, March–June 1862," 43–85.

8. Peter Cozzens, *General John Pope: A Life for the Nation* (Urbana: University of Illinois Press, 2000), 74–79; Peter Cozzens and Robert I. Girardi, eds., *The Military Memoirs of General John Pope* (Chapel Hill: University of North Carolina Press, 1998), 126–32; T. H. Williams, *Lincoln and His Generals*, 120.

9. T. H. Williams, *Lincoln and His Generals*, 135–39; Anders, *Henry Halleck's War*, 141–50.

10. K. P. Williams, *Lincoln Finds a General*, chap. 9; Cooling, *Symbol, Sword and Shield*, chap. 5.

11. Michael C. C. Adams, *Fighting for Defeat: Union Military Failure in the East, 1861–1865* (1978, rpt. Lincoln: University of Nebraska Press, 1992), 79–80, 96, 110, 115; ORA, I, 12, pt. 3, 437–38, 444; David G. Martin, *The Second Bull Run Campaign* (Conshohocken PA: Combined Books, 1997), 24.

12. Cozzens, *General John Pope*, 80; Stephen D. Engle, *Yankee Dutchman: The Life of Franz Sigel* (Baton Rouge: Louisiana State University Press, 1993), 128–29.

13. Willaim B. Styple, ed., *Writing and Fighting the Civil War: Soldier Correspondence to the New York Sunday Mercury* (Kearny NJ: Belle Grove Press, 2000), 112; Cozzens, *General John Pope*, 75–76; ORA, I, 12, pt. 3, 437, 483, 498–500, 503, 505–6, 507–8, 509, 510.

14. ORA, I, 12, pt. 3, 473–74; Cozzens, *General John Pope*, 80–87; Anders, *Henry Halleck's War*, 210; Robert K. Krick, *Stonewall Jackson at Cedar Mountain* (Chapel Hill: University of North Carolina Press, 1990), chap. 1.

15. John Mead Gould, *The Civil War Journals of John Mead Gould*, ed. William B. Jordan Jr. (Baltimore: Butternut and Blue Press, 1997), 111, 126; Cozzens, *General John Pope*, 85–87; Krick, *Jackson at Cedar Mountain*, 3–4, 7; Crist, *Papers of Jefferson Davis*, 8:309–11; ORA, I, 12, pt. 2, 50–51, and pt. 3, 509, 573, 577.

16. Jedediah Mannis and Galen R. Wilson, eds., *Bound to Be a Soldier: The Letters of Private James T. Miller, One Hundred Eleventh Pennsylvania Infantry, 1861–1864* (Knoxville: University of Tennessee Press, 2001), 28–29; Gould, *Civil War Journals*, 157.

17. Daniel E. Sutherland, "Abraham Lincoln, John Pope and the Origins of Modern War," *Journal of Military History* (October 1992): 575–78; ORA, IV, vol. 1, 1094–99.

18. David Donald, ed., *Inside Lincoln's Cabinet: The Civil War Diaries of Salmon P. Chase* (New York: Longmans, Green, 1954), 96–97; ORA, I, 11, pt. 3, 362–63, and 12, pt. 2, 50–53, and pt. 3, 509.

19. Sears, *Civil War Papers of McClellan*, 380–81; ORA, I, 11, pt. 3, 362–64; Sutherland, "Lincoln, Pope and Modern War," 579–81; Donald H. Wickman, ed., *Letters to Vermont from Her Civil War Soldiers* (Burlington VT: Images from the Past, 1998), vol. 2, August 13, 1862.

20. Dowdey and Manarin, *Wartime Papers of Lee*, 239; Crist, *Papers of Jefferson Davis*, 8:310; Percy G. Hamlin, *Richard Stoddert Ewell* (Richmond VA: Wittet and Shepperson, 1935), 12; Alexander, *Fighting for the Confederacy*, 123.

21. ORA, I, 12, pt. 3, 573, 574, and III, vol. 2, 301–9, 951; Crist, *Papers of Jefferson Davis*, 8:302, 310–12; Frank Freidel, *Francis Lieber: Nineteenth-Century*

Liberal (Baton Rouge: Louisiana State University Press, 1947), 317–41; War Department, Adjutant General's Office, *General Orders Affecting the Volunteer Forces, 1863* (Washington DC: U.S. Government Printing Office, 1864), 64–87.

22. *ORA*, I, 17, pt. 2, 150; Ulysses S. Grant, *Personal Memoirs* (New York: Charles Webster, 1885), 1:197–98.

23. Sutherland, "Lincoln, Pope and Modern War," 584; Daniel E. Sutherland, *Seasons of War: The Ordeal of a Confederate Community, 1861–1865* (New York: Free Press, 1995), 122–29; Daniel E. Sutherland, *The Emergence of Total War* (Fort Worth TX: Ryan Place, 1996), chap. 2; Joseph T. Durkin, ed., *Confederate Chaplain: A War Journal of Rev. James B. Sheeran, c.s.s.r., Fourteenth Louisiana, C.S.A* (Milwaukee: Bruce, 1960), 2; Randall Allen and Keith S. Bohannon, eds., *Campaigning with "Old Stonewall": Confederate Captain Ujanirtus Allen's Letters to His Wife* (Baton Rouge: Louisiana State University Press, 1998), 131, 135, 137; Hamlin, *Ewell*, 112; David S. Sparks, ed., *Inside Lincoln's Army: The Diary of Marsena Rudolph Patrick, Provost Marshal General, Army of the Potomac* (New York: Thomas Yoseloff, 1964), 109–10; Myrta Lockett Avary, *A Virginia Girl in the Civil War* (New York: D. Appleton, 1903), 49.

24. *New York Herald*, August 26, 1862; *Memphis Appeal*, August 20, 1862; Letter, John P. Hatch to father, August 13, 1862, Hatch Papers, Library of Congress; *ORA*, I, 12, pt. 2, 573.

25. Anders, *Halleck's War*, 210; K. P. Williams, *Lincoln Finds a General*, 1:257–59; Sparks, *Inside Lincoln's Army*, 109–10; Dowdey and Manarin, *Wartime Papers of Lee*, 248.

26. *ORA*, I, 12, pt. 3, 916–29, especially 925–26; W. J. Wood, *Civil War Generalship: The Art of Command* (1997, rpt. New York: Da Capo, 2000), 31–33, 36–37; Harsh, *Confederate Tide Rising*, 119–22.

27. *ORA*, I, 12, pt. 3, 525–26; Wood, *Civil War Generalship*, 46, 50–51; Edward J. Stackpole, *From Cedar Mountain to Antietam: August–September 1862* (Harrisburg: Stackpole, 1959), 31–32, 34–36; Martin, *Second Bull Run*, 58–59.

28. *Civil War Journals*, 162; Gould Milroy to wife, August 2, 1862, copy, Letter, R. H. Milroy Files, Library, Manassas National Battlefield, Manassas, Virginia.

29. Krick, *Jackson at Cedar Mountain*, 15–25, especially 22–24.

30. *ORA*, I, 12, pt. 3, 523–26; Wood, *Civil War Generalship*, 50; Stackpole, *From Cedar Mountain to Antietam*, 31–32.

31. *ORA*, I, 12, pt. 3, 551, 920, 924–25; William Thomas Venner, *Hoosier's Honor: The Iron Brigade's Nineteenth Indiana* (Shippensburg PA: Burd Street Press, 1998), 53, 57–60.

32. *ORA*, I, 12, pt. 3, 547, 922–23, 924–26; Wood, *Civil War Generalship*, 33; Stackpole, *From Cedar Mountain to Antietam*, 40–42.

33. Wood, *Civil War Generalship*, 31–33, 74–76.

34. Stackpole, *From Cedar Mountain to Antietam*, 46–54.

35. *ORA*, I, 12, pt. 2, 182; Krick, *Jackson at Cedar Mountain*, 14–15.

36. Krick, *Jackson at Cedar Mountain*, 21–30; James I. Robertson, *General A. P. Hill: The Story of a Confederate Warrior* (New York: Random House, 1987), 100–102.

37. Krick, *Jackson at Cedar Mountain*, 47–55; ORA, I, 12, pt. 2, 181.

38. Stackpole, *From Cedar Mountain to Antietam*, 57–60; Krick, *Jackson at Cedar Mountain*, 49–50; Gould, *Civil War Journals*, 161; Frederick Denison, *The Battle of Cedar Mountain: A Personal View, August 9, 1862* (Providence RI: N. Bangs Williams, 1881), 11; Steven S. Raab, ed., *With the Third Wisconsin Badgers: The Living Experience of the Civil War through the Journals of Van R. Willard* (Mechanicsburg PA: Stackpole, 1999), 73–76.

39. Denison, *Cedar Mountain*, 17, 19–20, 23; Wood, *Civil War Generalship*, 59.

40. Krick, *Jackson at Cedar Mountain*, 45–48.

41. Cozzens, *General John Pope*, 89; Cozzens and Girardi, *Military Memoirs of Pope*, 134–35.

42. Milo M. Quaife, ed., *From the Cannon's Mouth: The Civil War Letters of General Alpheus S. Williams* (1959, rpt. Lincoln: University of Nebraska Press, 1995), 100; Cozzens and Girardi, *Military Memoirs of Pope*, 135–36; Cozzens, *General John Pope*, 93–95; Fred Harvey Harrington, *Fighting Politician: Major General N. P. Banks* (Philadelphia: University of Pennsylvania Press, 1970), 81–82.

43. Wood, *Civil War Generalship*, 58–59; Krick, *Jackson at Cedar Mountain*, 95–97; John O. Casler, *Four Years in the Stonewall Brigade* (Guthrie: Oklahoma State Capital Printing Company, 1893), 142–44; Ezra J. Warner, *Generals in Gray: Lives of the Confederate Commanders* (Baton Rouge: Louisiana State University Press, 1959), 339–40; McHenry Howard to Alicia Winder, June 28, 1865, Item 97, Catalogue 33, Volume 2001, Brian and Maria Green, Inc., Kernersville NC.

44. Martin, *Second Bull Run*, 73–76; Wood, *Civil War Generalship*, 62–65; Krick, *Jackson at Cedar Mountain*, chap. 7.

45. Stackpole, *From Cedar Mountain to Antietam*, 66–67; "Register of Meterological Observations, Smithsonian Institution, Georgetown, D.C., August 1862," Archives of National Weather Records Center, Asheville NC, copy, Vertical file, Second Battle of Manassas, Weather Observations and Temperature, Library, Manassas National Battlefield, Virginia.

46. Blackford, *Letters from Lee's Army*, 104–5; Martin, *Second Bull Run*, 77–78; Wood, *Civil War Generalship*, 65–66; Krick, *Jackson at Cedar Mountain*, chaps. 8, 9.

47. Wood, *Civil War Generalship*, 65–69; Robertson, *Hill*, 104–6; John Wotring diary, August 9, 1862, courtesy of Joseph Rubenfine, West Palm Beach FL; W. B. Bean, *The Liberty Hall Volunteers: Stonewall's College Boys* (Charlottesville: University Press of Virginia, 1964), 129; Krick, *Jackson at Cedar Mountain*, chaps. 10, 11, 12.

48. Robert J. Trout, *With Pen and Saber: The Letters and Diaries of J. E. B. Stuart's Staff Officers* (Mechanicsburg PA: Stackpole, 1995), 90; Wotring diary, August 9, 1862; Quaife, *From the Cannon's Mouth*, 100–102; Stackpole, *From Cedar Mountain to Antietam*, 70–72; Martin, *Second Bull Run*, 80–81; Wood, *Civil War Generalship*, 69–71; Krick, *Jackson at Cedar Mountain*, chap. 14.

49. Blackford, *Letters from Lee's Army*, 106; Cozzens, *General John Pope*, 93–96; Robertson, *Hill*, 108; Wood, *Civil War Generalship*, 70–71.

50. Krick, *Jackson at Cedar Mountain*, chaps. 15, 26; Durkin, *Confederate Chaplain*, 4–5.

51. Wood, *Civil War Generalship*, 73–81; Robertson, *Hill*, 108; Stackpole, *Cedar Mountain to Antietam*, 75, 78–79; Krick, *Jackson at Cedar Mountain*, appendix 1.

52. ORA, I, 12, pt. 2, 185–86; Dowdey and Manarin, *Wartime Papers of Lee*, 251; Quaife, *From the Cannon's Mouth*, 100–101; William B. Styple, *Writing and Fighting the Confederate War: The Letters of Peter Wellington Alexander, Confederate War Correspondent* (Kearny NJ: Belle Grove, 2002), 91.

53. Martin, *Second Bull Run*, 82–83; Wood, *Civil War Generalship*, 69–74; ORA, I, 12, pt. 2, 135.

54. Quaife, *From the Cannon's Mouth*, 103; Trout, *With Pen and Saber*, 89; Letter, Allen to wife, August 11, 1862, in Allen and Bohannon, *Campaigning with Old Stonewall*, 141–42; Bean, *Liberty Hall Volunteers*, 129; Wotring diary, August 11, 1862.

55. Edwin C. Fishel, *The Secret War for the Union: The Untold Story of Military Intelligence in the Civil War* (Boston: Houghton Mifflin, 1996), 189; Gene Thorp, "The Front Line in Our Back Yard," Washington at War: 140 Years Ago series, *Washington Post*, August 11, 2002, Metro Section, C9.

56. Sears, *Civil War Papers of McClellan*, 391; Long, *Civil War Day by Day*, 247, 249, 253, 354; Coakley, *Role of Federal Military Forces*, 230.

3. Stonewall and a Virginia Reel

1. Stephen B. Oates, *A Woman of Valor: Clara Barton and the Civil War* (New York: Free Press, 1994), 63, and for background on Barton, see chaps. 1, 2.

2. Oates, *Woman of Valor*, 643–65; Clara Barton, "Notes from a Lecture," undated, Barton Papers, Library of Congress.

3. Gould, *Civil War Journals*, 168, 170, 171, 173; Mannis and Wilson, *Bound to Be a Soldier*, 32–38. especially 33.

4. Mannis and Wilson, *Bound to Be a Soldier*, 37; Cutrer and Parrish, *Brothers in Gray*, 123.

5. Mannis and Wilson, *Bound to Be a Soldier*, 37–38.

6. ORA, I, 12, pt. 3, 560; Krick, *Jackson at Cedar Mountain*, chap. 16.

7. Dowdey and Manarin, *Wartime Papers of Lee*, 238–39, 252–53, 258–59; Harsh, *Confederate Tide Rising*, 119–24; Kegel, *North with Lee and Jackson*, 139–40.

8. Martin, *Second Bull Run*, 89; David Homer Bates, *Lincoln in the Telegraph Office: Recollections of the United States Military Telegraph Corps During the Civil War* (1907, rpt. Lincoln: University of Nebraska Press, 1995), chap. 8.

9. Martin, *Second Bull Run*, 90–91; Harsh, *Confederate Tide Rising*, 124–25; John Hennessy, *Return to Bull Run: The Campaign and Battle of Second Manassas* (New York: Simon and Schuster, 1993), 34–35.

10. Durkin, *Confederate Chaplain*, 6; Henry Haupt, *Reminiscences* (Milwaukee: Wright and Joy, 1901), 69–70; ORA, I, 12, pt. 2, 571, 576.

11. Hennessy, *Return to Bull Run*, 42–45; Harsh, *Confederate Tide Rising*, 122–28.

12. Fishel, *Secret War*, 182–89, 191–93.

13. Hennessy, *Return to Bull Run*, 45–49; Heros von Borcke, *Memoirs of the Confederate War for Independence* (1866, rpt. Dayton OH: Morningside, 1985), 105–9.

14. *ORA*, I, 12, pt. 3, 589–95, especially 591; Stackpole, *From Cedar Mountain to Antietam*, 86; Fishel, *Secret War*, 193; K. P. Williams, *Lincoln Finds a General*, 1:277–78.

15. Armistead L. Long, *Memoirs of Robert E. Lee: His Military and Personal History* (New York, Stoddard, 1886), 186–87; Hennessy, *Return to Bull Run*, 85–87.

16. Raab, *With the Third Wisconsin Badgers*, 77; Cecil D. Eby Jr., ed., *A Virginia Yankee in the Civil War: The Diaries of David Hunter Strother* (Chapel Hill: University of North Carolina Press, 1961), 84; Margaret B. Paulus, ed., *Papers of General Robert Huston Milroy* (n.p., 1965), 1:74.

17. Hennessy, *Return to Bull Run*, 52–57; Wotring diary, August 18–20, 1862.

18. Hennessy, *Return to Bull Run*, 53, 58; Harsh, *Confederate Tide Rising*, 129–31; Stackpole, *From Cedar Mountain to Antietam*, 87; Fishel, *Secret War*, 195.

19. *ORA*, I, 12, pt. 3, 601–3.

20. Hennessy, *Return to Bull Run*, 62–63; K. P. Williams, *Lincoln Finds a* General, 1:280–81; Welch, *A Confederate Surgeon's Letters*, 21.

21. J. F. J. Caldwell, *History of a Brigade of South Carolinians Known as "Gregg's" and Subsequently as "McGowan's Brigade"* (1866, rpt. Dayton OH: Morningside Bookshop, 1951), 29; Robert G. Carroon, *From Freeman's Ford to Bentonville: The 61st Ohio Volunteer Infantry* (Shippensburg PA: Burd Street Press, 1998), 2, 4, 19; N. A. Davis, *The Campaign from Texas to Maryland*, 72–73.

22. Wotring diary, August 22, 1862; French Harding, *Civil War Memoirs*, ed. Victor L. Thacker (Parsons WV: McClain, 2000), 63; Stackpole, *From Cedar Mountain to Antietam*, 91; Engle, *Yankee Dutchman*, 137–38; Eugene M. Scheel, *The Civil War in Fauquier Co., Va.* (Waterford VA: Author, 1985), plate VII.

23. Engle, *Yankee Dutchman*, 138; K. P. Williams, *Lincoln Finds a General*, 1:284; Hennessy, *Return to Bull Run*, 72; *ORA*, I, 12, pt. 2, 331.

24. *ORA*, I, 12, pt. 2, 30–31, 59, and pt. 3, 622, 625, 627; T. D. Stamps and Department of Military Art and Engineering, United States Military Academy, *Civil War Atlas to Accompany Steele's American Campaigns* (West Point: United States Military Academy, 1941), plate 40.

25. Cozzens, *General John Pope*, 101; *ORA*, I, 12, pt. 3, 623; Stackpole, *From Cedar Mountain to Antietam*, 90–95; Hennessy, *Return to Bull Run* 76–81; Letter, T. Murray to Parents, Bristoe Station, August 25, 1862, copy, Vertical Files, Manassas National Battlefield Library, Manassas, Virginia; Harsh, *Confederate Tide Rising*, 131.

26. K. P. Williams, *Lincoln Finds a General*, 1:286–90; Haupt, *Reminiscences*, 78, 80, 82; *ORA*, I, 12, pt. 2, 60–64, and pt. 3, 630–38.

27 *ORA*, I, 12, pt. 2, 60–61, and pt. 3, 630–31, 642, 645–47.

28. Stackpole, *From Cedar Mountain to Antietam*, 96–101; K. P. Williams, *Lincoln Finds a General*, 1:284; Blackford, *Letters from Lee's Army*, 124–27.

29. Sears, *Civil War Papers of McClellan*, 399–400; Letter, Orlando Poe to wife, August 23, 1862, Poe Papers, Library of Congress; Henry Kyd Douglas, *I Rode with Stonewall* (Chapel Hill: University of North Carolina Press, 1940), 130–31; Charles W. Turner, ed., *Captain Greenlee Davidson, C.S.A. Diary and Letters 1851–1863* (Verona VA: McClure Press, 1975), 42–44; ORA, I, 12, pt. 2, 32, 673–74, and pt. 2, 642, 645, 649.

30. Basler, *Collected Works of Lincoln*, 5:388–89; Guelzo, *Lincoln's Emancipation Proclamation*, 132–38; Williams, "'Doing Less' and 'Doing More,'" 59, 62, 67.

31. Harsh, *Confederate Tide Rising*, 131–32; Dowdey and Manarin, *Wartime Papers of Lee*, 262–63; James D. Brewer, *The Raiders of 1862* (Westport CT: Praeger, 1997), pt. 1; James A. Ramage, *Rebel Raider: The Life of General John Hunt Morgan* (Lexington: University Press of Kentucky, 1986), chaps. 8, 9, 10.

32. Dowdey and Manarin, *Wartime Papers of Lee*, 263–65; Harsh, *Confederate Tide Rising*, 131–34.

33. Harsh, *Confederate Tide Rising*, 134–39; Stackpole, *From Cedar Mountain to Antietam*, 101–4; Hennessy, *Return to Bull Run*, 92–95; Martin, *Second Bull Run*, 105–8.

34. Stackpole, *From Cedar Mountain to Antietam*, 105–6; Martin, *Second Bull Run*, 108–9; Hennessy, *Return to Bull Run*, 96–101; Harsh, *Confederate Tide Rising*, 139–40; Robertson, *Hill*, 111–12; W. N. Wood, *Reminiscences of Big I*, 29; Harding, *Civil War Memoirs*, 64; Wotring diary, August 23, 24, 1862.

35. Fishel, *Secret War*, 198–99; Cozzens, *General John Pope*, 111–12; Harsh, *Confederate Tide Rising*, 140–41; ORA, I, 12, pt. 3, 653–58.

36. ORA, I, 12, pt. 2, 67, and pt. 3, 653; Martin, *Second Bull Run*, 109; Luther E. Alden, "Pope's Retreat," narrative, 12, 13, Vertical Files, Manassas National Battlefield Park Library.

37. ORA, I, 12, pt. 3, 653, 666–67; K. P. Williams, *Lincoln Finds a General*, 1:291–97.

38. Douglas, *I Rode with Stonewall*, 135; Martin, *Second Bull Run*, 109–10, 113–16; Cozzens, *General John Pope*, 110–11; Fishel, *Secret War*, 198.

39. ORA, I, 12, pt. 2, 65–66; Cozzens, *General John Pope*, 106–7; K. P. Williams, *Lincoln Finds a General*, 1:297–98.

40. Martin, *Second Bull Run*, 112–13; Hennessy, *Return to Bull Run*, chap. 7; Cozzens, *General John Pope*, 111–14; Rafuse, *McClellan's War*, 253–58.

41. Douglas, *I Rode with Stonewall*, 135–36; Harsh, *Confederate Tide Rising*, 146–48; Angus James Johnston II, *Virginia Railroads in the Civil War* (Chapel Hill: University of North Carolina Press, 1961), 85; Frances Trevelyan Miller, *Photographic History of the Civil War* (New York: Review of Reviews, 1911), 2:24–28, 5:283.

42. Martin, *Second Bull Run*, 118–20; Harding, *Civil War Memoirs*, 64; Wotring diary, August 26, 1862; K. P. Williams, *Lincoln Finds a General*, 1:302–4; Harsh, *Confederate Tide Rising*, 146–50.

43. ORA, I, 12, pt. 2, 401–4, 641–48, 654–57, 723–24, and pt. 3, 704, 732, 733.

44. Joseph Mills Hanson, *Bull Run Remembers: History, Traditions and Landmarks of the Manassas (Bull Run) Campaign before Washington 1861–1862* (Manassas VA: National Capital Publishers, 1953), 156–57.

45. *ORA*, I, 12, pt. 2, 404, 539–43; Hanson, *Bull Run Remembers*, 159; Haupt, *Reminiscences*, 95–104; K. P. Williams, *Lincoln Finds a General*, 1:303–5.

46. *ORA*, I, 12, pt. 2, 404, 539–43, 405–11, 697–99; Melinda Herzog, "The Battle of the Bull Run Railroad Bridge," *Hallowed Ground* [Civil War Preservation Trust] 5 (Summer 2004): 18–19; K. P. Williams, *Lincoln Finds a General*, 1:304.

47. Cozzens, *General John Pope*, 111; Hennessy, *Return to Bull Run*, 130.

48. Martin, *Second Bull Run*, 14–125; Cozzens, *General John Pope*, 115–16.

49. Martin, *Second Bull Run*, 125–26; Cozzens, *General John Pope*, 121–26; Stackpole, *From Cedar Mountain to Antietam*, 126–28.

50. K. P. Williams, *Lincoln Finds a General*, 1:312; Martin, *Second Bull Run*, 127–29; Hennessy, *Return to Bull Run*, 124.

51. Harsh, *Confederate Tide Rising*, 146–52; Hennessy, *Return to Bull Run*, 129–30, 136–37, 138–39; Martin, *Second Bull Run*, 129–31; Wotring diary, August 27, 1862.

52. Hennessy, *Return to Bull Run*, 139–40; Douglas, *I Rode with Stonewall*, 136.

53. Stackpole, *From Cedar Mountain to Antietam*, 132–45; Martin, *Second Bull Run*, 137; *ORA*, I, 12, pt. 2, 36, 70–72, 265, 272, 335, and pt. 3, 684; K. P. Williams, *Lincoln Finds a General*, 1:311.

54. *ORA*, I, 12, pt. 2, 37; Martin, *Second Bull Run*, 137; Harsh, *Confederate Tide Rising*, 153; K. P. Williams, *Lincoln Finds a General*, 1:314–17.

55. Thorp, "The Front Line," C9.

56. *ORA*, I, 11, pt. 1, 98; Rafuse, *McClellan's War*, 259; Hennesey, *Return to Bull Run*, 128–29; Styple, *Writing and Fighting the Confederate War*, 91.

4. Lee and Pope at Second Manassas

1. Cozzens, *General John Pope*, 115–17, especially 117; *ORA*, I, 12, pt. 2, suppl. 825.

2. K. P. Williams, *Lincoln Finds a General*, 1:288–89; Bruce Catton, *Mr. Lincoln's Army* (Garden City NY: Doubleday, 1955), 29–34; Rafuse, *McClellan's War*, 249–57.

3. Sears, *Civil War Papers of McClellan*, 389–99; Charles Dana Gibson with E. Kay Gibson, *Assault and Logistics: Union Army Coastal and River Operations 1861–1866* (Camden ME: Ensign Press, 1995), 216–18; *ORA*, I, 12, Pt. 3, 5.

4. *ORA*, I, 12, pt. 2, 5; Sears, *Civil War Papers of McClellan*, 399; Gibson and Gibson, *Assault and Logistics*, 617–18.

5. Sears, *Civil War Papers of McClellan*, 400–417, especially 406. See also Joseph T. Glatthaar, *Partners in Command: The Relationships between Leaders in the Civil War* (New York: Free Press, 1994), chap. 3; Marszalek, *Commander of all Lincoln's Armies*, 140–45.

6. Cozzens, *General John Pope*, 116–18; Sears, *Civil War Papers of McClellan*, 389–

90, 397, 404–16; Sears, *McClellan: The Young Napoleon*, 247–51; James M. Ridgway Jr., *Little Mac: Demise of an American Hero* (New York: Exlibris, 2000), 307–10.

7. Charles Francis Adams, *A Cycle of Adams Letters*, ed. Worthington C. Ford, 2 vols. (Boston: Houghton Mifflin, 1920), 2:277–78; *ORA*, I, 12, pt. 3, 691, and 11, pt. 1, 95; Sears, *Civil War Papers of McClellan*, 405–12.

8. Sears, *Civil War Papers of McClellan*, 416, 418; Sears, *McClellan: The Young Napoleon*, 254; *ORA*, I, 12, pt. 3, 697–98, 706, 723.

9. Sears, *Civil War Papers of McClellan*, 410–15; *ORA*, I, 12, pt. 3, 710, 725; Anders, *Henry Halleck's War*, 211; Rafuse, *McClellan's War*, 261–62, 263–65.

10. *ORA*, I, 12, pt. 1, 175–76, and pt. 2, 335–36.

11. Stackpole, *From Cedar Mountain to Antietam*, 146; Hennessy, *Return to Bull Run*, 139–43, 147–48; John Hennessy, *Second Manassas Battlefield Map Study* (Lynchburg VA: H. E. Howard, 1985), 1–2, map 1; *ORA*, I, 12, pt. 1, 195, 199, and pt. 2, 51, 131, 335–36, 393, 664, and suppl. 824–25, 829–38, 843–44, 861–65.

12. Stephen R. Potter et al., "'No Maneuvering and Very Little Tactics': Archaeology and the Battle of Brawner Farm," in *Archaeological Perspectives on the American Civil War*, ed Clarence R. Geier and Stephen R. Potter (Gainesville: University Press of Florida, 2000), 2–9; Hennessy, *Second Manassas Map Study*, 4, 19, 20, 30.

13. *ORA*, I, 12, pt. 2, 656, 710; Hennessy, *Second Manassas Map Study*, 29–30; Fishel, *Secret War*, 200–201; E-an Zen and Alta Walker, *Rocks and War: Geology and the Civil War Campaign of Second Manassas* (Shippensburg PA: White Mane, 2000), especially 55, map 9, and figures 2, 8, 9, 10.

14. Cozzens, *General John Pope*, 124–28; *ORA*, I, 12, pt. 2, 336–37, 360–61, 6644–665; Stamps and Department of Military Art and Engineering, *Civil War Atlas*, plate 43.

15. Hennessy, *Return to Bull Run*, 153–61; Hennessy, *Second Manassas Map Study*, 15–18, 22–29; Stackpole, *From Cedar Mountain to Antietam*, 145–48; Martin, *Second Bull Run*, 252–54; Joseph T. Durkin, ed., *John Dooley, Confederate Soldier: His War Journal* (Washington DC: Georgetown University Press, 1945), 14–16; George Skoch and Mark W. Perkins, eds., *Lone Star Confederate: A Gallant Soldier of the Fifth Texas Infantry* (College Station: Texas A&M University Press, 2003), 60–63.

16. *ORA*, I, 12, pt. 2, 384, 386–87, 564; Hennessy, *Return to Bull Run*, 153–61; Noel G. Harrison, "Action at Chapman's (Beverley's) Mill August 1862," *Junction* [The Manassas Museum News] 8, (March–April 1990): 1–4; James Burgess, "The Battle for Thoroughfare Gap, August 28, 1862," Vertical Files, Manassas National Park Library, Manassas National Battlefield; Skoch and Perkins, *Lone Star Confederate*, 62.

17. Hennessy, *Second Manassas Map Study*, 49, 52; Martin, *Second Bull Run*, 154; Zen and Walker, *Rocks and War*, 53–55, figures 4, 7, and maps 11, 12; Fishel, *Secret War*, 201–2.

18. Hennessy, *Return to Bull Run*, 164–66; *ORA*, I, 12, pt. 2, 337, 369, 371, 373–74, 375–76, 377–78, 380–81, 645.

19. Hennessy, *Return to Bull Run*, 167.

20. Potter et al., "No Maneuvering and Very Little Tactics," 8–13; Hennessy, *Return to Bull Run*, chap. 10; Hennessy, *Second Manassas Map Study*, 30–31, map 4.

21. Ropes, *The Army under Pope*, chap. 4; Martin, *Second Bull Run*, 145–51; Hennessy, *Return to Bull Run*, especially 177–87; Hennessy, *Second Manassas Map Study*, 31–32; *ORA*, I, 12, pt. 2, 369, 371, 375–76, 378, 380–82.

22. Dawes quoted in Hennessy, *Return to Bull Run*, 193; Hennessy, *Second Manassas Map Study*, 39–59; Taliaferro quoted in Alan D. Gaff, *Brave Men's Tears: The Iron Brigade at Brawner Farm* (Dayton OH: Morningside Press, 1985), 164.

23. *ORA*, I, 12, pt. 1, 206–8; Hennessy, *Second Manassas Map Study*, 39, 60–61, map 3; Wotring diary, August 28, 1862.

24. Cozzens, *General John Pope*, 130; Hennessy, *Second Manassas Map Study*, 61, map 3; Hennessy, *Return to Bull Run*, 195.

25. *ORA*, I, 12, pt. 3, 733; Eby, *Virginia Yankee*, 91–92; Hennessy, *Second Manassas Map Study*, 73; Ropes, *The Army under Pope*, chaps. 6–10.

26. *ORA*, I, 12, pt. 2, 76, and pt. 2, suppl., 832; Hennessy, *Second Manassas Map Study*, 73–74, 86.

27. *ORA*, I, 12, pt. 3, 729, 730, and pt. 2, suppl., 831–32, 851–52, 902–3, 1010–12.

28. Hennessy, *Return to Bull Run*, 226; Hennessy, *Second Manassas Map Study*, 63, 96, 100–106, 118, map 4. Kenneth P. Williams is less critical of the tone and content of the "Joint Order"; see *Lincoln Finds a General*, 1:325–27.

29. Hennessy, *Return to Bull Run*, 221–22; Hennessy, *Second Manassas Map Study*, 61–79, 125, maps 3, 4, 5.

30. Hennessy, *Second Manassas Map Study*, 87–104, 114–19, map 4.

31. Hennessy, *Second Manassas Map Study*, 100–101, 120; Martin, *Second Bull Run*, 172; Cozzens, *General John Pope*, 170–71; *ORA*, I, 12, pt. 2, 39; Eby, *Virginia Yankee*, 92.

32. DeWitt B. Stone Jr., ed., *Wandering to Glory: Confederate Veterans Remember Evans' Brigade* (Columbia: University of South Carolina Press, 2002), 45–47; Skoch and Perkins, *Lone Star Confederate*, 64; Martin, *Second Bull Run*, 173–77; Hennessy, *Second Manassas Map Study*, 76–85, 110–19, maps 3, 4; Harsh, *Confederate Tide Rising*, 156.

33. Hennessy, *Return to Bull Run*, 226–28; Hennessy, *Second Manassas Map Study*, 110–14, 134–37, 145, maps 5, 6.

34. Hennessy, *Return to Bull Run*, 229–31; Hennessy, *Second Manassas Map Study*, 134, 162, and map 7; Skoch and Perkins, *Lone Star Confederate*, 65; Harsh, *Confederate Tide Rising*, 157.

35. Hennessy, *Return to Bull Run*, 243; Hennessy, *Second Manassas Map Study*, 120–92, 196–201, maps 5, 6, 7.

36. Hennessy, *Return to Bull Run*, 259, citing Letter, H. S. Thomas to Porter, July 13, 1878, Porter Papers, Library of Congress; Martin, *Second Bull Run*, 171–72; Stackpole, *From Cedar Mountain to Antietam*, 183–92.

37. Hennessy, *Return to Bull Run*, 259–69; Hennessy, *Second Manassas Map Study*, maps 6, 7.

38. *ORA*, I, 12, pt. 2, suppl., 826; Hennessy, *Return to Bull Run*, 270–71, 306; Hennessy, *Second Manassas Map Study*, 169, 175, map 7; Martin, *Second Bull Run*, 178–85.

39. Hennessy, *Return to Bull Run*, chap. 15; Hennessy, *Second Manassas Map Study*, 194–201, map 7; Martin, *Second Bull Run*, 185–88; Stackpole, *From Cedar Mountain to Antietam*, 190–92.

40. Skoch and Perkins, *Lone Star Confederate*, 66; Hennessy, *Second Manassas Map Study*, 175–81, 196–99, map 7; Martin, *Second Bull Run*, 188–91.

41. Martin, *Second Bull Run*, 190–91; Hennessy, *Second Manassas Map Study*, 202, map 7.

42. Hennessy, *Return to Bull Run*, 288–89, 291; Hennessy, *Second Manassas Map Study*, 192; Martin, *Second Bull Run*, 191.

43. D. B. Stone, *Wandering to Glory*, 49; Hennessy, *Return to Bull Run*, 291–300; Hennessy, *Second Manassas Map Study*, 204–10, 215–22, map 7; Martin, *Second Bull Run*, 190–91.

44. Skoch and Perkins, *Lone Star Confederate*, 64–70; Fishel, *Secret War*, 202.

45. Fishel, *Secret War*, 202–3; Hennessey, *Second Manassas Map Study*, 202, map 8.

46. *ORA*, I, 12, pt. 3, 741, 742; Stackpole, *From Cedar Mountain to Antietam*, 214–15; Hennessy, *Return to Bull Run*, 304–8; Hennessy, *Second Manassas Map Study*, 202; Martin, *Second Bull Run*, 194.

47. Fishel, *Secret War*, 204; Hennessy, *Second Manassas Map study*, 204.

48. Dowdey and Manarin, *Wartime Papers of Lee*, 266–67, also 260–65; Crist, *Papers of Jefferson Davis*, 8:347, 350, 354–55, 357–59, 366, 367–68, 369; Hennessy, *Return to Bull Run*, 313.

49. Hennessy, *Return to Bull Run*, 314–15; Hennessy, *Second Manassas Map Study*, 248–50 and map 9; Martin, *Second Bull Run*, 203–5.

50. *ORA*, I, 12, pt. 3, 741, 742; Skoch and Perkins, *Lone Star Confederate*, 70–73.

51. *ORA*, I, 11, pt. 1, 97–100, and 12, pt. 3, 706, 739–40.

52. *ORA*, I, 11, pt. 1, 101–2, and 12, pt. 3, 738, 744–45; also see Rafuse, *McClellan's War*, 261–67.

53. Eby, *Virginia Yankee*, 94–95; Martin, *Second Bull Run*, 208–9; Hennessy, *Second Manassas Map Study*, 226–27, map 9.

54. Cozzens, *General John Pope*, 164–65; Hennessy, *Second Manassas Map Study*, 227–47, map 9.

55. Hennessy, *Second Manassas Map Study*, 227–47, 261, maps 9, 10; Martin, *Second Bull Run*, 209–10.

56. Hennessy, *Return to Bull Run*, 334–61; Hennessy, *Second Manassas Map Study*, 283–316, map 11; Martin, *Second Bull Run*, 209–10.

57. Hennessy, *Second Manassas Map Study*, 316–31, 332, map 12.

58. Quoted in Hennessy, *Return to Bull Run*, 373, also 366–73; Hennessy,

Second Manassas Map Study, 316–42, map 12, D. B. Stone, *Wandering to Glory*, 50–53; Skoch and Perkins, *Lone Star Confederate*, 74.

59. Skoch and Perkins, *Lone Star Confederate*, 77; Martin, *Second Bull Run*, 227–29; Hennessy, *Second Manassas Map Study*, 343–73, map 13.

60. Skoch and Perkins, *Lone Star Confederate*, 78; Wotring diary, August 30, 1862; Hennessy, *Return to Bull Run*, 401–2.

61. ORA, I, 12, pt. 2, 77–78; Martin, *Second Bull Run*, 233–35; Hennessy, *Second Manassas Map Study*, 403–8, map 14.

62. Hennessy, *Return to Bull Run*, 242, 468; Hennessy, *Second Manassas Map Study*, 403–25, 441, maps 14, 15; Cozzens, *General John Pope*, 163; Sears, *McClellan: The Young Napoleon*, 254; Rafuse, *McClellan's War*, 266, 271.

63. Todd S. Berkoff, "'A Fierce and Bloody Encounter': The Cavalry Battle at Lewis Ford," *Hallowed Ground* [Civil War Preservation Trust] 5 (Summer 2004): 28–31; Martin, *Second Bull Run*, 242–45; Hennessy, *Second Manassas Map Study*, 426–40, maps 14, 15.

64. ORA, I, 12, pt. 2, 78–79; Walcott, quoted in Hennessy, *Return to Bull Run*, 437; Hennessy, *Second Manassas Map Study*, 441–52, map 16; Bayard quoted in Rafuse, *McClellan's War*, 266.

65. ORA, I, 12, pt. 2, 78–79; Dowdey and Manarin, *Wartime Papers of Lee*, 268.

66. William P. Buck, ed., *Sad Earth, Sweet Heaven: The Diary of Lucy Rebecca Buck During the War between the States* (Birmingham AL: Cornerstone, 1973), 138; Wiley Sword, *Southern Invincibility: A History of the Confederate Heart* (New York: St. Martin's, 1999), 134, 158.

5. In the Rain at Chantilly

1. ORA, I, 11, pt. 1, 102, and pt. 3, 771–72. For the battle of Richmond and the Kentucky situation, see James Lee McDonough, *War in Kentucky: From Shiloh to Perryville* (Knoxville: University of Tennessee Press, 1994), chap. 5; Earl J. Hess, *Banners to the Breeze: The Kentucky Campaign, Corinth, Stones River* (Lincoln: University of Nebraska Press, 2000), 38–42; Kenneth W. Noe, *Perryville: This Grand Havoc of Battle* (Lexington: University Press of Kentucky, 2001), 39–40; Kenneth A. Hafendorfer, *Perryville, Battle for Kentucky* (Owensboro KY: McDowell, 1981), pt. 1.

2. Putnam, *Richmond During the War*, 166; Bill, *Beleaguered City*, 148–49; news coverage can be traced in J. Cutler Andrews, *The South Reports the Civil War* (1970, rpt. Pittsburgh: University of Pittsburgh Press, 1985), 200–203; Jean V. Berlin, ed., *A Confederate Nurse: The Diary of Ada W. Bacot 1860–1863* (Columbia: University of South Carolina Press, 1994), 143; J. B. Jones, *A Rebel War Clerk's Diary*, 96.

3. Casualty figures (however typically suspect) can be computed in ORA, I, 12, pt. 2, 249–62 (Union) and 560–62, 568, 811–13 (Confederate), from which the estimate cited here appears in F. H. Kennedy, *Civil War Battlefield Guide*, 109–11. Percentages appear in Martin, *Second Bull Run*, 248–49; Andrews, *South Reports the Civil War*, 199–200, treats landscape disfiguration.

4. *ORA*, I, 12, pt. 3, 768; Asbury Coward, *The South Carolinians*, ed. Natalie Bond and Osmun Coward (New York: Vantage Press, 1968), 53.

5. *ORA*, I, 12, pt. 2, 557; Hennessy, *Return to Bull Run*, 442–43; Martin, *Second Bull Run*, 255; Freeman, *Lee's Lieutenants*, 2:130.

6. David A. Welker, *Tempest at Ox Hill: The Battle of Chantilly* (New York: Da Capo, 2002), 103, 104; *ORA*, I, 12, pt. 2, 557–58, 566, 647, 743; Paul Taylor, *He Hath Loosed the Fateful Lightning: The Battle of Ox Hill (Chantilly) September 1, 1862* (Shippensburg PA: White Mane, 2003), 20–30.

7. *ORA*, I, 11, pt. 1, 103, and 12, pt. 3, 771–72; Sears, *Civil War Papers of McClellan*, 423–24.

8. Sears, *Civil War Papers of McClellan*, 427; Rafuse, *McClellan's War*, 265–68; *ORA*, I, 12, pt. 3, 773.

9. *ORA*, I, 12, pt. 2, 44, 79–81, 437, and pt. 3, 769, also suppl., 843, 1066; Hennessy, *Return to Bull Run*, 440; Fishel, *Secret War*, 206–8; Cozzens, *General John Pope*, 188–89; Welker, *Tempest at Ox Hill*, 92–93; Taylor, *He Hath Loosed*, chap. 2.

10. *ORA*, I, 12, pt. 2, 81–82, and pt. 3, 770–71; Welker, *Tempest at Ox Hill*, 123–25.

11. *ORA*, I, 12, pt. 2, 82–83, and pt. 3, 963; Hennessy, *Return to Bull Run*, 443–45; Cozzens, *General John Pope*, 189–90.

12. *ORA*, I, 12, pt. 2, 84, and pt. 3, 785; Welker, *Tempest at Ox Hill*, 130.

13. *ORA*, I, 12, pt. 2, 83, 85–86, and pt. 3, 785; Welker, *Tempest at Ox Hill*, 128–29.

14. Cozzens, *General John Pope*, 190–92; Welker, *Tempest at Ox Hill*, 123–29.

15. Welker, *Tempest at Ox Hill*, 129–36.

16. Welker, *Tempest at Ox Hill*, 137–44; Martin, *Second Bull Run*, 256–59; Taylor, *He Hath Loosed*, 36–40.

17. Welker, *Tempest at Ox Hill*, 145–46; *ORA*, I, 12, pt. 3, 788.

18. The battle receives comprehensive coverage in Taylor, *He Hath Loosed*, chaps. 4, 5; Welker, *Tempest at Ox Hill*, chaps. 7, 8, 9; Stackpole, *From Cedar Mountain to Antietam*, chap. 13; shorter accounts in Martin, *Second Bull Run*, chap. 10, and essays such as Robert Ross Smith, "Ox Hill: The Most Neglected Battle of the Civil War," in Fairfax County Civil War Commission, *Fairfax County and the War between the States* (1961, rpt. Fairfax VA: Office of Comprehensive Planning, 1985), 19–64; A. Van Loan Naisawald, "A Nasty Little Battle in the Rain," *Civil War Times Illustrated* (June 1964): 10–16; Robert James, "Stonewall's Surprise at Ox Hill," *America's Civil War* (January 1985): 54–61; Joseph W. Whitehorne, "A Beastly, Comfortless Conflict: The Battle of Chantilly," *Blue and Gray Magazine* (May 1987): 7–23, 46–56; John Hennessy, "Thunder at Chantilly: The Second Manassas Campaign Closes amidst Blood and a Torrent," *North and South* (March 2000): 47–60.

19. James Longstreet, *From Manassas to Appomattox: Memoirs of the Civil War in America* (1895, rpt. New York: Da Capo, 1992), 194; Welker, *Tempest at Ox Hill*, 192–93.

20. Taylor, *He Hath Loosed*, 100; F. H. Kennedy, *Civil War Battlefield Guide*, 112;

Welker, *Tempest at Ox Hill,* 229; Martin, *Second Bull Run,* 265; Harsh, *Confederate Tide Rising,* 171, 172; Welch, *A Confederate Surgeon's Letters,* 28–31.

21. Horatio Belcher diary, William Fenton Papers, Bentley Historical Library, University of Michigan, Ann Arbor, quoted in Taylor, *He Hath Loosed,* 110; Hennessy, *Return to Bull Run,* 450; Martin, *Second Bull Run,* 265; Harsh, *Confederate Tide Rising,* 170; Cozzens, *General John Pope,* 192; Stackpole, *From Cedar Mountain to Antietam,* 253; Cooling, *Symbol, Sword and Shield,* 126–27.

22. Cozzens, *General John Pope,* 192–93; Welker, *Tempest at Ox Hill,* 206–8; Taylor, *He Hath Loosed,* 104–5, 107; *ORA,* I, 12, pt. 3, 785; Michael C. Hardy, *The Thirty-Seventh North Carolina Troops: Tar Heels in the Army of Northern Virginia* (Jefferson NC: McFarland, 2003), 94.

23. *ORA,* I, 12, pt. 2, 771–79.

24. Oates, *Woman of Valor,* 66–67; Taylor, *He Hath Loosed,* 100–107.

25. Oates, *Woman of Valor,* 76–77.

26. Samuel Heintzelman journal, August 31, 1862, Library of Congress; Oliver Otis Howard, *Autobiography* (New York: Baker & Taylor, 1908), 1:271; Warren Lee Goss, *Recollections of a Private: A Story of the Army of the Potomac* (New York: Thomas Y. Crowell, 1890), 92–93; *ORA,* I, 12, pt. 3, 796–97; Gideon Welles, *Diary* (Boston: Houghton-Mifflin, 1911), 1:105–6.

27. *ORA,* I, 12, pt. 3, 786, 797, 719–30; Sears, *McClellan: The Young Napoleon,* 259–30; Cooling, *Symbol, Sword and Shield,* 131–34.

28. Sears, *McClellan: The Young Napoleon,* 260–61; Bates, *Lincoln in the Telegraph Office,* 118–22; Donald, *Inside Lincoln's Cabinet,* 116–20.

29. McClellan, *McClellan's Own Story,* 537; Hennessy, *Return to Bull Run,* 453–54; Cozzens, *General John Pope,* 195; Welker, *Tempest at Ox Hill,* 224–25; Sears, *McClellan: The Young Napoleon,* 261–62; Sears, *Civil War Papers of McClellan,* 429–31; Rafuse, *McClellan's War,* 269–74.

30. Tyler Dennett, ed., *Lincoln and the Civil War in the Diaries and Letters of John Hay* (New York: Dodd, Mead, 1939), 46–47; *ORA,* I, 12, pt. 2, 787–88.

31. Jacob D. Cox, *Military Reminiscences of the Civil War* (New York: Scribner's, 1900), 1:259; Cozzens, *General John Pope,* 196–201; *ORA,* I, 12, pt. 3, 816–27.

32. *ORA,* I, 12, pt. 3, 805; Anders, *Henry Halleck's War,* 252; Sears, *McClellan: The Young Napoleon,* 262; Taylor, *He Hath Loosed,* 122–23; Rafuse, *McClellan's War,* 271–72.

33. *ORA,* I, 23, pt. 3, 706–73, 791; Cooling, *Symbol, Sword and Shield,* 130–31; James A. Mowris, *A History of the One Hundred Seventeenth Regiment, New York Volunteers* (Hartford CT: Case, Lockwood, 1866), 25–35.

34. Wayne Mahood, *General Wadsworth: The Life and Times of Brevet Major General James S. Wadsworth* (Cambridge MA: Da Capo Press, 2003), 101. On the navy's role, see *ORA,* I, 11, pt. 3, 384, and 12, pt. 2, 737, 794–95. On Aquia destruction, see *ORA,* I, 12, pt. 3, 813–16.

35. *ORA,* I, 12, pt. 2, 798–810; D. Scott Harwig, "Who Would Not Be a Soldier: The Volunteers of '62 in the Maryland Campaign," in *The Antietam Campaign,* ed. Gary Gallagher (Chapel Hill: University of North Carolina Press, 1999), 143–68.

36. McClellan, *McClellan's Own Story*, 536, 538; Heintzelman journal, August 31, 1862, Library of Congress; Cooling, *Symbol, Sword and Shield*, 134.

37. Dowdey and Manarin, *Wartime Papers of Lee*, 269–70, 292–94. For recent scholarship analyzing Lee's decision, see Kegel, *North with Lee and Jackson*, 151–55, as well as background in chaps. 1–13; Michael A. Palmer, *Lee Moves North: Robert E. Lee on the Offensive* (New York: Wiley, 1998), chap. 1; Joseph L. Harsh, *Taken at the Flood: Robert E. Lee and Confederate Strategy in the Maryland Campaign of 1862* (Kent OH: Kent State University Press 1999), chap. 1; Joseph L. Harsh, *Sounding the Shallows: A Confederate Companion for the Maryland Campaign of 1862* (Kent OH: Kent State University Press, 2000), chap. 5.

38. Rafuse, *McClellan's War*, 276–78.

39. Dowdey and Manarin, *Wartime Papers of Lee*, 294–96; ORA, I, 19, pt. 2, 591–94; Keith S. Bohannon, "Dirty, Ragged and Ill-Provided For: Confederate Logistical Problems in the 1862 Maryland Campaign," in Gallagher, *The Antietam Campaign*, 102–8.

40. McGuire, *Diary of a Southern Refugee*, 151; William Blair, *Virginia's Private War: Feeding Body and Soul in the Confederacy, 1861–1865* (New York: Oxford University Press, 1998), 77–79; Sutherland, *Seasons of War*, 190–91.

6. Maryland, My Maryland

1. Douglas, *I Rode with Stonewall*, 147–48; D. B. Stone, *Wandering to Glory*, 57.

2. J. B. Polley, *A Soldier's Letters to Charming Nellie* (1908, rpt. Gaithersburg MD: Butternut Press, 1984), 80; Hardy, *Thirty-Seventh North Carolina*, 95–96.

3. Paul Gordon and Rita Gordon, *A Playground of the Civil War: Frederick County, Maryland* (Frederick MD: Heritage Partnership, 1994), 25; C. W. Turner, *Captain Greenlee Davidson*, 46.

4. Joseph C. G. Kennedy, *Preliminary Report on the Eighth Census, 1860* [U.S. Congress, 37th, 2d Session, Senate] (Washington DC: U.S. Government Printing Office, 1862), 131; William C. Wright, *The Secession Movement in the Middle Atlantic States* (Rutherford NJ: Fairleigh Dickinson University Press, 1973), chap. 1.

5. Robert J. Brugger, *Maryland: A Middle Temperament* (Baltimore: Johns Hopkins University Press, 1988), 270–79, 287; W. C. Wright, *Secession Movement*, 27–40; *Baltimore Sun* quoted in Gordon and Gordon, *A Playground of the Civil War*, 25.

6. W. C. Wright, *Secession Movement*, 34, 71–73; Brugger, *Maryland*, 272. Recent pro-secessionist scholarship includes Lawrence M. Denton, *A Southern Star for Maryland: Maryland and the Secession Crisis* (Baltimore: Publishing Concepts, 1995), and Bart Rhett Talbert, *Maryland: The South's First Casualty* (Charlottesville VA: Howell Press, 1995). Other possibilities might be seen in Jerre Garrett, *Muffled Drums and Mustard Spoons, Cecil County, Maryland, 1860–1865* (Shippensburg PA: Burd Street Press, 1996), chaps. 1, 2.

7. W. C. Wright, *Secession Movement*, 71–73; Brugger, *Maryland*, 272; Denton, *A Southern Star*, chaps. 4, 5; Frank Towers, *The Urban South and the Coming of the Civil War* (Charlottesville: University of Virginia Press, 2004), chap. 5; Scott Sumter

Sheads and Daniel Carroll Toomey, *Baltimore During the Civil War* (Linthicum MD: Toomey Press, 1997), chaps. 1–3; Daniel Carroll Toomey, *The Civil War in Maryland* (Baltimore: Toomey Press, 1983), chap. 3; Robert I. Cottom Jr. and Mary Ellen Hayward, *Maryland in the Civil War: A House Divided* (Baltimore: Maryland Historical Society, 1994), chaps. 3, 4; George William Brown, *Baltimore and the Nineteenth of April, 1861: A Story of the War* (Baltimore: Johns Hopkins University Press, 2001), introduction; Glenn F. Williams, "Under the Despot's Heel," *America's Civil War* (May 2000): 22–28.

8. Eric Mills, *Chesapeake Bay in the Civil War* (Centreville MD: Tidewater, 1996), 91.

9. Irwin Silber, ed. and comp., *Songs of the Civil War* (New York: Columbia University Press, 1960), 70–73.

10. Lori Montgomery, "Resurrecting a Slogan: Imprint Befuddles the Free—Make That 'Old Line'—State," *Washington Post*, March 14, 2000, B1, B4; Kevin Conley Ruffner, *Maryland's Blue and Gray* (Baton Rouge: Louisiana State University Press, 1997), especially chaps. 1–6; Craig L. Symonds, *Confederate Admiral: The Life and Wars of Franklin Buchanan* (Annapolis MD: Naval Institute Press, 1999), chaps. 9, 10.

11. Mills, *Chesapeake Bay in the Civil War*, chaps. 1–4.

12. Mary Alice Wills, *The Confederate Blockade of Washington, D.C. 1861–1862* (Parsons WV: McClain, 1975), 58.

13. Mills, *Confederate Blockade*, 58–59; Hanson, *Bull Run Remembers*, 42–64; Donald G. Shomlette, *Lost Towns of Tidewater Maryland* (Centreville MD: Tidewater, 2000), 126–27.

14. Gene Thorp, "Capital in Crisis: Union Fortifies Washington as Confederate Troops Invade Maryland," *Washington Post*, August 18, 2002, C9.

15. *Baltimore Sun*, September 23, 1862, quoting *Richmond Examiner*, September 12, 1862; also John Esten Cooke, *A Life of Gen. Robert E. Lee* (New York: D. Appleton, 1871), 125–28; Bohannon, "Dirty, Ragged," 101–42.

16. *ORA*, I, 19, pt. 2, 596–97; Harsh, *Taken at the Flood*, 105–7; Gordon and Gordon, *Playground of the Civil War*, 62–63; Karen Gardner, "Digging History: Archaeologists Opening Windows on the Past," *Frederick News-Post Weekend Guide*, May 2, 2002, 4, 6.

17. *ORA*, I, 19, pt. 2, 596, also 592–93; Harsh, *Taken at the Flood*, 124–25.

18. *ORA*, I, 19, pt. 2, 597–98, 600.

19. *ORA*, I, 19, pt. 2, 601–2.

20. Longstreet, *From Manassas to Appomattox*, 285; *ORA*, I, 19, pt. 2, 601–2; Toomey, *Civil War in Maryland*, dust jacket back cover.

21. *ORA*, I, 19, pt. 2, 601–2; Louis H. Manarin, "A Proclamation: 'To the People of ____,'" *North Carolina Historical Review* (Spring 1964): 246–51.

22. *ORA*, I, 19, pt. 2, 600–606; Dowdey and Manarin, *Wartime Papers of Lee*, 297–300, 303, 304–5.

23. Margaret Leech, *Reveille in Washington 1860–1865* (New York: Harper and Brothers, 1941), 197; Flavius Bellamy letter, September 8, 1862, Indiana State Library, Indianapolis.

24. Dennett, *Lincoln and the Civil War*, 47; Sears, *Civil War Papers of McClellan*, 440; Stephen W. Sears, *Controversies and Commanders: Dispatches from the Army of the Potomac* (Boston: Houghton Mifflin, 1999), chap. 4; Marszalek, *Commander of All Lincoln's Armies*, 146–47; Anders, *Henry Halleck's War*, chaps. 8, 9.

25. Sears, *Controversies and Commanders*, 101; Sears, *McClellan: The Young Napoleon*, 266–67; Cooling, *Symbol, Sword and Shield*, 134–35; Richard B. Irwin, "Washington under Banks," in Johnson and Buel, *Battles and Leaders*, 2:542–44; D. Scott Hartwig, "Who Would Not Be a Soldier: The Volunteers of '62 in the Maryland Campaign," in Gallagher, *The Antietam Campaign*, 143–68; Wert, *Sword of Lincoln*, 141–47.

26. Stackpole, *From Cedar Mountain to Antietam*, 305; Sears, *McClellan: The Young Napoleon*, 431; Anders, *Henry Halleck's War*, 252–54; Dennett, *Lincoln and the Civil War*, 47; Welles, *Diary*, 1:101–5; *ORA*, I, 19, pt. 2, 169.

27. Sears, *McClellan: The Young Napoleon*, 266–67; Sears, *Controversies and Commanders*, 101–3; Ridgway, *Little Mac*, 322–23.

28. Adam Gurowski, *Diary from March 4, 1861 to November 12, 1862* (Boston: Lee and Shepard, 1862), 263–64, 267; Welles, *Diary*, 1:111, 114–15; Sears, *McClellan: The Young Napoleon*, 268–69.

29. Welles, *Diary*, 1:100–118.

30. McClellan, *McClellan's Own Story*, 552–53; Rafuse, *McClellan's War*, 280–81.

31. Fishel, *Secret War*, 213–17; Charles T. Jacobs, *Civil War Guide to Montgomery County, Maryland* (1983, rpt. Rockville MD: Montgomery County Historical Society, 1996), 4, 41; Wert, *Sword of Lincoln*, 147.

32. Jacobs, *Civil War Guide*, 7–8, 12, 14–15, 19, 20, 29, 31, 34, 35, 36, 39, 44, 46–47; McClellan, *McClellan's Own Story*, 553.

33. Jacobs, *Civil War Guide*, 58; Harsh, *Taken at the Flood*, 151; Wert, *Sword of Lincoln*, 147.

34. Welles, *Diary*, 1:115–17; Rafuse, *McClellan's War*, 291–93.

35. Von Borcke, *Memoirs*, 1:91–98; Gordon and Gordon, *A Playground of the Civil War*, 65–68; Burke Davis, *Jeb Stuart: The Last Cavalier* (New York: Rinehart, 1957), 193–94.

36. Harsh, *Taken at the Flood*, 122, 166–67; B. Davis, *Jeb Stuart*, 199; von Borcke, *Memoirs*, 198–99.

37. Harsh, *Taken at the Flood*, 133–52; *ORA*, I, 19, pt. 2, 281–82, 603–4.

38. Harsh, *Taken at the Flood*, 152–57, 180, 186–87, 190, 192, 237, 238 dissects Special Orders 191 in great detail.

39. Sears, *McClellan: Young Napoleon*, 281–82; Sears, *Controversies and Commanders*, chap. 5; Wert, *Sword of Lincoln*, 149; Rafuse, *McClellan's War*, 291–92; Wilbur D. Jones Jr., *Giants in the Cornfield: The Twenty-Seventh Indiana Infantry* (Shippensburg PA: White Mane, 1997), preface and appendix A; Richard C. Datzman, "Who Found Lee's Lost Orders?," unpublished study, 1973, files, Antietam National Battlefield Library; *ORA*, 19, pt. 2, 281; *Harper's Weekly*, September 27, 1862.

40. Harsh, *Taken at the Flood*, 241; Sears, *McClellan: The Young Napoleon*, 281–83; *ORA*, I, 19, pt. 2, 281–82; Ridgway, *Little Mac*, 328–29.

41. McClellan, *McClellan's Own Story*, 555–61; Quaife, *From the Cannon's Mouth*, 121.

42. Thorp, "A Capital in Crisis"; Gene Thorp, "Union Fortifies Washington as Confederate Troops Invade Maryland," and "America's Bloodiest Day: Union and Confederate Armies Meet in the Battle of Antietam," *Washington Post*, both August 25, 2002, C9.

43. Letter, John B. Bashler, cousin, September 9, 1862, author's collection.

7. South Mountain and Harpers Ferry

1. Robert L. Bee, ed., *The Boys from Rockville: Civil War Narratives of Sgt. Benjamin Hirst, Company D. Fourteenth Connecticut Volunteers* (Knoxville: University of Tennessee Press, 1998), 19; Harsh, *Taken at the Flood*, 171; ORA, I, 19, pt. 2, 260–70. A picture of the destroyed bridge appears in John Cannan, *The Antietam Campaign* (New York: Wieser and Wieser, 1990), 75.

2. Gordon and Gordon, *A Playground of the Civil War*, 78–80.

3. Silber, *Songs of the Civil War*, 73; Parks and Steiner quoted in Cottom and Hayward, *Maryland in the Civil War*, 65, 66.

4. George O. Seilheimer, "The Historical Basis of Whittier's Barbara Frietchie," in Johnson and Buel, *Battle and Leaders*, 2: 618–19; Gordon and Gordon, *Playground of the Civil War*, 69–76; D. B. Stone, *Wandering to Glory*, 57; George Wilson Booth, *A Maryland Boy in Lee's Army: Personal Reminiscences of a Maryland Soldier in the War between the States, 1861–1865* (1898, rpt. Lincoln: University of Nebraska Press, 2000), 70.

5. Sears, *Civil War Papers of McClellan*, 449, 450, 454.

6. Gordon and Gordon, *A Playground of the Civil War*, 78–96; Bradley M. Gottfried, *Stopping Pickett: The History of the Philadelphia Brigade* (Shippensburg PA: White Mane, 1999), 111; Mike Pride and Mark Travis, *My Brave Boys: To War with Colonel Cross and the Fighting Fifth* (Hanover NH: University Press of New England, 2001), 122–23; Bee, *The Boys from Rockville*, 16–17; Steven J. Keillor, *No More Gallant a Deed: A Civil War Memoir of the First Minnesota Volunteers*, ed. James A. Wright (St. Paul: Minnesota Historical Society, 2001), 195; Griffin A. Stedman, "Reminiscences of the Eleventh," *Connecticut War Record* 2 (November 1864), copy, Antietam National Battlefield Library, Sharpsburg, Maryland.

7. Palfrey, *The Antietam and Fredericksburg*, 22–23; John Gibbon, *Personal Recollections of the Civil War* (New York: Putnam's, 1928), 7–73; Lance J. Herdegen, *The Men Stood Like Iron: How the Iron Brigade Won Its Name* (Bloomington: Indiana University Press, 1997), 139–40.

8. Turner, *Captain Greenlee Davidson*, 48, 49; Gordon and Gordon, *Playground of the Civil War*, 72–73; Douglas, *I Rode with Stonewall*, 151; David G. Colwell, *The Bitter Fruits: The Civil War Comes to a Small Town in Pennsylvania* (Carlisle PA: Cumberland County Historical Society, 1998), 131.

9. Palfrey, *The Antietam and Fredericksburg*, 23–24; Harsh, *Taken at the Flood*, 173–77, 182–83, 186–87, 198–203.

10. Sears, *Civil War Papers of McClellan*, 443–44; Anders, *Henry Halleck's War*, 266–69, 274–75.

11. *ORA*, I, 19, pt. 2, 253–55, 275, and pt. 1, 758–59; Harsh, *Taken at the Flood*, 189–90, 209–11, 237–41; Rafuse, *McClellan's War*, 287–92.

12. Harsh, *Taken at the Flood*, 190–209; Dowdey and Manarin, *Wartime Papers of Lee*, 304–5.

13. Harsh, *Taken at the Flood*, chap. 5, especially 252; Harsh, *Sounding the Shallows*, 16; Stackpole, *From Cedar Mountain to Antietam*, 324–25; Cannan, *Antietam Campaign*, 88; *ORA*, I, 19, pt. 1, 816–17, 839, 853–54, 953, and pt. 2, 606–7.

14. *ORA*, I, 19, pt. 1, 26, 42–46, 48, and pt. 2, 267–69, 272, 281–82, 287, 288; Mark A. Snell, *From First to Last: The Life of Major General William B. Franklin* (New York: Fordham University Press, 2002), 175–76.

15. Sears, *Civil War Papers of McClellan*, 455, n. 5; *ORA*, I, 19, pt. 1, 44–45, and 51, pt. 1, 826–27.

16. *ORA*, I, 19, pt. 1, 145, and pt. 2, 606–7; Chester G. Hearn, *Six Years of Hell: Harpers Ferry During the Civil War* (Baton Rouge: Louisiana State University Press, 1996), 150–51; Paul R. Teetor, *A Matter of Hours: Treason at Harper's Ferry* (Rutherford NJ: Fairleigh Dickinson University Press, 1982), chaps. 15, 16; Helen Trimpi, "Lafayette McLaws' Aide-de-Camp," *Civil War Regiments* 6, no. 2 (1998): 32–33.

17. Palfrey, *The Antietam and Fredericksburg*, 25; Hearn, *Six Years of Hell*, 1, 101–11; Teetor, *A Matter of Hours*, chap. 10.

18. *ORA*, I, 19, pt. 1, 728; Hearn, *Six Years of Hell*, 159–61; Teetor, *A Matter of Hours*, chaps. 10, 16, 17.

19. Hearn, *Six Years of Hell*, chap. 7; Teetor, *A Matter of Hours*, chaps. 2, 3, 4, also 73–75.

20. Sears, *Civil War Papers of McClellan*, 458; *ORA*, I, 19, pt. 1, 758; Herdegen, *The Men Stood Like Iron*, 138–39.

21. *ORA*, I, 19, pt. 1, 47–48; Stackpole, *From Cedar Mountain to Antietam*, 324–25; Timothy J. Reese, "The Cavalry Clash at Quebec Schoolhouse," *Blue and Gray Magazine* (February 1993): 24–30. Harsh, *Taken at the Flood*, 200–201; Stackpole, *From Cedar Mountain to Antietam*, 320–30.

22. *ORA*, I, 19, pt. 1, 47–49; Sears, *McClellan: The Young Napoleon*, 283–87; Cannan, *Antietam Campaign*, 90; Teetor, *A Matter of Hours*, 154–58.

23. Harsh, *Taken at the Flood*, 267; John Michael Priest, *Before Antietam: The Battle for South Mountain* (Shippensburg PA: White Mane, 1993), chap. 12; Herdegen, *The Men Stood Like Iron*, chap. 17, especially 146.

24. Priest, *Before Antietam*, chap. 10; Stackpole, *From Cedar Mountain to Antietam*, 325–36; Terry A. Johnston Jr., "From Fox's Gap to the Sherrick Farm," *Civil War Regiments* 6, no. 2 (1998): 66–67.

25. *ORA*, I, 19, pt. 1, 45–46, and pt. 2, 290, and 51, pt. 1, 833; see also Wert, *Sword of Lincoln*, 151–53.

26. Priest, *Before Antietam*, chaps. 11, 12; Cannan, *Antietam Campaign*, 92–94; Stackpole, *From Cedar Mountain to Antietam*, 328–32; Gottfried, *Stopping Pickett*, 111; William J. K. Beaudot and Lance J. Herdegen, *An Irishman in the Iron Brigade:*

The Civil War Memoirs of James P. Sullivan, Sergt., Company K, Sixth Wisconsin Volunteers (New York: Fordham University Press, 1993), 62–63; Pride and Travis, *My Brave Boys*, 122–23; John J. Hennessy, *Fighting with the Eighteenth Massachusetts: The Civil War Memoir of Thomas H. Mann* (Baton Rouge: Louisiana State University Press, 2002), 100–101.

27. Bee, *The Boys from Rockville*, 18; Jerome M. Loving, *Civil War Letters of George Washington Whitman* (Durham NC: Duke University Press, 1975), 66–67; Sears, *Civil War Papers of McClellan*, 461; Cannan, *Antietam Campaign*, 98; Herdegen, *The Men Stood Like Iron*, 152–54.

28. Harsh, *Taken at the Flood*, 271, 284–85, 287–89.

29. Dennis E. Frye, "Drama between the Rivers: Harpers Ferry in the 1862 Maryland Campaign," in *Antietam: Essays on the 1862 Maryland Campaign*, ed. Gary Gallagher (Kent OH: Kent State University Press, 1989), 31; Priest, *Before Antietam*, chap. 13; Timothy J. Reese, *Sealed with Their Lives: The Battle for Crampton's Gap, Burkittsville, Maryland, September 14, 1862* (Baltimore: Butternut and Blue, 1998), chaps. 1–7.

30. Kennedy, *Civil War Battlefield Guide*, 115–17; Reese, *Sealed with Their Lives*, chaps. 4, 5; Stackpole, *From Cedar Mountain to Antietam*, 317–20; Cannan, *Antietam Campaign*, 98–100; ORA, I, 19, pt. 1, 47, and pt. 2, 289.

31. Trimpi, "Lafayette McLaws' Aide-de-Camp," 36; Frye, "Drama between the Rivers," quoting McLaws, 32; Reese, *Sealed with Their Lives*, chap. 6; ORA, I, 19, pt. 1, 47; Sears, *Civil War Papers of McClellan*, 461.

32. Teetor, *A Matter of Hours*, 156; Priest, *Before Antietam*, chap. 14; Snell, *From First to Last*, 176–77, 185–87.

33. ORA, I, 19, pt. 2, 289–95; Sears, *Civil War Papers of McClellan*, 457–63.

34. ORA, I, 19, pt. 1, 951; Teetor, *A Matter of Hours*, chap. 20; Hearn, *Six Years of Hell*, chap. 11; Cannan, *Antietam Campaign*, 102.

35. ORA, I, 19, pt. 1, 45; Hearn, *Six Years of Hell*, 77–80; Teetor, *A Matter of Hours*, chap. 21; Allan L. Tischer, *The History of the Harpers Ferry Cavalry Expedition, September 14 and 15, 1862* (Winchester VA: Five Cedars Press, 1993), pt. 1, chap. 2, also pts. 3, 4; Bohannon, "Dirty, Ragged," 115–16.

36. Kennedy, *Civil War Battlefield Guide*, 113–15; ORA, I, 19, pt. 1, 539, 540, and pt. 2, 951; Teetor, *A Matter of Hours*, chaps. 22, 23; Hearn, *Six Years of Hell*, chap. 12.

37. Harsh, *Taken at the Flood*, 298–301; Trimpi, "Lafayette McLaws' Aide-de-Camp," 36.

38. Harsh, *Taken at the Flood*, 301–5.

39. Sears, *Civil War Papers of McClellan*, 463; Sears, *McClellan: The Young Napoleon*, 292–93; ORA, I, 19, pt. 1, 294–95.

40. ORA, I, 19, pt. 2, 294, 295–96, 307, 308; Stackpole, *From Cedar Mountain to Antietam*, 362–63; Rafuse, *McClellan's War*, 300–305.

41. ORA, I, 19, pt. 2, 296–97, 307, and 51, pt. 1, 836; Reese, *Sealed with Their Lives*, 177–82.

42. Sears, *McClellan: The Young Napoleon*, 292–93; Stackpole, *From Cedar Mountain to Antietam*, 364–65; McClellan, *McClellan's Own Story*, 585–86.

43. Sears, *McClellan: The Young Napoleon*, 293–95.

44. Gene Thorp, "America's Bloodiest Day," *Washington Post*, August 25, 2002, C9; Rafuse, *McClellan's War*, 305–7.

8. The Bridges of the Antietam

1. Helen Ashe Hays, *The Antietam and Its Bridges* (New York: Putnam, 1910), 3.

2. Hays, *Antietam and Its Bridges*, chaps. 1–6; "America's Deadliest Day," the title of the *Antietam Commemorative Issue*, published by editors of *America's Civil War*, *Civil War Times*, *MHQ: The Quarterly Journal of Military History*, September 2002; McPherson, *Crossroads of Freedom*; Stephen W. Sears, *Landscape Turned Red: The Battle of Antietam* (New York: Tichnor and Fields, 1983).

3. Hays, *Antietam and Its Bridges*, 41, 42, 55; Harsh, *Taken at the Flood*, 298–308; Wert, *Sword of Lincoln*, 156.

4. *ORA*, I, 19, pt. 1, 53, 55.

5. Sears, *Civil War Papers of McClellan*, 466; *ORA*, I, 19, pt. 2, 307–8.

6. *ORA*, I, 19, pt. 1, 41; Snell, *From First to Last*, 189–91.

7. Booth, *A Maryland Boy*, 71–72; *ORA*, I, 19, pt. 1, 54–55; William Marvel, *Burnside* (Chapel Hill: University of North Carolina Press, 1992), 127–31.

8. *ORA*, I, 19, pt. 1, 211.

9. *ORA*, I, 19, pt. 1, 30, 55; McClellan, *McClellan's Own Story*, 590.

10. *ORA*, I, 19, pt. 1, 217; Herdegen, *The Men Stood Like Iron*, 159–60; Rafuse, *McClellan's War*, 310.

11. *ORA*, I, 19, 140–41; Rafuse, *McClellan's War*, 308–14.

12. James V. Murfin, *The Gleam of Bayonets: The Battle of Antietam and the Maryland Campaign of 1862* (New York: Yoseloff, 1965), 208; Sears, *Landscape Turned Red*, 162–79; Harsh, *Taken at the Flood*, chap. 8; Harsh, *Sounding the Shallows*, 193–94.

13. Harsh, *Taken at the Flood*, chap. 8; Dawes quoted in Herdegen, *The Men Stood Like Iron*, 160.

14. Hooker quoted in Murfin, *Gleam of Bayonets*, 208; *ORA*, I, 19, pt. 1, 218.

15. Murfin, *Gleam of Bayonets*, chap. 8; Sears, *Landscape Turned Red*, chap. 6; Herdegen, *The Men Stood Like Iron*, chaps. 19, 20; Curt Johnson and Richard C. Anderson Jr., *Artillery Hell: The Employment of Artillery at Antietam* (College Station: Texas A&M Press, 1995), chaps. 1, 3–5; Jay Luvaas and Harold W. Nelson, eds., *The U.S. Army War College Guide to the Battle of Antietam: The Maryland Campaign of 1862* (Carlisle PA: South Mountain Press, 1987), 121–87; Wert, *Sword of Lincoln*, 157–63.

16. *ORA*, I, 19, pt. 1, 218–19; Harsh, *Taken at the Flood*, 370–80, especially 374–75; Robert C. Cheeks, "Carnage in a Cornfield," *Antietam Commemorative Issue*, special issue of *America's Civil War* (2002): 32–40.

17. Marion V. Armstrong, *Disaster in the West Woods: General Edwin V. Sumner and the II Corps at Antietam* (Sharpsburg: Western Maryland Interpretive Association, 2002), 1–38; Gottfried, *Stopping Pickett*, 112–15.

18. Armstrong, *Disaster in the West Woods*, 39–65; Harsh, *Taken at the Flood*, 275–76, 305–8, 311–12, 313, 314–15, 505–6, 574–76, 820, 857–60, 874–75,

914–17, 969, 970–71; Robert E. L. Krick, "Defending Lee's Flank: J. E. B. Stuart, John Pelham, and Confederate Artillery on Nicodemus Heights," in Gallagher, *The Antietam Campaign,* 192–210; Gottfried, *Stopping Pickett,* 116–21; J. A. Wright, *No More Gallant a Deed,* 199; Wert, *Sword of Lincoln,* 162–63.

19. U.S. Department of the Interior, National Park Service, Antietam National Battlefield, Handout, "Angel of the Battlefield," undated; Oates, *Woman of Valor,* 80–91.

20. Harsh, *Taken at the Flood,* 394–95; Luvaas and Nelson, *Army War College Guide,* 184–213; Murfin, *Gleam of Bayonets,* chap. 9; Sears, *Landscape Turned Red,* 236–47; Cannan, *Antietam Campaign,* 139–58, especially 141; Eby, *Virginia Yankee,* 111; Rafuse, *McClellan's War,* 317.

21. Murfin, *Gleam of Bayonets,* 246–66, especially 262; Sears, *Landscape Turned Red,* 236–47, 251–54; Cannan, *Antietam Campaign,* 144–47; *ORA,* I, 19, pt. 1, 193, 308–9, 323–24, 326, 327–28, 331, 336, 915–16, 1022–23, 1036–38.

22. Rafuse, *McClellan's War,* 318–20; Robert K. Krick, "It Appeared As Though Mutual Extermination Would Put a Stop to the Awful Carnage: Confederates in Sharpsburg's Bloody Lane," in Gallagher, *The Antietam Campaign,* 223–58; Bee, *The Boys from Rockville,* 18–23; Pride and Travis, *My Brave Boys,* 131–39.

23. Harsh, *Taken at the Flood,* 397; Cannan, *Antietam Campaign,* 156–57; Murfin, *Gleam of Bayonets,* 264.

24. Harsh, *Taken at the Flood,* 408–12.

25. *ORA,* I, 19, pt. 1, 376–77; Snell, *From First to Last,* 194–95; Rafuse, *McClellan's War,* 323–24.

26. *ORA,* I, 19, pt. 1, 211–12; Luvaas and Nelson, *Army War College Guide,* 212; Sears, *Landscape Turned Red,* 270–71; Rafuse, *McClellan's War,* 318–20.

27. Sears, *Civil War Papers of McClellan,* 467–68; *ORA,* I, 19, pt. 1, 312–13, and 51, pt. 1, 846–47.

28. Cannan, *Antietam Campaign,* 157–58; Sears, *Landscape Turned Red,* 274–75; Krick, "Defending Lee's Flank," 210–11.

29. *ORA,* I, 19, pt. 1, 55, 63, 418–19, 423–34, and 51, pt. 1, 844; Marvel, *Burnside,* 127–35, especially 134–35; Wert, *Sword of Lincoln,* 167–69; Rafuse, *McClellan's War,* 318–19, 320, 322–25.

30. Phillip Thomas Tucker, *Burnside's Bridge: The Climactic Struggle of the Second and Twentieth Georgia at Antietam Creek* (Mechanicsburg PA: Stackpole, 2000), ix–x, 64–65, 154; Murfin, *Gleam of Bayonets,* 269–73; *ORA,* I, 19, pt. 1, 424.

31. Cannan, *Antietam Campaign,* 162–67; Tucker, *Burnside's Bridge,* chaps. 4—8; Douglas, *I Rode with Stonewall,* 172; Wright, *No More Gallant a Deed,* 199; Thomas G. Clemens, "Why Did Burnside Cross the Bridge?," *Antietam Commemorative Issue* (2002): 64–71.

32. Tucker, *Burnside's Bridge,* 139–43; R. Keith Toney, "Dying as Brave Men Should Die: The Attack and Defense of Burnside's Bridge," in *The Maryland Campaign of 1862 and Its Aftermath,* ed. Mark Snell (Campbell CA: Savas, 1998), 111–12; Theodore Alexander, *Forgotten Valor: Off the Beaten Path at Antietam* (Columbus OH: Blue & Gray Enterprises, 2002), 18–20.

33. Catton, *Mr. Lincoln's Army*, 314; Rafuse, *McClellan's War*, 325.

34. Harsh, *Taken at the Flood*, 416–17; Rafuse, *McClellan's War*, 325–26.

35. *ORA*, I, 19, pt. 1, 886–87, 981, 987–88; Luvaas and Nelson, *Army War College Guide*, 228, 243; Lesley J. Gordon, "All Who Went into That Battle Were Heroes: Remembering the Sixteenth Connecticut Volunteers at Antietam," in Gallagher, *The Antietam Campaign*, 169–91; Loving, *Civil War Letters*, 68; Tucker, *Burnside's Bridge*, 150, 151; Peter S. Carmichael, "D. R. Jones and A. P. Hills Rescued the Right," *Civil War* (June 1999): 54–59; U.S. Department of the Interior, National Park Service, Antietam National Battlefield, Handout, "Zouaves," undated; Hardy, *Thirty-Seventh North Carolina*, 99–100.

36. Harsh, *Sounding the Shallows*, 19, 201, 202, 214; U.S. Department of the Interior, National Park Service, Antietam National Battlefield, Handout, "Casualties of Battle," undated; Charles W. Rouse diary, September 17, 1862, copy, Antietam National Battlefield Park Library; Sears, *McClellan: The Young Napoleon*, 316–17; Sears, *Landscape Turned Red*, 291–92.

37. Booth, *A Maryland Boy*, 72; U.S. Department of the Interior, National Park Service, Antietam National Battlefield, Handout, "Medal of Honor: The Bravest of the Brave," undated.

38. Harsh, *Sounding the Shallows*, 207–11; Harsh, *Taken at the Flood*, 424–29; *ORA*, I, 19, pt. 1, 151; Eby, *Virginia Yankee*, 112.

39. Rafuse, *McClellan's War*, 327–28; *New York Tribune*, September 29, 1862, quoted in Murfin, *Gleam of Bayonets*, 300; Stone, *Wandering to Glory*, 65; Rhodes, *All for the Union*, 73; Wert, *Sword of Lincoln*, 170.

40. Palfrey, *The Antietam and Fredericksburg*, 128; James A. Huston, *The Sinews of War: Army Logistics 1775–1953* (Washington DC: Office of the Chief of Military History, Department of the Army, 1966), 204–6; *ORA*, I, 19, pt. 2, 323–30; Harsh, *Taken at the Flood*, 437–40; Stackpole, *From Cedar Mountain to Antietam*, 439–40; Murfin, *Gleam of Bayonets*, 300–302; Sears, *Civil War Papers of McClellan*, 468–69; Sears, *McClellan: The Young Napoleon*, 319.

41. *ORA*, I, 19, pt. 1, 65, 219, and pt. 2, 312–14, 322–23; Palfrey, *The Antietam and Fredericksburg*, 127; Sears, *Civil War Papers of McClellan*, 473; Sears, *McClellan: Young Napoleon*, 319; Paul E. Steiner, *Medical-Military Portraits of Union and Confederate Generals* (Philadelphia: Whitmore, 1968), 16–17.

42. Harsh, *Taken at the Flood*, 440–44.

43. *ORA*, I, 19, pt. 2, 330, and 51, pt. 1, 847–50, 853; Stackpole, *From Cedar Mountain to Antietam*, 440–41; Murfin, *Gleam of Bayonets*, 302–4; Sears, *McClellan: Young Napoleon*, 320–21; Harsh, *Sounding the Shallows*, 214, 215–18.

44. *ORA*, I, 19, pt. 1, 957, 982, and pt. 2, 330, 626; Rafuse, *McClellan's War*, 329–31.

45. Hennessy, *Fighting with the Eighteenth Massachusetts*, 104; Peter S. Carmichael, "'We Don't Know What on Earth to Do with Him': William Nelson Pendleton and the Affair at Shepherdstown," in Gallagher, *The Antietam Campaign*, 259–88; Harsh, *Taken at the Flood*, 452–71; Harsh, *Sounding the Shallows*, 212–20; Hardy, *Thirty-Seventh North Carolina*, 101–2.

46. *ORA*, I, 19, pt. 1, 69, 152; Rhodes, *All for the Union*, 74; Harsh, *Taken at the Flood*, 465–66.

47. Sears, *Civil War Papers of McClellan*, 473, 476; Wert, *Sword of Lincoln*, 172–73; Rafuse, *McClellan's War*, 331–33; Brian Holden Reid, *Robert E. Lee: Icon for a Nation* (London: Weidenfeld & Nicholson, 2005), 133–34; Thorp, "America's Bloodiest Day," C9.

9. Opportunities Found and Lost

1. Oates, *Woman of Valor*, 84; Mary Bedinger Mitchell, "A Woman's Recollections of Antietam," in Johnson and Buel, *Battles and Leaders*, 2:691; Wright, *No More Gallant a Deed*, 203.

2. Wright, *No More Gallant a Deed*, 206, 214; Otho Nesbitt, "Antietam: An Eyewitness Account," in *Maryland Time Exposures 1840–1640*, ed. Mame Warren and Mario E. Warren (Baltimore: Johns Hopkins University Press, 1984), 275–77; Kathleen A. Ernst, *Too Afraid to Cry: Maryland Civilians in the Antietam Campaign* (Mechanicsburg PA: Stackpole, 1999), chaps. 6, 7.

3. William Frassanito, *Antietam: The Photographic Legacy* (New York: Scribner's, 1978), 51–54, 286; Roy Meredith, *Mr. Lincoln's Camera Man* (New York: Scribner's, 1946), chap. 13; J. Cutler Andrews, *The North Reports the War* (1953, rpt. Pittsburgh: University of Pittsburgh Press, 1983), 275–85 (on Smalley, 64–65); J. Cutler Andrews, *The South Reports the War* (1970 rpt. Pittsburgh: University of Pittsburgh Press, 1985), 208–26; Berlin, *Confederate Nurse*, 149–50; Styple, *Writing and Fighting the Confederate War*, 105–9; Bill, *Beleaguered City*, 149; Gary W. Gallagher, "The Net Result of the Campaign Was in Our Favor: Confederate Reaction to the Maryland Campaign," in Gallagher, *The Antietam Campaign*, 3–43.

4. Coakley, *Role of Federal Military Forces*, 230–36. On feelings and conditions in the Army of the Potomac after Antietam, see Brooks D. Simpson, "General McClellan's Bodyguard: The Army of the Potomac after Antietam," in Gallagher, *The Antietam Campaign*, 44–73.

5. Guelzo, *Lincoln's Emancipation Proclamation*, 153; for the text of the two proclamations, see Basler, *Collected Works of Lincoln*, 5:433–37, or John G. Nicolay and John Hay, eds., *Complete Works of Abraham Lincoln* (Harrogate TN: Lincoln Memorial University, 1894), 8:36–42; William K. Klingaman, *Abraham Lincoln and the Road to Emancipation* (New York: Viking, 2001), 179–80, 185–86; F. J. Williams, "'Doing Less' and 'Doing More,'" 62–65; Syrett, *Confiscation Acts*, 60–61.

6. Charles S. Wainwright, *A Diary of Battle: The Personal Journals of Colonel Charles S. Wainwright, 1861–1865*, ed. Allan Nevins (1962, rpt. New York: Da Capo, 1998), 109; Donald, *Inside Lincoln's Cabinet*, 149–51; Welles, *Diary*, 1:142–43; F. J. Williams, "'Doing Less' and 'Doing More,'" 67.

7. *ORA*, I, 24, pt. 3, 157; McPherson, *Crossroads of Freedom*, 139; Sutherland, *Emergence of Total War*, 91; Murfin, *Gleam of Bayonets*, 311; Sears, *Landscape Turned Red*, 319; Stackpole, *From Cedar Mountain to Antietam*, 443; Guelzo, *Lincoln's*

Emancipation Proclamation, 1; F. J. Williams, "'Doing Less' and 'Doing More,'" 66–67; Syrett, *Confiscation Acts*, 61.

8. Basler, *Collected Works of Lincoln*, 5:537, 424–25; Nicolay and Hays, *Complete Works of Lincoln*, 8:33; Edward L. Ayers, *In the Presence of Mine Enemies* (New York: Norton, 2003), 320; Virginia Jeans Laas, ed., *Wartime Washington: The Civil War Letters of Elizabeth Blair Lee* (Urbana: University of Illinois Press, 1991), 187, n. 5.

9. Ervin B. Jordan Jr., *Black Confederates and Afro-Yankees in Civil War Virginia* (Charlottesville: University Press of Virginia, 1995), 254–55; J. B. Jones, *A Rebel War Clerk's Diary*, 101; Donald, *Inside Lincoln's Cabinet*, 151–52; Welles, *Diary*, 1:144–45.

10. Russell Duncan, ed., *Blue-Eyed Child of Fortune: The Civil War Letters of Colonel Robert Gould Shaw* (Athens: University of Georgia Press, 1992), 245, 252; McGuire, *Diary of a Southern Refugee*, 159; Ayers, *In the Presence of Mine Enemies*, 318, quoting Joseph Waddell diary, September 24, 27, October 1, 2, 1862, University of Virginia Library, Charlottesville.

11. William Alan Blair, ed., *A Politician Goes to War: The Civil War Letters of John White Geary* (University Park: Pennsylvania State University Press, 1995), 56; M. C. C. Adams, *Fighting for Defeat*, 126; Grimsley, *Hard Hand of War*, 133–34, 135, 137n; McGuire, *Diary of a Southern Refugee*, 159; Herdegen, *The Men Stood Like Iron*, 199; Vivian Zollinger, "'I Take My Pen in Hand': Civil War Letters from Owen County, Indiana Soldiers," *Indiana Magazine of History* (June 1997): 173–74s.

12. Wright, *No More Gallant a Deed*, 208, 209; Wainwright, *Diary of Battle*, 108–9; Hennessy, *Fighting with the Eighteenth Massachusetts*, 107; John J. Hennessy, "Father Abraham's Paper Wad: The Army of the Potomac," *Civil War* (June 1999): 47–48; Eby, *Virginia Yankee*, 116, 119; Wert, *Sword of Lincoln*, 176–77.

13. H. Jones, *Union in Peril*, chaps. 7–10, especially 175–79, also 105–9, 115–22; Howard R. Jones, *Abraham Lincoln and a New Birth of Freedom: The Union and Slavery in the Diplomacy of the Civil War* (Lincoln: University of Nebraska Press, 1999), chaps. 4, 5, 6, especially 84; E. D. Adams, *Great Britain and the American Civil War* (New York: Russell and Russell, 1925), vol. 2, chap. 11; Lynn M. Case and Warren F. Spencer, *The United States and France: Civil War Diplomacy* (Philadelphia: University of Pennsylvania Press, 1970), 325–32; Klingaman, *Lincoln and the Road to Emancipation*, 203–4.

14. C. F. Adams, *Cycle of Adams Letters*, 1:192; James M. McPherson, *Battle Cry of Freedom: The Civil War Era* (New York: Oxford University Press, 1988), 556; Mahin, *One War at a Time*, 128–29. Understanding European mediation and intervention exceeds the parameters of this study, but other useful works include George M. Blackburn, *French Newspaper Opinion on the American Civil War* (Westport CT: Greenwood, 1997), chap. 6; Alfred Grant, *The American Civil War and the British Press* (Jefferson NC: McFarland, 2000); Philip S. Foner, *British Labor and the American Civil War* (New York: Holmes and Meier, 1985); and Eugene H. Berwanger, *The British Foreign Service and the American Civil War* (Lexington: University Press of Kentucky, 1994), 167–69.

15. Jones, *The Union in Peril*, 210–18, also chap. 8; E. D. Adams, *Britain and*

the American Civil War, 2:39–44, 54–55, 62–64, 74; James B. McPherson, "The Saratoga That Wasn't: The Impact of Antietam Abroad," *Catoctin History* (Fall 2002): 10–15; McPherson, *Crossroads of Freedom*, 141–42; Joseph A. Fry, *Dixie Looks Abroad: The South and U.S. Foreign Relations, 1789–1973* (Baton Rouge: Louisiana State University Press, 2002), 88–91.

16. Sears, *Civil War Papers of McClellan*, 473, 476, 477–78, 481–82, 485–86, 490; Sears, *McClellan: The Young Napoleon*, 323–30; Welles, *Diary*, 1:158; Marszalek, *Commander of All Lincoln's Armies*, 150–51; Williams, "'Doing Less' and 'Doing More,'" 67.

17. Sears, *McClellan: The Young Napoleon*, 323; ORA, I, 19, pt. 2, 339, 342–43, 353, 359–60, 365, and pt. 1, 10, 70–71, 181, and III, 2, 586; Sears, *Civil War Papers of McClellan*, 487–88; Snell, *From First to Last*, 199; Pride and Travis, *My Brave Boys*, 146, 149; Herdegen, *The Men Stood Like Iron*, 200; J. A. Wright, *No More Gallant a Deed*, 109–10; ORA, I, 19, pt. 2, 417.

18. Simpson, "General McClellan's Bodyguard," 54–57; Sears, *Civil War Papers of McClellan*, 477, 488; Basler, *Collected Works of Lincoln*, 5:442–43, 444; Dennett, *Lincoln and the Civil War*, 51; Gordon and Gordon, *A Playground of the Civil War*, 132–33; Wert, *Sword of Lincoln*, 175–76.

19. Sears, *Civil War Papers of McClellan*, 490; Blair, *A Politician Goes to War*, 58–59; Wainwright, *Diary of Battle*, 110; Herdegen, *The Men Stood Like Iron*, 151, 200–201; Robert Garth Scott, ed., *Forgotten Valor: The Memoirs, Journals and Civil War Letters of Orlando B. Willcox* (Kent OH: Kent State University Press, 1999), 370; Quaife, *From the Cannon's Mouth*, 136; Marvel, *Burnside*, 151.

20. Sears, *Civil War Papers of McClellan*, 487–88; Sears, *McClellan: The Young Napoleon*, 330–31.

21. Laas, *Wartime Washington*, 185; Welles, *Diary*, 1:176, 177; Donald, *Inside Lincoln's Cabinet*, 166, 169; Basler, *Collected Works of Lincoln*, 5:448, 460; Sears, *McClellan: The Young Napoleon*, 331; Gordon and Gordon, *A Playground of the Civil War*, 133–34; Janice Ferraro Pruchinski, *Divine Soldier: A Biography of Samuel Wheelock Fiske, from Pastor to Civil War Soldier* (Guilford CT: Quickstep, 2000), 38.

22. ORA, I, 19, pt. 1, 72, pt. 2, 393, 689; Rafuse, *McClellan's War*, 362.

23. ORA, pt. 1, 11–24, and pt. 2, 395; Sears, *Civil War Papers of McClellan*, 492; Herdegen, *The Men Stood Like Iron*, 199; Gottfried, *Stopping Pickett*, 122, 125; Simpson, "General McClellan's Bodyguard," 58–59; Rafuse, *McClellan's War*, 348–49.

24. ORA, I, 19, pt. 1, 152; Crist, *Papers of Jefferson Davis*, 8:421–22.

25. Rhodes, *All for the Union*, 77; ORA, pt. 1, 73, 152, and pt. 2, 28–81; John W. Thompson, *Horses, Hostages and Apple Cider: JEB Stuart's 1862 Pennsylvania Raid* (Mercersburg PA: Mercersburg Printing, 2002); Rafuse, *McClellan's War*, 349–54.

26. ORA, pt. 2, 421, also 51; Trout, *With Pen and Saber*, 105–13, especially 107; Eby, *Virginia Yankee*, 122–24; Cooke, *Life of Lee*, 161–63; Kevin E. O'Brien, *My Life in the Irish Brigade: The Civil War Memoirs of Private William McCarter, 116th Pennsylvania* (Campbell CA: Savas, 1996), chap. 2.

27. *ORA*, pt. 1, 13–14, 16.

28. See Cooling, *Symbol, Sword and Shield*, chap. 6; John Gross Barnard, *A Report on the Defenses of Washington* (Washington DC: U.S. Government Printing Office, 1871); Laas, *Wartime Washington*, 187.

29. *ORA*, I, 19, pt. 1, 1092, and pt. 2, 633, 634–38, 640, 642–54, 655–60, 661–66, 668, 670–71, 678, 684–85; John C. Oeffinger, ed., *A Soldier's General: The Civil War Letters of Major General Lafayette McLaws* (Chapel Hill: University of North Carolina Press, 2002), 156; G. Moxley Sorrel, *At the Right Hand of Longstreet: Recollections of a Confederate Staff Officer* (1905, rpt. Lincoln: University of Nebraska Press, 1999), chap. 14; Alexander, *Fighting for the Confederacy*, 155–56.

30. *ORA*, I, 19, pt. 2, 669, 671–74, 682, 683.

31. *ORA*, I, 19, pt. 1, 152, 1091–91, and pt. 2, 497, 675, 678, 686, 687.

32. Letter, "Morris" to parents, November 1, 1862, author's files; Patrick J. Brennan, "Little Mac's Last Stand," *Blue and Gray Magazine* (December 1999): 8; Pharris Deloach Johnson, comp. and ed., *Under the Southern Cross: Soldier Life with Gordon Bradwell and the Army of Northern Virginia* (Macon GA: Mercer University Press, 1999), 97–98; Rafuse, *McClellan's War*, 360–66.

33. Strength figures in *ORA*, I, 19, pt. 1, 13, 15, 16–17, 17–20, 81, and pt. 2, 66, 336, 374, 410, 417, 421–22, 454, 476, 484–85, 490–91, 569, 621, 639–40, 660, 674, 683–84, 713; Palfrey, *The Antietam and Fredericksburg*, 131; Sears, *Civil War Papers of McClellan*, 491, 507–8, 511, 513; Pride and Travis, *My Brave Boys*, 151–54; Hennessy, *Fighting with the Eighteenth Massachusetts*, 110–12; Loving, *Civil War Letters*, 73, 150; Wright, *No More Gallant a Deed*, 222–24.

34. Rafuse, *McClellan's War*, 362–72; Sears, *Civil War Papers of McClellan*, 511–20.

35. *ORA*, I, 19, pt. 2, 415, 494, 498, 519.

36. *ORA*, I, 19, pt. 2, 549; von Borcke, *Memoirs*, 60; Walter Taylor, *Four Years with General Lee*, ed. James I. Robertson Jr. (1962, rpt. Bloomington: Indiana University Press, 1996), 76; Johnson, *Under the Southern Cross*, 94; Brennan, "Little Mac's Last Stand," 10–20, 48–56; Hardy, *Thirty-Seventh North Carolina*, 111.

37. Rafuse, *McClellan's War*, 371; Sears, *Landscape Turned Red*, 331, 337–38; Sears, *McClellan: The Young Napoleon*, 338–43; McClellan, *McClellan's Own Story*, 653.

38. Wainwright, *Diary of Battle*, 122, 124; Gibbon quoted in Herdegen, *The Men Stood Like Iron*, 199, 212; O'Brien, *My Life in the Irish Brigade*, 33–34.

39. Sears, *McClellan: The Young Napoleon*, 336–37, 339–41; Sears, *Civil War Papers of McClellan*, 519–20.

40. *ORA*, I, 19, pt. 1, 551; McClellan, *McClellan's Own Story*, 653; Sears, *Landscape Turned Red*, 341–43; Sears, *McClellan: The Young Napoleon*, 341–43.

41. McPherson, *Battle Cry of Freedom*, 561–62; Sears, *McClellan: The Young Napoleon*, 338, 342; Johnson, *Under the Southern Cross*, 94; Freeman, *Lee's Lieutenants*, 2:313; Welles, *Diary*, 1:182–83; Gurowski, *Diary*, 313–14; Pride and Travis, *My Brave Boys*, 155; Gottfried, *Stopping Pickett*, 126.

42. McPherson, *Crossroads of Freedom*, 149, 153–54.

43. Adams, *Britain and the American Civil War*, 2:39–44, 62–64, 74; Jones, *Union in Peril*, 210–18; Fry, *Dixie Looks Abroad*, 88–92; Philip Paludan, *"A People's Contest": The Union and the Civil War* (New York: Harper and Row, 1988), 100–101; Philip Paludan, *The Presidency of Abraham Lincoln* (Lawrence: University Press of Kansas, 1994), 157; McPherson, *Crossroads of Freedom*, 141–43; Oeffinger, *A Solider's General*, 158; Syrett, *Confiscation Acts*, 122–23; Williams, "'Doing Less' and 'Doing More,'" 68–69.

44. Ayers, *In the Presence of Mine Enemies*, 320–21.

45. Kegel, *North with Lee and Jackson*, 186–87.

46. Thorp, "America's Bloodiest Day," C9.

47. Reid, *Lee*, 133–34; Gallagher, "The Net Result of the Campaign Was in Our Favor," 34.

48. E. B. Long, *Civil War Day by Day*, 282; Michael G. Mahon, ed., *Winchester Divided: The Civil War Diaries of Julia Chase and Laura Lee* (Mechanicsburg PA: Stackpole, 2002), 58–70.

Bibliographic Essay

Chapter note references to unit histories, memoirs, and personal reminiscences need no repetition here. They attest to the variety of sources embracing the people and events associated with the war in the East from the Peninsula to the Antietam. This essay focuses on more synthesized literature of importance. There remains no better place to begin than with original government documents published as U.S. War Department, *The War of the Rebellion: A Compilation of the Official Records of the Union and Confederate Armies* (Washington DC: Government Printing Office, 1880–1901), especially Series I, volumes 11, 12, 19, and 51, and the accompanying *Atlas* (Washington DC: Government Printing Office, 1891–1895), as well as U.S. Department of the Navy, *Official Records of the Union and Confederate Navies in the War of the Rebellion* (Washington DC: Government Printing Office, 1894–1922), Series I, volumes 5 and 7. Janet B. Hewett and other editors have been compiling an ongoing *Supplement to the Official Records of the Union and Confederate Armies* (Wilmington NC: Broadfoot, 1994–) to eventually encompass upwards of a hundred additional volumes of Civil War documents. Similarly, presidential correspondence for both Lincoln and Davis provides superb integrative approaches to political, diplomatic, military, and sociocultural phenomena. Particularly essential are John G. Nicolay and John Hay, eds., *Complete Works of Abraham Lincoln* (Harrogate TN: Lincoln Memorial University, 1894), volume 8; Roy P. Basler, ed., *The Collected Works of Abraham Lincoln* (New Brunswick NJ: Rutgers University Press, 1953–1955), volume 5; and Lynda Lasswell Crist, ed., *The Papers of Jefferson Davis* (Baton Rouge: Louisiana State University Press, 1995), volume 8: 1862. Other documentary volumes of importance include Clifford Dowdey and Louis H. Manarin, eds., *The Wartime Papers of R. E. Lee* (Boston:

Little, Brown, 1961) and Stephen W. Sears, ed., *The Civil War Papers of George B. McClellan: Selected Correspondence 1860–1865* (New York: Ticknor and Fields, 1989).

Military operations form the principal feature of this book. The reader might begin with Colin R. Ballard, *The Military Genius of Abraham Lincoln* (Cleveland: World, 1952), then move to essays in Gabor S. Borritt's anthologies, *Lincoln's Generals* (New York: Oxford University Press, 1994) and *Jefferson Davis's Generals* (New York: Oxford University Press, 1999) and Gary Gallagher, ed., *Lee and His Army in Confederate History* (Chapel Hill: University of North Carolina Press, 2001), before consulting R. Steven Jones, *The Right Hand of Command: Use and Disuse of Personal Staffs in the Civil War* (Mechanicsburg PA: Stackpole, 2000) on that vital underpinning of leadership and command. Edward Hagerman, *The American Civil War and the Origins of Modern Warfare: Ideas, Organization, and Field Command* (Bloomington: Indiana University Press, 1988); Paddy Griffith, *Battle Tactics of the Civil War* (New Haven: Yale University Press, 1989); Grady McWhiney and Perry D. Jamieson, *Attack and Die: Civil War Military Tactics and the Southern Heritage* (Tuscaloosa: University of Alabama Press, 1984); Archer Jones, *Civil War Command and Strategy: The Process of Victory and Defeat* (New York: Free Press, 1992); and Brent Noteworthy, *The Bloody Crucible of Courage: Fighting Methods and Combat Experience of the Civil War* (New York: Carroll & Graf, 2003) are absolutely indispensable for understanding the operational art from Cedar Mountain to Antietam. Indispensable for understanding the overall context of the war are Herman Hattaway and Archer Jones, *How the North Won the Civil War: A Military History of the Civil War* (Urbana: University of Illinois Press, 1983) and Richard E. Beringer, Herman Hattaway, Archer Jones, and William N. Still Jr., *Why the South Lost the Civil War* (Athens: University of Georgia Press, 1986).

General narratives pertinent to the 1862 war in Virginia and Maryland include a handy *Civil War Reader, 1862* by the editors of *Civil War Times* and *America's Civil War* (New York: Ibooks, 2002) and Jim Miles, *Forged in Fire: A History and Tour Guide of the War in the East from Manassas to Antietam, 1861–1862* [The Civil War Explorer Series] (Nashville TN: Cumberland House, 2000). Despite its title, James M. McPherson, *Crossroads of Freedom: Antietam, the Battle That Changed the Course of the Civil War* (New York: Oxford University Press, 2002) deftly places the episodic in a holistic setting. Writing more traditional military history, Joseph L. Harsh uses the Maryland campaign as the leitmotiv for a multivolume study suggested in his titles, *Robert E. Lee and the Making of Southern Strategy, 1861–862* (Kent OH: Kent University Press, 1998), *Taken at the Flood: Robert E. Lee and Confederate Strategy in the Maryland Campaign of 1862* (Kent OH: Kent University Press, 1999), and *Sounding the Shallows: A Confederate Companion for the Maryland Campaign of 1862* (Kent OH: Kent University Press, 2000). Michael A. Palmer, *Lee Moves North: Robert E. Lee on the Offensive* (New York: Wiley, 1998) and James A. Kegel, *North with Lee and Jackson: The Lost Story of Gettysburg* (Mechanicsburg PA: Stackpole, 1996) add to the body of literature concerning Confederate offensives north of the Potomac. The second volume of the now classic four-volume set edited by Robert Underwood Johnson and Clarence Clough Buel, *Battles and Leaders of the Civil War* (New York: Century, 1887) offers early contributions by participants to the summer and fall events. The crucial but overlooked theme of guarding the nation's capital comes in B. Franklin Cooling, *Symbol, Sword and Shield: Defending Washington During the Civil War* (1975, rpt. Shippensburg PA: White Mane, 1991).

Individual battle and campaign studies in this period remain central to this study. Paralleling the approach taken in this book, early volumes in Scribner's Campaigns of the Civil War series include John C. Ropes, *The Army under Pope* (New York: Scribner's 1881) and Francis Winthrop Palfrey, *The Antietam and Fredericksburg* (New York: Scribner's, 1882). Retired Lt. Gen. Edward J. Stackpole adds a more modern primer in *From Cedar Mountain to Antietam* (Harrisburg PA: Stackpole, 1959). Other general modern accounts include David G. Martin, *The Second Bull Run Campaign, July-August 1862* (Conschohocken PA: Combined Books, 1997); Robert K. Krick, *Stonewall Jackson at Cedar Mountain* (Chapel Hill: University of North Carolina Press, 1990); and John J. Hennessy, *Return to Bull Run: The Campaign and Battle of Second Manassas* (New York: Simon & Schuster, 1993) as well as his intensive *Second Manassas Battlefield Map Study* (Lynchburg VA: H. E. Howard, 1985). Four chapters in W. J. Wood, *Civil War Generalship: The Art of Command* (1997, rpt. Cambridge MA: Da Capo, 2000) are devoted to Cedar Mountain. A brief but incisive National Park Civil War Series pamphlet with text by A. Wilson Greene, *The Second Battle of Manassas* (Washington DC: Eastern Park and Monument Association, 1995) provides a primer, and an intriguing piece by E-an Zen and Alta Walker, *Rocks and War: Geology and the Civil War Campaign of Second Manassas* (Shippensburg PA: White Mane, 2000) lends an eclectic perspective. Paul Taylor, *He Hath Loosed the Fateful Lightning: The Battle of Ox Hill (Chantilly) September 1, 1862* (Shippensburg PA: White Mane, 2003) and David A. Welker, *Tempest at Ox Hill: The Battle of Chantilly* (Cambridge MA: Da Capo, 2002) conclude the summer story.

Far greater coverage has been accorded the Maryland campaign. One should begin with D. Scott Hartwig's annotated *The Battle of Antietam and the Maryland Campaign of 1862: A Bibliography* (Westport CT: Meckler, 1990). Joseph Pierro, editor. *The Maryland Campaign of September 1862; Ezra A. Carman's Definitive Study of the Union and Confederate Armies at Antietam* (New York: Routledge, 2007). John Cannan, *The Antietam Campaign, July–November, 1862* (New York: Wieser and Wieser, 1990) provides a primer, and niche essays in Mark A. Snell, ed., *The Maryland Campaign of 1862*, Vol. 6, No. 2 of *Civil War Regiments: A Journal of the American Civil War* (Campbell CA: Savas, 1998) and Gary W. Gallagher, ed., *The Antietam Campaign* (Chapel Hill: University of North Carolina Press, 1999) and Gary W. Gallagher, ed., *Antietam: Essays on the 1862 Maryland Campaign* (Kent OH: Kent State University Press, 1989) treat special aspects of the subject. Donald R. Jermann's *Antietam: The Lost Order* (Gretna LA: Pelican, 2006) uses that important scrap of paper to explain why Harper's Ferry was the key to Union victory. The two preferred works for South Mountain are John Michael Priest's excruciatingly detailed *Before Antietam: The Battle for South Mountain* (Shippensburg PA: White Mane, 1982) and Timothy J. Reese, *Sealed with Their Lives: The Battle for Crampton's Gap, Burkittsville, Maryland, September 14, 1862* (Baltimore: Butternut & Blue, 1998). The Harpers Ferry surrender receives coverage by Paul R. Teetor, *A Matter of Hours: Treason at Harper's Ferry* (Rutherford NJ: Fairleigh Dickinson University Press, 1982) and Chester G. Hearn, *Six Years of Hell: Harpers Ferry During the Civil War* (Baton Rouge: Louisiana State University Press, 1996). Allan L. Tischler, *The History of the Harpers Ferry Cavalry Expedition, September 14 and 15, 1862* (Winchester VA: Five Cedars Press, 1993) recounts that little-known episode. Tone to the subsequent bloodiest day in American history comes from Helen Ashe Hays, *The Antietam and Its Bridges: The Annals of an Historic Stream* (New York: G. P. Putnam's Sons, 1910) and John W. Schildt, *Roads to Antietam* (Chewsville MD: Antietam Publications, 1985).

The best histories of the battle of Antietam continue to be James V. Murfin, *The Gleam of Bayonets: The Battle of Antietam and Robert E. Lee's Maryland Campaign, September 1862* (New York: Thomas Yoselof, 1965) and Stephen W. Sears, *Landscape Turned Red: The Battle of Antietam* (New Haven: Ticknor & Fields, 1983). John Michael Priest once again provides the most detailed account of the fighting in *Antietam: The Soldier's Battle* (Shippensburg PA: White Mane, 1989), and Perry D. Jamieson, *Death in September: The Antietam Campaign* (Fort Worth TX: Ryan Place, 1995) offers a delightful read. Two worthwhile specialized accounts are Curt Johnson and Richard C. Anderson Jr., *Artillery Hell: The Employment of Artillery at Antietam* (College Station: Texas A&M University Press, 1995) and Phillip Thomas Tucker, *Burnside's Bridge: The Climactic Struggle of the Second and Twentieth Georgia at Antietam Creek* (Mechanicsburg PA: Stackpole, 2000). Stuart's post-Antietam antics find unique treatment in John W. Thompson IV, *Horses, Hostages, and Apple Cider: J. E. B. Stuart's 1862 Pennsylvania Raid* (Mercersburg PA: Mercersburg Printers, 2002). Finally, one should not overlook William A. Frassanito's pioneering work juxtaposing period imagery and modern location, *Antietam: The Photographic Legacy of America's Bloodiest Day* (New York: Scribner's, 1978).

The contending civilian leaders' responses to events can be studied in William J. Cooper Jr., *Jefferson Davis, American* (New York: Knopf, 2000); William C. Davis, *Jefferson Davis: The Man and His Hour* (New York: Harper Collins, 1991) and *Lincoln's Men: How President Lincoln Became Father to an Army and a Nation* (New York: Free Press, 1999); David Herbert Donald, *Lincoln* (New York: Simon and Schuster, 1995); and William E. Gienapp, *Abraham Lincoln and Civil War America: A Biography* (New York: Oxford University Press, 2002). The significance of Lincoln and his Emancipation Proclamation appear in Harold Holzer, Edna Greene Medford, and Frank J. Williams, *The Emancipation Proclamation: Three Views* (Baton Rouge: Louisiana State University Press, 2006); Richard Striner, *Father Abraham: Lincoln's Relentless Struggle to End Slavery* (Oxford: Oxford University Press, 2006); Allen C. Guelzo, *Lincoln's Emancipation Proclamation: The End of Slavery in America* (New York: Simon and Schuster, 2004); William K. Klingaman, *Abraham Lincoln and the Road to Emancipation 1861–1865* (New York: Penguin, 2001); and James M. McPherson, *Abraham Lincoln and the Second American Revolution* (New York: Oxford University Press, 1990). The essays by La Wanda Cox, "Lincoln and Black Freedom," and Hans L. Trefousse, "Lincoln and Race Relations," in Martin H. Greenberg and Charles G. Waugh, eds., *The Price of Freedom: Slavery and the Civil War*, Vol. 2, *The Preservation of Liberty* (Nashville TN: Cumberland House, 2000) are equally crucial. Readers would also do well to ponder Bruce Levine, *Confederate Emancipation: Southern Plans to Free and Arm Slaves During the Civil War* (New York: Oxford University Press, 2006). Cabinet officers like Gideon Welles should be consulted in John Niven, *Gideon Welles: Lincoln's Secretary of the Navy* (New York: Oxford University Press, 1973); Howard K. Beale, ed., *Diary of Gideon Welles*, 3 vols. (New York: Norton, 1960); and David Donald, ed., *Inside Lincoln's Cabinet: The Civil War Diaries of Salmon P. Chase* (New York: Longmans, Green, 1954). These add to our knowledge of administration affairs.

The armies themselves have had their share of attention. Douglas Southall Freeman's classic *Lee's Lieutenants*, 3 vols. (New York: Scribner's, 1942–1944) is more than just a study of Confederate command, but rather a treatment of the emerging Army of Northern Virginia and its leaders in this crucial developmental period. Bruce Catton similarly analyzed the "odyssey" of McClellan and the Army of the Potomac through *Mr. Lincoln's Army* (Garden City NJ: Doubleday, 1955), as did Kenneth P. Williams in volumes 1 and 2 of his multi-volume *Lincoln Finds a General* (New York: Macmillan, 1949–1959), although Jeffrey D. Wert, *The Sword of Lincoln: The Army of the Potomac* (New York: Simon and Schuster, 2005) offers a more recent perspective. Stephen R. Taafe, *Commanding the Army of the Potomac* (Lawrence: University Press of Kansas, 2006) and Stephen W. Sears, *Controversies and Commanders: Dispatches from the Army of the Potomac* (Boston: Houghton Mifflin, 1999) add analysis of command and civil-military relations. Michael C. C. Adams, *Our Masters the Rebels* (Cambridge MA: Harvard University Press, 1978), reprinted as *Fighting for Defeat: Union Military Failure in the East, 1861–1865* (Lincoln: University of Nebraska Press, 1978), suggests that Confederate arms simply "psyched-out" their opponents.

Surely the most controversial general of that moment, if not the war, was George B. McClellan. Over the years biographies pro and con have illumined his personality and career. Taking off from the general's apologia, *McClellan's Own Story* (New York: Charles L. Webster, 1887), the modern "McClellan-Go-Round" (as Joseph Harsh once styled it) commenced with Warren W. Hassler Jr.'s favorable *General*

George B. McClellan: Shield of the Union (Baton Rouge: Louisiana State University Press, 1957) and has been critically revisited in Stephen W. Sears, *George B. McClellan: The Young Napoleon* (New York: Da Capo, 1988); Thomas J. Rowland, *George B. McClellan and Civil War History: In the Shadow of Grant and Sherman* (Kent OH: Kent State University Press, 1998); and James M. Ridgway Jr., *Little Mac: Demise of an American Hero* (New York: Xlibris, 2000), and Edward H. Bonekemper III, *McClelland Failure: A Study of Civil War Fear, Incompetence and Worse* (Jefferson NC: McFarland, 2006). In truth, the man who organized and reorganized the Army of the Potomac so brilliantly but who failed to fight it well will be forever shrouded in controversy, although Ethan S. Rafuse has added a distinctive revisionist touch in *McClellan's War: The Failure of Moderation in the Struggle for the Union* (Bloomington: Indiana University Press, 2005)—as much analytical biography as war study. Union General-in-Chief Henry Halleck remains even more opaque with John F. Marszalek, *Commander of all Lincoln's Armies: A Life of General Henry W. Halleck* (Cambridge MA: Belknap Press, 2004) effectively updating the classic Stephen A. Ambrose, *Halleck: Lincoln's Chief of Staff* (Baton Rouge: Louisiana State University Press, 1962) and Curt Anders, *Henry Halleck's War: A Fresh Look at Lincoln's Controversial General-in-Chief* (Carmel: Guild Press of Indiana, 1999). John Pope's story emerges from Peter Cozzens, *General John Pope: A Life for the Nation* (Urbana: University of Illinois Press, 2000) and Peter Cozzens and Robert I. Girardi, eds., *The Military Memoirs of General John Pope* (Chapel Hill: University of North Carolina Press, 1998). For corps commanders, readers should consult Fred Harvey Harrington, *Fighting Politician, Major General N. P. Banks* (Philadelphia: University of Pennsylvania Press, 1944); Walter H. Hebert, *Fighting Joe Hooker* (Indianapolis: Bobbs-Merrill, 1944); William Marvel, *Burnside* (Chapel Hill: University of North Carolina, 1991); Stephen D. Engle, *Yankee Dutchman: The Life of Franz Sigel* (Baton Rouge: Louisiana State University Press, 1993); William F. McConnell, *Remember Reno: A Biography of Major General Jesse Lee Reno* (Shippensburg PA: White Mane, 1996); Mark A. Snell, *From First to Last: The Life of Major General William B. Franklin* (New York: Fordham University Press, 2002); and Ethan S. Rafuse, *Fitz John Porter, The Campaign of Second Manassas and the Problem of Command and Control in the 19th Century* [The Papers of the Blue and Gray education Society, Number 7] (Danville VA: Blue and Gray Education Society, 1998). Lower on the command ladder, Edward G. Longacre, *General John Buford* (Conshohocken PA: Combined Books, 1996) and David M. Jordan, *"Happiness Is Not My Companion": The Life of General G. K. Warren* (Bloomington: Indiana University Press, 2001) stand out.

Who can fail to appreciate the pillar of Confederate biography, Douglas Southall Freeman's masterful four-volume *R. E. Lee: A Biography* (New York: Scribner's, 1934–1935). Yet critical reexaminations of Lee's generalship have emerged with Emory M. Thomas's delicate probe, *Robert E. Lee: A Biography* (New York: Norton, 1995), counterbalancing Alan T. Nolan's controversial *Lee Considered: General Robert E. Lee and Civil War History* (Chapel Hill: University of North Carolina Press, 1991); Thomas L. Connelly, *The Marble Man: Robert E. Lee and His Image in American Society* (New York: Knopf, 1977); and Thomas L. Connelly and Barbara Bellows, *God and General Longstreet* (Baton Rouge: Louisiana State University Press, 1982). Lesser known examinations of Lee include John D. McKenzie, *Uncertain Glory: Lee's Generalship Re-Examined* (New York: Hippocrene Books, 1997); Robert G. Tanner, *Retreat to Victory? Confederate Strategy Reconsidered* (Wilmington DE: Scholarly Resources, 2001); Michael Fellman, *Making of Robert E. Lee* (New York: Random House, 2000); and Bevin Alexander, *Robert E. Lee's Civil War* (Avon MA: Adams Media Corporation, 1998). Edward H. Bonekeeper's measure is captured in the title *How Robert E. Lee Lost the Civil War* (Fredericksburg VA: Sergeant Kirkland's Press, 1997). Of special note is *Robert E. Lee: Icon for a Nation* (London: Weidenfeld & Nicolson, 2005) by renowned British military historian Brian Holden Reid.

Recent biographies of some of Lee's lieutenants deserve note: William Garrett Piston, *Lee's Tarnished Lieutenant: James Longstreet and His Place in Southern History* (Athens: University of Georgia Press, 1987); Jeffrey D. Wert, *General James Longstreet, the Confederacy's Most Controversial soldier: A Biography* (New York: Simon & Schuster, 1993); and R. L. DiNardo and Albert A. Nofi, eds., *James Longstreet the Man, the Soldier, the Controversy* (Conshohocken PA: Combined Books, 1998). Jackson biographies that command attention include the classic Frank Everson Vandiver, *Mighty Stonewall* (New York: McGraw Hill, 1957) and newer studies by Byron Farwell, *Stonewall: A Biography of General Thomas Jackson* (New York: Norton, 1992); Bevin Alexander, *Lost Victories: The Military Genius of Stonewall Jackson* (New York: Henry Holt, 1992); and James I. Robertson Jr. *Stonewall Jackson: The Man,*

The Soldier, the Legend (New York: Macmillan, 1997). Key division commanders may be approached through James I. Robertson Jr., *General A. P. Hill: The Story of a Confederate Warrior* (New York: Random House, 1987); Samuel J. Martin, *Road to Glory: Confederate General Richard S. Ewell* (Indianapolis: Guild Press of Indiana, 1991); Donald C. Pfanz, *Richard S. Ewell: A Soldier's Life* (Chapel Hill: University of North Carolina Press, 1998); John C. Oeffinger, ed., *A Soldier's General: The Civil War Letters of Major General Lafayette McLaws* (Chapel Hill: University of North Carolina Press, 2002); Hal Bridges, *Lee's Maverick General: Daniel Harvey Hill* (New York: McGraw-Hill, 1961); and Emory M. Thomas, *Bold Dragoon: The Life of J. E. B. Stuart* (New York: Harper and Row, 1986).

The complex relationship between war and diplomatic affairs looms large in this time frame. The classic works remain Ephraim Douglass Adams's two-volume *Great Britain and the American Civil War* (New York: Longmans Green, 1925) and Lynn M. Case and Warren F. Spencer, *The United States and France: Civil War Diplomacy* (Philadelphia: University of Pennsylvania Press, 1970). Possibly the best overall integrative work is Dean B. Mahin, *One War at a Time: The International Dimensions of the American Civil War* (Washington DC: Brassey's 1999). Joseph A. Fry has added a fresh interpretation in *Dixie Looks Abroad: The South and U.S. Foreign Relations, 1789–1973* (Baton Rouge: Louisiana State University Press, 2002), as has Charles M. Hubbard, *The Burdens of Confederate Diplomacy* (Knoxville: University of Tennessee Press, 1998). Howard Jones discusses the provocative linkage between emancipation and the international scene in *Union in Peril: The Crisis over British Intervention and the Civil War* (Chapel Hill: University of North Carolina Press, 1992) and *Abraham Lincoln and a New Birth of Freedom: The Union and Slavery in the Diplomacy of the Civil War* (Lincoln: University of Nebraska Press, 1999). Niche works of value to the Peninsula-Antietam story include Philip S. Foner, *British Labor and the American Civil War* (New York: Holmes and Meier, 1981); Alfred Grant, *The American Civil War and the British Press* (Jefferson NC: McFarland, 2000); and George M. Blackburn, *French Newspaper Opinion on the American Civil War* (Westport CT: Greenwood, 1997).

Judging the vagaries of public will points to Phillip Shaw Paludan, *"A People's Contest": The Union and Civil War 1861–1865* (New York: Harper and Row, 1988); Frank Freidel's pivotal two-volume *Union Pamphlets of the Civil War, 1861–1865* (Cambridge MA: Harvard

University Press, 1967); Earl J. Hess, *Liberty, Virtue and Progress: Northerners and Their War for the Union* (New York: Fordham University Press, 1997); as well as the copiously illustrated *The Union Image: Popular Prints of the Civil War North,* by Mark E. Neely Jr. and Harold Holzer (Chapel Hill: University of North Carolina Press, 2000). The Confederate experience can be discerned from Emory H. Thomas, *The Confederate Nation, 1861–1865* (New York: Harper and Row, 1979); George C. Rable, *The Confederate Republic: A Revolution against Politics* (Chapel Hill: University of North Carolina Press, 1994); and Wiley Sword, *Southern Invincibility: A History of the Confederate Heart* (New York: St. Martin's, 1999). Niche works in this regard include E. Lawrence Abel, *Singing the New Nation: How Music Shaped the Confederacy, 1861–1865* (Mechanicsburg PA: Stackpole, 2000), which covers the role of Stephen Randall's "Maryland, My Maryland," and Steven E. Woodworth, *While God Is Marching On: The Religious World of Civil War Soldiers* (Lawrence: University Press of Kansas, 2001). The relationship between battles and politics comes to the forefront in Christopher Dell, *Lincoln and the War Democrats: The Grand Erosion of Conservative Tradition* (Cranberry NJ: Associated University Presses, 1975) and Mark E. Neely Jr., *The Union Divided: Party Conflict in the Civil War North* (Cambridge MA: Harvard University Press, 2002). The role of the press has been told best in J. Cutler Andrews's classic *The South Reports the War* (1970, rpt. Pittsburgh: University of Pittsburgh Press, 1985) and *The North Reports the War* (1955, rpt. Pittsburgh: University of Pittsburgh Press, 1983).

As historians focus increasingly on the interface between war and society from 1861 to 1865, the transformation from "soft" to "hard" or repressive war commands center stage. John Syrett, *The Civil War Confiscation Acts: Failing to Reconstruct the South* (New York: Fordham University Press, 2005) is a pioneer study in that regard. Mark Grimsley, *The Hard Hand of War: Union Military Policy toward Southern Civilians 1861–1865* (New York: Cambridge University Press, 1995) and Daniel E. Sutherland, *The Emergence of Total War* (Fort Worth TX: Ryan Place, 1996) as well as *Seasons of War: The Ordeal of a Confederate Community, 1861–1865* (New York: Free Press, 1995) establish the mark. William Blair, *Virginia's Private War: Feeding Body and Soul in the Confederacy 1861–1865* (New York: Oxford University Press, 1998) and Ervin L. Jordan Jr., *Black Confederates and Afro-Yankees in Civil War Virginia* (Charlottesville: University Press of Virginia, 1995) address race relations in the countryside. Alfred Hoyt Bill, *The Beleaguered City: Richmond, 1861–1865* (New York: Knopf, 1946); Ernest B. Ferguson, *Ashes of Glory: Richmond at War* (New York: Vintage Books, 1996); and Virginia Hale, *Four Valiant Years in the Lower Shenandoah Valley* (Strasburg VA: Shenandoah Publishing House, 1968) supplement the personal diaries and accounts of Confederate civilians noted in the present volume's notes. Home front and war coverage north of the Potomac can begin in no better place than the nation's capital with Ernest B. Ferguson, *Freedom Rising: Washington dc in the Civil War* (New York: Knopf, 2004) and Margaret Leech's Pulitzer prize–winning *Reveille in Washington, 1860–1865* (New York: Harper, 1941). Robert I. Cottom Jr. and Mary Ellen Hayward, *Maryland in the Civil War: A House Divided* (Baltimore: Maryland Historical Society, 1994); Daniel Carroll Toomey, *The Civil War in Maryland* (Baltimore: Toomey Press, 1983); and Susan Cooke Soderberg, *A Guide to Civil War Sites in Maryland: Blue and Gray in a Border State* (Shippensburg PA: White Mane, 1998) offer primers on the Old Line State in the period. The appropriate chapter in William C. Wright, *The Secession Movement in the Middle Atlantic States* (Rutherford NJ: Fairleigh Dickinson University Press, 1973) and Harold R. Manakee, *Maryland in the Civil War* (Baltimore: Maryland Historical Society, 1961) offer more balanced explanations to Maryland's allegiance than Lawrence M. Denton, *A Southern Star for Maryland: Maryland and the Secession Crisis* (Baltimore: Publishing Concepts, 1995) or Bart Rhett Talbert, *Maryland: The South's First Casualty* (Charlottesville VA: Howell Press, 1995). Essential local studies include Daniel Toomey and Scott Sumpter Sheads, *Baltimore During the Civil War* (Lithicum MD: Toomey Press, 1997); appropriate Baltimore chapters and passages in Frank Towers, *The Urban South and the Coming of the Civil War* (Charlottesville: University of Virginia Press, 2004); Roger Keller, *Crossroads of War: Washington County, Maryland in the Civil War* (Shippensburg PA: Burd Street Press, 1997); and Paul Gordon and Rita Gordon, *Frederick County, Maryland: A Playground in the Civil War* (Frederick MD: Heritage Partnership, 1994) and *Never the Like Again: Frederick County, Maryland 1860–1865* (Shippensburg PA: Burd Street Press, 1996). Carlisle, Pennsylvania, a town tangentially caught up in the effects of the Maryland campaign, gains attention in David G. Colwell, *The Bitter Fruits: The Civil War Comes to a Small Town in Pennsylvania* (Carlisle PA: Cumberland County Historical Society, 1998).

Recognition of the pivotal nature of Civil War logistics lags far behind operational history. Nonetheless, Edwin C. Fishel, *The Secret War for the Union: The Untold Story of Military Intelligence in the Civil War* (Bloomington: Indiana University Press, 1996) is crucial for understanding the maneuvers of Lee, Pope, and McClellan. Thomas Weber, *The Northern Railroads in the Civil War, 1861–1865* (1951, rpt. Bloomington: Indiana University Press, 1999) and Charles Dana and E. Kay Gibson, *Assault and Logistics: Union Army Coastal and River Operations 1861–1866* [The Army's Navy Series, Vol. 2] (Camden ME: Ensign Press, 1995) are rich explanations of moving men and matériel. Medical treatment has been explored in Terry Reimer, *One Vast Hospital: The Civil War Hospital Sites in Frederick, Maryland after Antietam* (Frederick MD: National Museum of Civil War Medicine, 2001). Earl J. Hess, *Field Armies and Fortifications in the Civil War: The Eastern Campaigns 1861–1864* (Chapel Hill: University of North Carolina Press, 2005) ably introduces that neglected subject area.

Last but hardly least are the historic sites themselves, with attendant research and interpretive facilities. Essays in Clarence R. Geier and Stephen R. Potter, *Archaeological Perspectives on the American Civil War* (Gainesville: University Press of Florida, 2000) and Clarence R. Geier and Susan E. Winter, eds., *Look to the Earth: Historical Archaeology and the American Civil War* (Knoxville: University of Tennessee Press, 1994) provide interdisciplinary ways to study events from the Peninsula to the Antietam. National Park Service visitor center libraries and museums at Manassas, Harpers Ferry, and Antietam offer a plethora of documentation sources (material and manuscript) for further study. Lest preservation stewardship be forgotten, see Joan M. Zenzen's insightful *Battling for Manassas: The Fifty-Year Preservation Struggle at Manassas National Battlefield Park* (University Park PA: Pennsylvania State University Press, 1998). Finally, appropriate historic site visitation guides include Joseph W. A Whitehorne, *The Battle of Second Manassas: Self-Guided Tour* (Washington DC: U.S. Army Center of Military History, 1990) and Jay Luvaas and Harold W. Nelson, eds., *Guide to the Battle of Antietam: The Maryland Campaign of 1862* (Lawrence: University Press of Kansas, 1996).

Index

Benning, Henry, 248
Best family, 175, 188
Beverly, William, 105
Beverly's ford, 75–76, 80
Blackford, Charles Minor, 23, 59, 61; on
    battle at Cedar Mountain, 62–63; at
    Sulphur Springs, 80
Blackford, William, 197
"Black Hatters," 215
Blair, Francis Preston, 271, 272, 287, 288
Blair, Montgomery, 20, 265
Blair, William, 19–20
Blue Ridge Mountains, 285
Bolivar Heights, 201
Boonsboro MD, 191, 201, 215, 217, 222,
    224; pike, 247. *See also* South Mountain
Booth, George Wilson, 198, 231, 251
Booth, John Wilkes, 174
Boston Journal, 260–61
Boteler, Andrew, 6
Boteler's ford, 223, 236, 255
Bowie, Richard J., 188
Braddock, Edward, 210
Bradford, A. W., 172, 261
Bradwell, Gordon, 289
Bragg, Braxton, xiii, 5, 100, 138, 291
Branch, Lawrence O'Brien, 250
Brawner, John, 103
Brawner's Woods, 107
Breckinridge, John C., 44, 167
Bristoe Station, 86, 87–88, 92, 102, 133
Brodhead, Thornton F., 72
Brookeville MD, 167
Brown, George, 169
Brown, John, 13, 207
Brown, Ridgely, 187
Brownsville MD, 216, 218
Brugger, Robert J., 167, 168
Buchanan, Franklin, 170
Buchanan, James, 36, 167
Buck, Lucy, 136, 137, 164
Buck Hill, headquarters on, 114, 127, 130
Buckingham, Catharinus P., 286, 287
Buell, Don Carlos, 15, 29, 138, 261, 291
Buford, Beverly, 134
Buford, John, 48, 49, 75, 85, 105, 112
Bull Run, 2, 12, 39, 89–90, 94, 105; First,
    208; Stone Bridge crossing, 134. *See also*
    Second Manassas

Bull's Hill, 220
Burgwyn, Harry, 136
Burgwyn, William H. S., 23
Burkittsville MD, 216, 274
Burney, Samuel A., 4
Burnside, Ambrose, 10–11, 47, 71, 94,
    110, 158, 182, 214, 224, 233, 250,
    271, 272, 287; Clara Barton and, 65;
    conflict with Pope, 99; at Hanover
    Junction, 69; and IX Corps, 231, 240;
    liberation of Frederick MD by, 199; and
    plans obtained by Stuart, 78–79; at
    Richmond, 25–28
Butler, Benjamin, 17, 169
Butterfield, Daniel, 8

Campbell, Robert, 104, 114, 115, 125,
    132; on the loss of life, 131; on victory
    at Second Manassas, 119
Cannan, James, 243
casualties, war, xiv, 63–64, 65–67, 152–53,
    215, 251
Catlett's Station, 78–79, 82, 86, 91, 94
Catoctin Mountain, 199
Caton, Bruce, 249
Cedar Mountain, battle at, xi, 49–50, 78,
    85; advancement of troops toward,
    53–57; casualties of, 63–64, 65–67;
    Jackson's success and, 58–63; survivors
    of, 66–67
Cemetery Hill, 223, 233, 247
Centreville VA, 103–4
Chain Bridge, 156, 160
Chambersburg PA, 200, 276
Chandler, Zachariah, 17
Chantilly, battle of, xi, xiii, 182, 246;
    contested action at, 162–63; evacuation
    of casualties from, 152–53; immediate
    limelight after, 157; map of, September
    1, 1862, 149; retirement from, 151–52;
    significance of, 151; weather conditions
    at, 148–49
"Chantilly Fumble," 151
Charles County, 173
Charleston Daily Courier, 198, 260
Charleston WV, 281
Chase, Julia, 292–93

Brigade," 107; troops at Culpeper and, 57–60, 67–69; on victory at Second Manassas, 119

James River, xx, 82–83; McClellan ordered to assume control over ships on, 97–98

Johnson, Bradley, 103, 178

Johnson, Frederick Countian Bradley, 170

Johnston, Joseph E., 2, 6; at Fair Oaks, 3

"Joint Order" controversy, 111–12, 118

Jones, D. R., 115, 247, 249

Jones, Howard, 268

Jones, John B., 5, 139, 266

Jones, William E., 61

"Jug" Bridge, 199

Kanawha Valley VA, 276, 280

Kearny, Philip, 25, 93, 94, 97, 147, 149–50, 150; conflict with Pope, 99; ordered to reopen rail line from Bristoe Station to Manassas, 96; reactions to Pope's orders, 109–10; at Second Manassas, 113, 118–19

Keedysville MD, 222, 224, 225, 236

Kelly's ford, 78, 80

Kemp Hall, 166

Kentucky, 261, 291

Kerus, Mark, 131

Kettle Run, 90–91, 92, 94

Keyes, Erasmus, 11, 18, 26

Killiansburg Cave MD, 260

Kilpatrick, H. Judson, 48, 121

King, Henry Lord Page, 222

King, Rufus, 38, 49, 112; move to Warrenton by, 50; withdrawal toward Manassas of, 107

Lange, Gottfried, 3

Larkin, James, 288

Law, Evander, 121

Lawton, Alexander R., 236

Lawton, Hugh, 60, 77, 80

Lee, Elizabeth Blair, 265, 274, 279

Lee, Fitzhugh, 72, 87, 89, 90, 102, 104

Lee, Laura, 293

Lee, Mary Custis, 83

Lee, Robert E., xii, 35, 82, 98, 101, 165, 169, 174, 186, 190, 204, 215, 234, 245, 256; at Antietam, 225, 260, 261; and Antietam withdrawal results, 260, 261; arrives at Clark's Mountain, 73; assumes command, 3; attacked at Sharpsburg MD, xx; at Boonesboro, 219; communications with Longstreet, 104–5; communications with Stonewall Jackson, 46–47, 51; critics of, 5; flanking maneuver of, 124–25; foot soldiers, superiority of, 284; impact of Antietam offensive, 268; injuries, 140; intent to attack Pope, xx, 71–72; Jackson's direct orders to, 132; on John Pope, 43–44, 46–47; letters to Davis by, 160–62; on liberating Maryland, 124; Lincoln's advice to McClellan on, 278; and Maryland campaign, xiii, xv; McClellan, final battles with, 285–87; McClellan's movements against, 281–82; military difficulties of, 279–81; orders attack on Harrison's Landing, 24; plans stolen from, 72; post-Antietam strategy of, 274–75, 276, 277; proclamation to Maryland by, 203; reinforcement of troops by, 22–23; relationship with Davis, 3, 7, 31, 280–81; retreat to Virginia, 290; rivalry with George McClellan, xiii, xx, 8; and the Seven Day's battles, 3–4; "signal victory" announcement and, 139; spies used by, 71; strategic decisions made by, 69–70, 82–83, 94–95

Lee, Samuel Phillips, 274

Lee, Stephen Dill, 85, 129, 254

Leech, Margaret, 181

Leesburg VA, 165

Letterman, Jonathan, 8

Lewis, Francis, 133

Lewis, George Cornewall, 269–70

Lieber, Francis W., 45

Lincoln, Abraham, 174, 185, 246, 260, 262, 263, 275, 280–82, 285–86, 291, 294; appoints Henry Halleck general in chief, xii, 21–22, 31, 36, 37; and battle of Chantilly, 154–55; communications with McClellan, 8–9, 10, 220, 271–74; concern over conflict between Pope and McClellan, 98; confiscation laws signed by, 13–15, 18–19, 21, 46;

ordered to assume control of ships, 97–98; ordered to withdraw from the James River, xx; orders to Miles, 221; personal conflicts of, 10, 80; and philosophy of war, 185; reorganization of Union Army by, 181–82; reply to Halleck, 142; rivalry with Robert E. Lee, xiii, xx, 8; and the Seven Days battles, 2–4; strategic errors by, 25–28, 206, 231; Stuart's maneuvers against, 276–77; troop support for, 8–9, 25–26; at Turner's and Fox's gaps, 211; Washington guarded by, 91

McClellan, Mary Ellen, 9, 11, 181, 204, 270, 285, 287–88

McDowell, Irvin, 38–39, 46, 49, 71, 85, 93, 101, 146; at Beverly's ford, 75, 80; blamed by James Miller for not taking Richmond, 67; communications with Pope, 93; at Culpepper, 56, 61; moves toward Manassas, 90, 102; moves to Warrenton, 49–50, 80; orders Reynolds to strike at Manassas Junction, 103–4; at Rappahannock Station, 74; at Second Manassas, 106; at Warrenton, 84

McDowell, Irvine, 111

McGuire, Hunter, 56

McGuire, Judith W., 3, 164, 266

McKinley, William, 248

McLaws, Lafayette, 85, 191, 201, 207–8, 216–18, 225, 280, 289

McLean, Nathaniel C., 130

McPherson, James, xv–xvi, 229, 264

McReynolds, A. T., 209

Meade, George Gordon, 215, 237

Mechanicsville MD, 187

Meigs, Montgomery, 18, 25–26, 28, 29

Memphis Appeal, 46, 261

Memphis TN, 174

Middlebrook MD, 187, 190

Middle Orndorff Bridge, 223, 225, 229, 244

Middletown MD, 200, 201

Miles, Dixon, 190, 193, 201–2, 207–8; death of, 221; instructed to retake Maryland Heights, 213; surrender by, 218, 219, 222; treason and, 221

Militia Act, 19–20

Millan farm, 148

Miller, D. R., 236

Miller, James T., 41–42; on the battle at Cedar Mountain, 66–67

Milroy, Robert, 48, 73, 75, 80, 133

Mitchel, Ormsby MacKnight, 17

Mitchell, Mary Bedinger, 259

Molly Maguires, 291

Monocacy Bridge, 253

Monocacy Church, 186

Monocacy River, 175, 186, 190

Montgomery, Richard, 123

Montgomery County MD, 173, 186, 187

Moor, Augustus, 210

Morgan, John Hunt, 82, 172

Morrell, George, 253

Morrill Act, 12

Morris, William G., 166

Mountain Church Road, 216

Mt. Tabor Church, 214

Muddy Branch, 187

Mumma, Samuel, 238

Munford, Thomas T., 87, 216, 223

Murfin, James, 242, 264

Nagle, James, 117

Napoleon III, 21, 268, 269

National pike, 211

National Road, 186, 187

National War College, xiv

Nelson, William "Bull," 138

Nesbin, Otho, 260

New York Herald, 46, 63, 72, 81

"New York Rebel," 189

New York Sunday Mercury, 40

New York Times, xiv, 18

New York Tribune, 252, 260–61

New York World, 265

Nicodemus Heights, 238, 252, 253

Nicodemus Hill, 239

Norton, Oliver, 8

nurses, army, 65–66

Occoquan River, 173

Offutt's Crossroads, 187

Old Hagerstown Road, 214

Old Line State, 166, 172

Old Sharpsburg Road, 201, 210, 214, 224

Orange Court House, 71, 72

Orange VA, 52–53, 99
Owen County IN, 266
Ox Hill. *See* Chantilly, battle of
Ox Road, 148

Palfrey, Francis, 200, 207, 253, 254, 282–83
Palmerston, Henry John Temple, 268, 269, 270, 289–90
Palmerston, Lord, 64
Paludan, Philip, 289
Parks, Leighton, 197
Parr's Ridge, 186
Patrick, Marsena, 147
Pegram, Willie, 60–61
Pelham, John, 107, 237
Pender, Dorsey, 150
Pendleton, Sandy, 55
Pendleton, William, 5, 222, 236, 256
Pennsylvania, 276, 277, 279, 281, 291; Reserves, 108, 131
Petty, Cornelia, 56
Philadelphia Inquirer, 186
Phillips, Philo D., 221
Phillips, Wendell, 17
Pierson, Reuben Allen, 4, 66
Pinkerton, Allan, 214
Pittsburgh PA, 281
Pleasant Valley, 216, 218, 225
Pleasonton, Alfred, 30, 186, 219, 224, 244; Antietam scouting by, 232, 255, 256; Frederick scouting by, 203; Harpers Ferry scouting by, 205; Turner's Gap scouting by, 209
Poe, Orlando, 81
Poffenberger, Samuel, 237, 259
Polley, J. B., 166
Poolesville MD, 186, 189
Pope, Clara Horton, 36
Pope, Douglass, 118
Pope, John, xii, xx, 24, 25, 31, 70, 175, 182, 185, 192; after-action report by, 121; anger towards Porter of, 121–22; appointed to oversee the Union Army, 21–22, 36; background of, 36–37; and battle at Cedar Mountain, 58–63; as Bully Pope, 195; communications with Halleck, 43–45, 72, 79, 84–85,

86, 94; conflicts with McClellan, 80, 96–98; decision to cover Washington, 90–91; decision to stand and fight, 122; and defeat at Chantilly, 163; dispatch to Porter from, 110; Edwin Stanton and, 36–37; final line of defense of, 133; gathers troops at Culpeper after Cedar Mountain, 67–69; and "Joint Order" controversy, 111–12; on King's withdrawal, 110; lack of ammunition and, 125; leadership style of, 39–41; Lee's intent to attack, xx, 71; moves troops south toward Jackson's troops, 47–49; ordered to halt advance by Halleck, 50–51; orders advance to Cedar Mountain, 49–50; orders advance to Manassas, 91; orders rail line from Bristoe Station to Manassas reopened, 96; orders regarding property confiscation and treatment of citizens given by, 40–47; orders Sigel to strike at Lee across Kelly's ford, 78; order to hold fast, 107; plans for Manassas, 101–2; plans to concentrate at Centreville, 108; promises to attack Lee, 145–46; at Rappahannock Station, 73–75; reinforcements sent to, 27–28, 34; renewed efforts at Second Manassas by, 109–10; request for help made by, 144–45; at Second Manassas, 84; strategic decisions made by, 94–95; testimony at Porter's court-martial of, 111; treatment of citizens by, 42–44; troops sent to Culpeper by, 56–58; at Warrenton, 76–78
Porter, Fitz John, 11, 78, 80, 91, 94, 97, 99, 202, 223, 286; at Antietam, 241, 244, 250, 255, 256; arrival at Manassas Junction of, 110–11; at Chantilly, 140, 143; ordered to Bristoe Station, 96; ordered to Manassas, 102; on Pope's decision to stand and fight, 143; reinstated, 182–83
Port Tobacco MD, 173
Potomac River, 165, 172, 229, 276, 277, 281
Price, R. Channing, 277
Price, Sterling, 291

Seneca Bridge, 187
Seneca Creek, 186
Seven Days' battle, xv, 2–4, 13, 18, 35, 237;
    George McClellan and, 80; John Pope
    and, 39
Seward, William H., 20–21, 288
Sharpsburg MD, 228, 236, 246, 259, 260,
    292. *See also* Antietam
Sharpsburg VA, 191, 216, 224, 225
Shaw, Robert Gould, 266
Sheeran, James, 46, 61, 70
Shenandoah Valley, 166, 179, 271, 274–
    75, 276, 279
Shepherdstown MD, 236, 249
Shiloh, 139
ships, Union Army, 34–35
Sigel, Franz, 38–39, 49, 80, 97, 101, 112,
    113, 146, 183, 286; at Cedar Mountain,
    62; communications with Pope, 79; at
    Culpeper, 56, 61; at Freeman's ford,
    77; moves toward Fayetteville, 84–85,
    86; moves toward Manassas, 92, 102;
    ordered to strike at Lee across Kelly's
    ford, 78; at the Rappahannock River,
    74–76; in Warrenton, 76–77
Silver Springs MD, 187
Slaughter, Philip, 53
slaves: abolitionists and, xii, 17–18, 64;
    arrest of fugitive, 81, 88; conscription
    of, 19; emancipated in the District
    of Columbia, 14; George McClellan
    on, 16–17; Harpers Ferry revolt and,
    13; moderate views on, 18; as private
    property, 13–14; and Santo Domingo
    revolt, 175. *See also* emancipation;
    freedmen
Sliddell, John, 269
Slocum, Henry, 216
Slough, John P., 158
Smalley, George E., 260–61
Smith, Edmund Kirby, 5, 51, 100, 138, 291
Smith, Gustavus W., 69, 281
Smith, Thomas W., 26
Smith, William, 216
Sneden, Robert Knox, 9, 11, 15; on
    the relocation of troops away from
    Richmond, 32–33
South Mountain MD, xi, xx, 193, 215,

222, 240, 260, 269, 272, 273, 292–93;
    Brownsville Gap, 216, 218; Burkittsville
    Gap at, 216; casualties at, 217; Catoctin
    Mountain and, 199; Crampton's Gap
    at, 197, 201, 205, 211, 213, 216; death
    of Reno at, 199, 214; Fox's Gap at, 210,
    211, 224; Frosttown Gap at, 211, 215;
    Hagan's Gap at, 210; National pike
    crossing at, 203; Turner's Gap at, 209,
    210, 211, 215, 224
Special Order 191, 190–94, 203, 206, 211
spies, Confederate, 71–72
Sprague, William, 37
Springfield Republican, 274
St. Luke's Episcopal Church, 218
Stackpole, Edward J., 51, 151, 182–83,
    217, 264
Stahel, Julius, 76
Stanton, Edwin M., 9, 10, 25, 30, 153, 159,
    184, 270, 274; blamed by James Miller
    for not taking Richmond, 67; eastern
    armies merged by, 35–36; George
    McClellan and, 98–100, 99; John Pope
    and, 36–37; strategic decisions made
    by, 47, 69
Stedman, Griffin, 199
Steiner, Lewis H., 197
Stenart, George H., 280
Steuart, George M., 170
Stevens, Isaac Ingalls, 119, 147, 150
Stevens, Thaddeus, 17
Stevenson, Charles, xiv
Stone, Charles P., 182, 187
Stone, Edward W., 32
Stony Ridge, 115
Strother, David, 73, 77, 110, 241, 251,
    267; on Pope's command system, 127
Stuart, James Ewell Brown, 5, 24, 60,
    63, 82, 140, 186, 188, 197, 203–4,
    210–11, 216–17, 219; ambushed near
    Verdiersville, 72; at Antietam, 234, 239,
    246, 251; battle of Antietam and, 276,
    277, 282, 289; at Catlett's Station, 78–
    79, 86, 94; in Gainesville, 87; Maryland
    campaign papers obtained by, 82;
    railroad interdictions by, 75–76, 78–79;
    at the Rappahannock River, 75–76;
    "sabers and roses" ball, 188–89

University of Nebraska Press

Also of Interest in the Great Campaigns of the Civil War series:

And Keep Moving On
The Virginia Campaign, May–June 1864
By Mark Grimsley

Mark Grimsley places the Virginia Campaign in the political context of the 1864 presidential election; appraises the motivation of soldiers; appreciates the impact of the North's sea power advantage; questions conventional interpretations; and examines the interconnections among the major battles, subsidiary offensives, and raids.

ISBN: 978-0-8032-7119-7 (paper)

Now for the Contest
Coastal and Oceanic Naval Operations in the Civil War
By William H. Roberts

Now for the Contest tells the story of the Civil War at sea in the context of three campaigns: the blockade of the southern coast, the raiding of Union commerce, and the projection of power ashore. Retired U.S. Navy commander William H. Roberts also examines how both sides mobilized and employed their resources for a war that proved to be of unprecedented intensity and duration.

ISBN: 978-0-8032-3861-9 (cloth)

Vicksburg Is the Key
The Struggle for the Mississippi River
By William L. Shea and Terrence J. Winschel

This fast-paced, gripping narrative of the Civil War struggle for the Mississippi River is the first comprehensive single-volume account to appear in over a century. *Vicksburg Is the Key* tells the story of the series of campaigns the Union conducted on land and water to conquer Vicksburg and of the many efforts by the Confederates to break the siege of the fortress.

ISBN: 978-0-8032-9344-1 (paper)

Order online at www.nebraskapress.unl.edu or call 1-800-755-1105. Mention the code "BOFOX" to receive a 20% discount.